FRIENDS IS FRIENDS

by GREG COOK

:01

First Second
New York

Thank you to Tom Devlin and friends at Highwater Books who
helped get this going, to my agent Neeti Madan at Sterling Lord
Literistic, to all the Sad Paraders and Pity Partiers, and to Mark
Siegel, Robyn Chapman, Gina Gagliano, Danielle Ceccolini,
and friends at First Second who helped get this done.

—Greg Cook

:01

First Second

Published by First Second
First Second is an imprint of Roaring Brook Press, a division of
Holtzbrinck Publishing Holdings Limited Partnership
175 Fifth Avenue, New York, New York 10010

Library of Congress Control Number: 2015944385

ISBN: 978-1-59643-105-8

Our books may be purchased in bulk for promotional, educational,
or business use. Please contact your local bookseller or the Macmillan
Corporate and Premium Sales Department at (800) 221-7945 ext.
5442 or by e-mail at MacmillanSpecialMarkets@macmillan.com.

First Edition 2016
Book design by Danielle Ceccolini
Additional production work by Jonathan Rotsztain

Printed in the United States of America

10 9 8 7 6 5 4 3 2 1

Hand drawn with graphite pencils, blue pencils, sumi ink, and brushes
on copier paper and bristol board.

For Ulysses,
Jasper, and Kari.
♡ Forever.

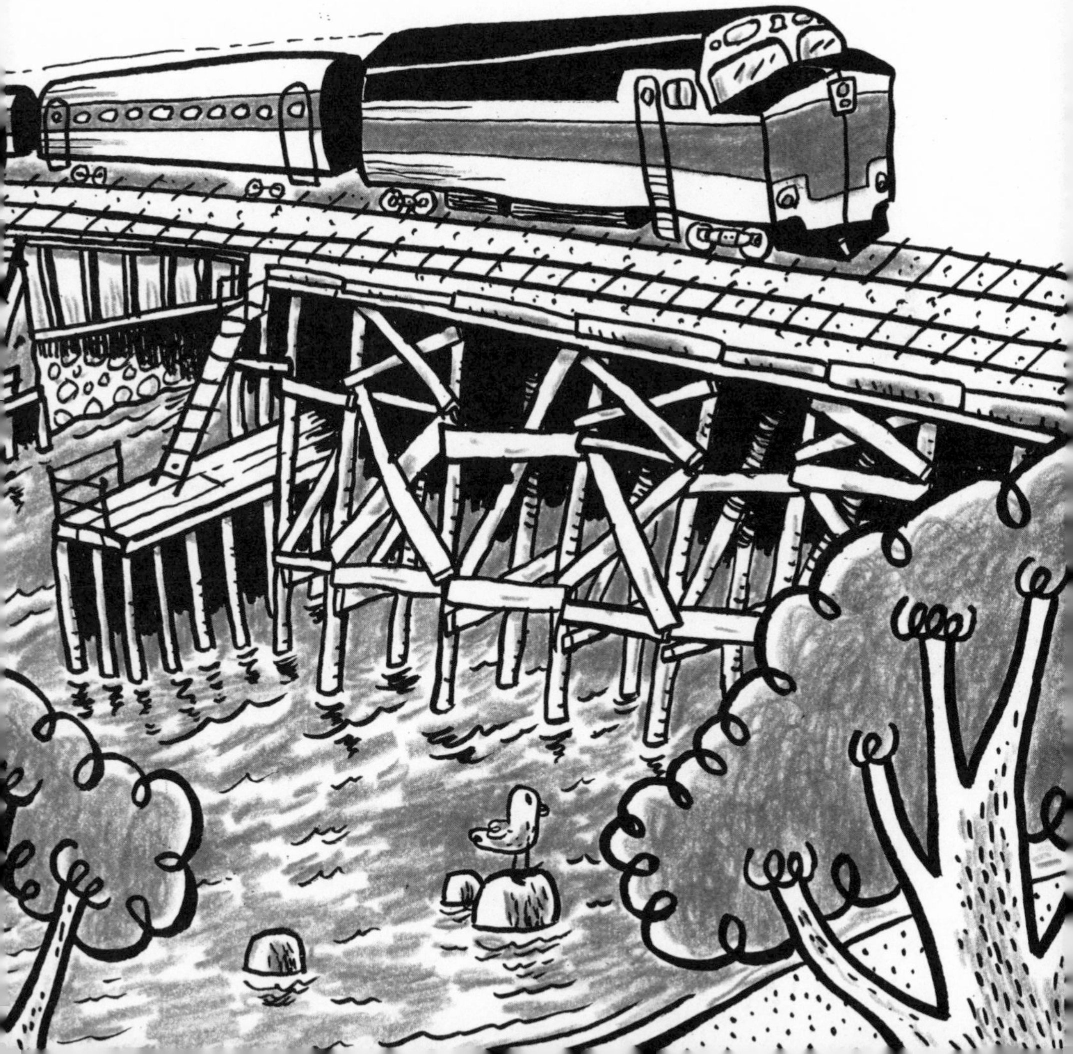

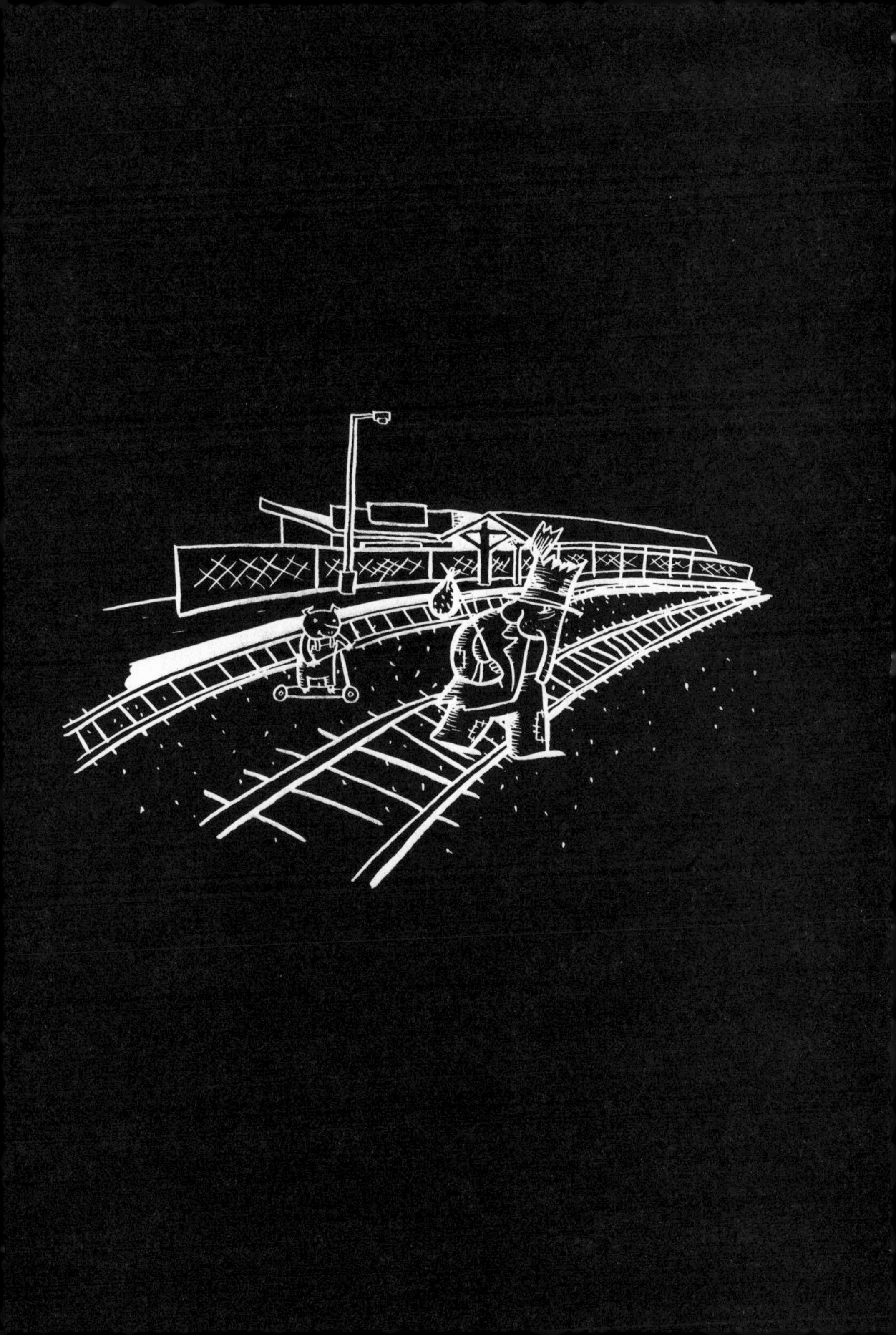

GREG COOK

FRIENDS IS FRIENDS

GLOUCESTER, MASS.
to MALDEN, MASS.

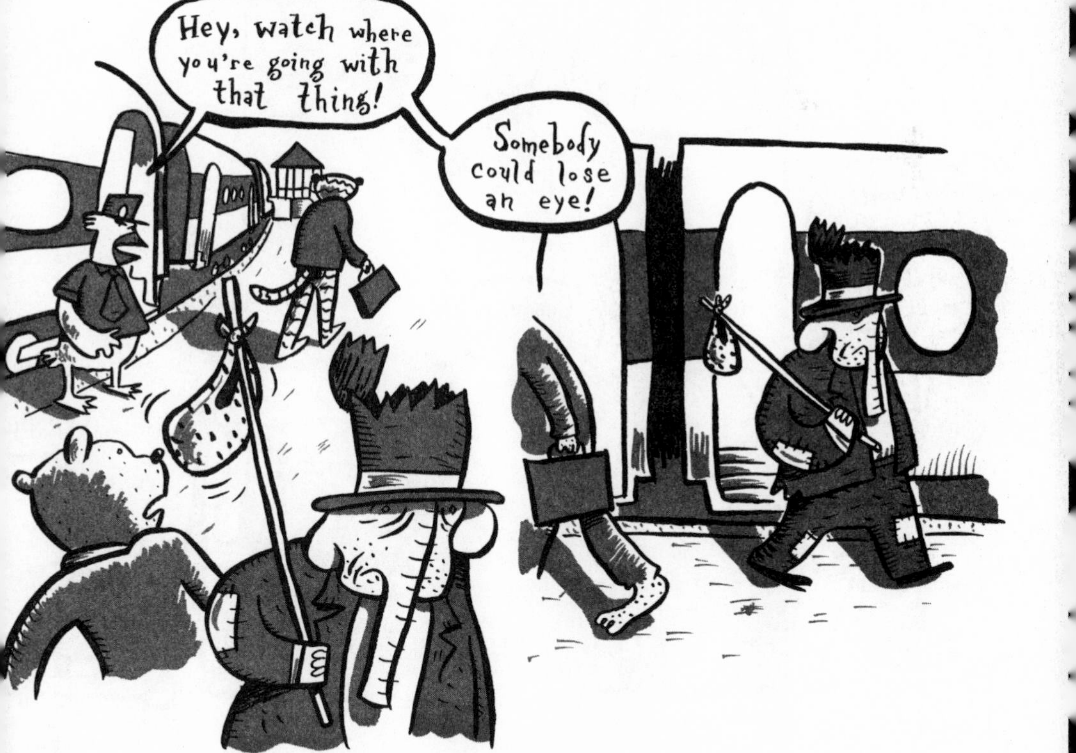
Hey, watch where you're going with that thing!
Somebody could lose an eye!

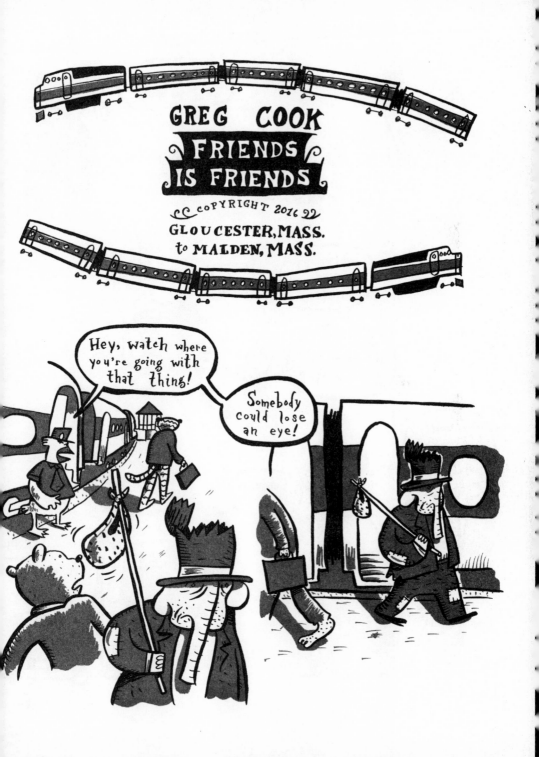

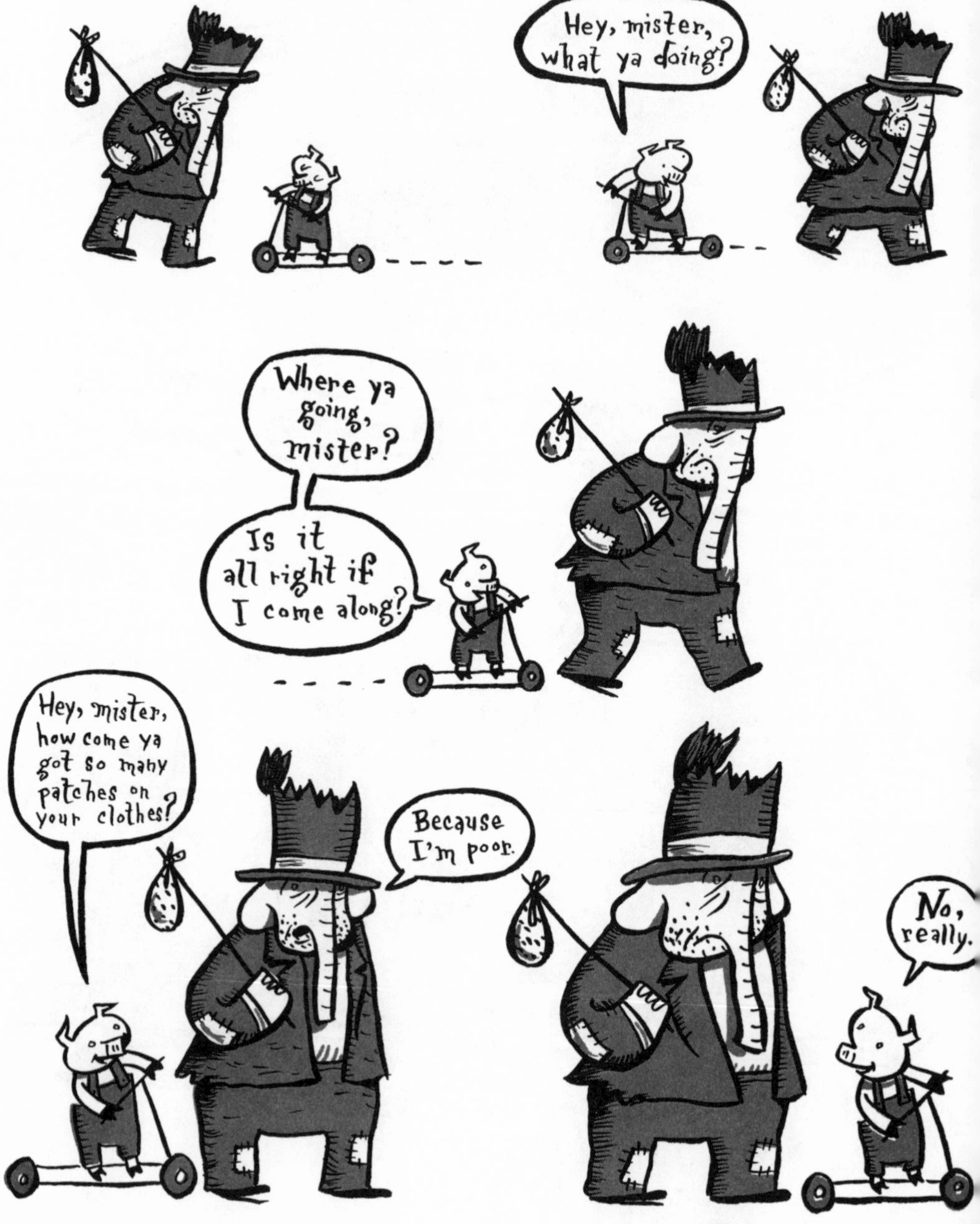

Hey, mister, what ya doing?
Where ya going, mister?
Is it all right if I come along?
Hey, mister, how come ya got so many patches on your clothes?
Because I'm poor.
No, really.

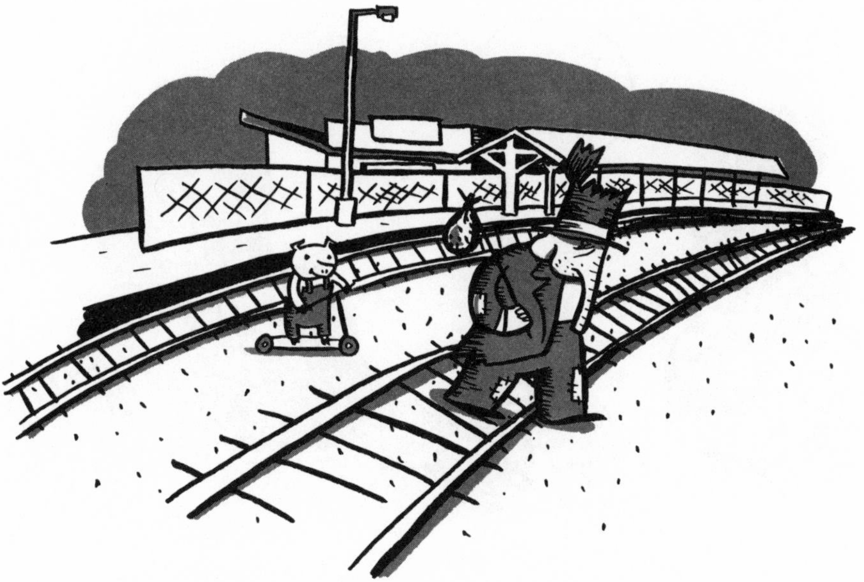

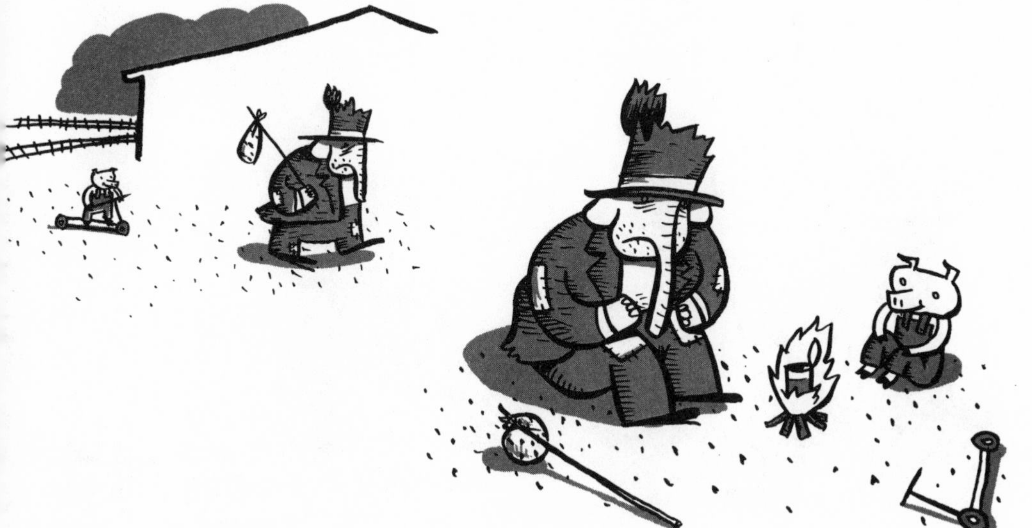

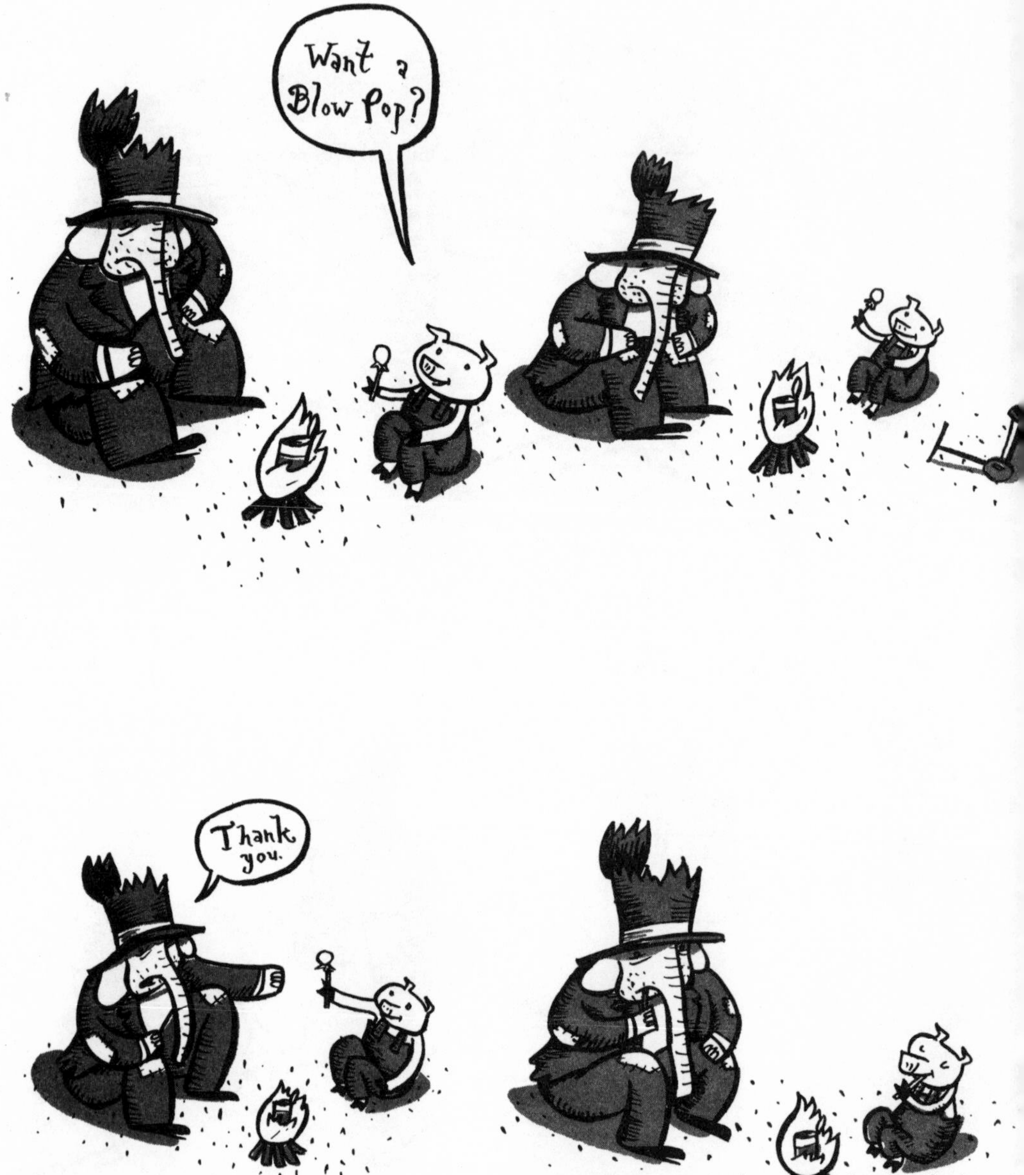
Want a Blow Pop?
Thank you.

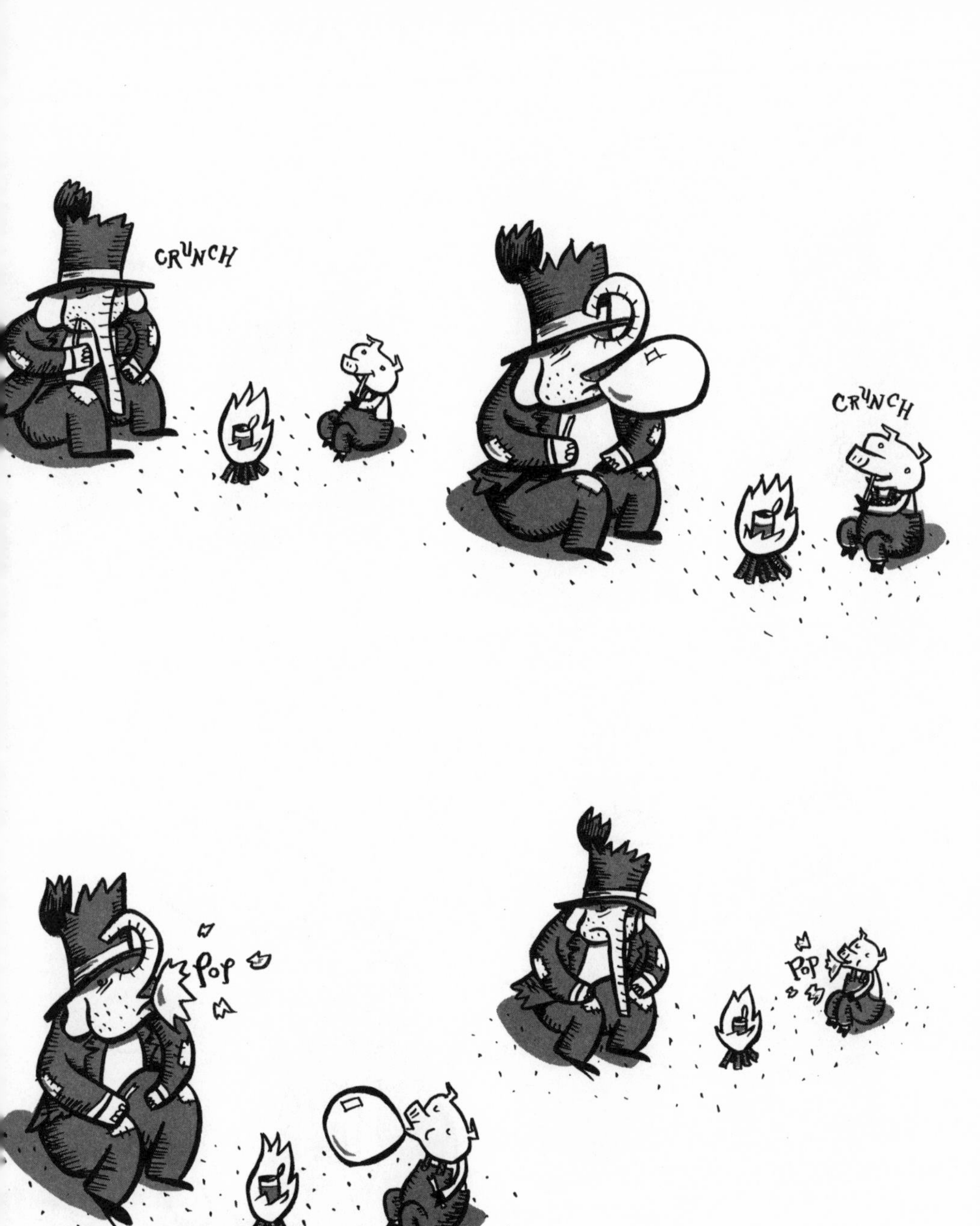
CRUNCH
CRUNCH
POP
POP

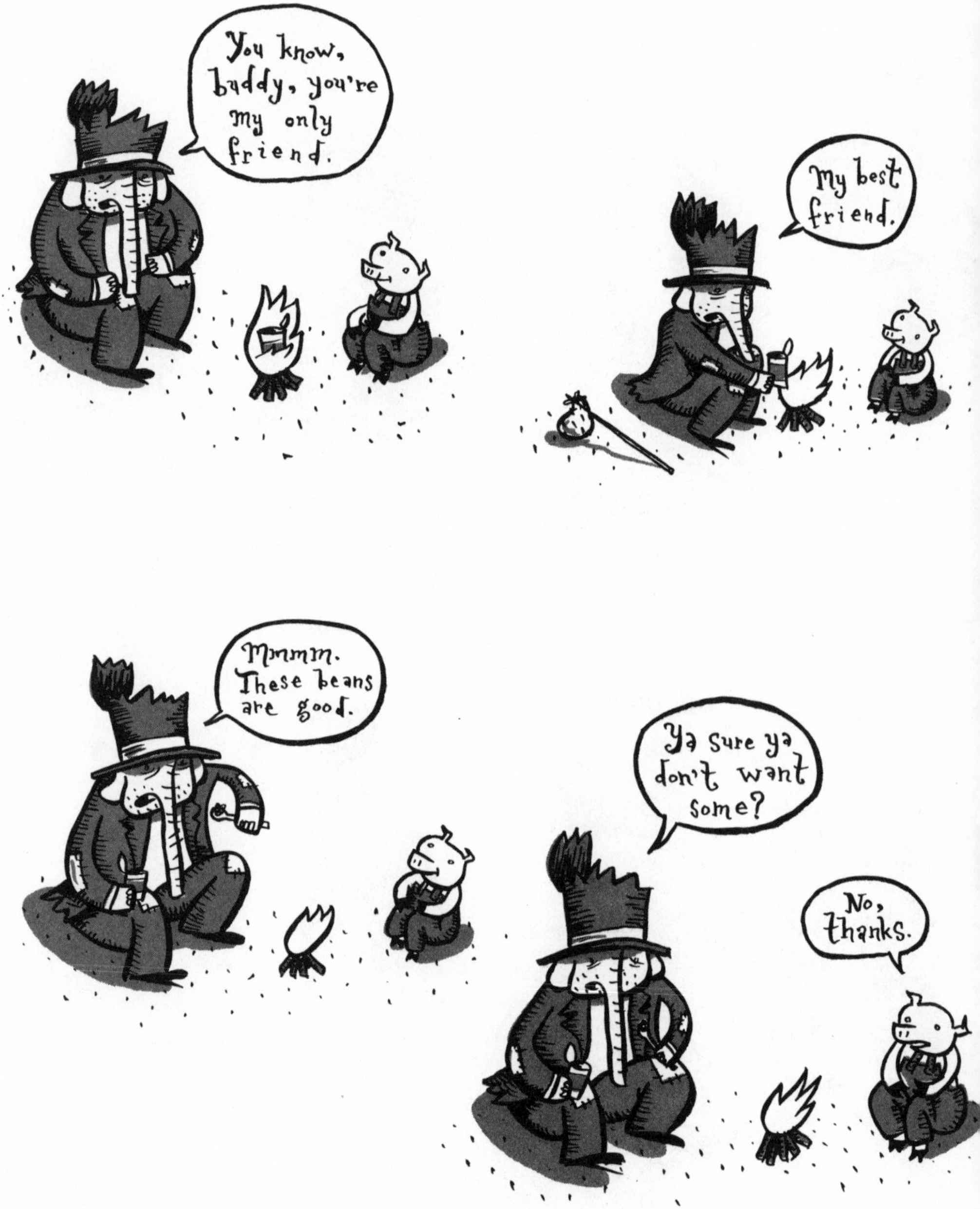
You know, buddy, you're my only friend.
My best friend.
Mmmm. These beans are good.
Ya sure ya don't want some?
No, thanks.

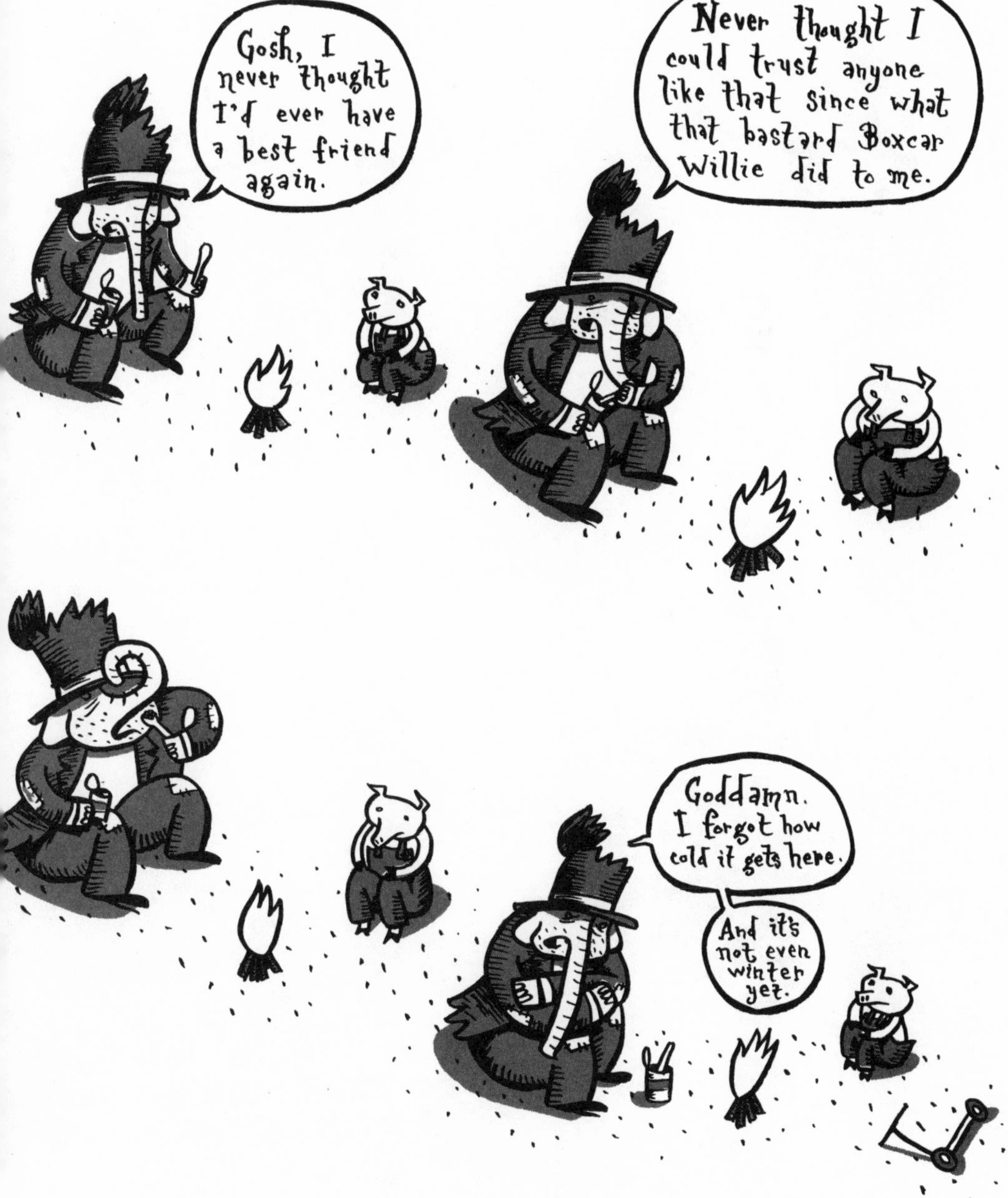
Gosh, I never thought I'd ever have a best friend again.
Never thought I could trust anyone like that since what that bastard Boxcar Willie did to me.
Goddamn. I forgot how cold it gets here.
And it's not even winter yet.

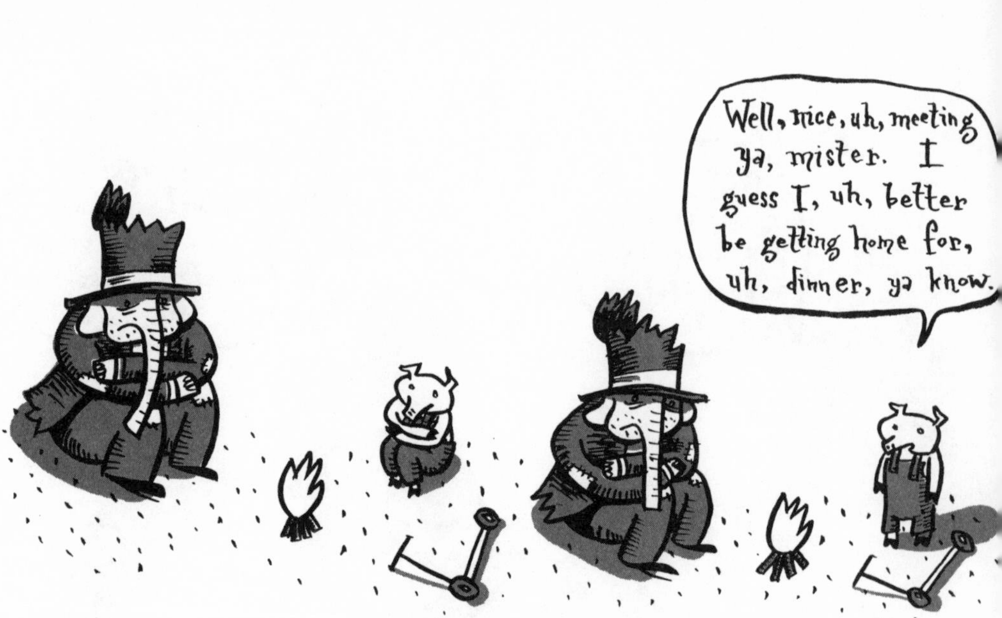
Well, nice, uh, meeting ya, mister. I guess I, uh, better be getting home for, uh, dinner, ya know.

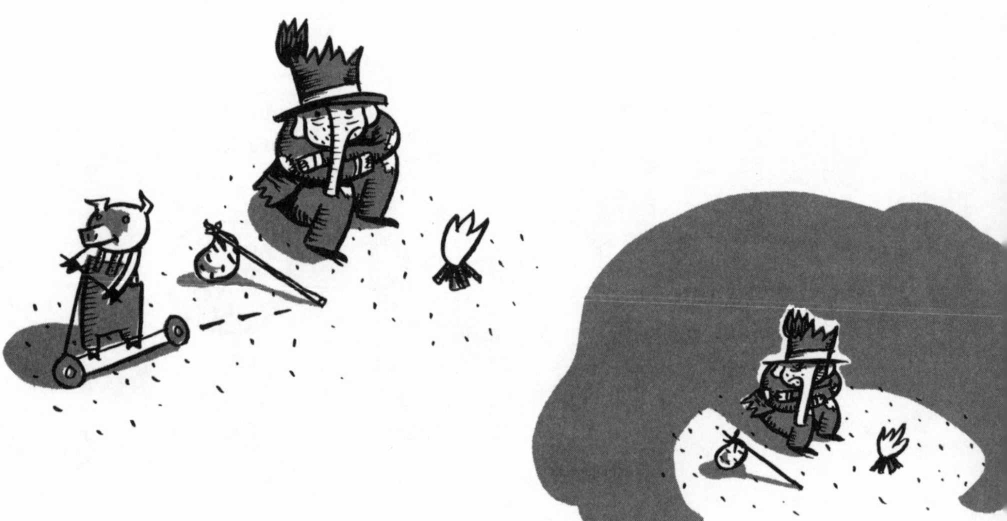

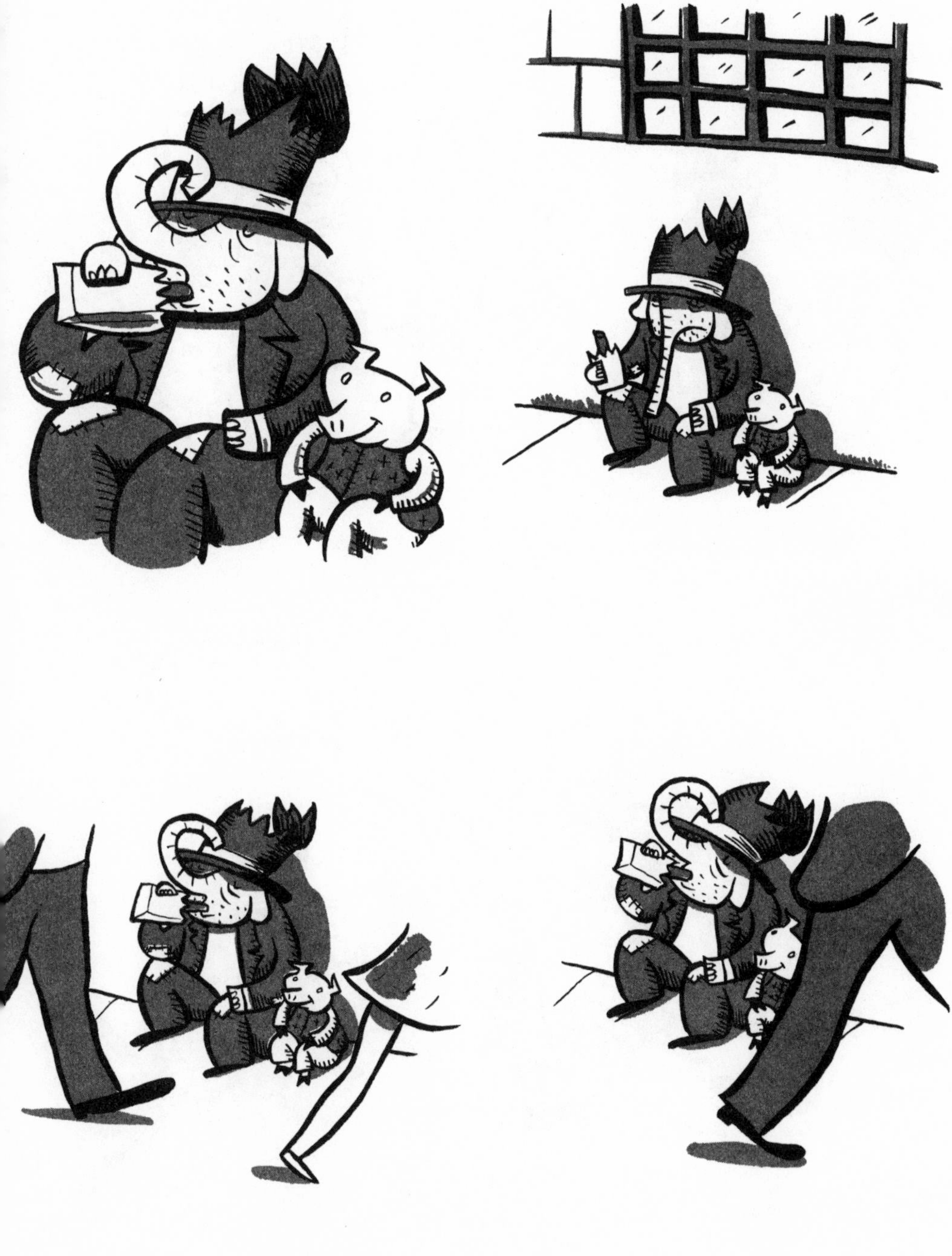

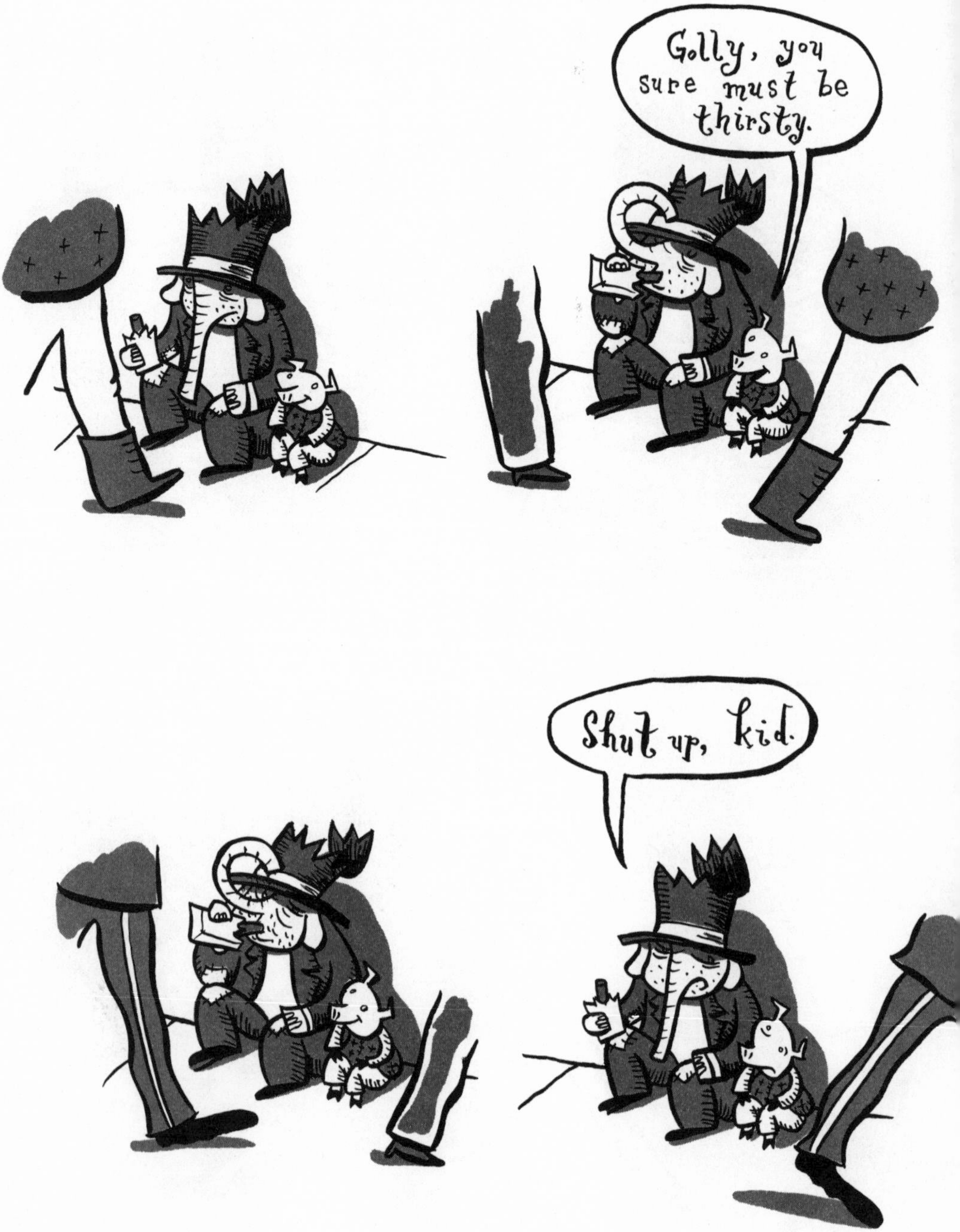
Golly, you sure must be thirsty.
Shut up, kid.

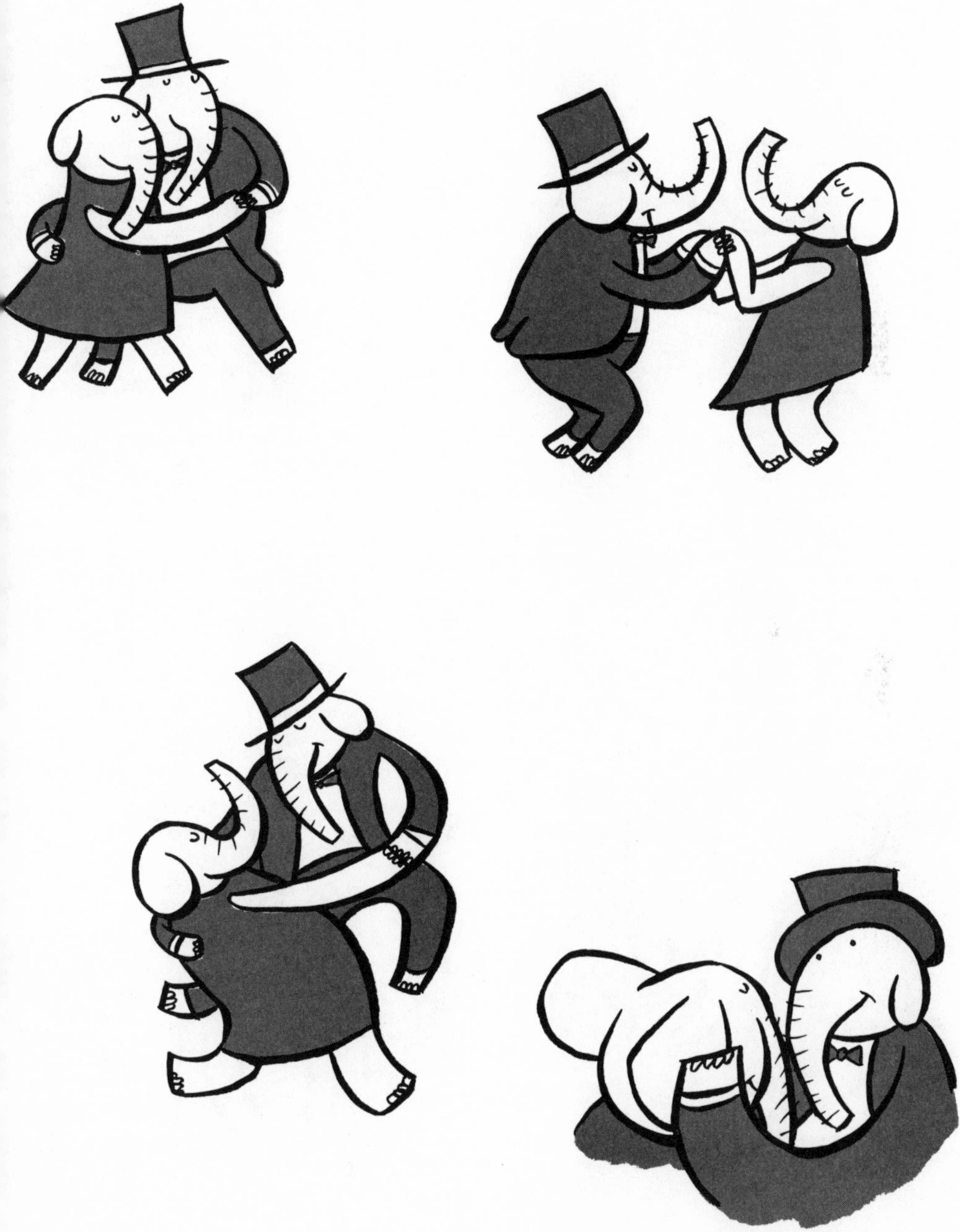

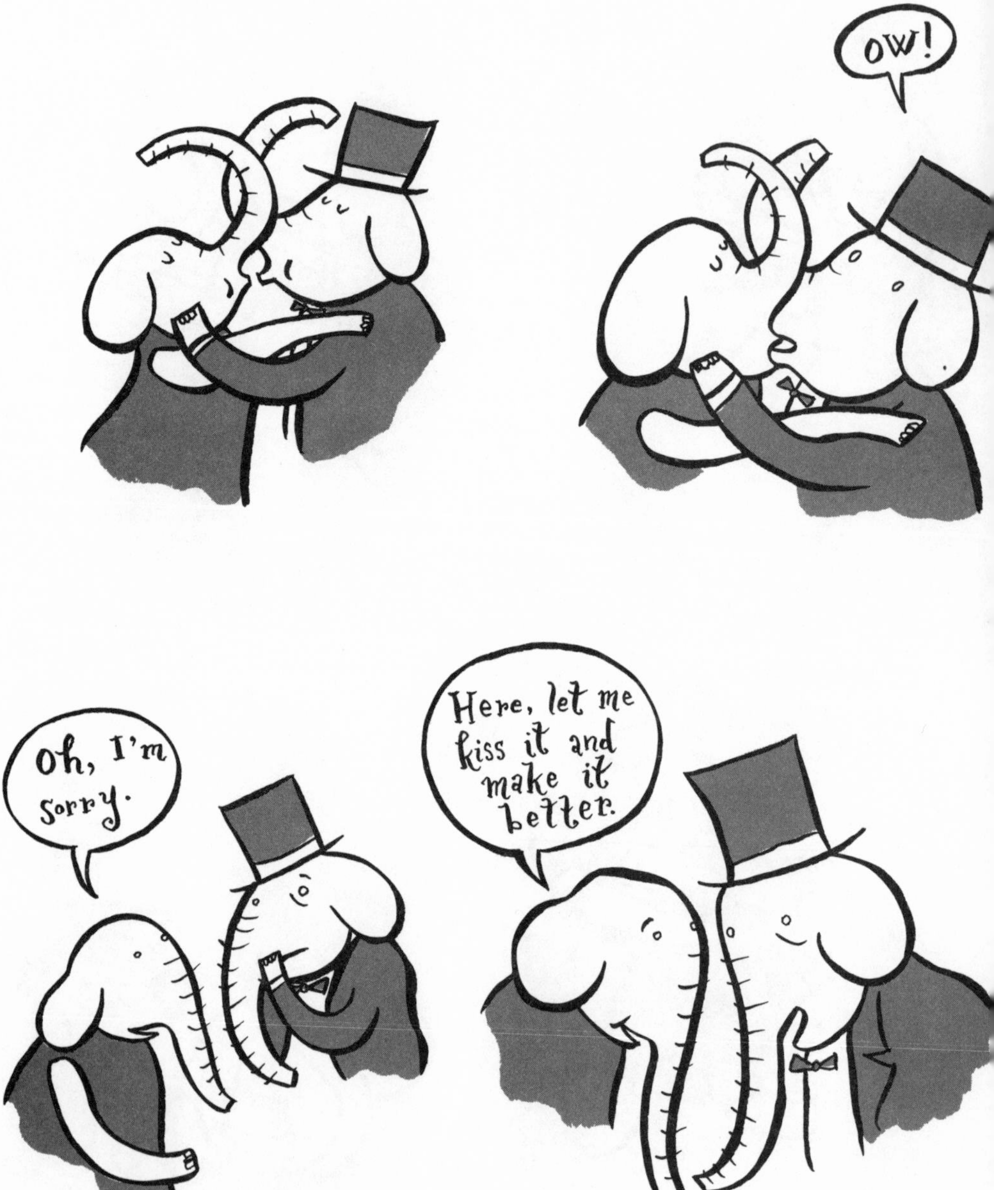
OW!
Oh, I'm sorry.
Here, let me kiss it and make it better.

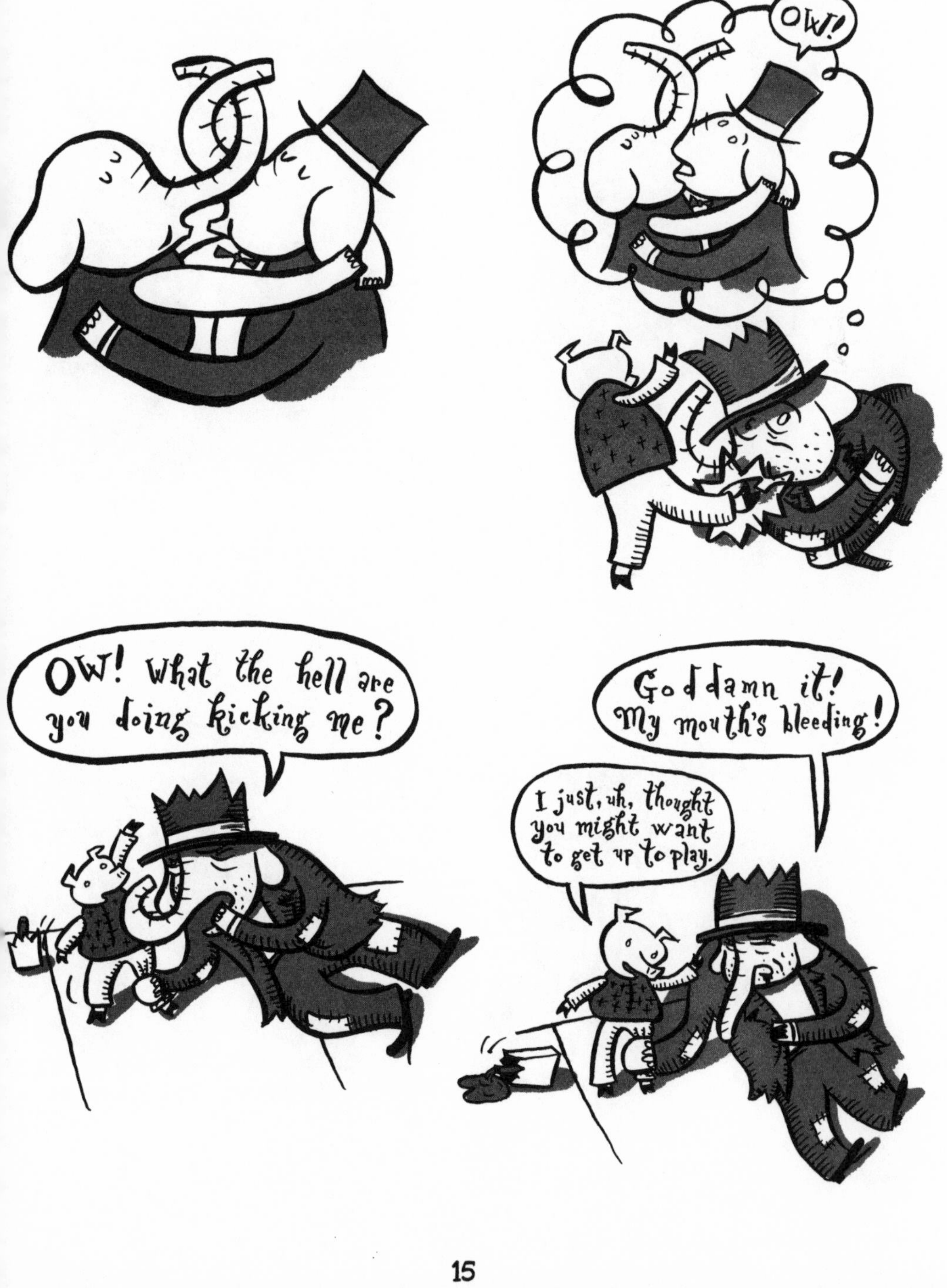
OW!
OW! What the hell are you doing kicking me?
Goddamn it! My mouth's bleeding!
I just, uh, thought you might want to get up to play.

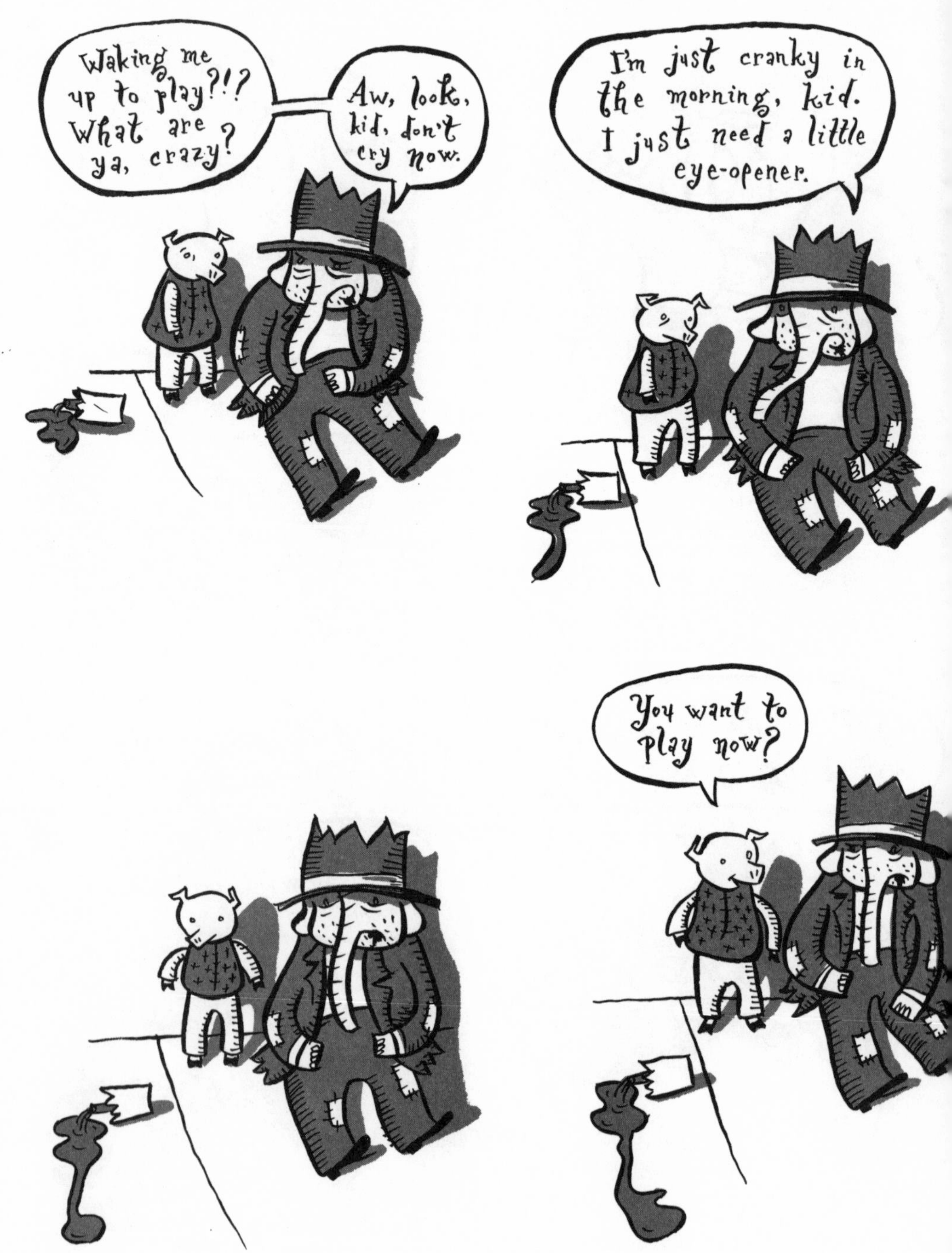
Waking me up to play?!? What are ya, crazy?
Aw, look, kid, don't cry now.
I'm just cranky in the morning, kid. I just need a little eye-opener.
You want to play now?

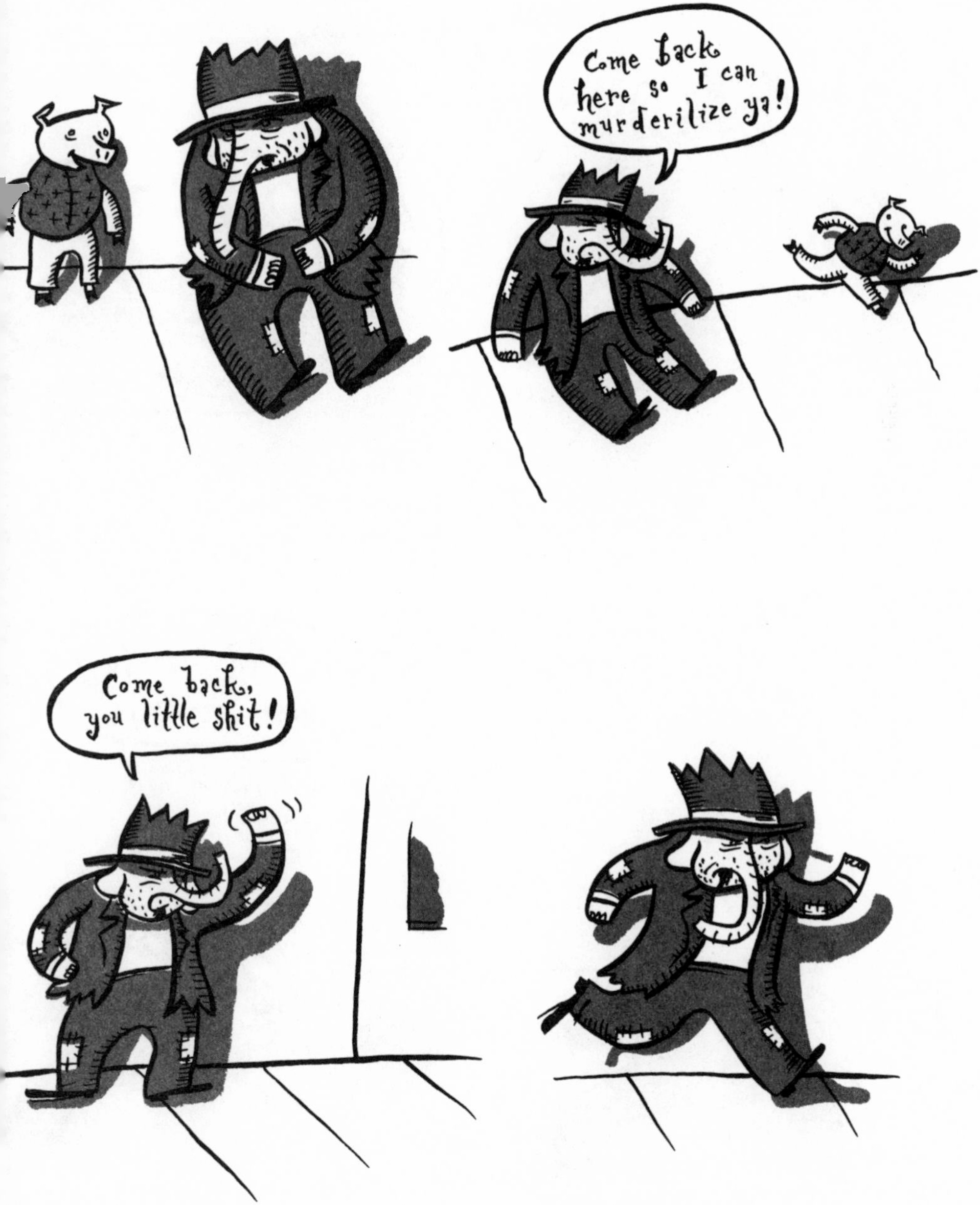
Come back here so I can murderilize ya!
Come back, you little shit!

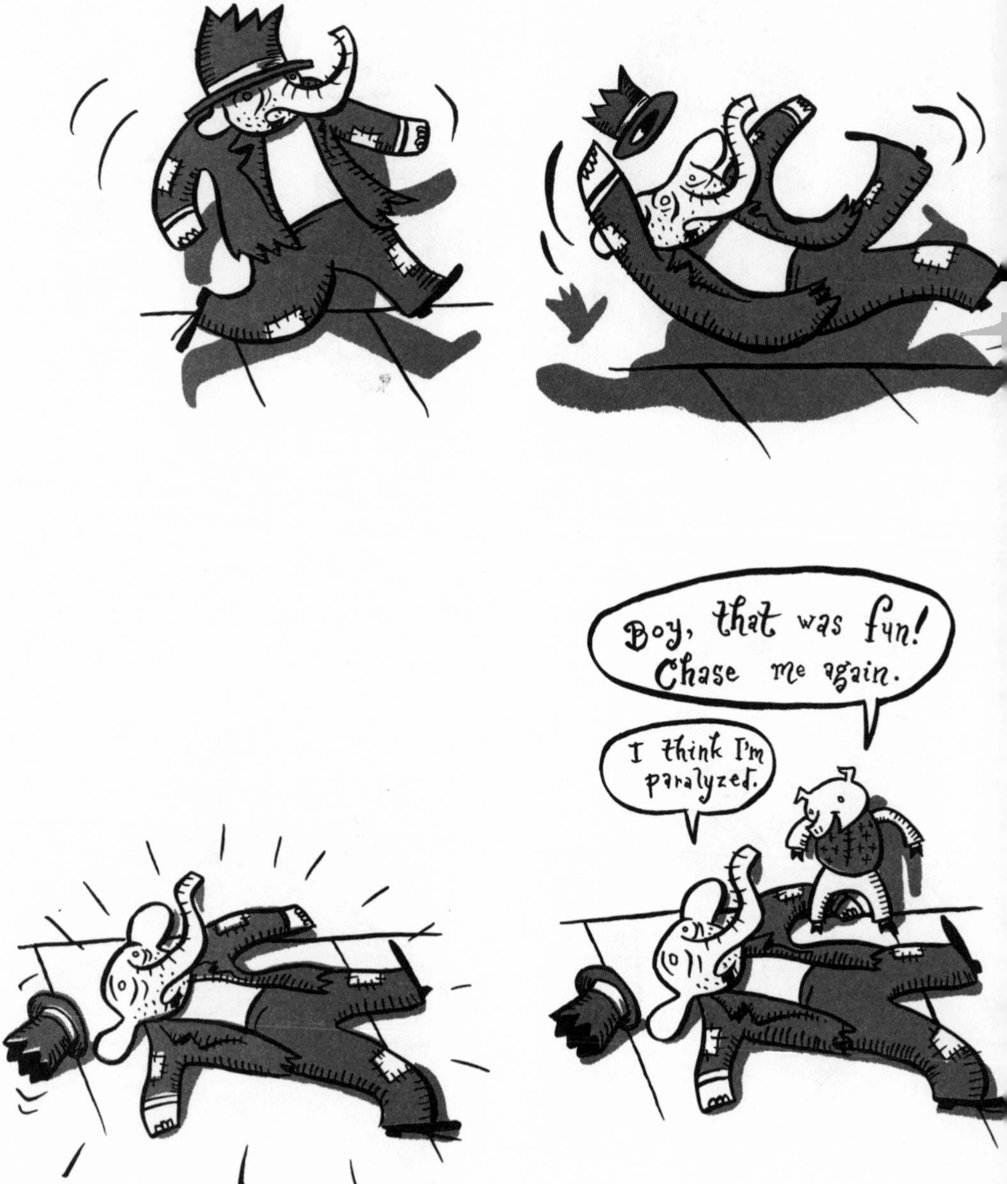
Boy, that was fun! Chase me again.
I think I'm paralyzed.

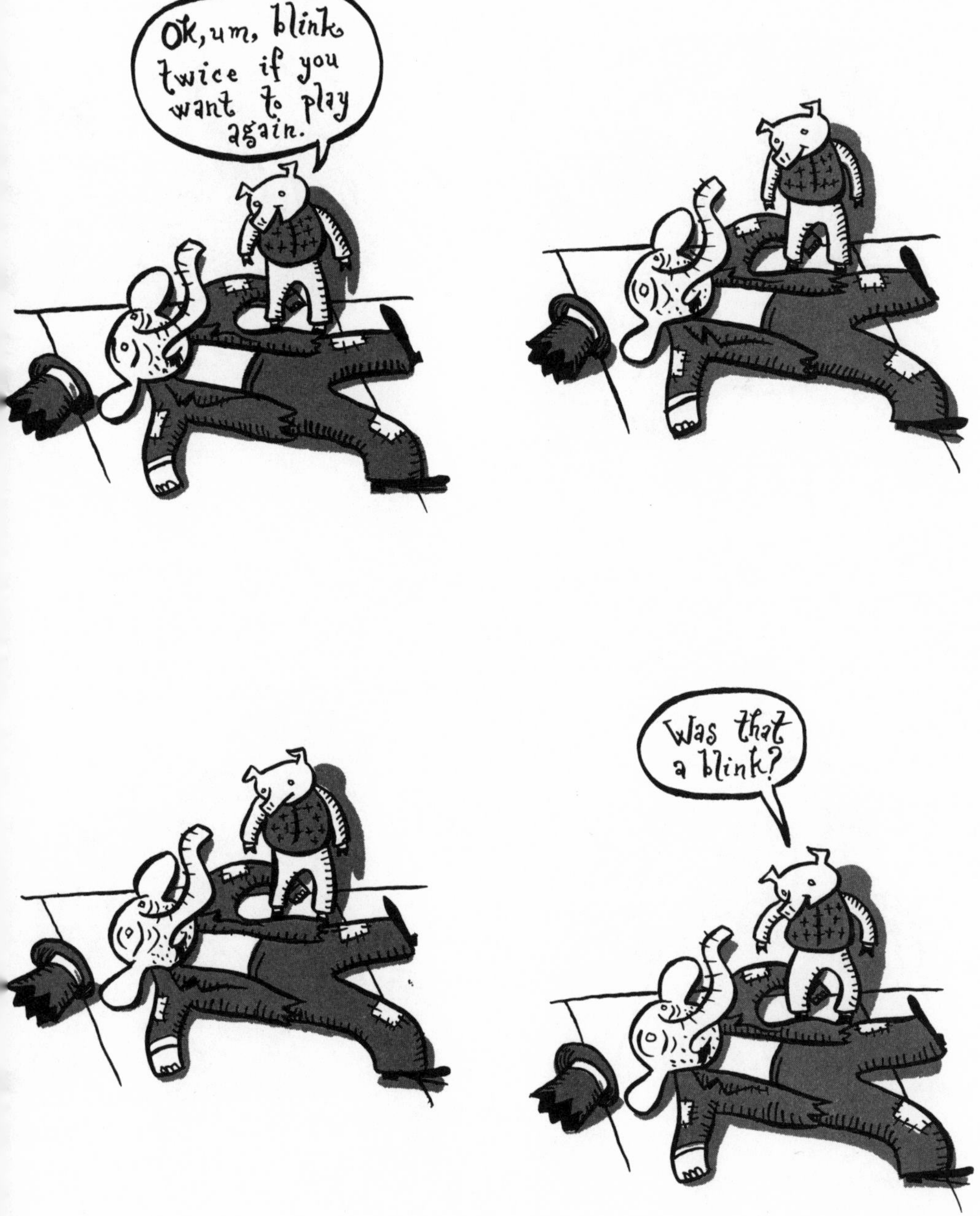
Ok, um, blink twice if you want to play again.
Was that a blink?

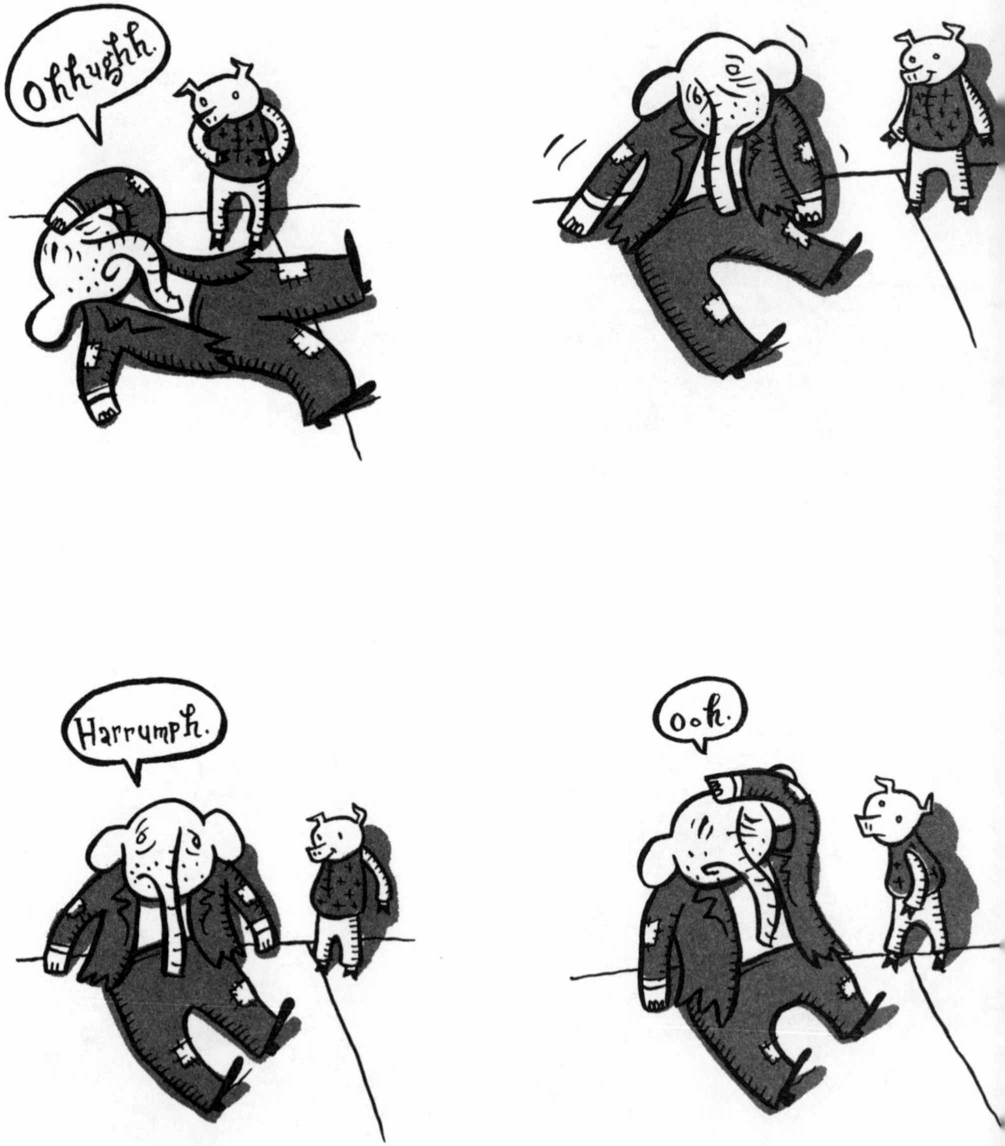
Ohhughh.
Harrumph.
Ooh.

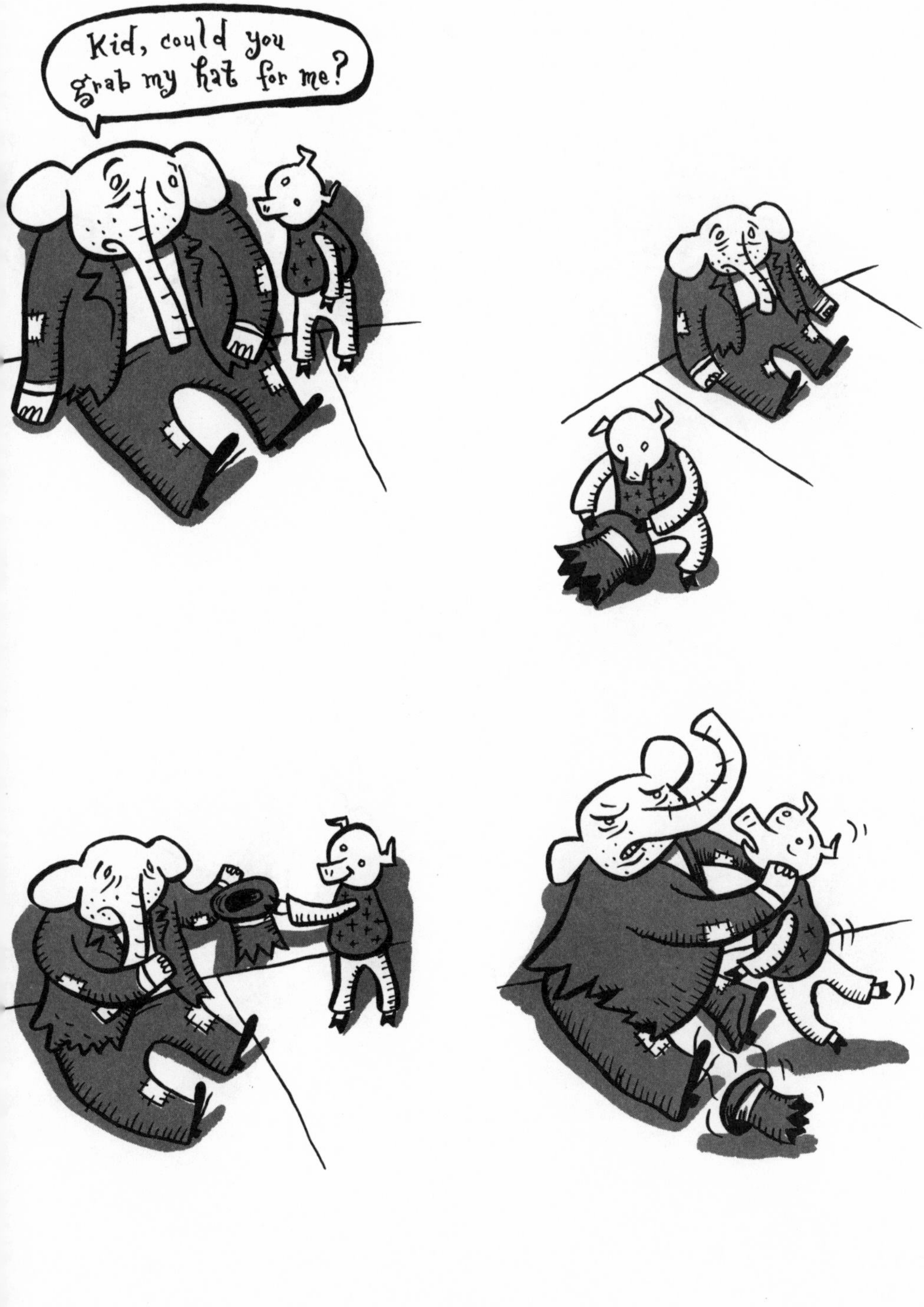
Kid, could you grab my hat for me?

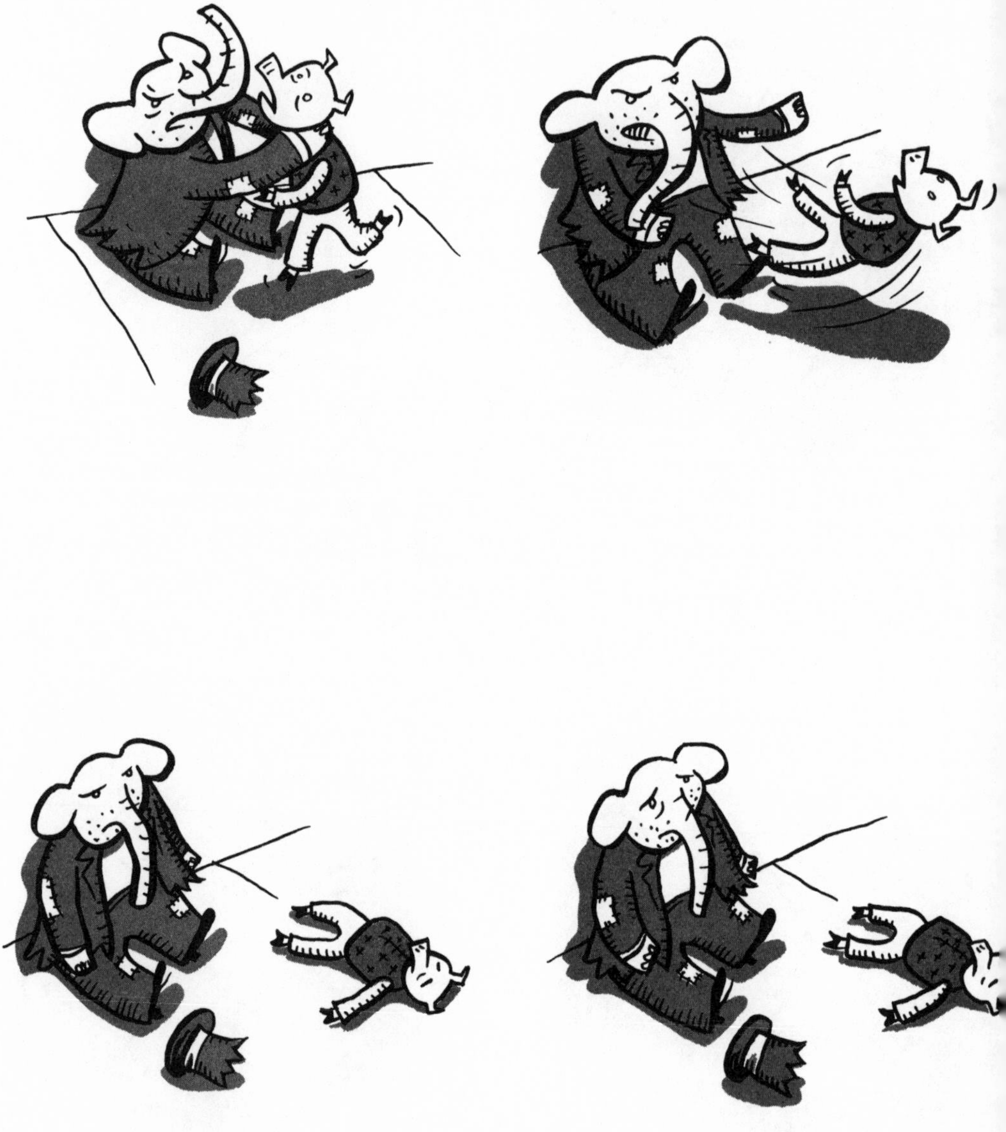

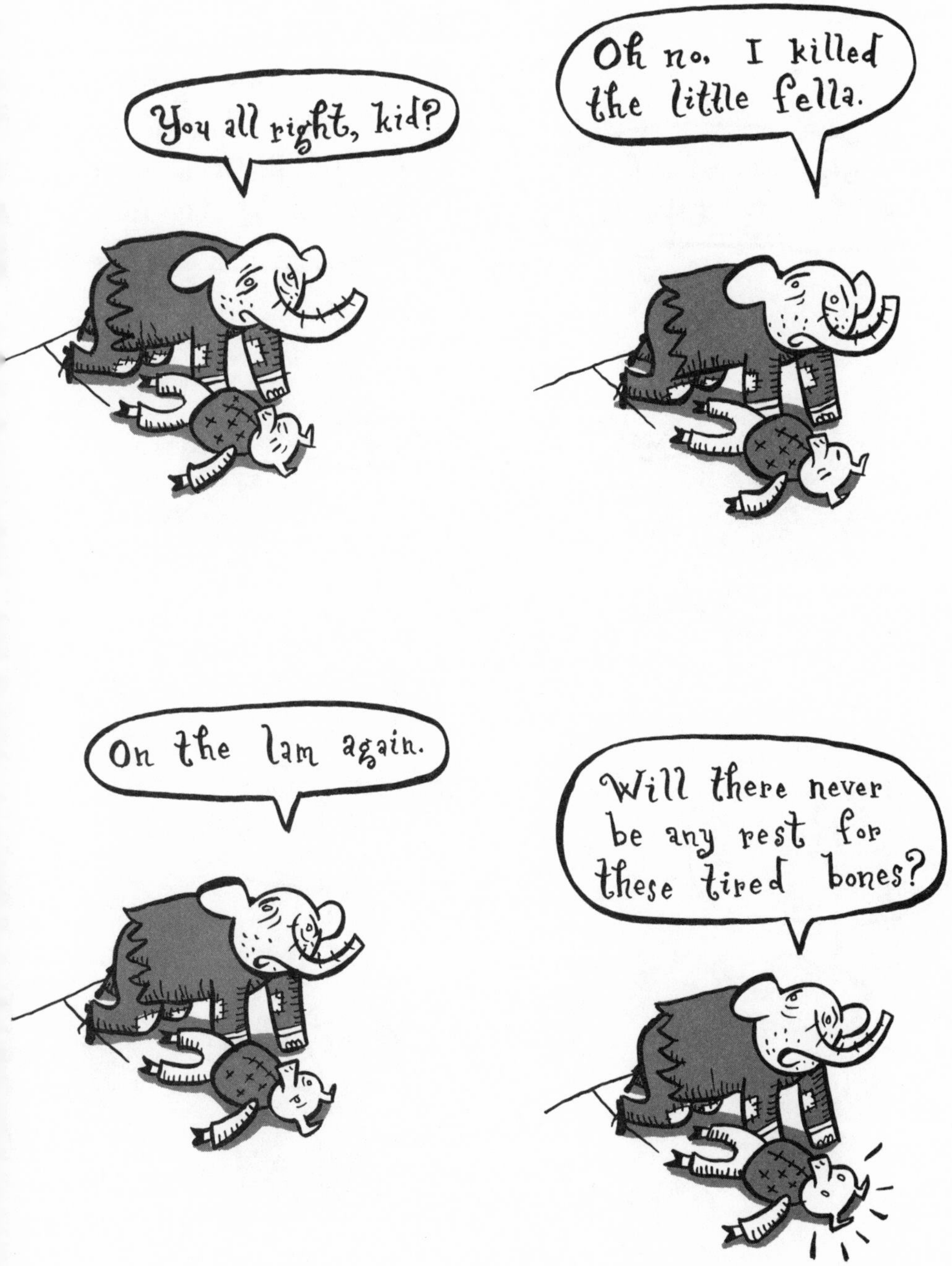
You all right, kid?
Oh no. I killed the little fella.
On the lam again.
Will there never be any rest for these tired bones?

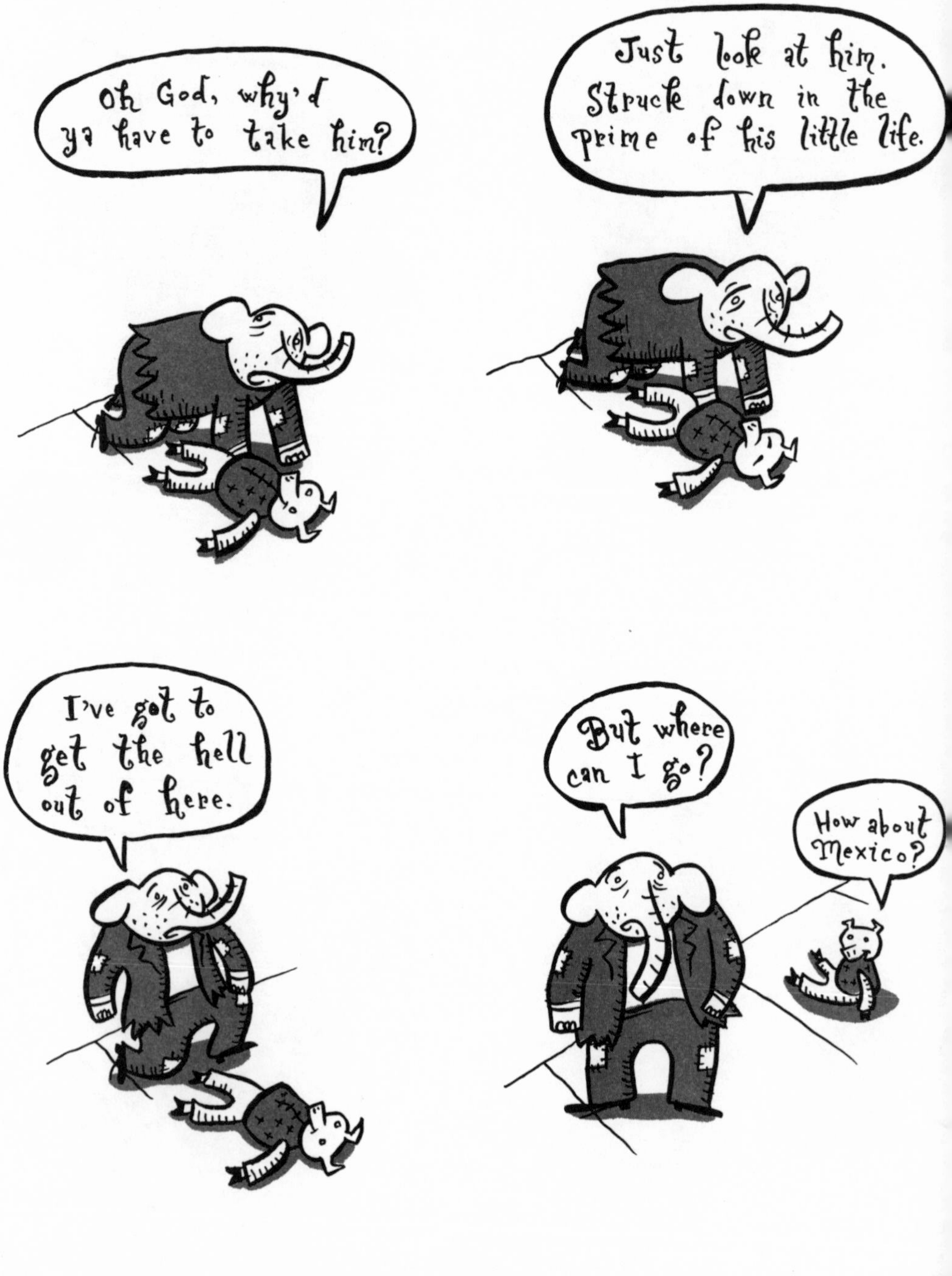
Oh God, why'd ya have to take him?
Just look at him. Struck down in the prime of his little life.
I've got to get the hell out of here.
But where can I go?
How about Mexico?

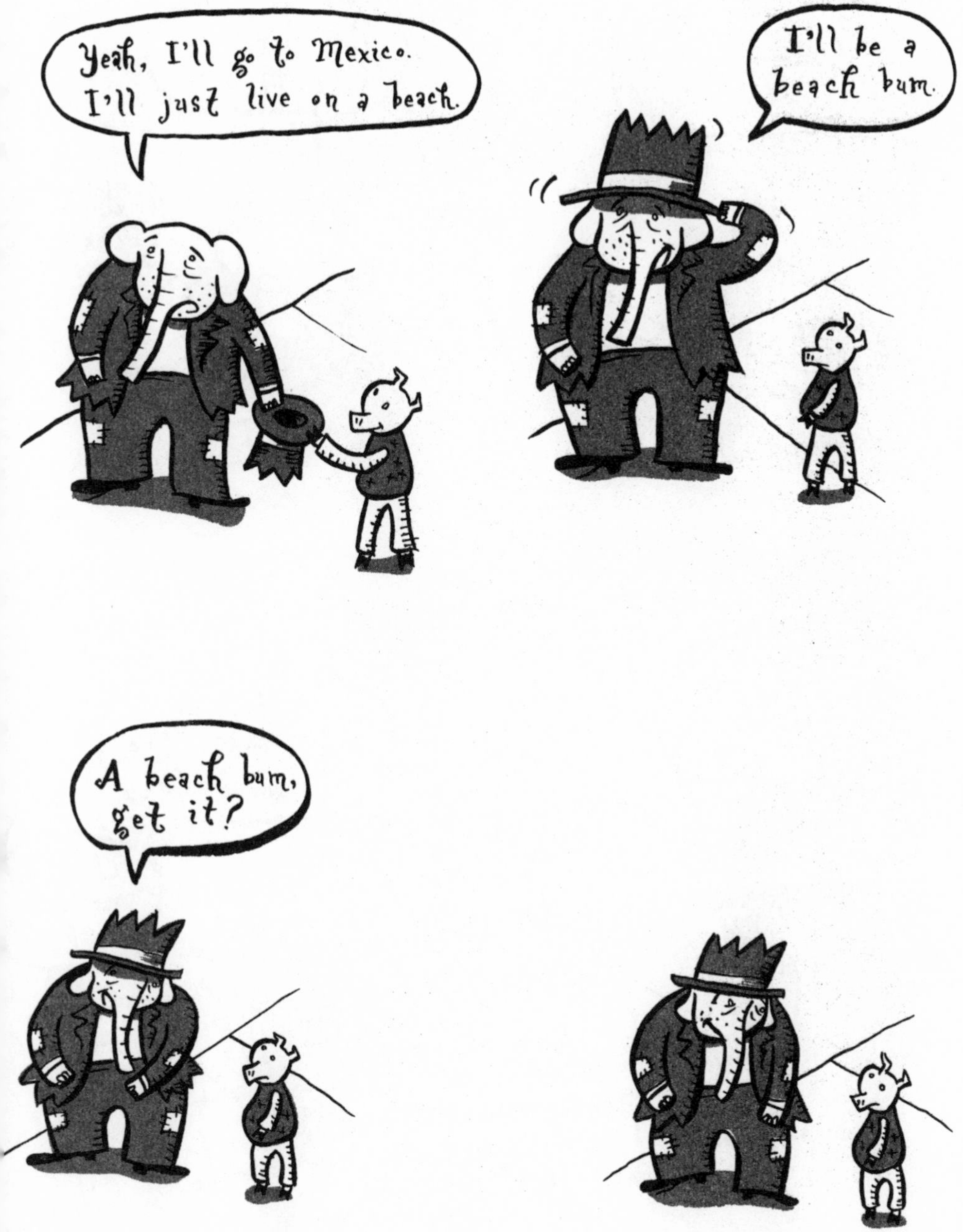
Yeah, I'll go to Mexico. I'll just live on a beach.
I'll be a beach bum.
A beach bum, get it?

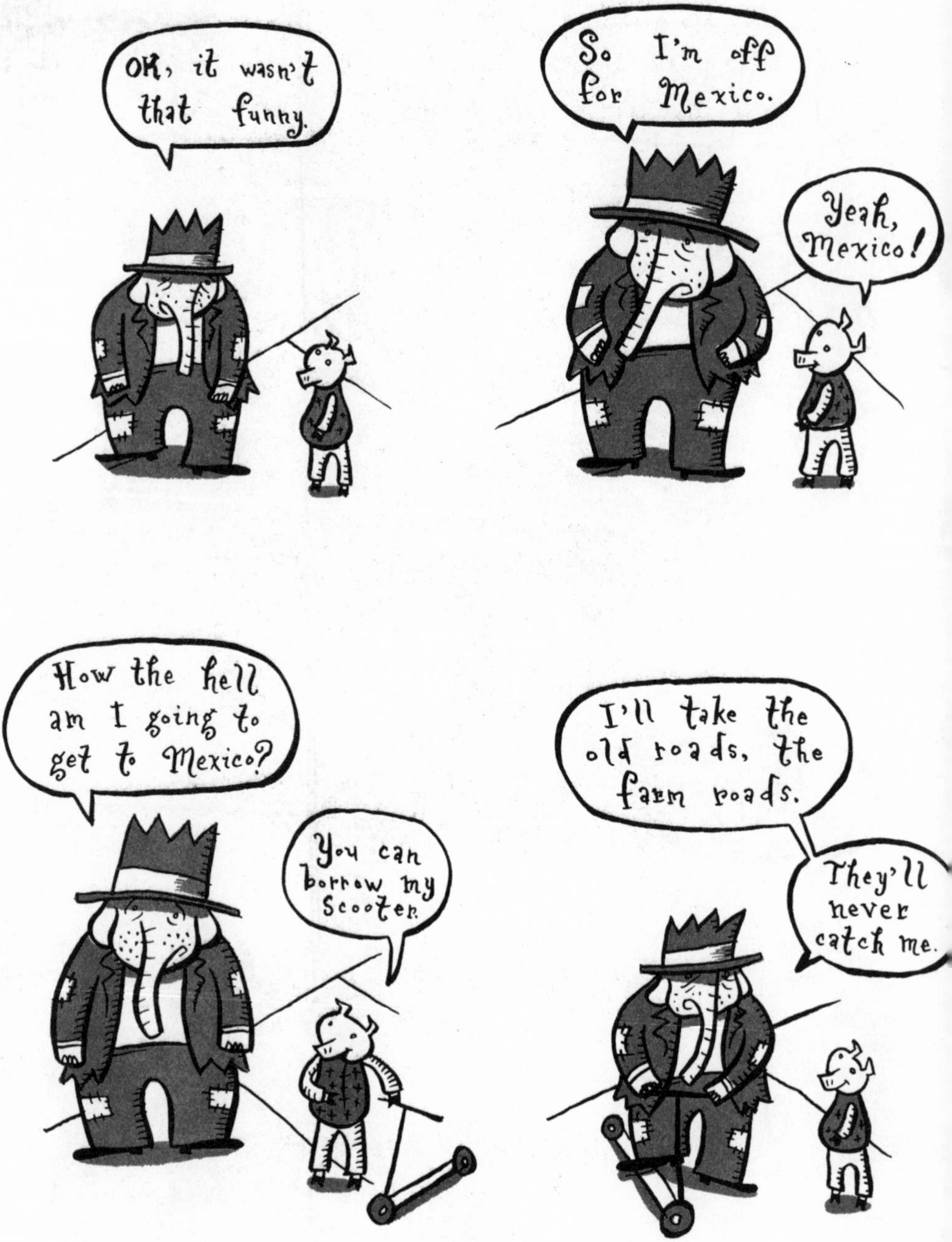
OK, it wasn't that funny.
So I'm off for Mexico.
Yeah, Mexico!
How the hell am I going to get to Mexico?
You can borrow my Scooter.
I'll take the old roads, the farm roads.
They'll never catch me.

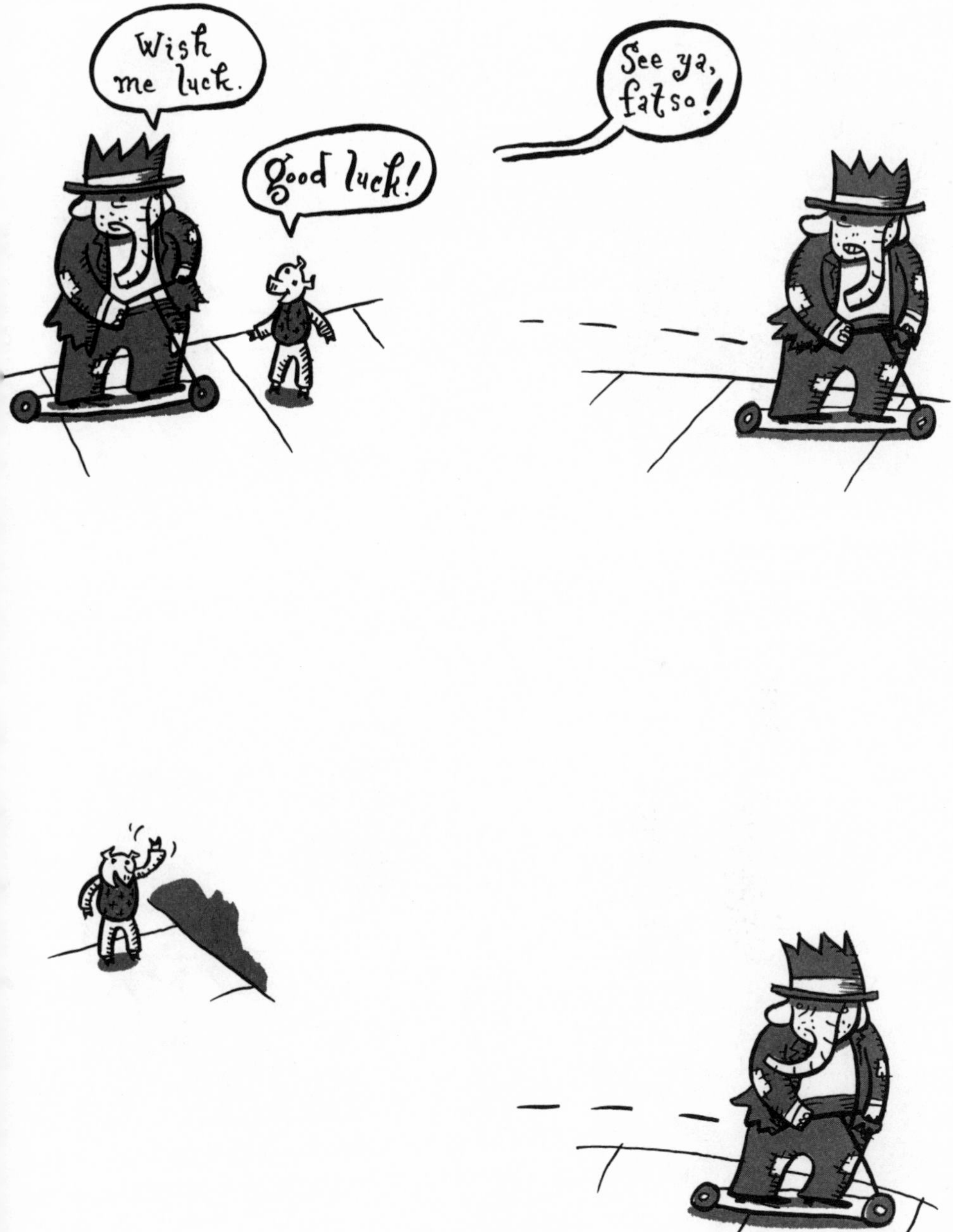
Wish me luck.
Good luck!
See ya, fatso!

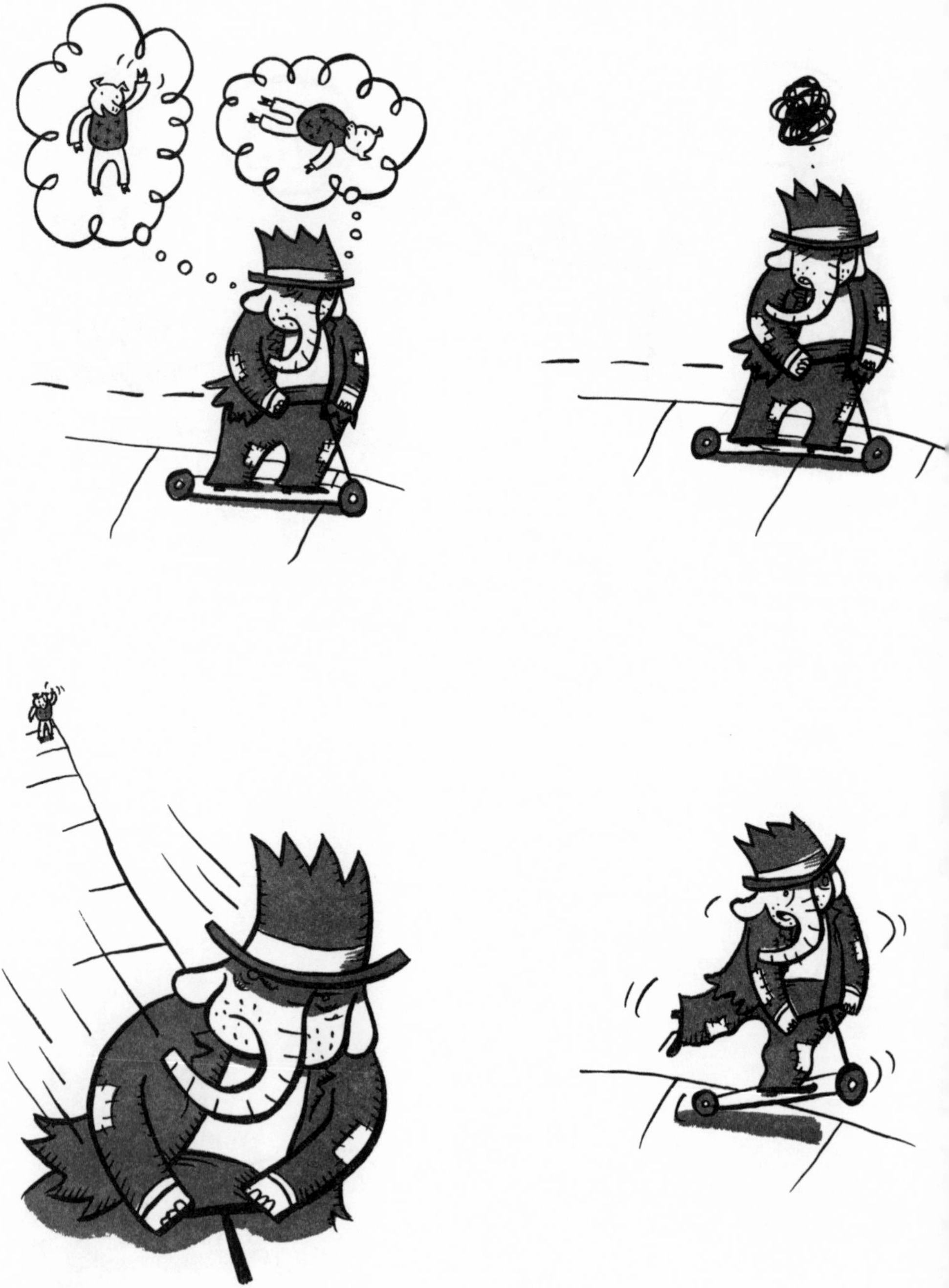

I hate you, fatso. I hope you die!

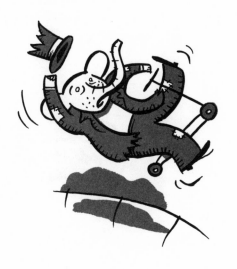

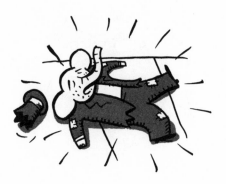

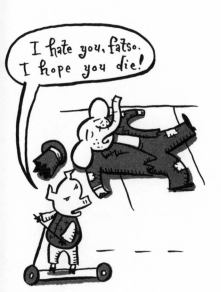

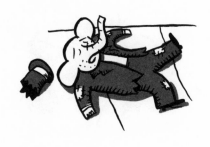

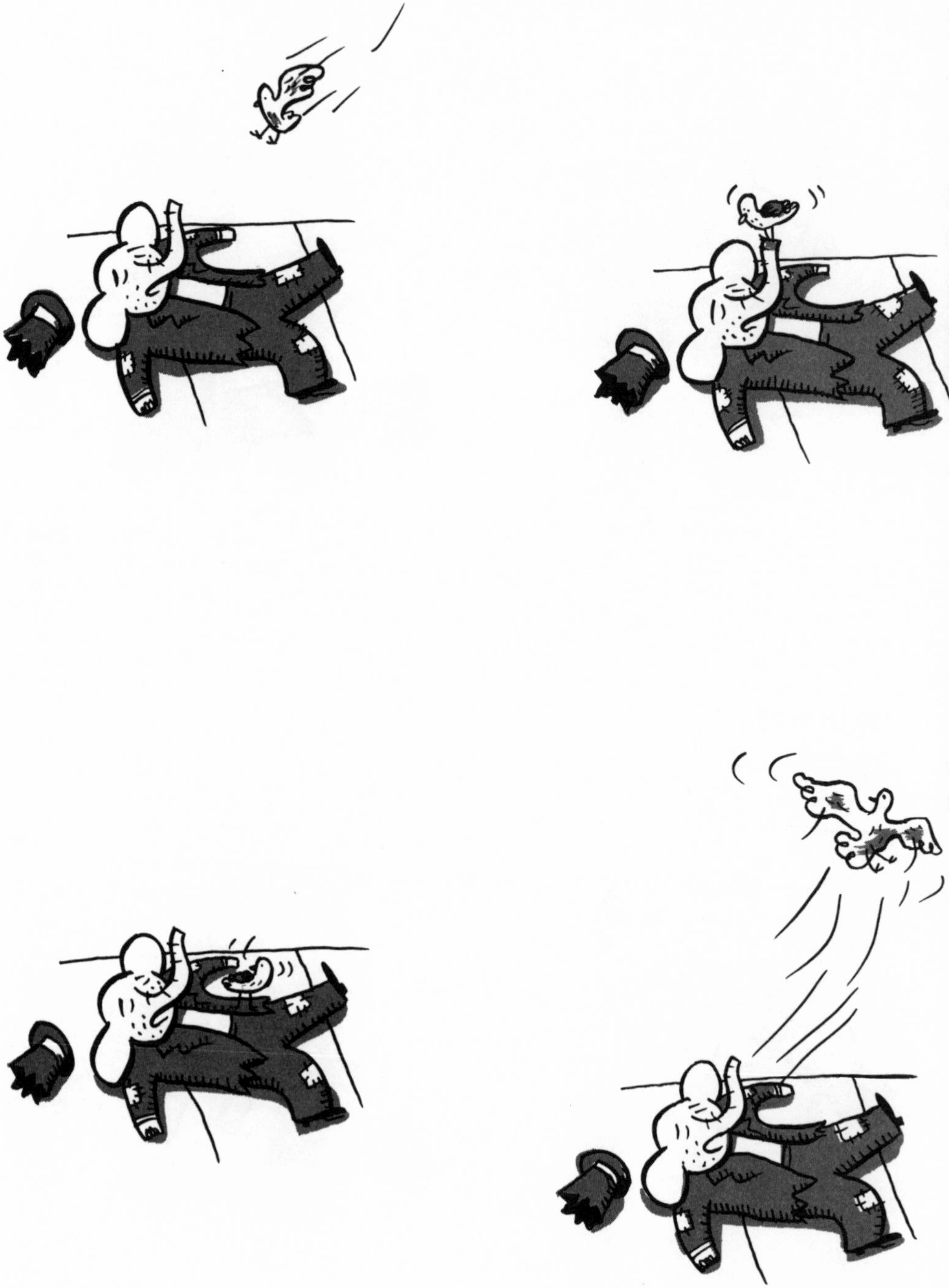

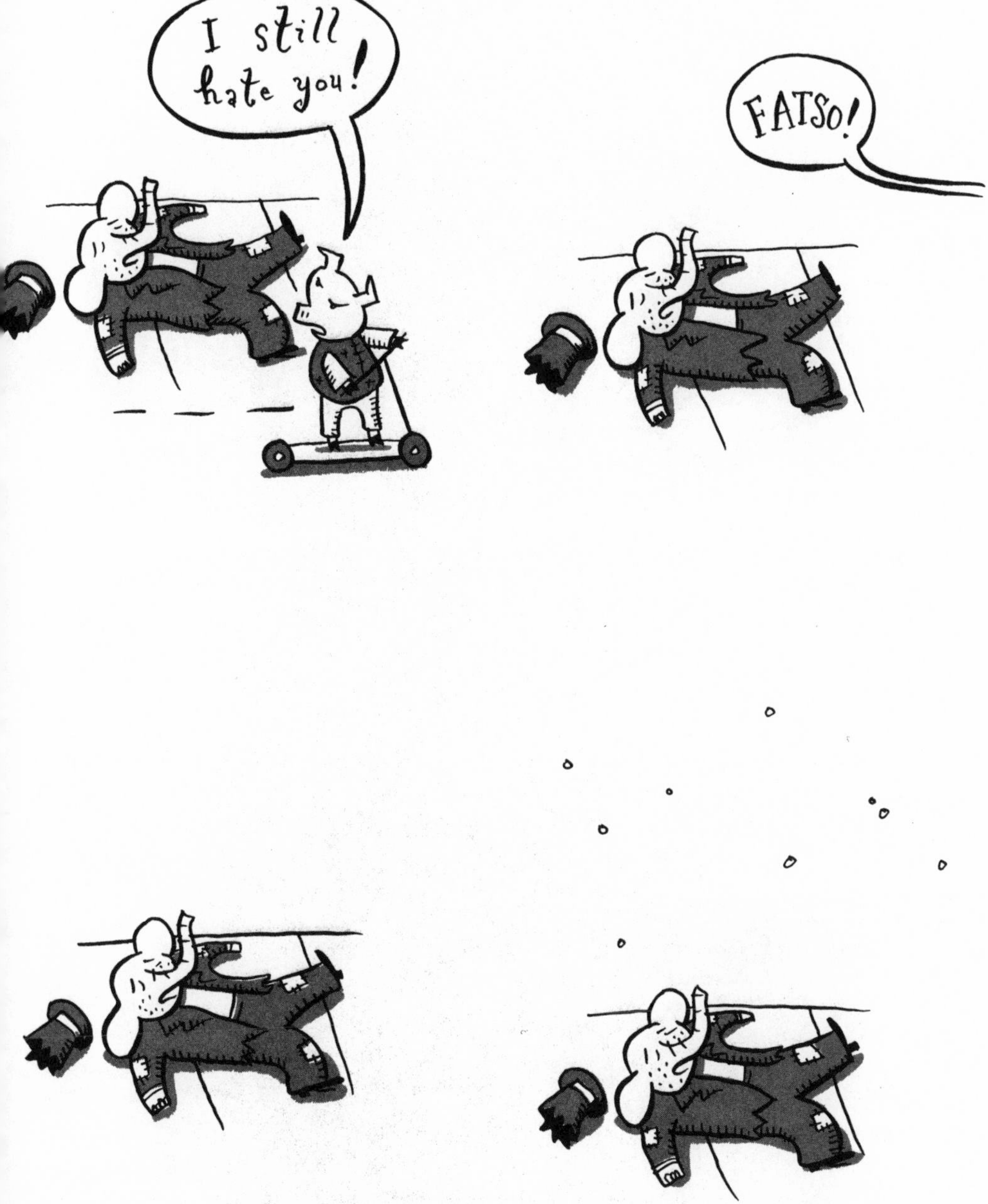
I still hate you!
FATSO!

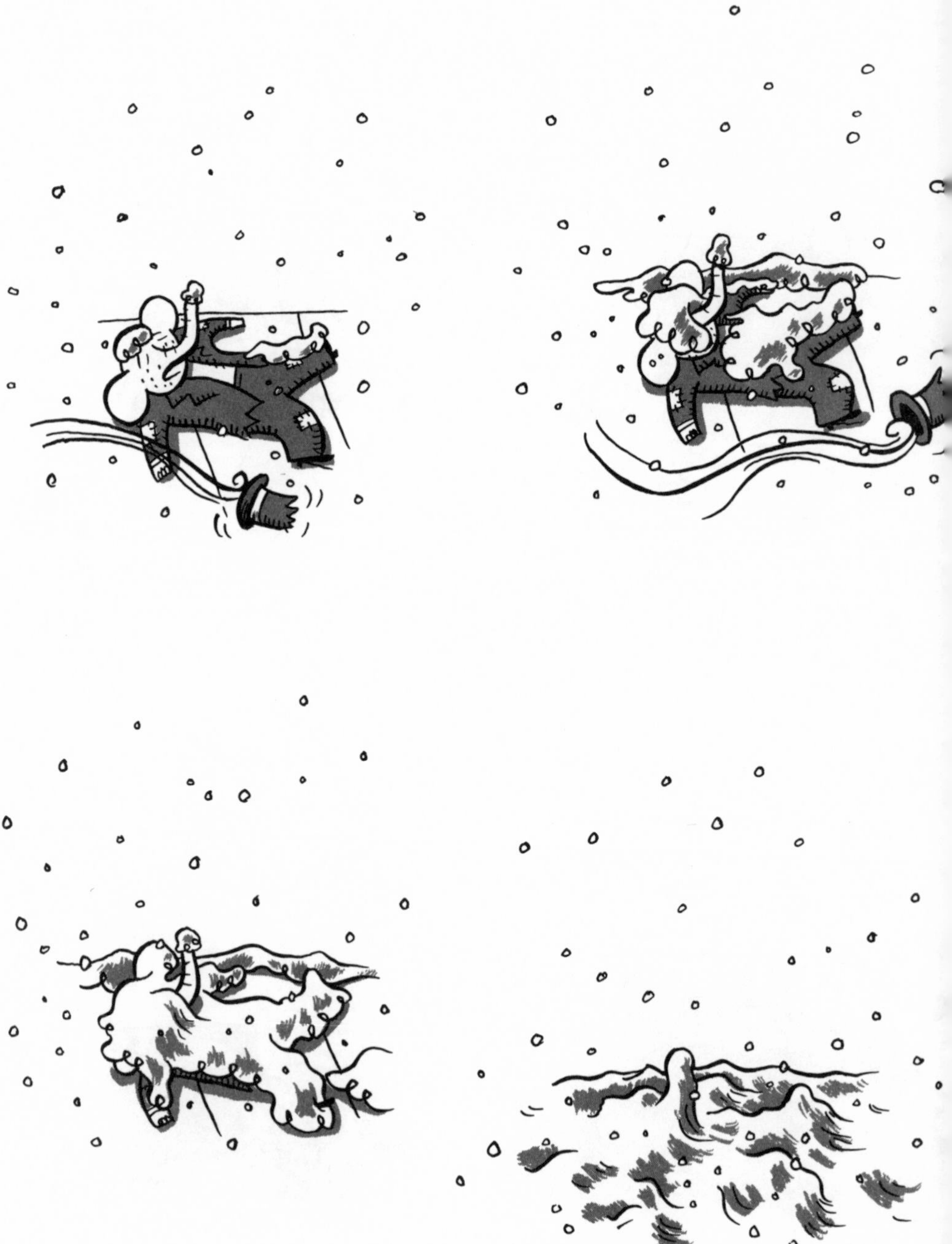

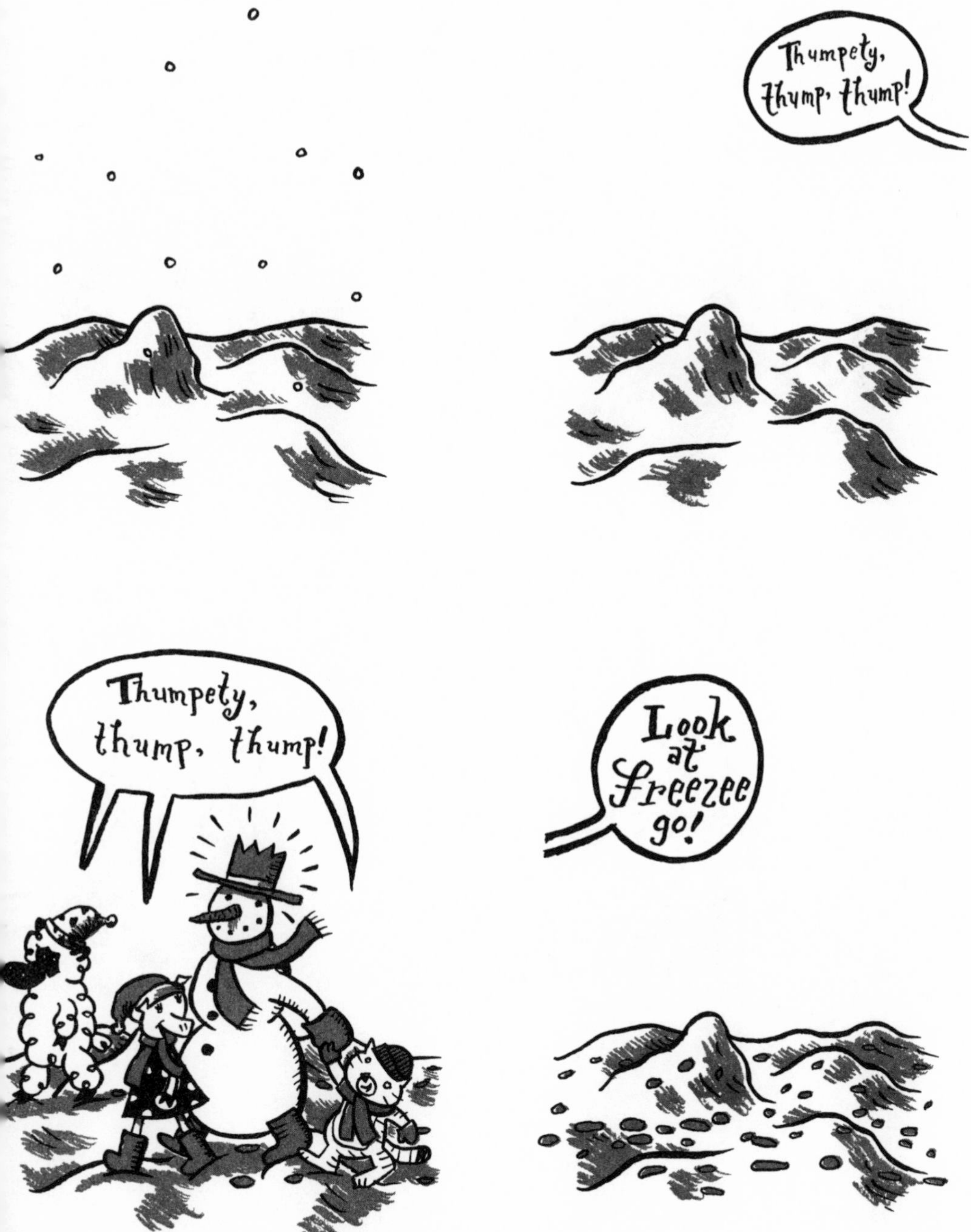
Thumpety, thump, thump!
Thumpety, thump, thump!
Look at Freezee go!

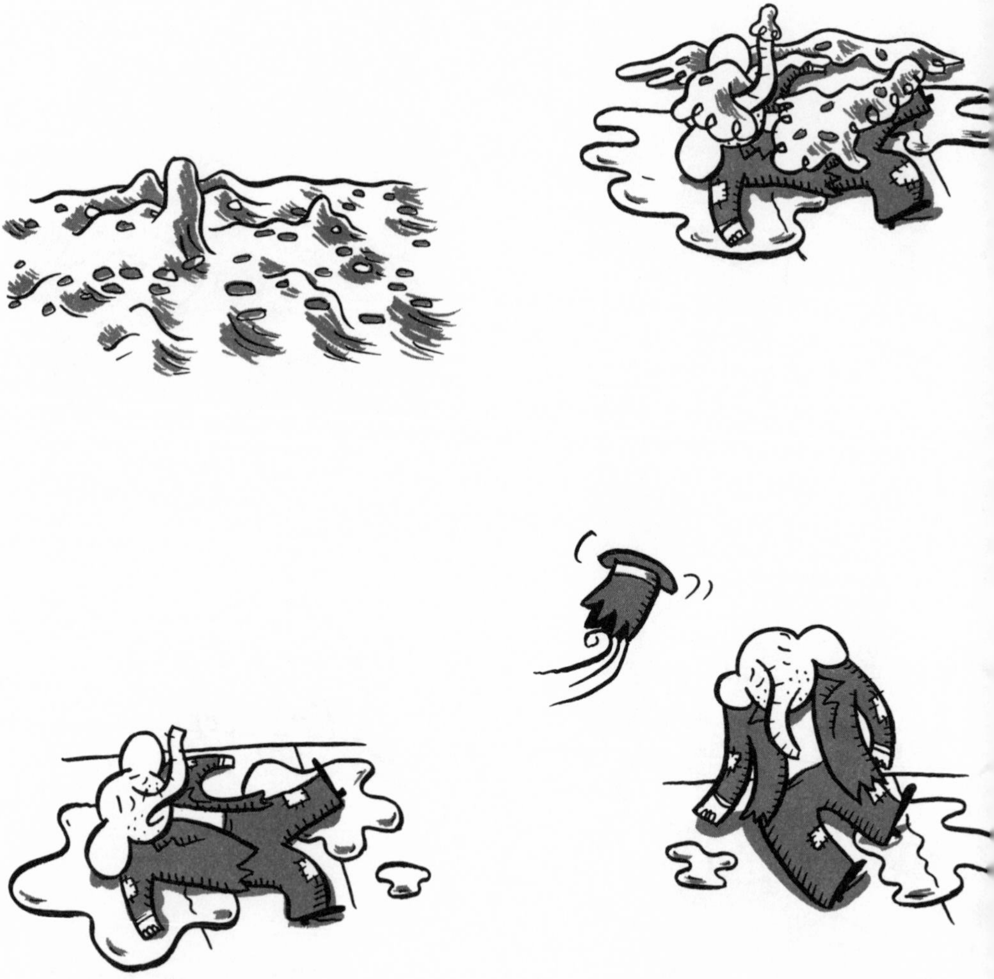

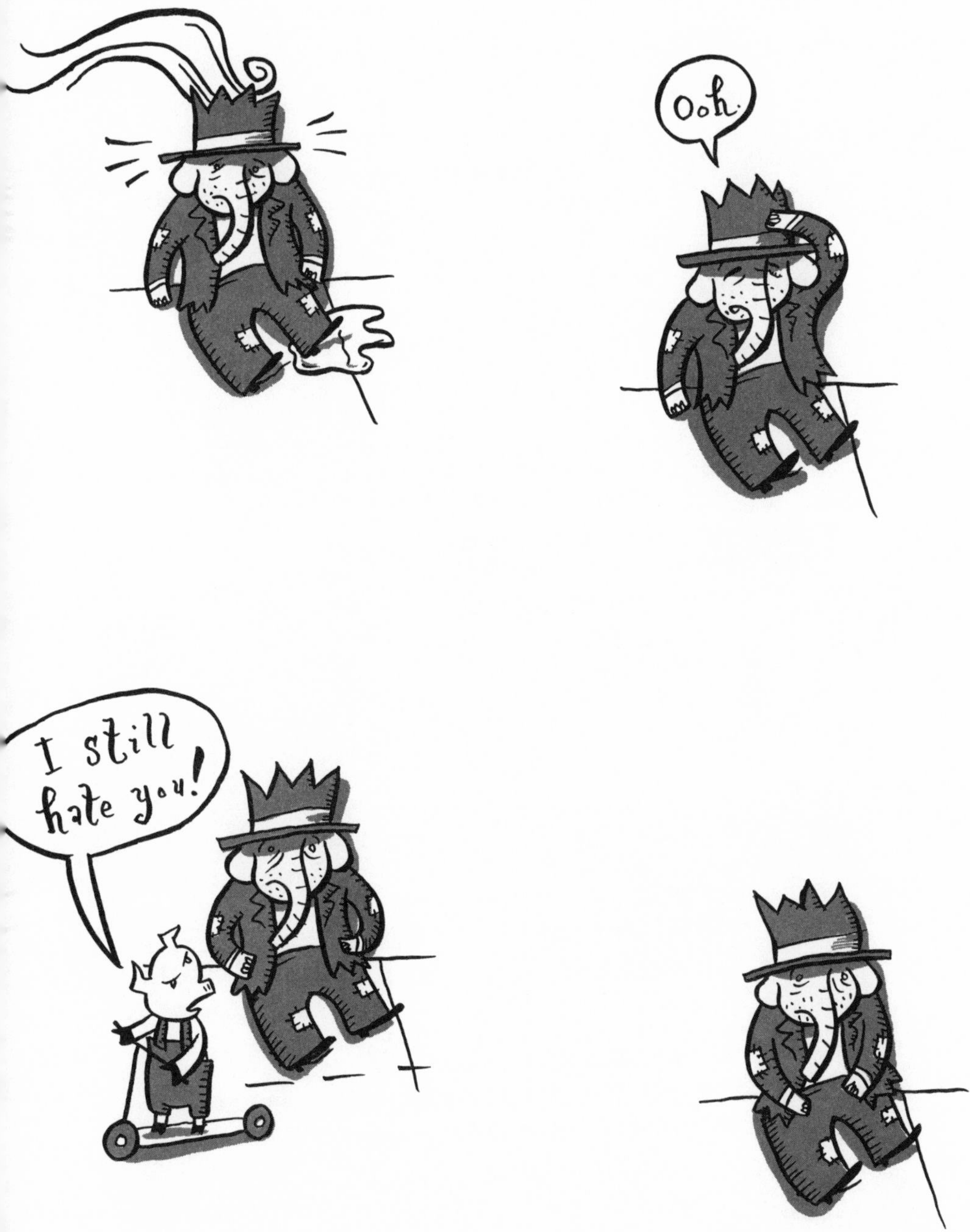
Ooh.
I still hate you!

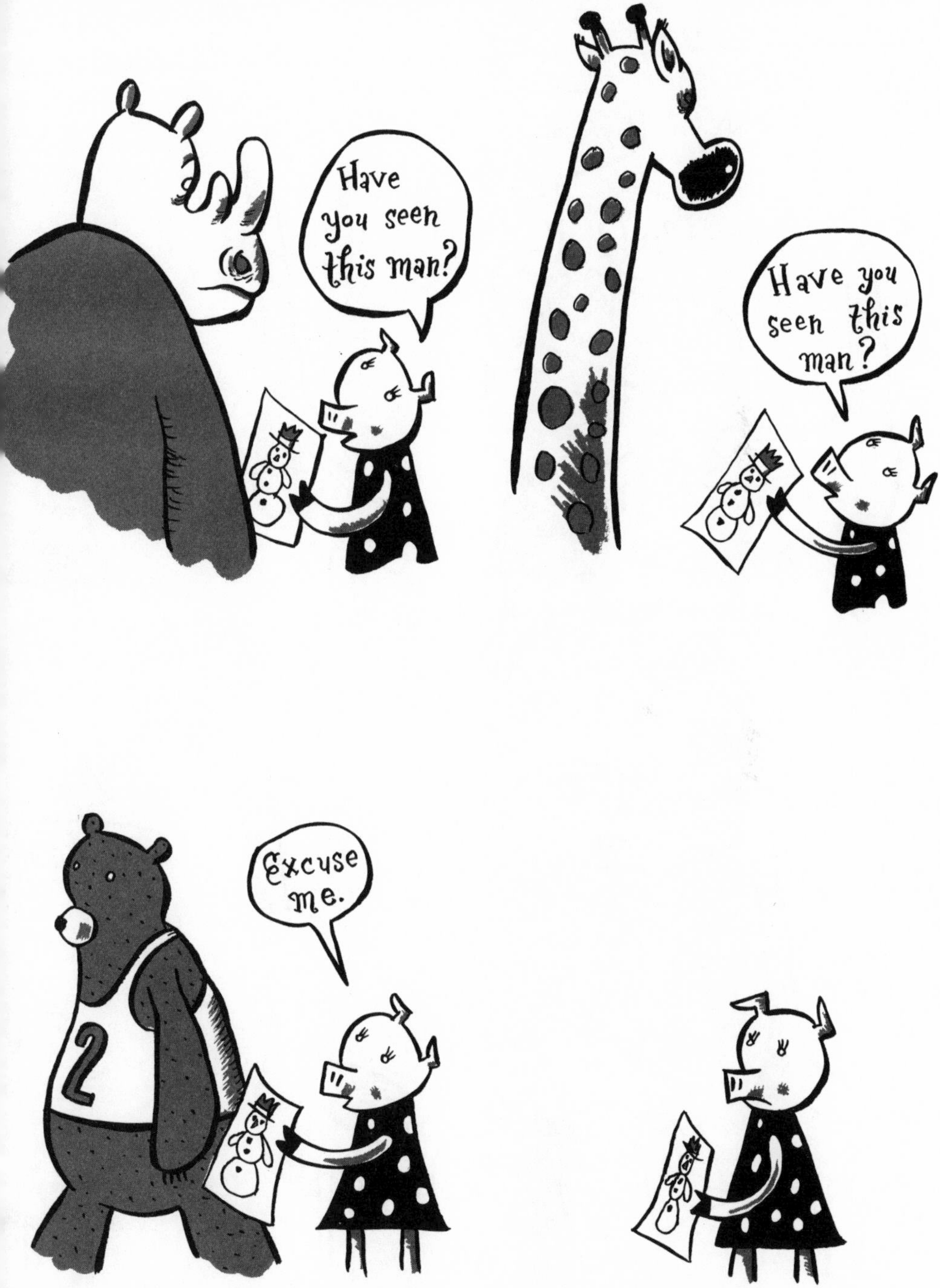
Have you seen this man?
Have you seen this man?
Excuse me.

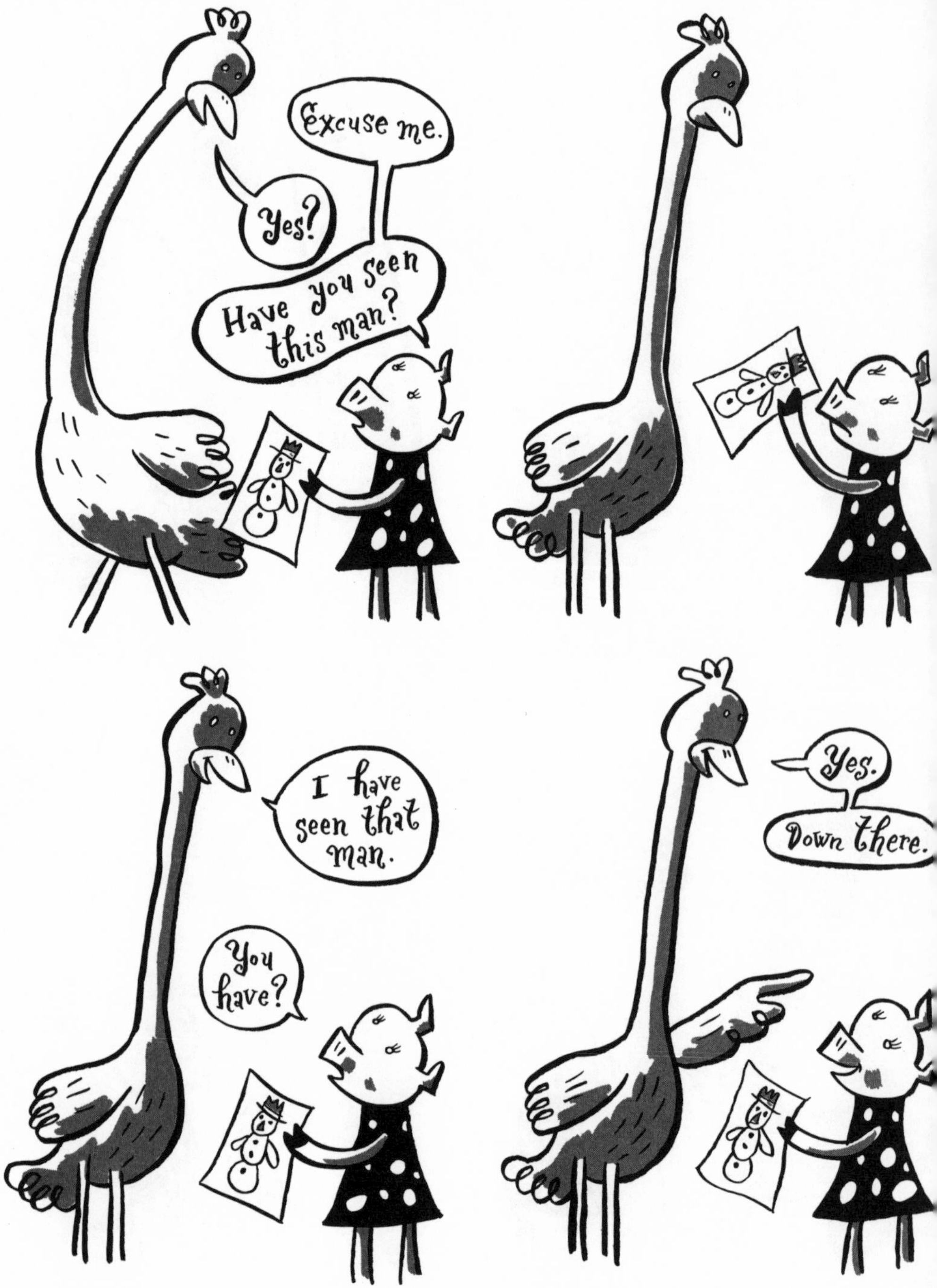
Excuse me.
Yes?
Have you seen this man?
I have seen that man.
You have?
Yes.
Down there.

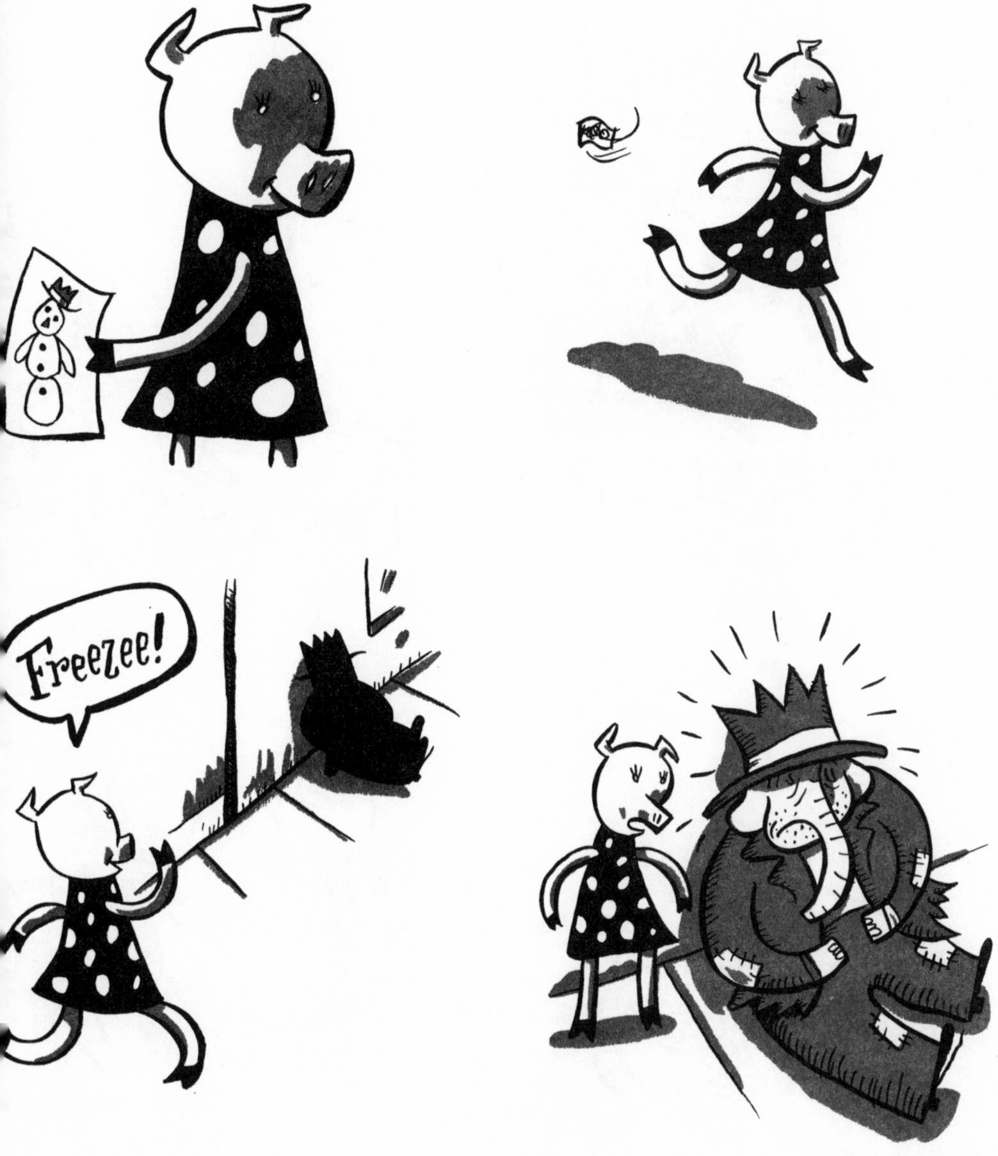
Freezee!

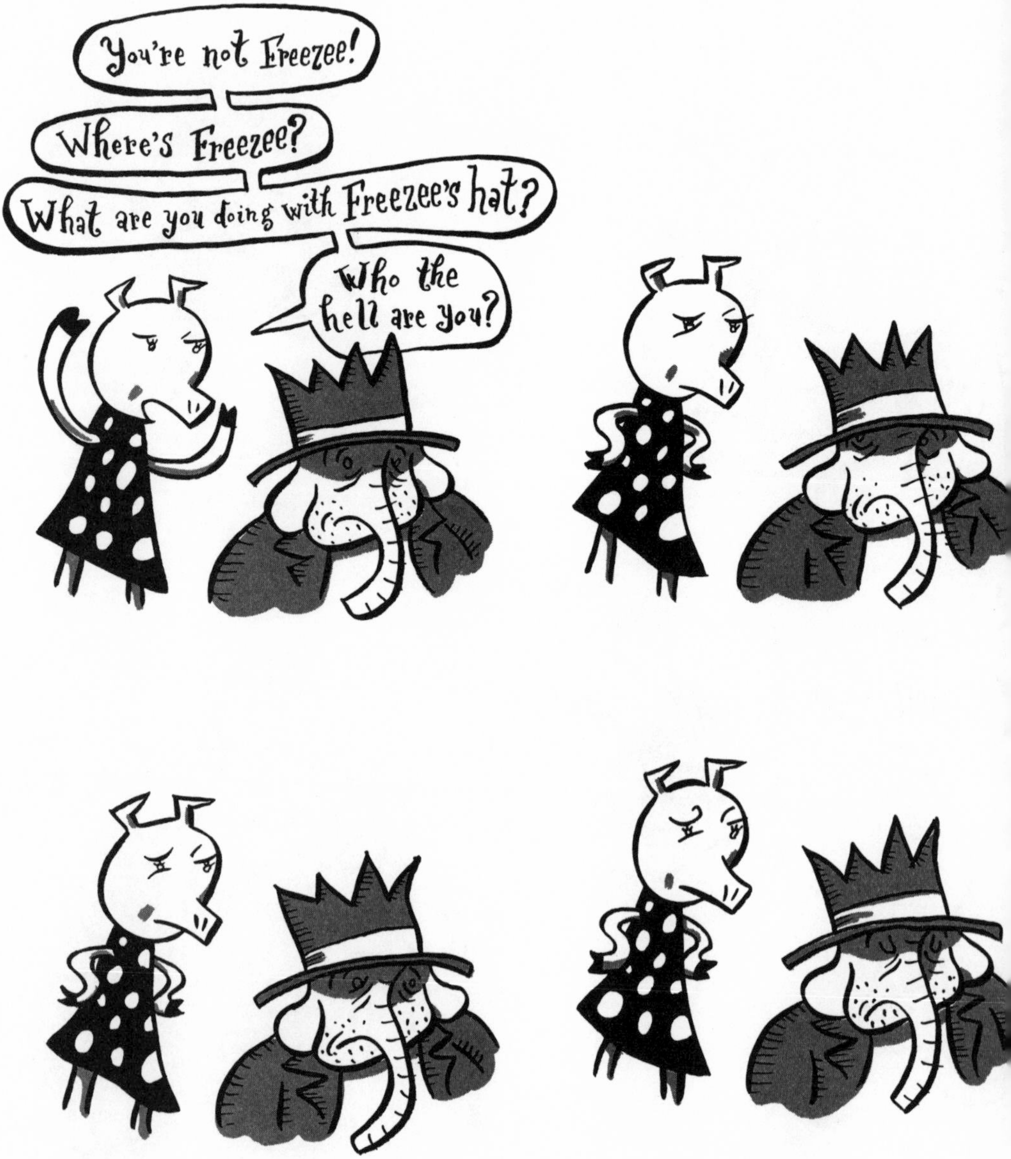
You're not Freezee!
Where's Freezee?
What are you doing with Freezee's hat?
Who the hell are you?

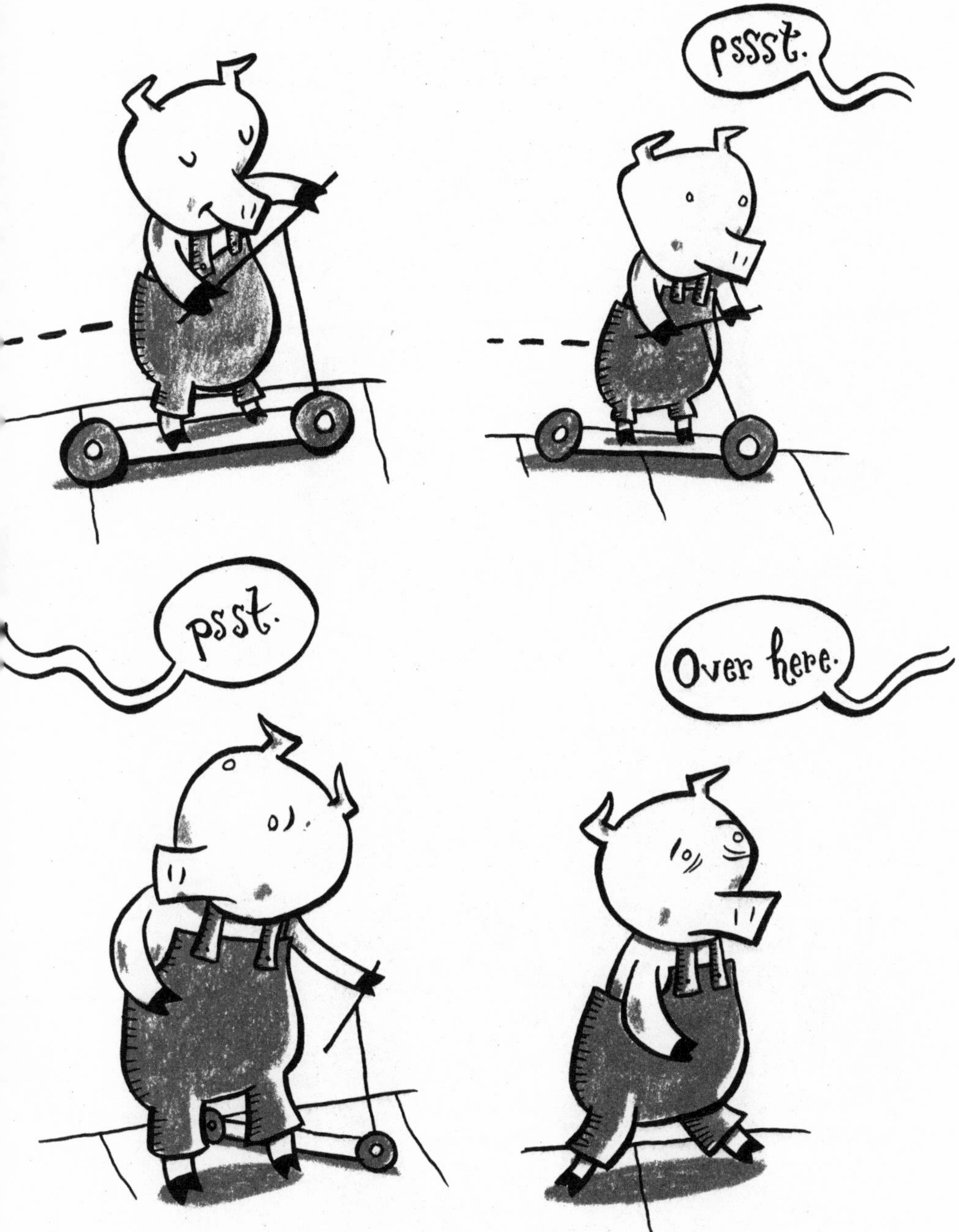
pssst.
psst.
Over here.

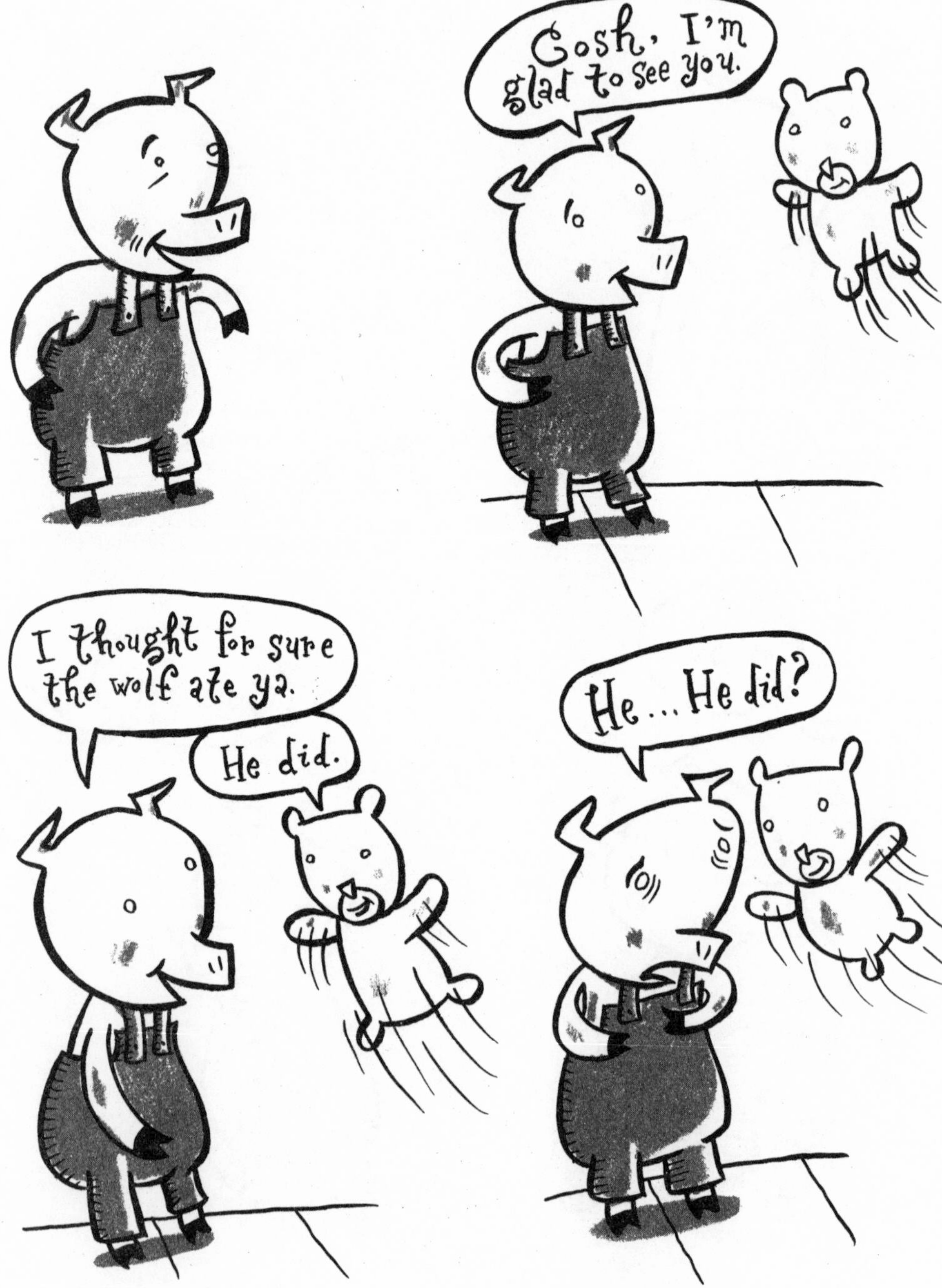
Gosh, I'm glad to see you.
I thought for sure the wolf ate ya.
He did.
He... He did?

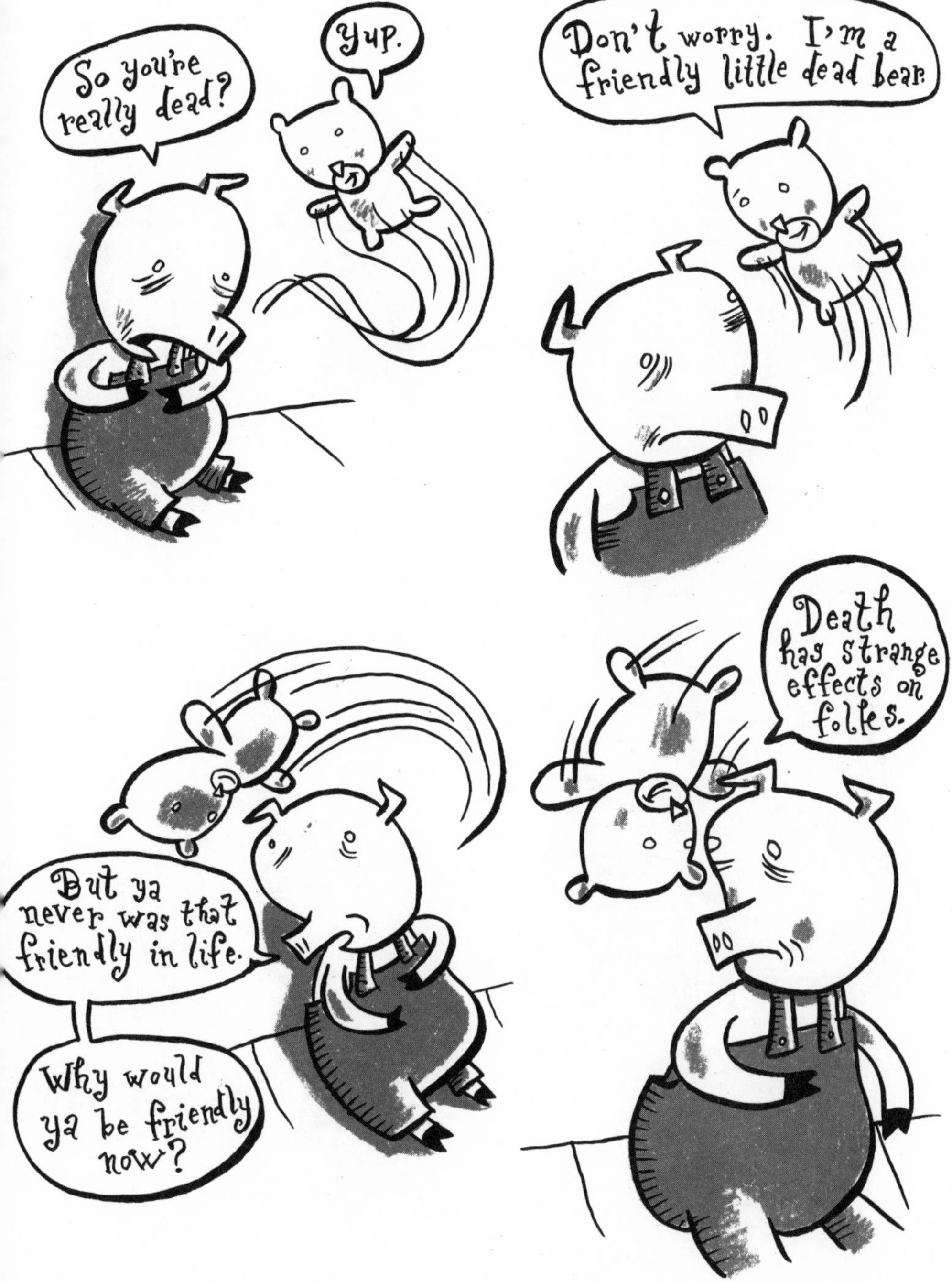
So you're really dead?
Yup.
Don't worry. I'm a friendly little dead bear.
But ya never was that friendly in life.
Why would ya be friendly now?
Death has strange effects on folks.

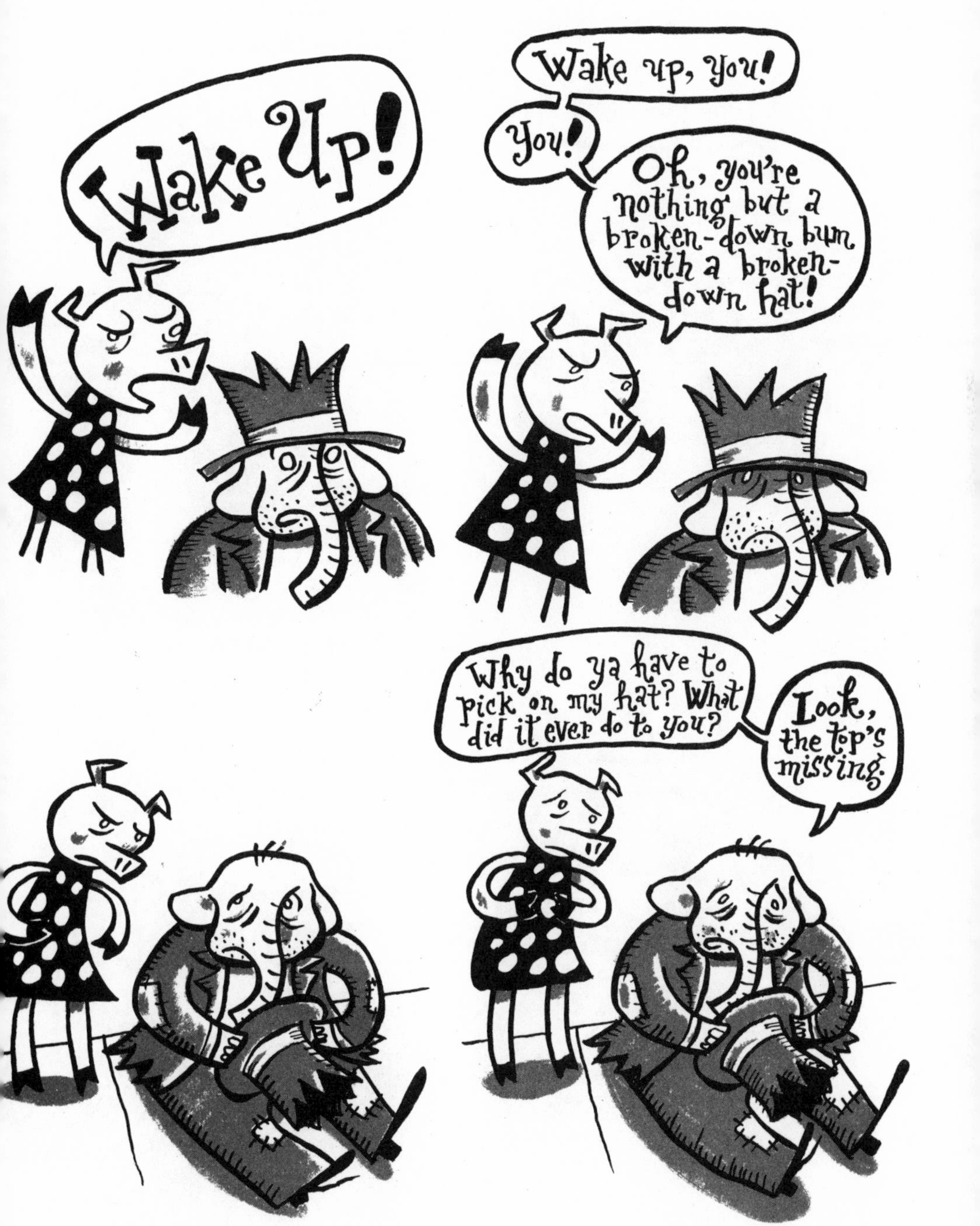

Wake Up!
Wake up, you!
You!
Oh, you're nothing but a broken-down bum with a broken-down hat!
Why do ya have to pick on my hat? What did it ever do to you?
Look, the top's missing.

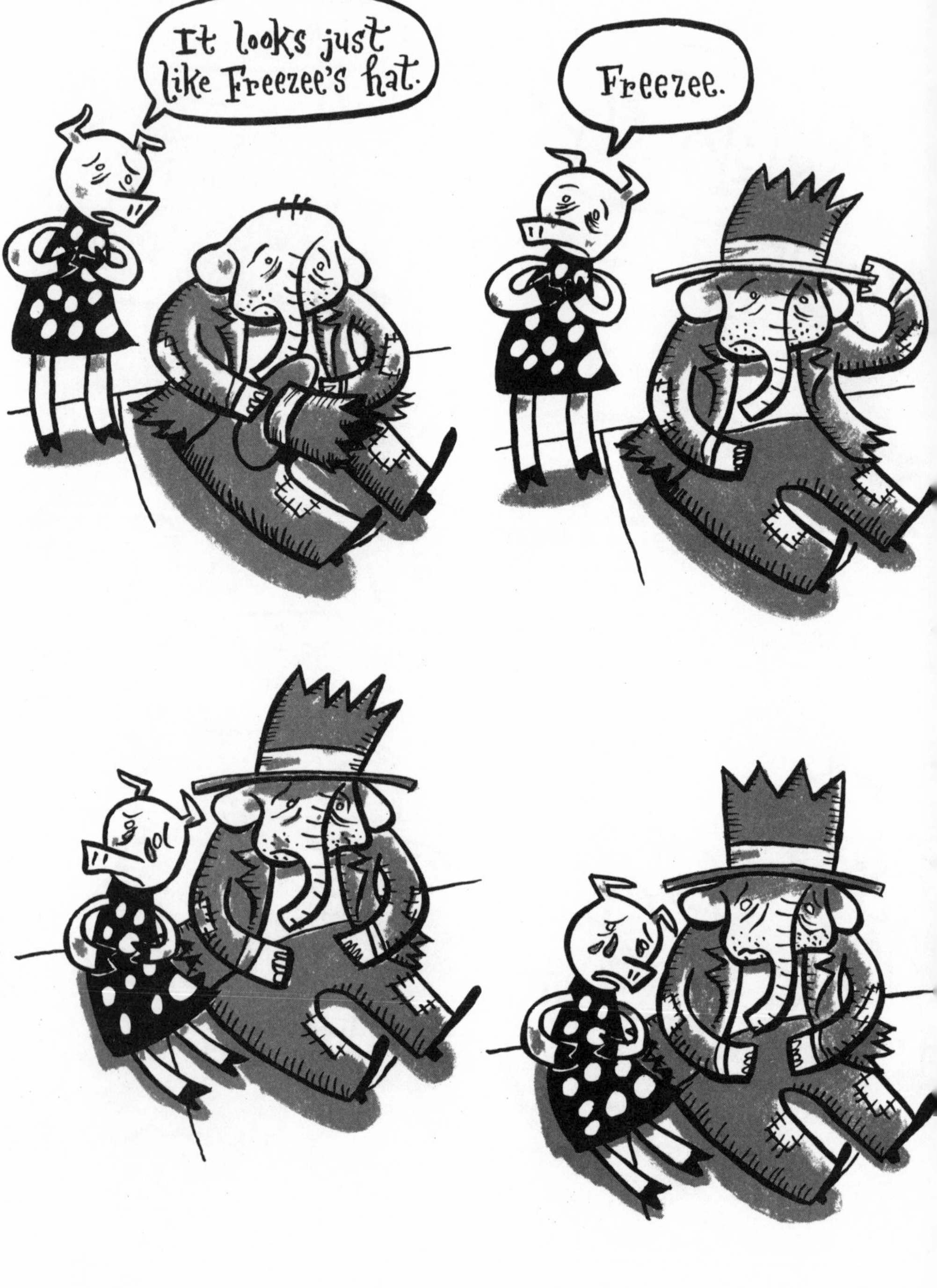
It looks just like Freezee's hat.
Freezee.

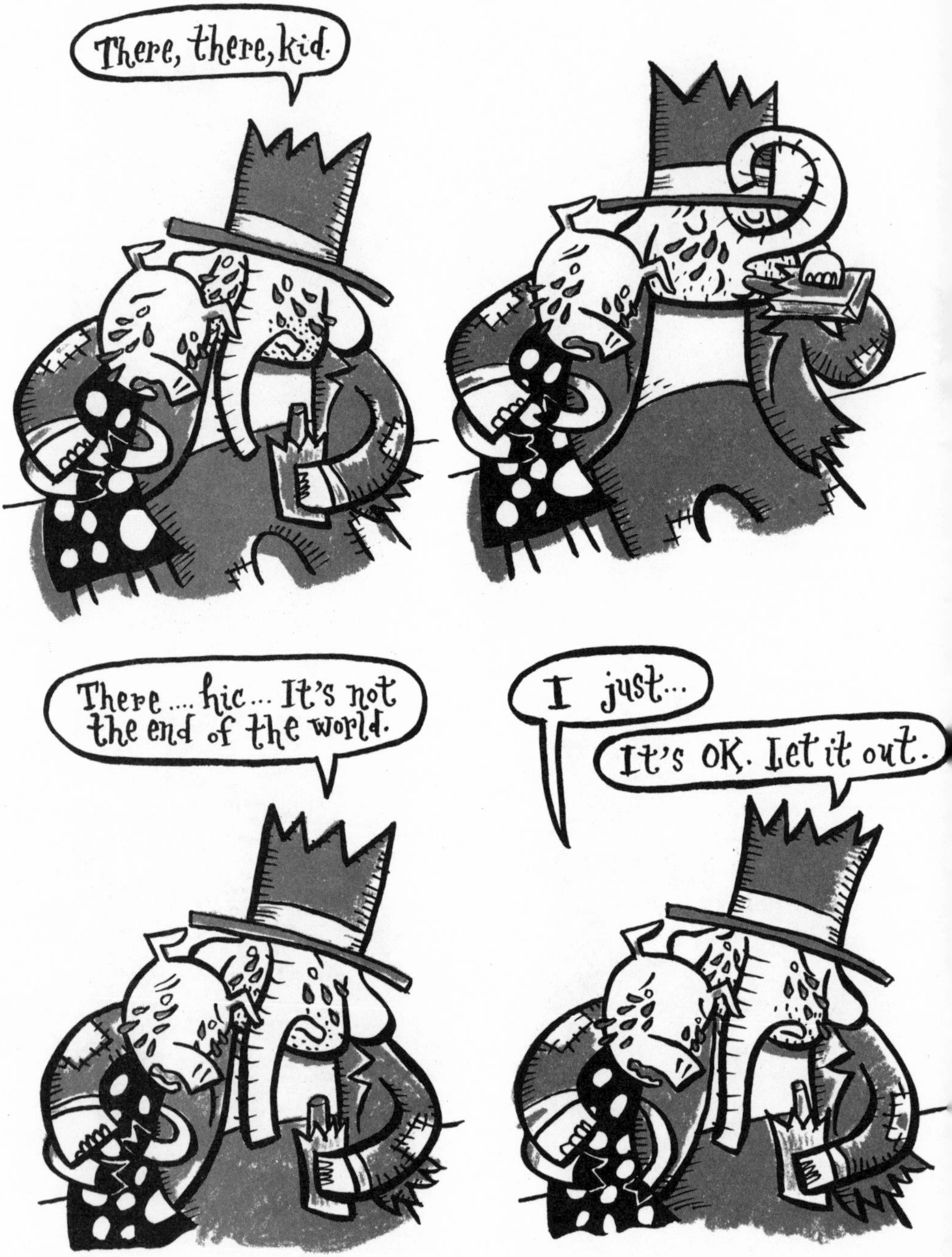
There, there, kid.
There.... hic... It's not the end of the world.
I just...
It's OK. Let it out.

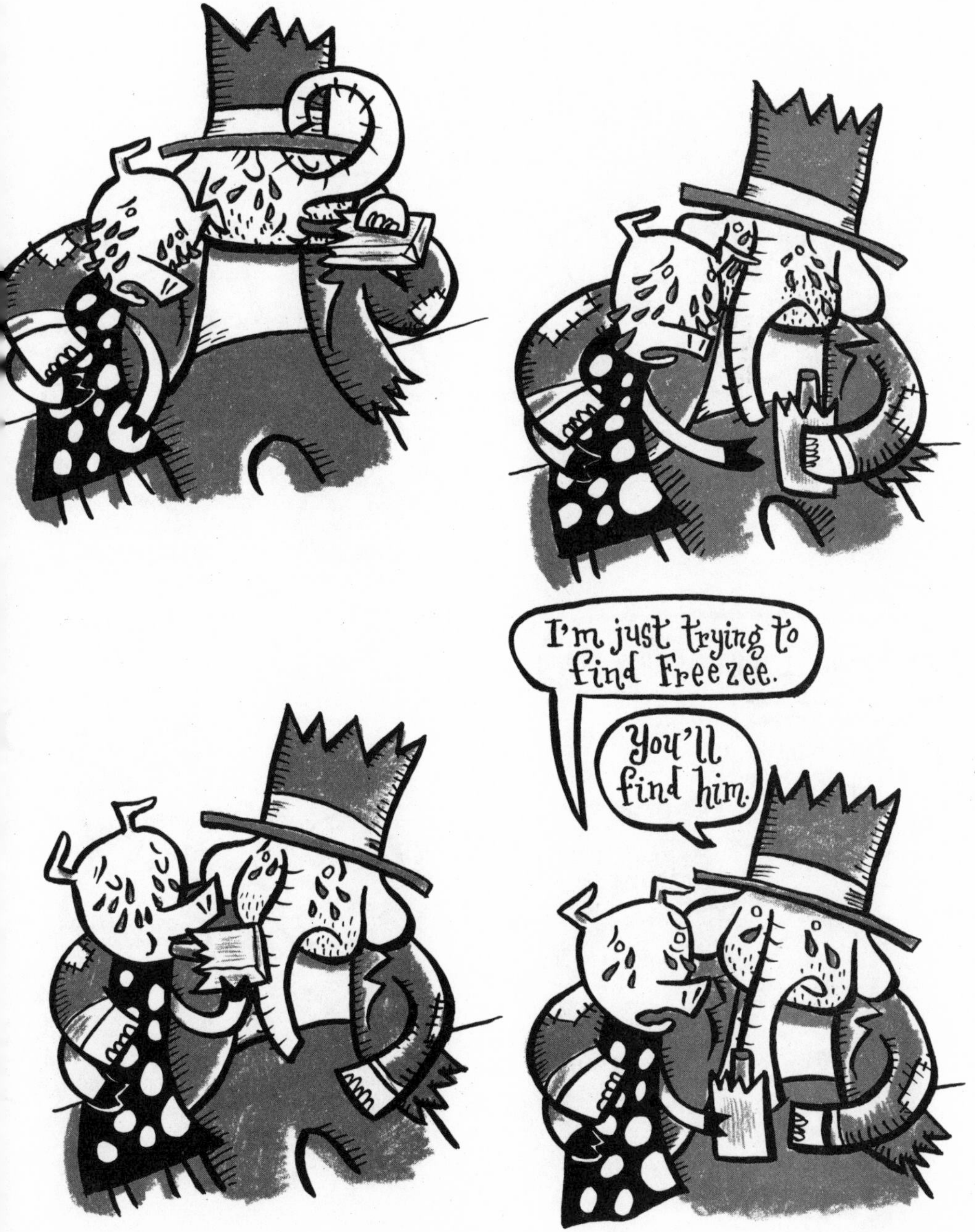
I'm just trying to find Freezee.
You'll find him.

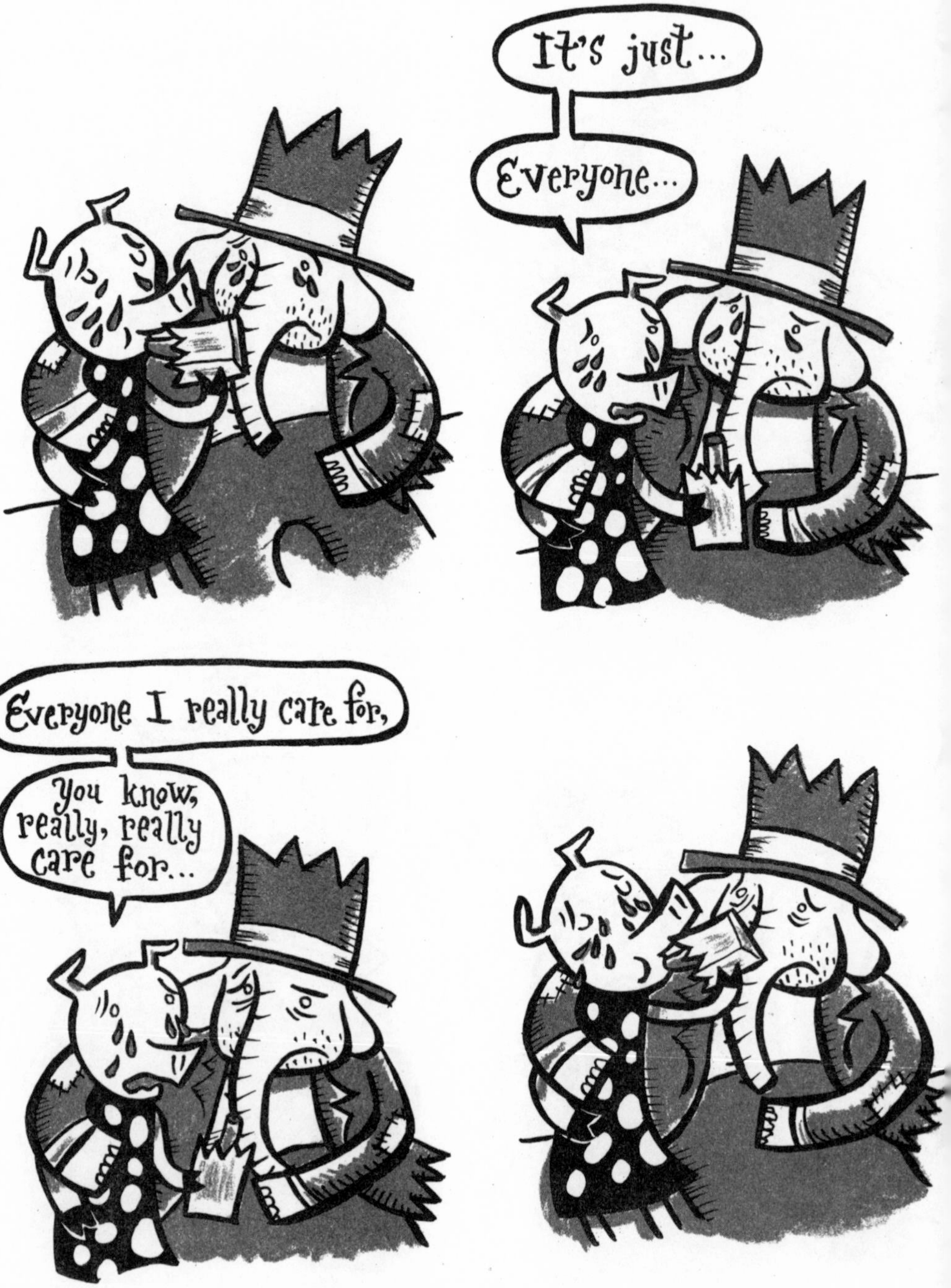
It's just...
Everyone...
Everyone I really care for,
you know, really, really care for...

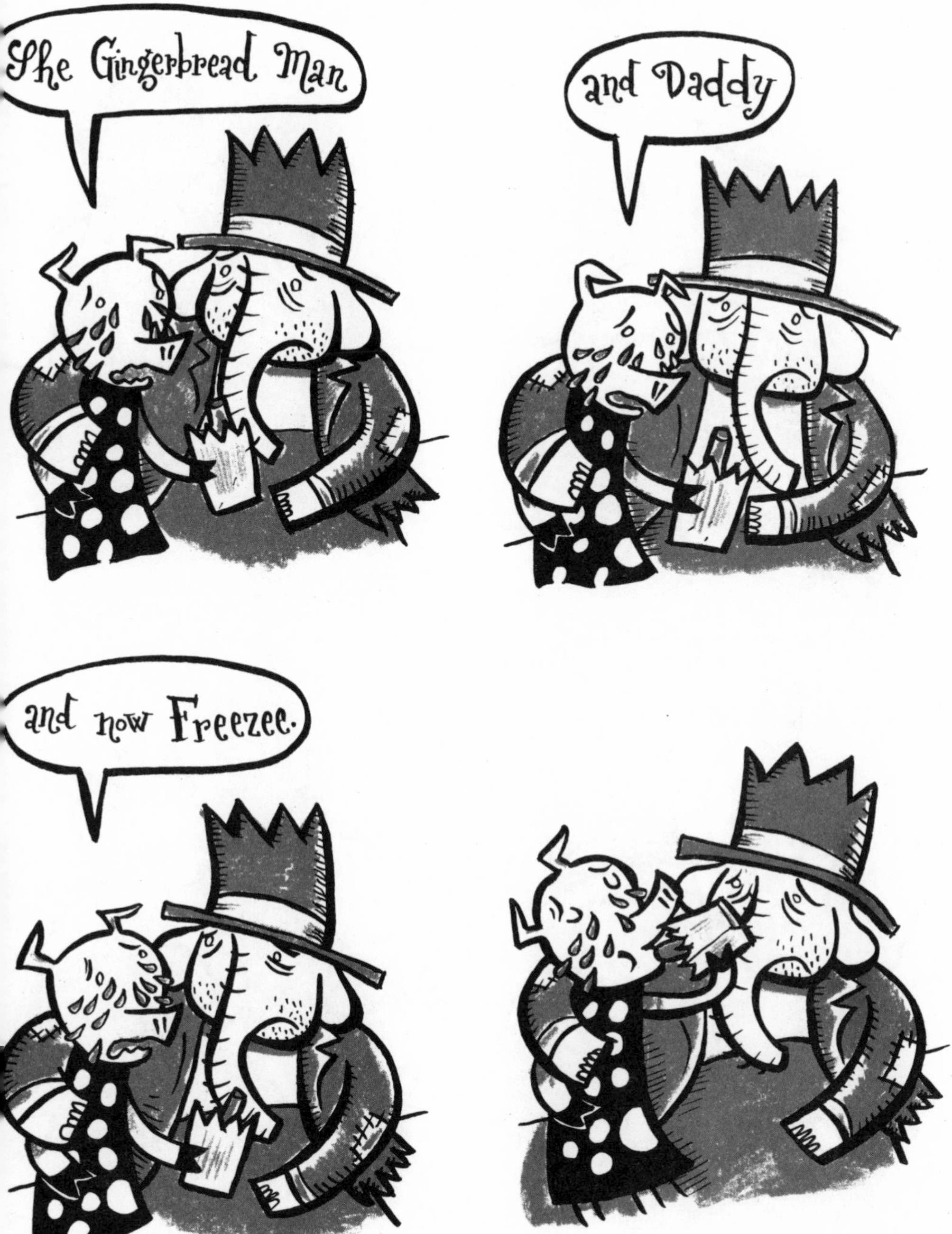

The Gingerbread Man
and Daddy
and now Freezee.

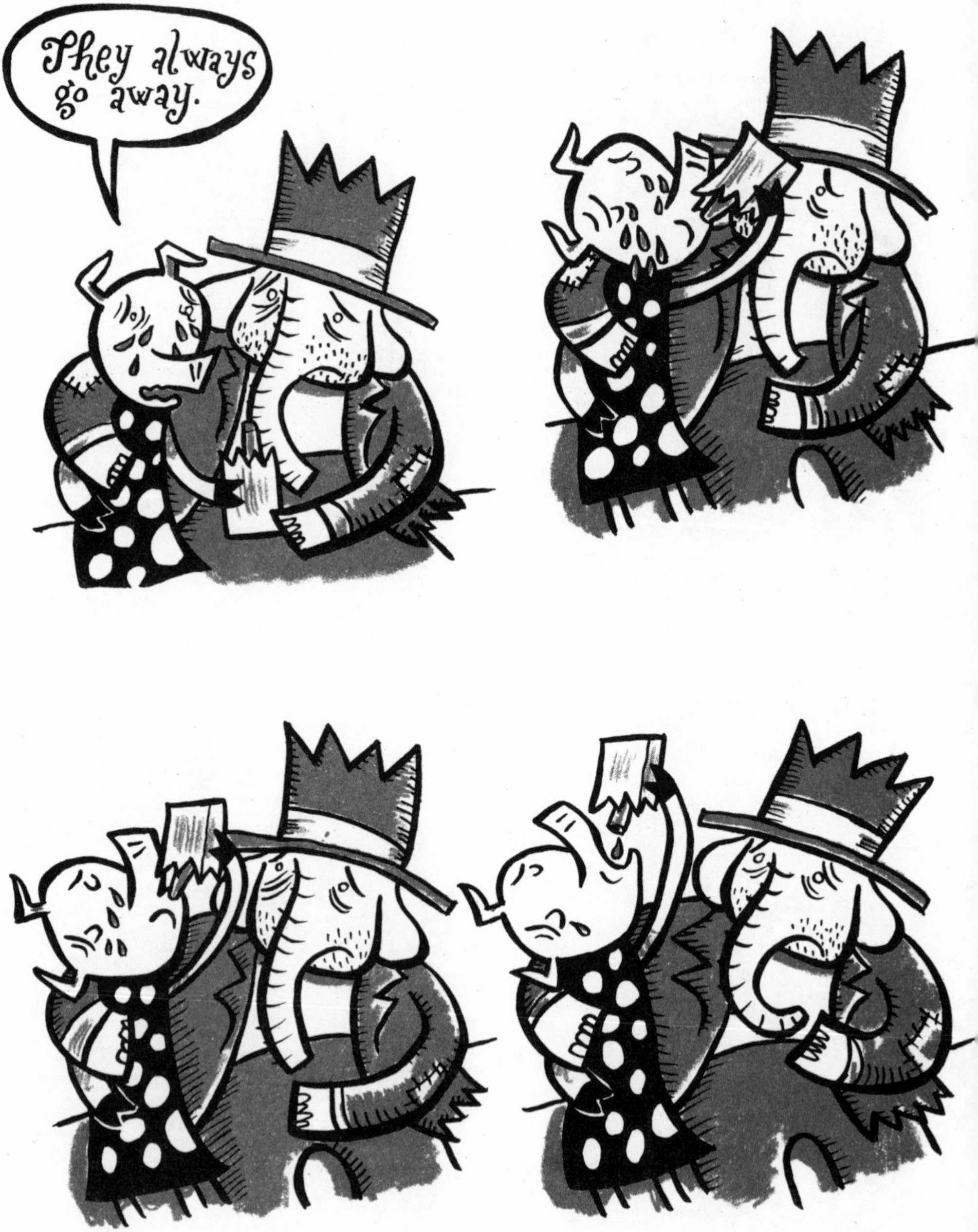
They always go away.

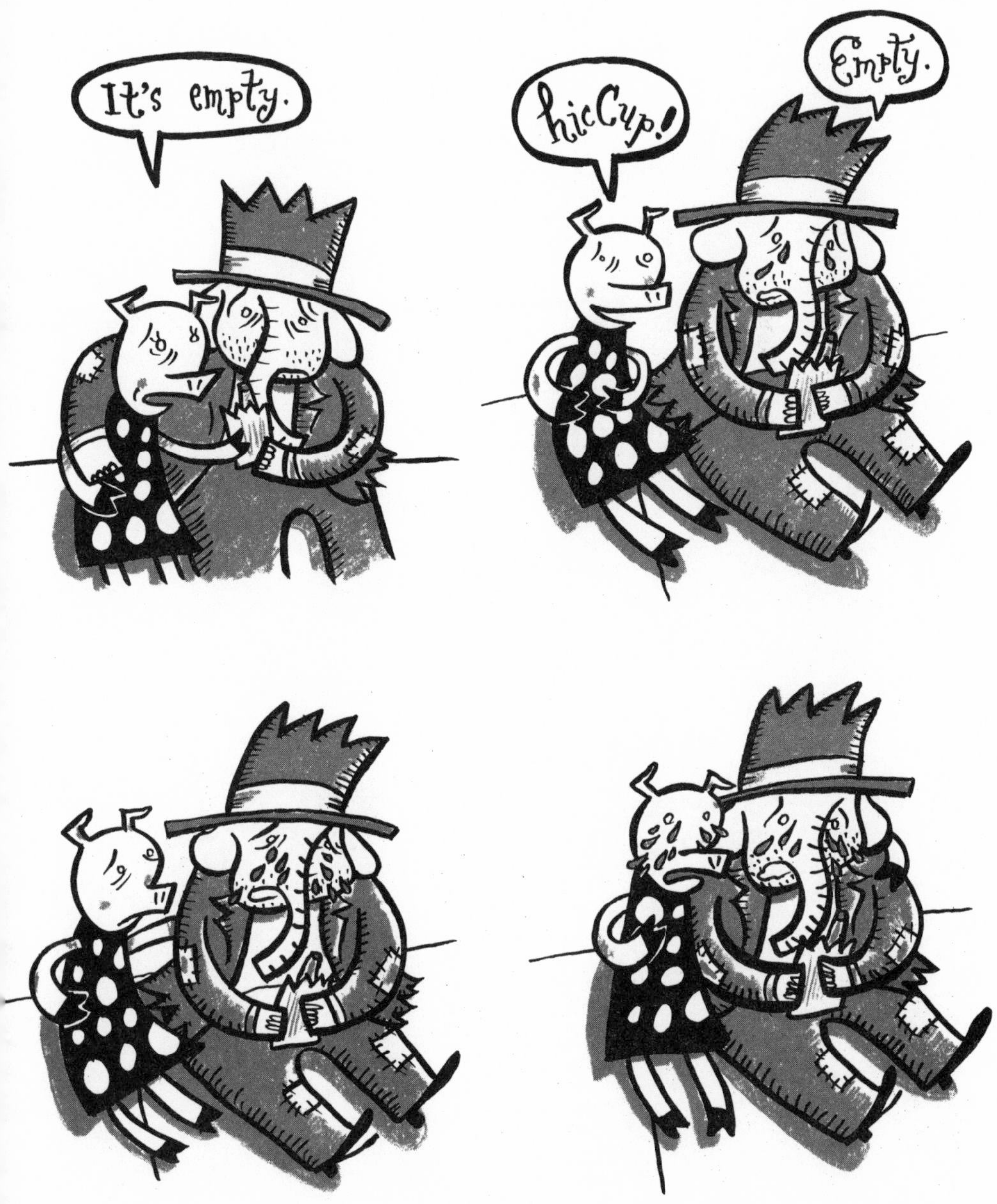
It's empty.
hicCup!
Empty.

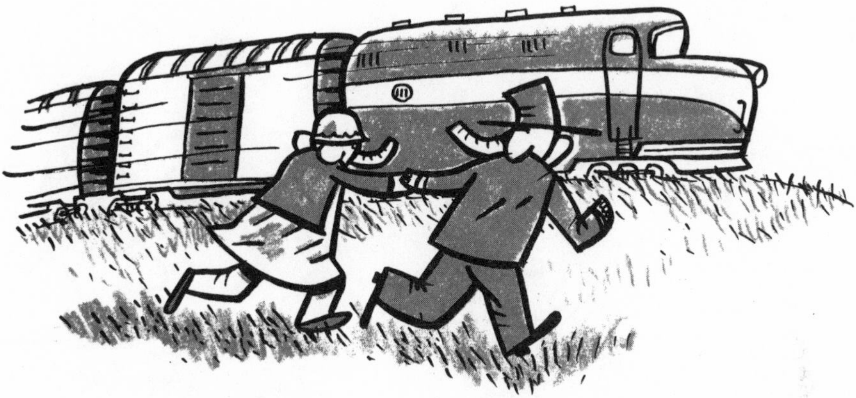

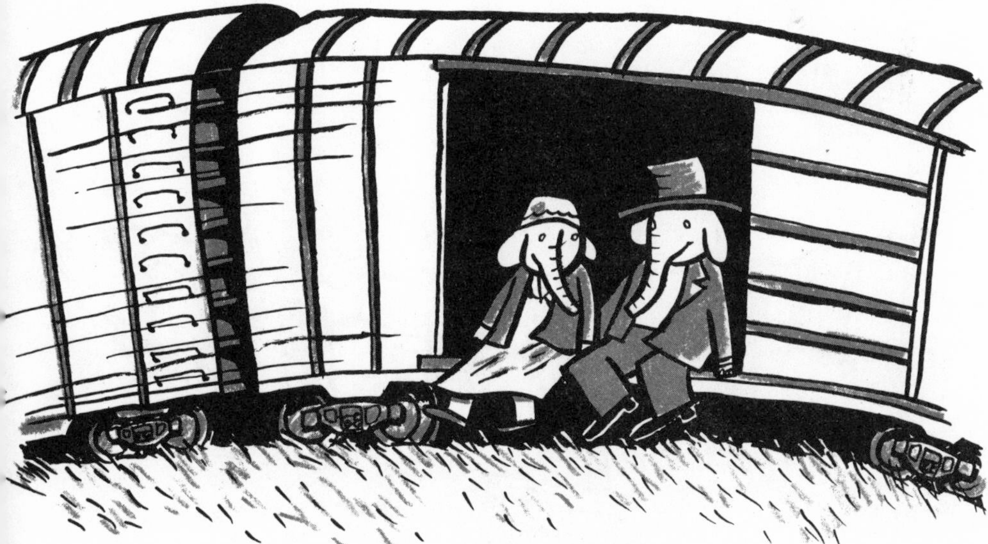

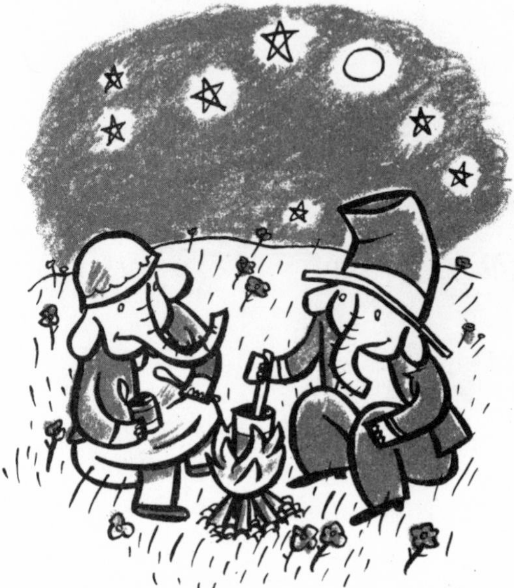

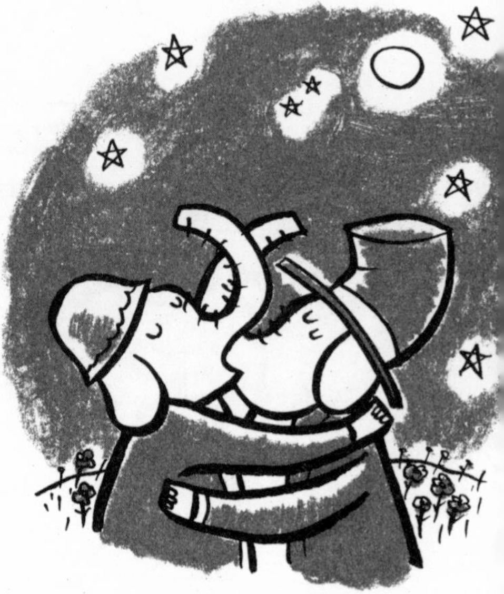

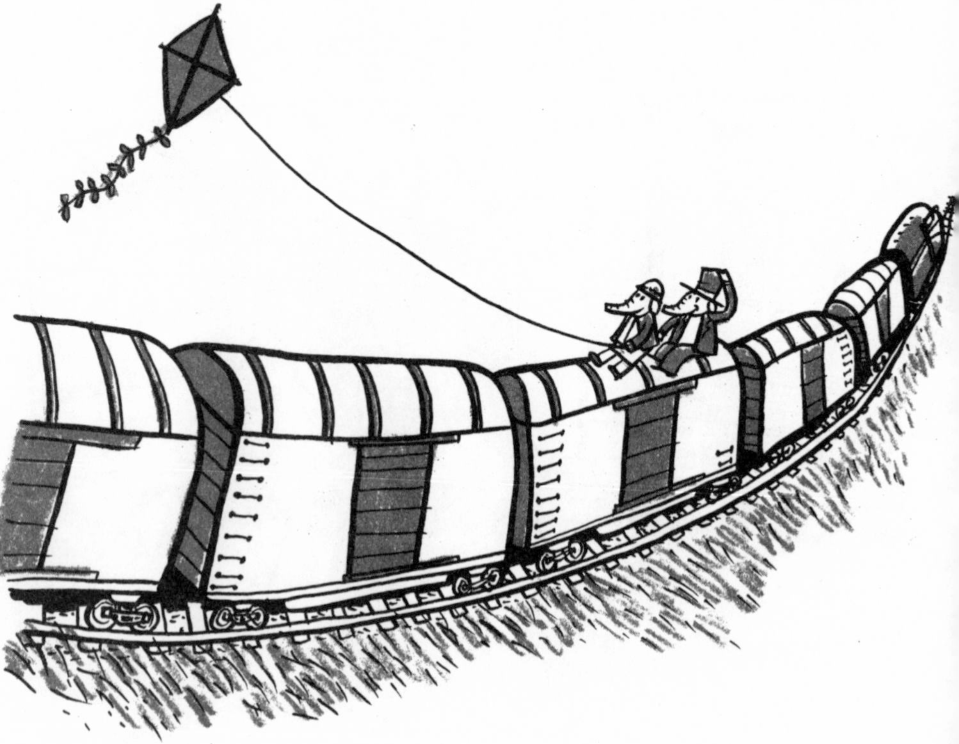

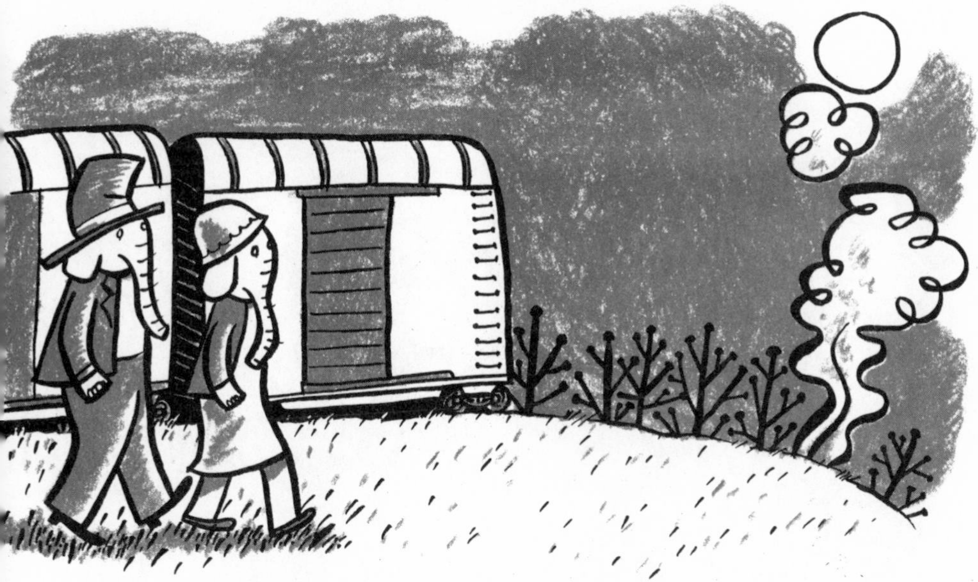

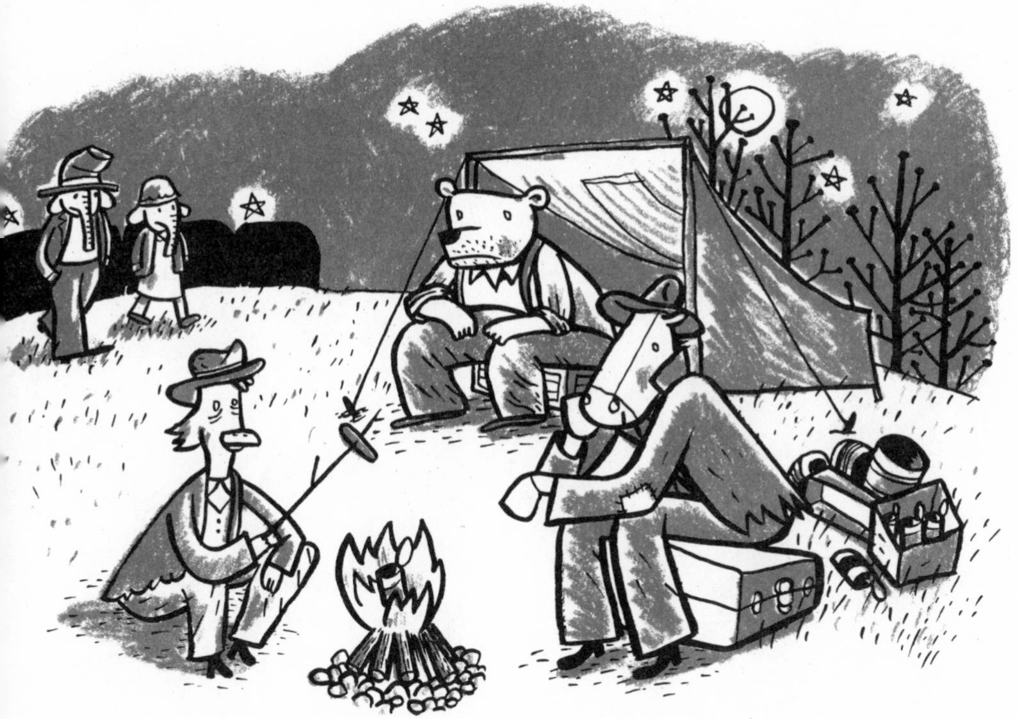

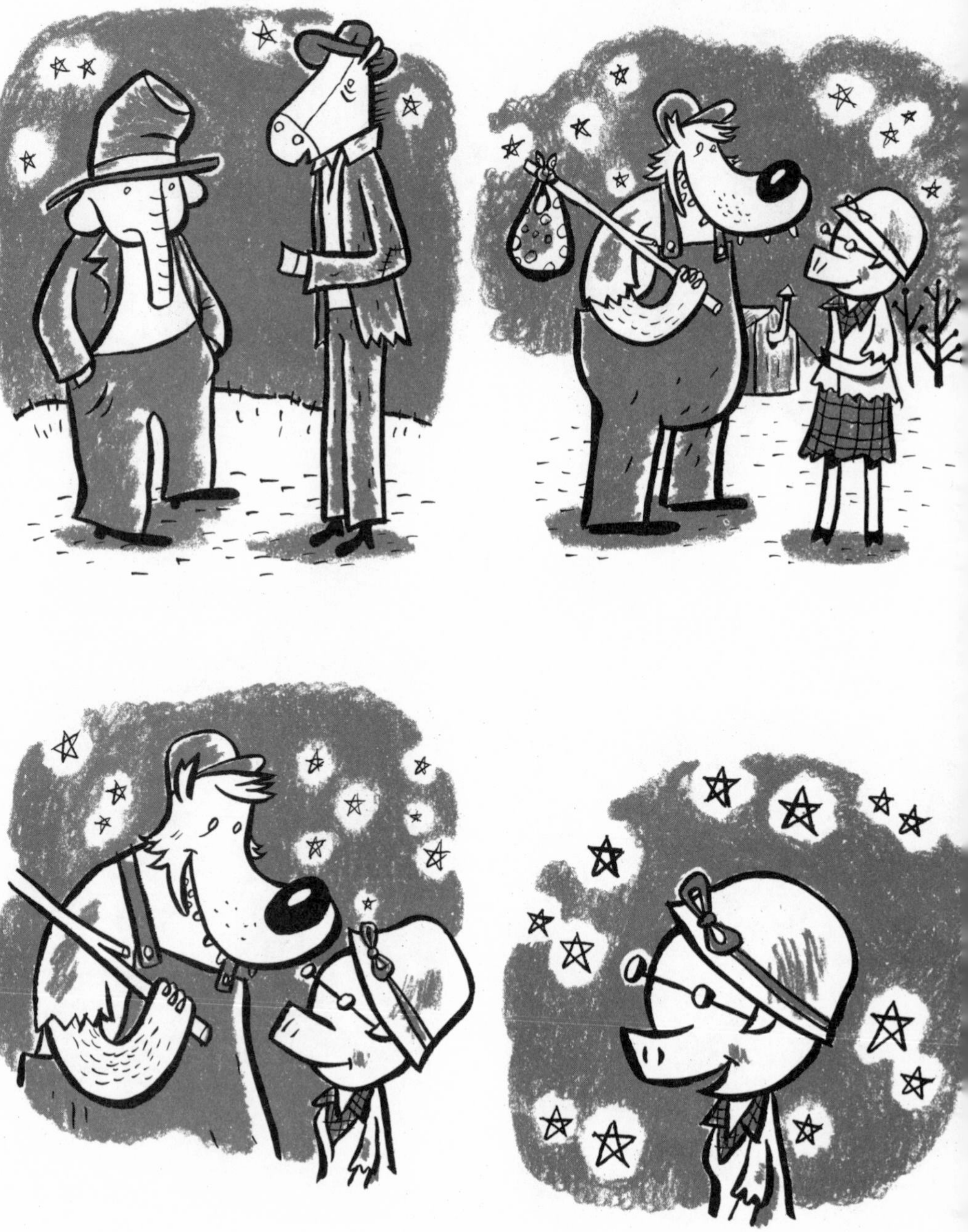

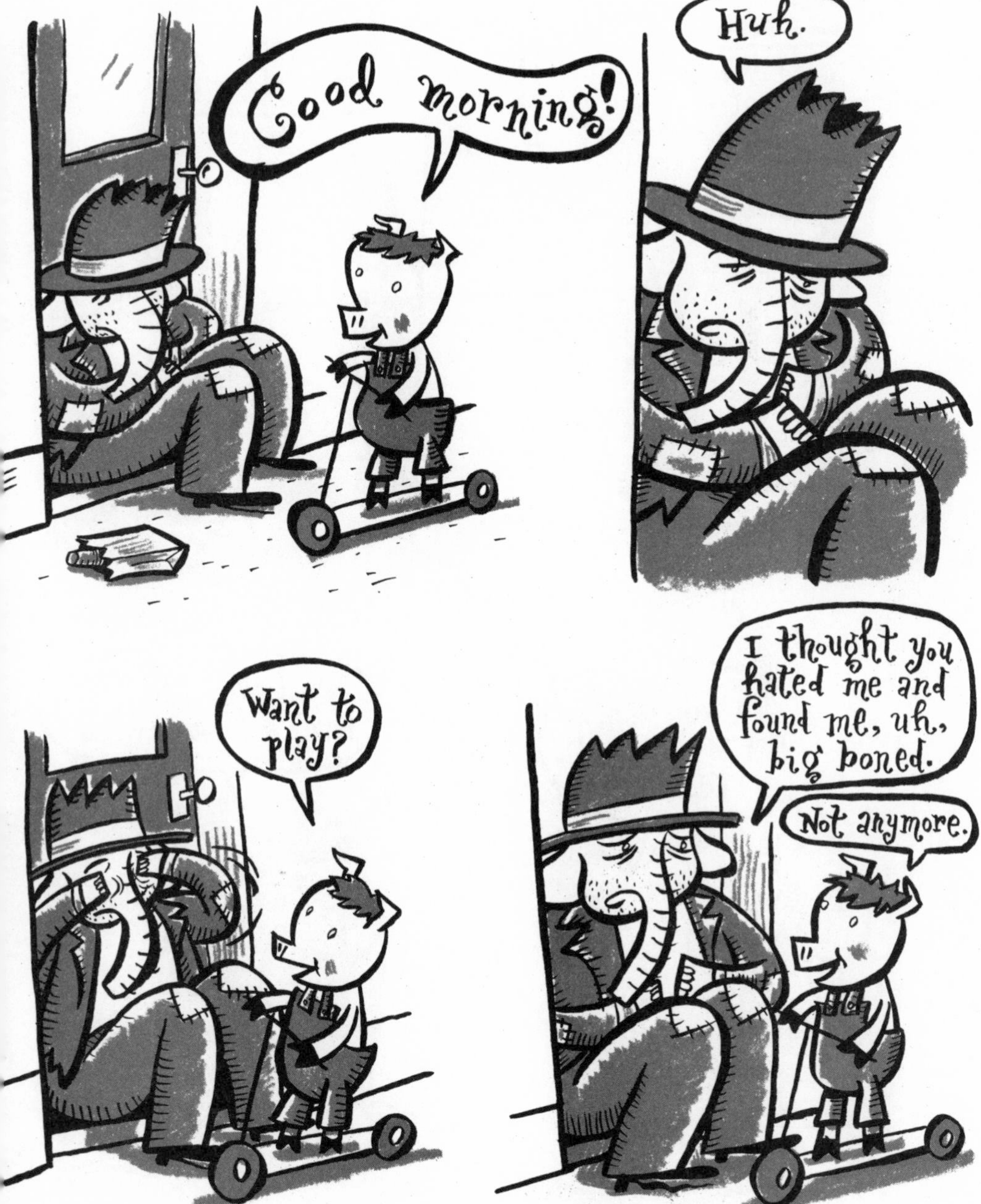
Good morning!
Huh.
Want to play?
I thought you hated me and found me, uh, big boned.
Not anymore.

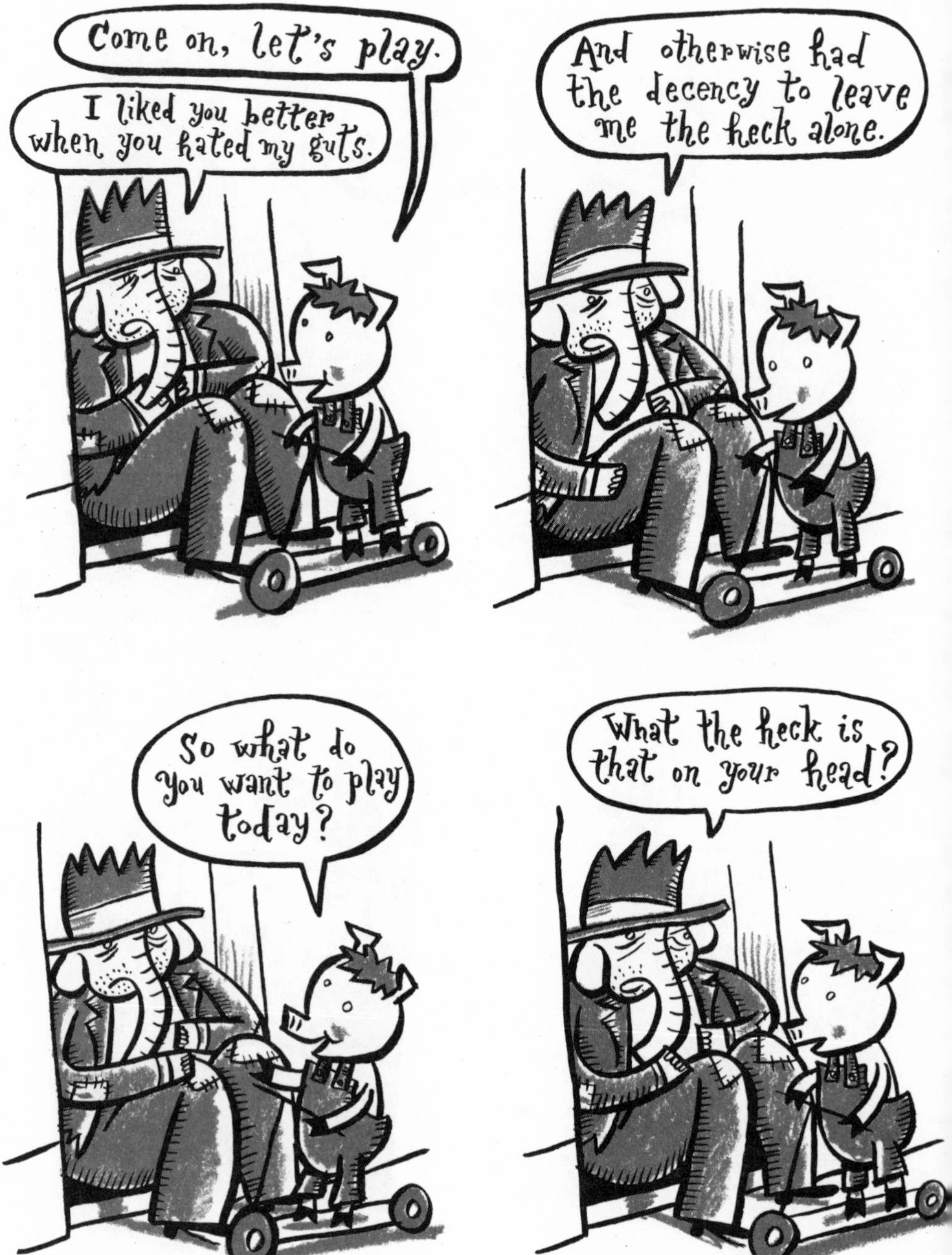
Come on, let's play.
I liked you better when you hated my guts.
And otherwise had the decency to leave me the heck alone.
So what do you want to play today?
What the heck is that on your head?

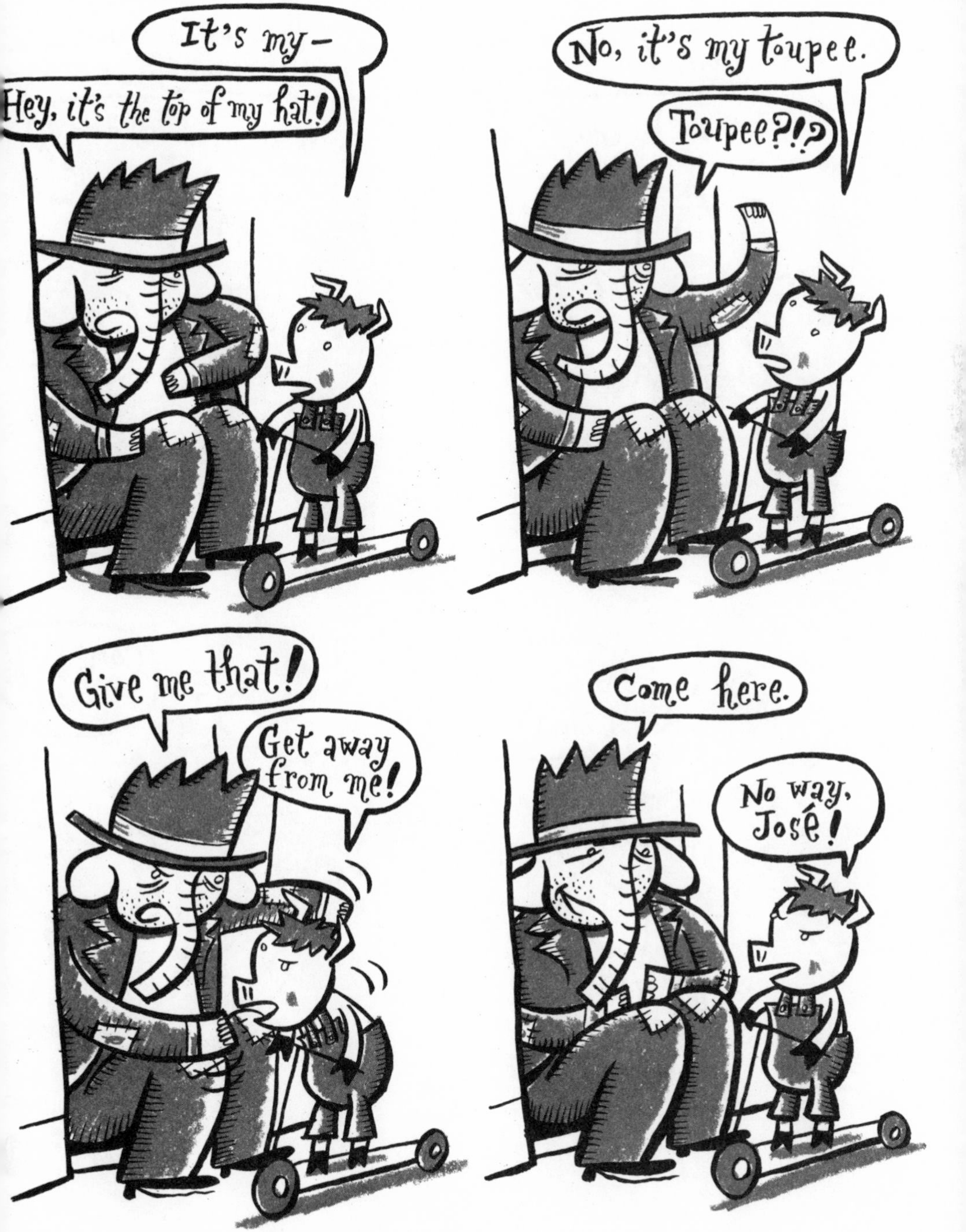
It's my–
Hey, it's the top of my hat!
No, it's my toupee.
Toupee?!?
Give me that!
Get away from me!
Come here.
No way, José!

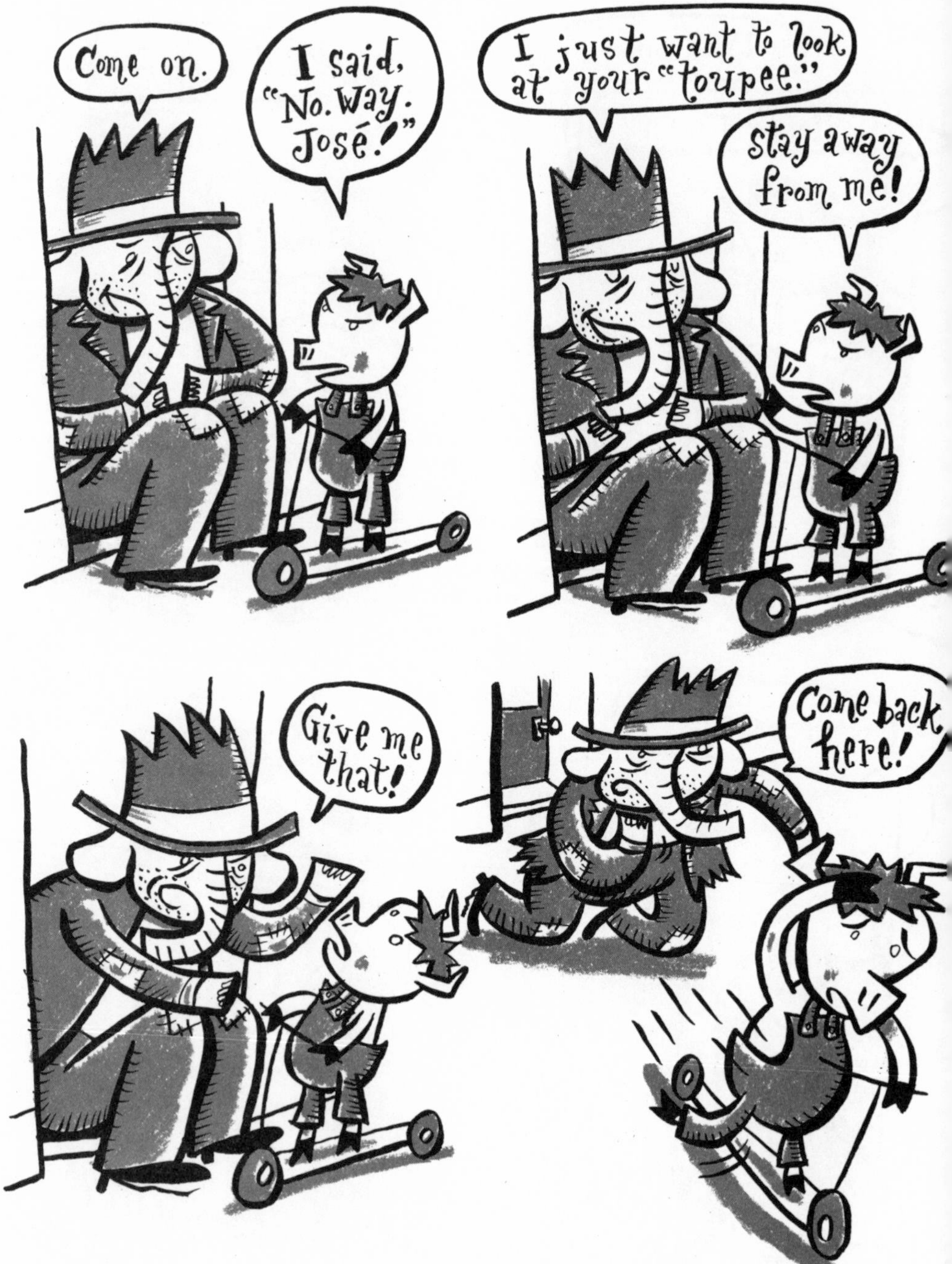
Come on.
I said, "No. Way. José!"
I just want to look at your "toupee."
Stay away from me!
Give me that!
Come back here!

Ya know, I don't think things are

Working out so great with that hobo guy.

You've just got to give him a chance.

On the outside, sure he's ugly and smelly and unshaven and surly and unkept and drunk and mean...a real poopyhead...

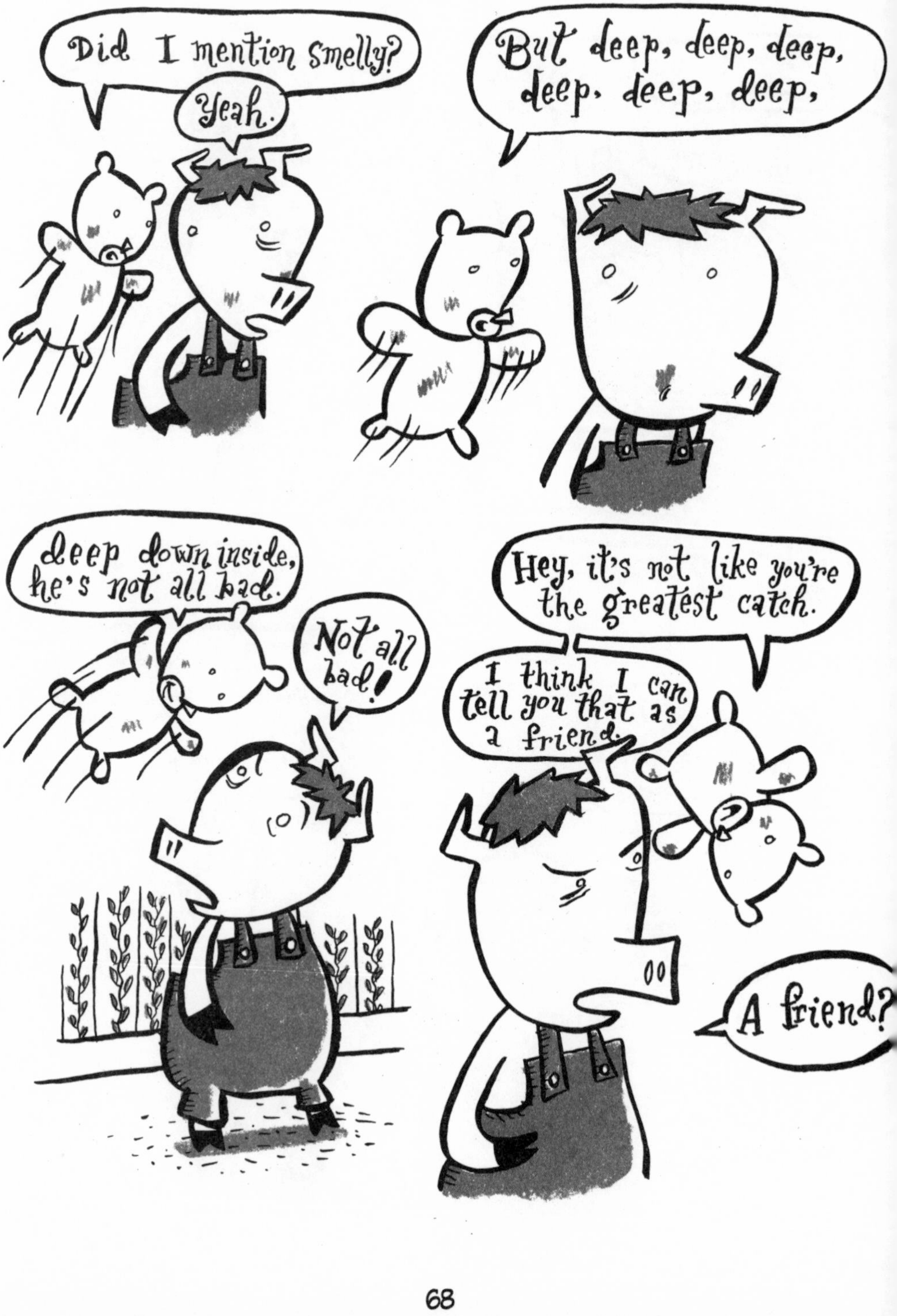

Did I mention smelly?
Yeah.
But deep, deep, deep, deep, deep, deep,
deep down inside, he's not all bad.
Not all bad!
Hey, it's not like you're the greatest catch.
I think I can tell you that as a friend.
A friend?

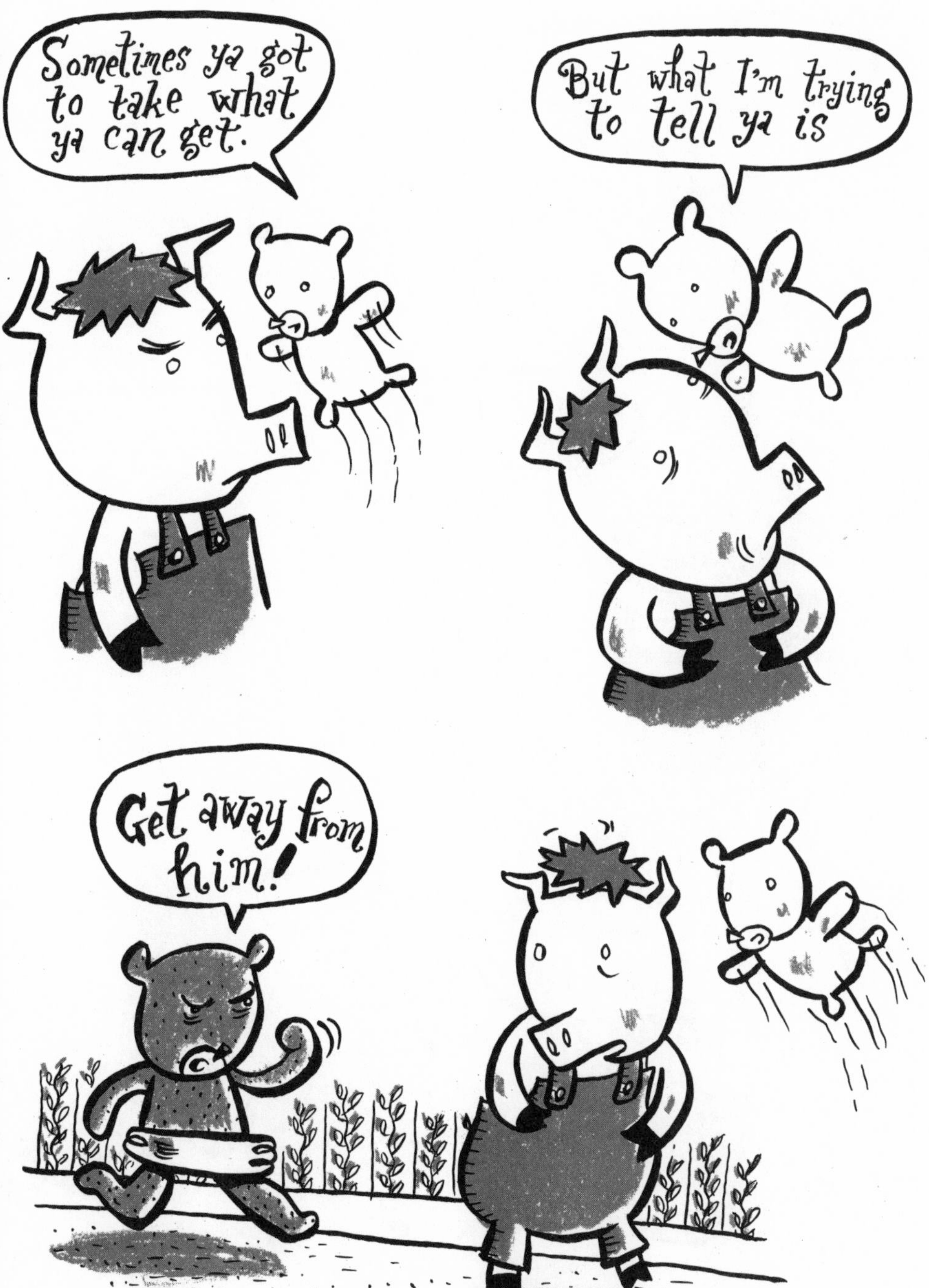
Sometimes ya got to take what ya can get.
But what I'm trying to tell ya is
Get away from him!

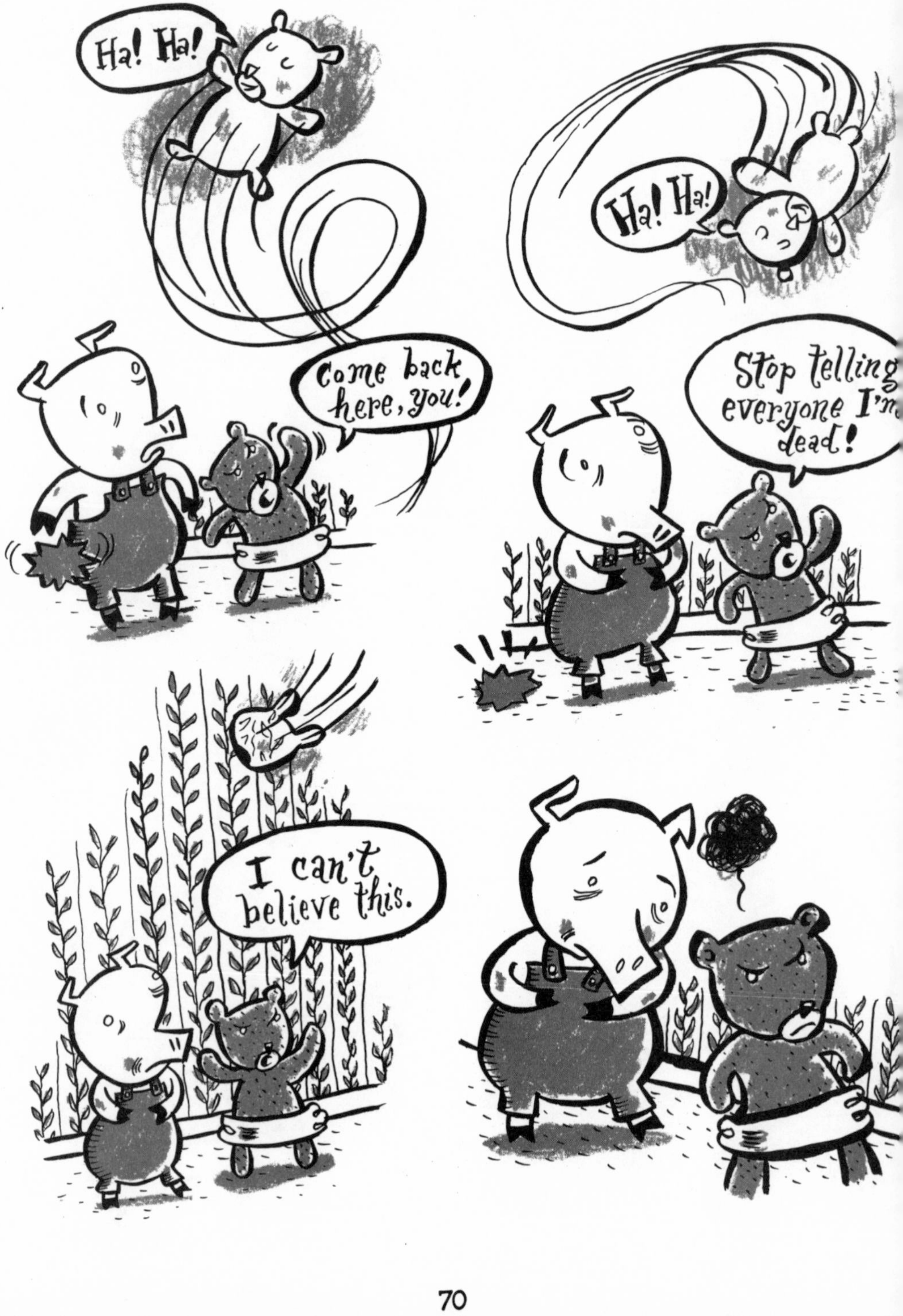
Ha! Ha!
Ha! Ha!
Come back here, you!
Stop telling everyone I'm dead!
I can't believe this.

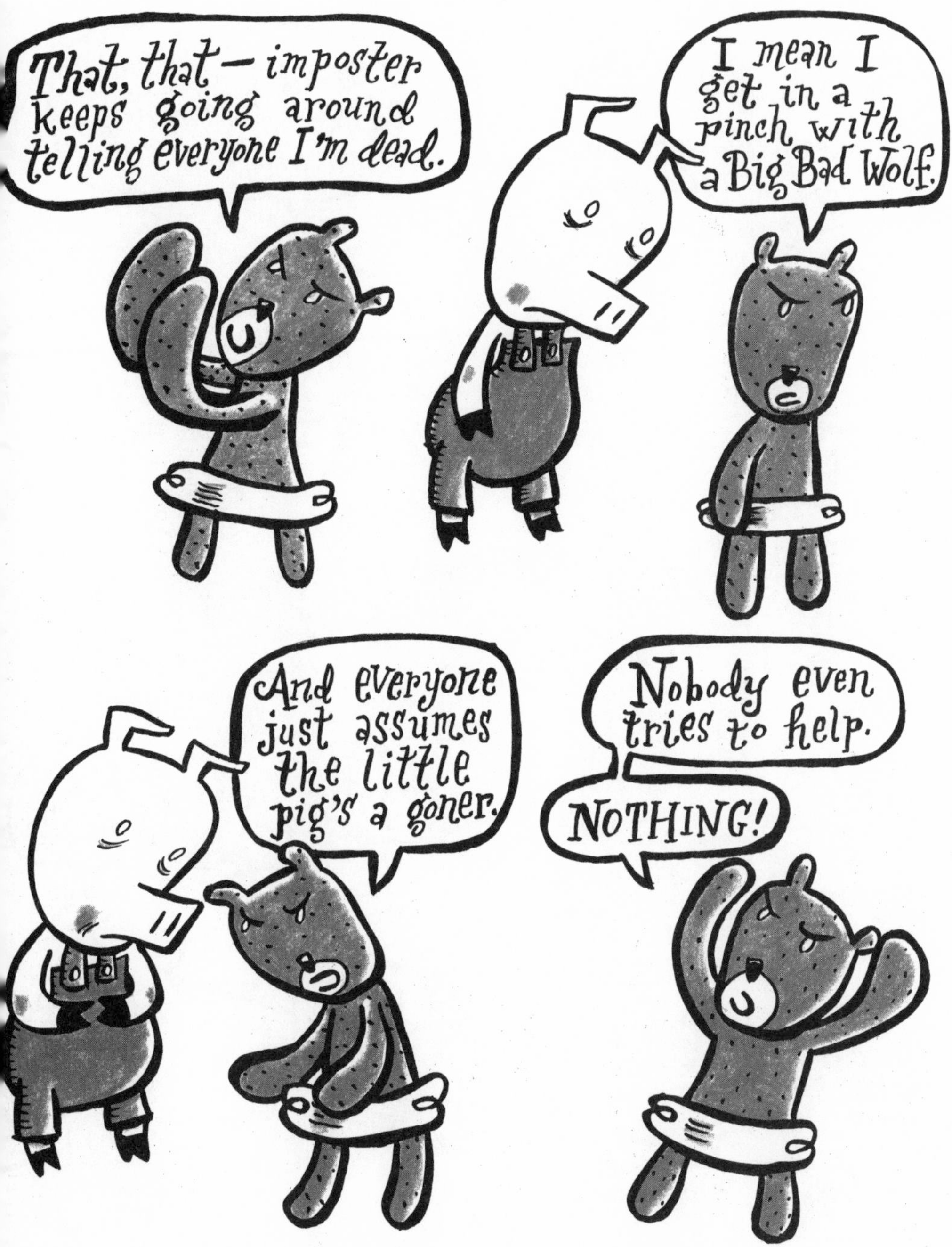
That, that— imposter keeps going around telling everyone I'm dead.
I mean I get in a pinch with a Big Bad Wolf.
And everyone just assumes the little pig's a goner.
Nobody even tries to help.
NOTHING!

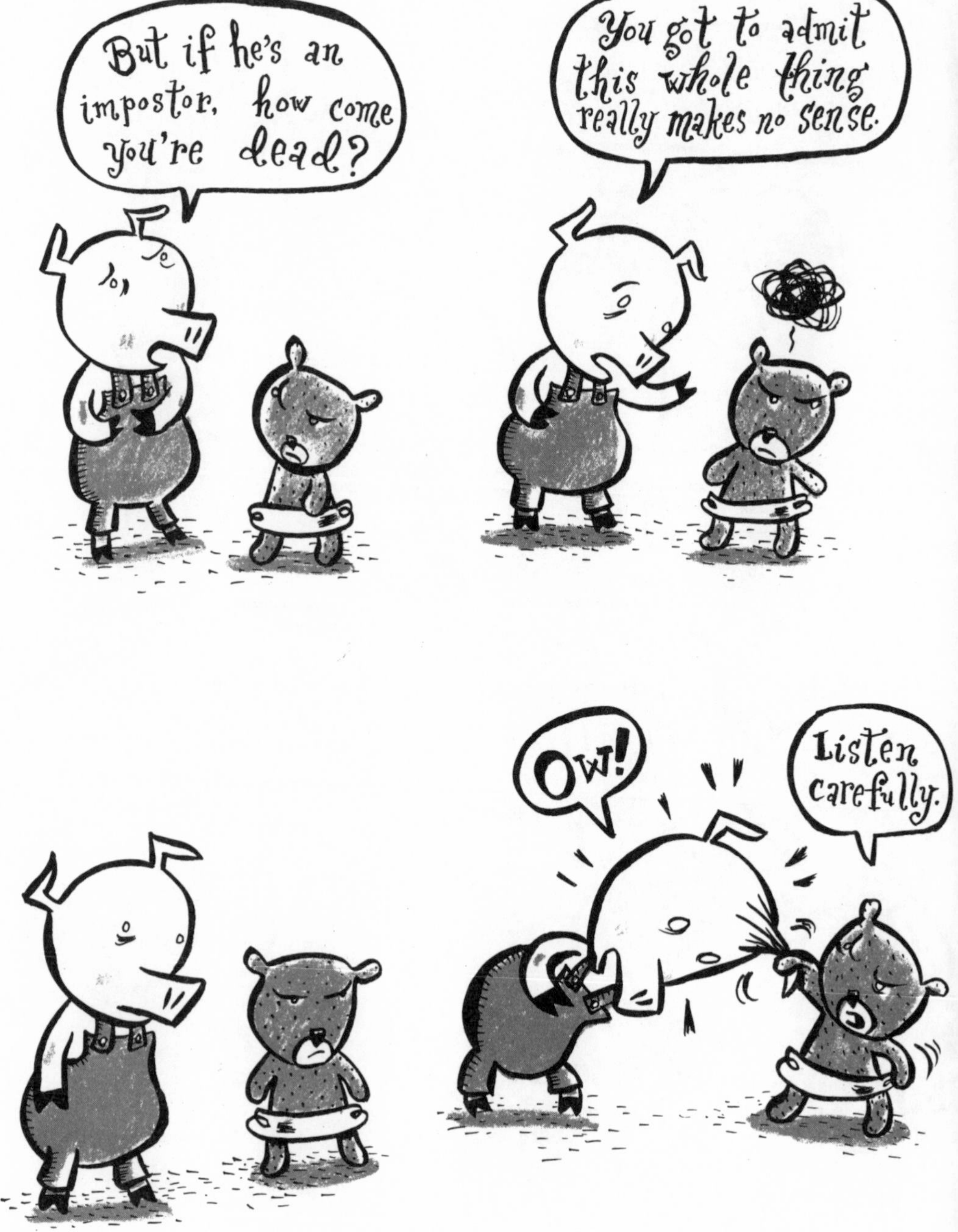
But if he's an impostor, how come you're dead?
You got to admit this whole thing really makes no sense.
Ow!
Listen carefully.

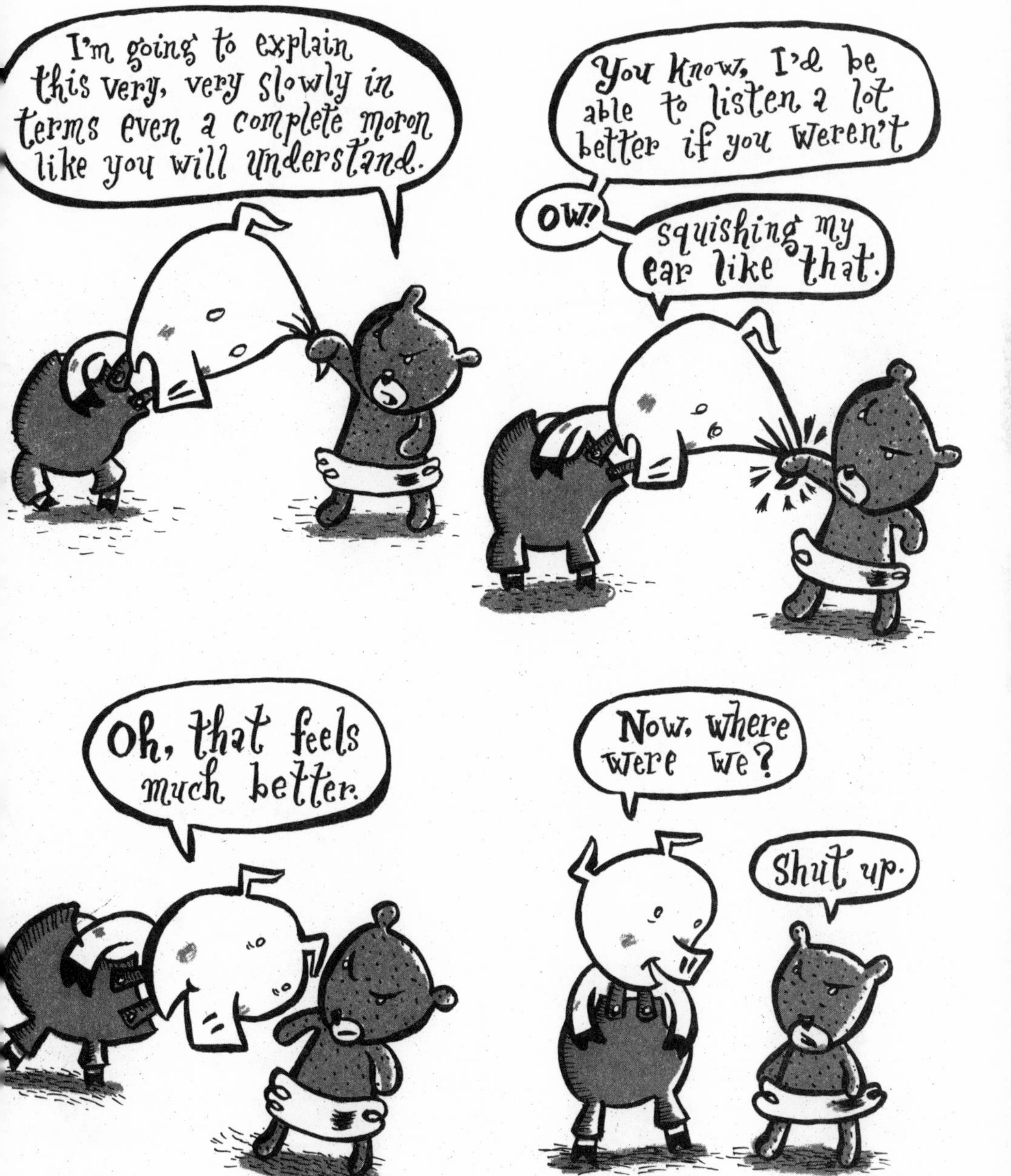
I'm going to explain this very, very slowly in terms even a complete moron like you will understand.
You know, I'd be able to listen a lot better if you weren't
OW!
squishing my ear like that.
Oh, that feels much better.
Now, where were we?
Shut up.

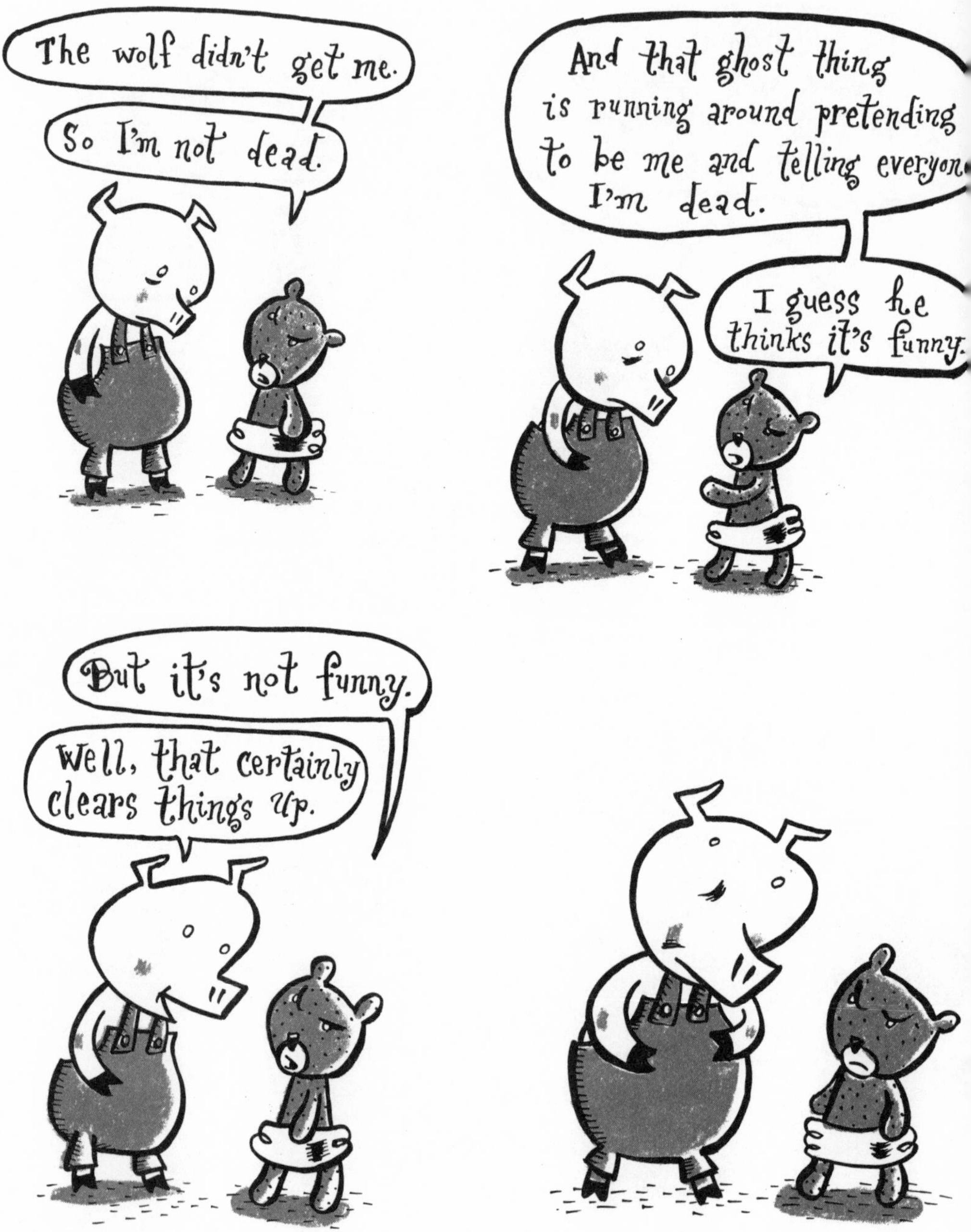
The wolf didn't get me.
So I'm not dead.
And that ghost thing is running around pretending to be me and telling everyone I'm dead.
I guess he thinks it's funny.
But it's not funny.
Well, that certainly clears things up.

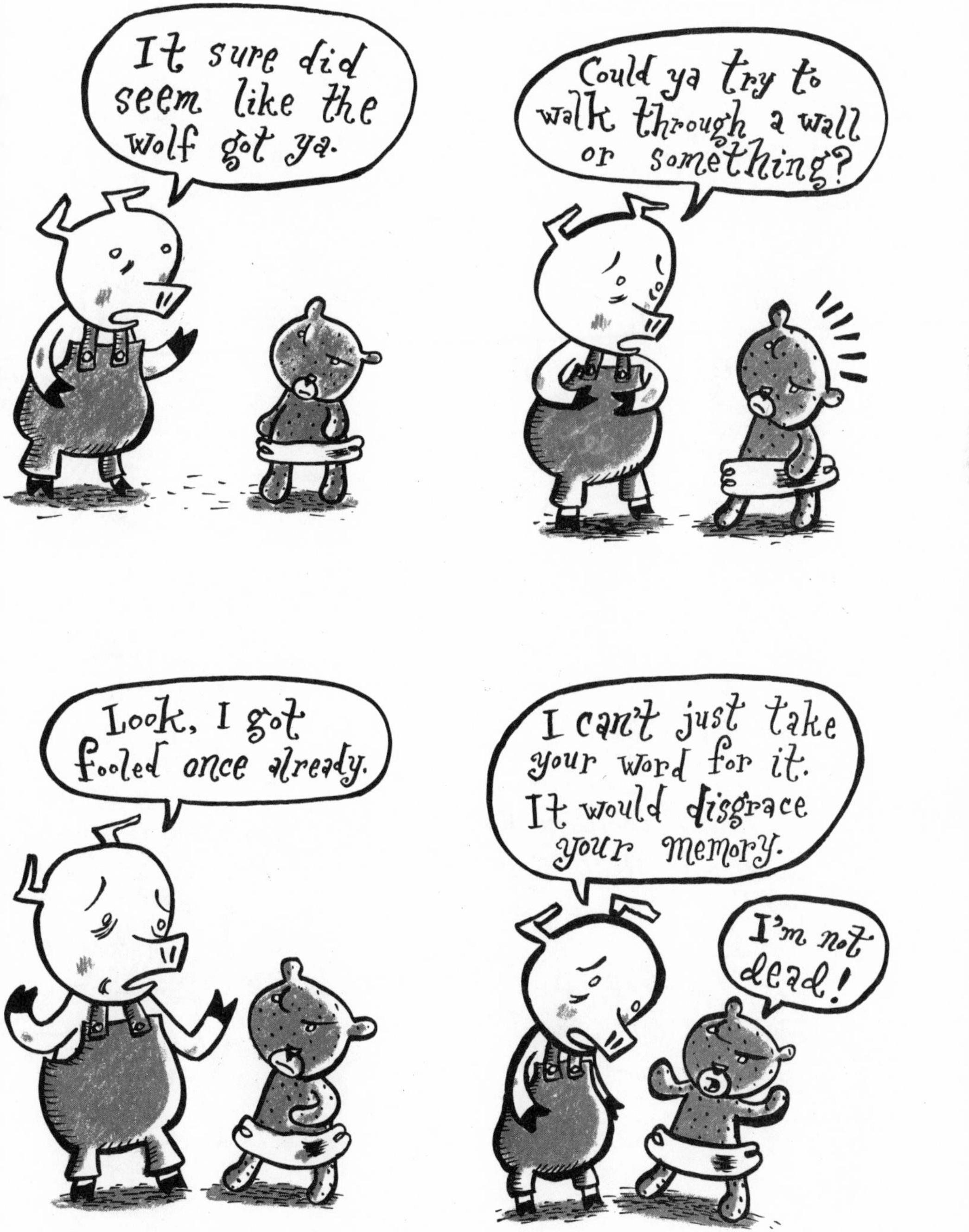
It sure did seem like the wolf got ya.
Could ya try to walk through a wall or something?
Look, I got fooled once already.
I can't just take your word for it. It would disgrace your memory.
I'm not dead!

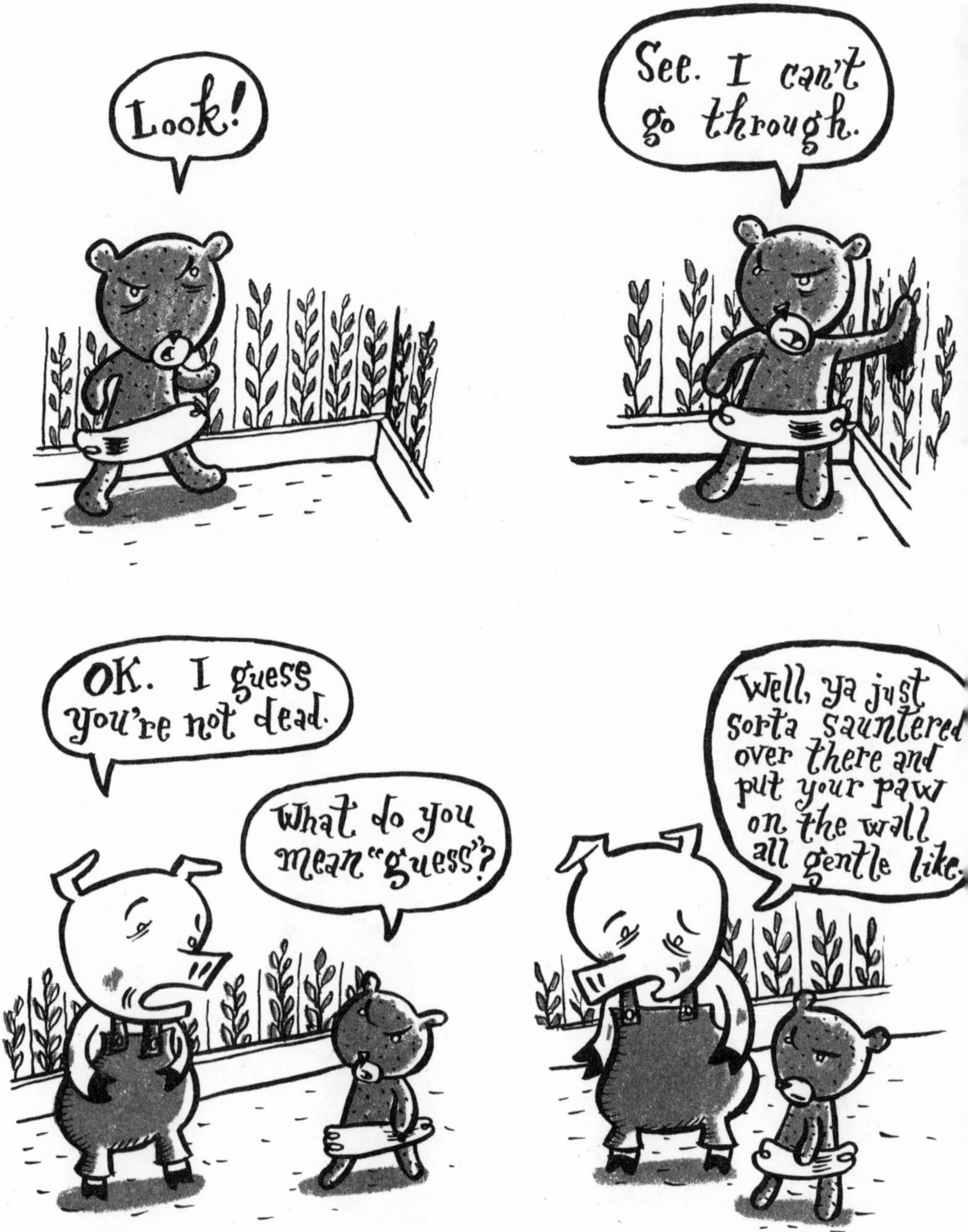
Look!
See. I can't go through.
OK. I guess you're not dead.
What do you mean "guess"?
Well, ya just sorta sauntered over there and put your paw on the wall all gentle like.

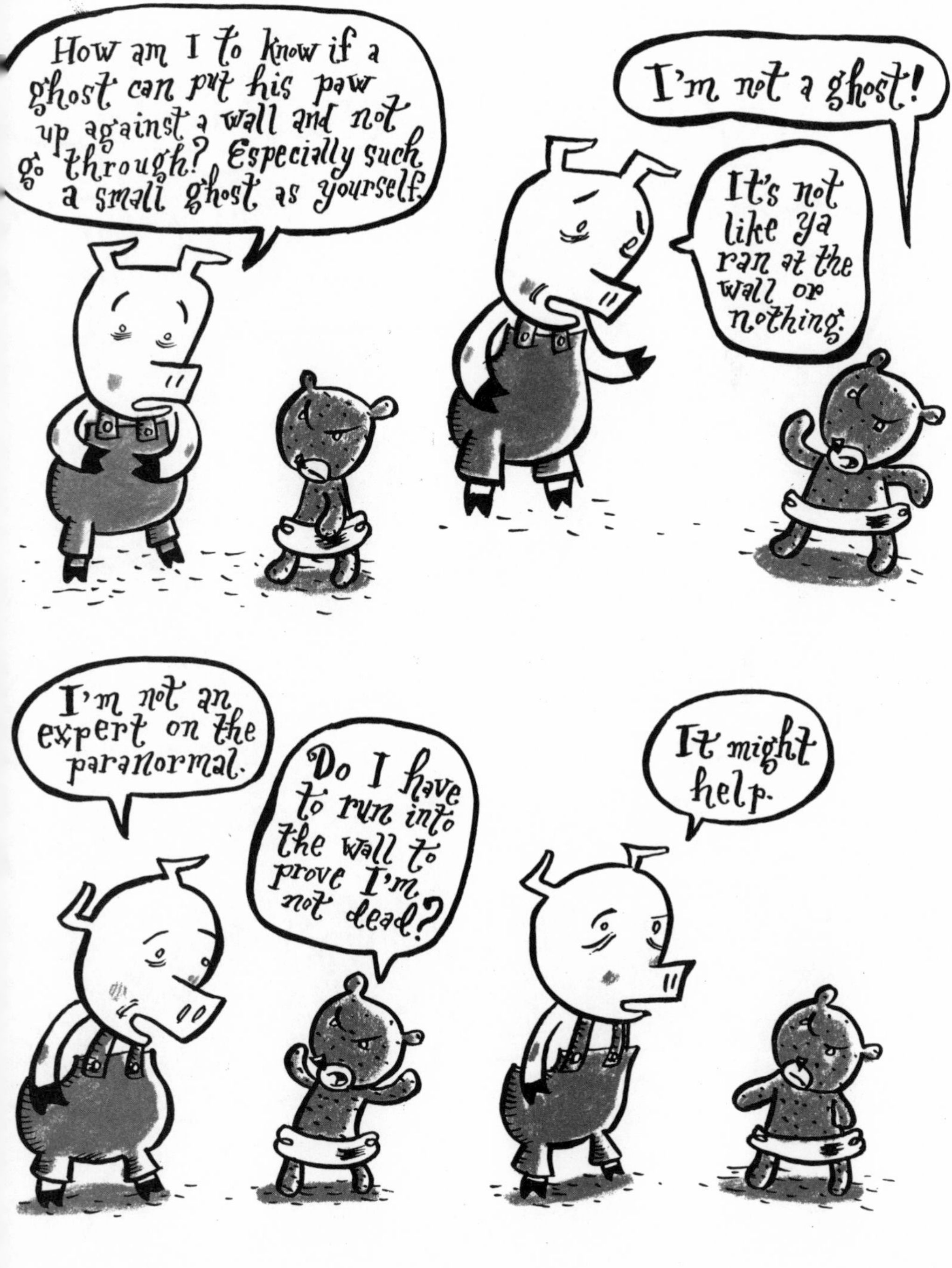
How am I to know if a ghost can put his paw up against a wall and not go through? Especially such a small ghost as yourself.
I'm not a ghost!
It's not like ya ran at the wall or nothing.
I'm not an expert on the paranormal.
Do I have to run into the wall to prove I'm not dead?
It might help.

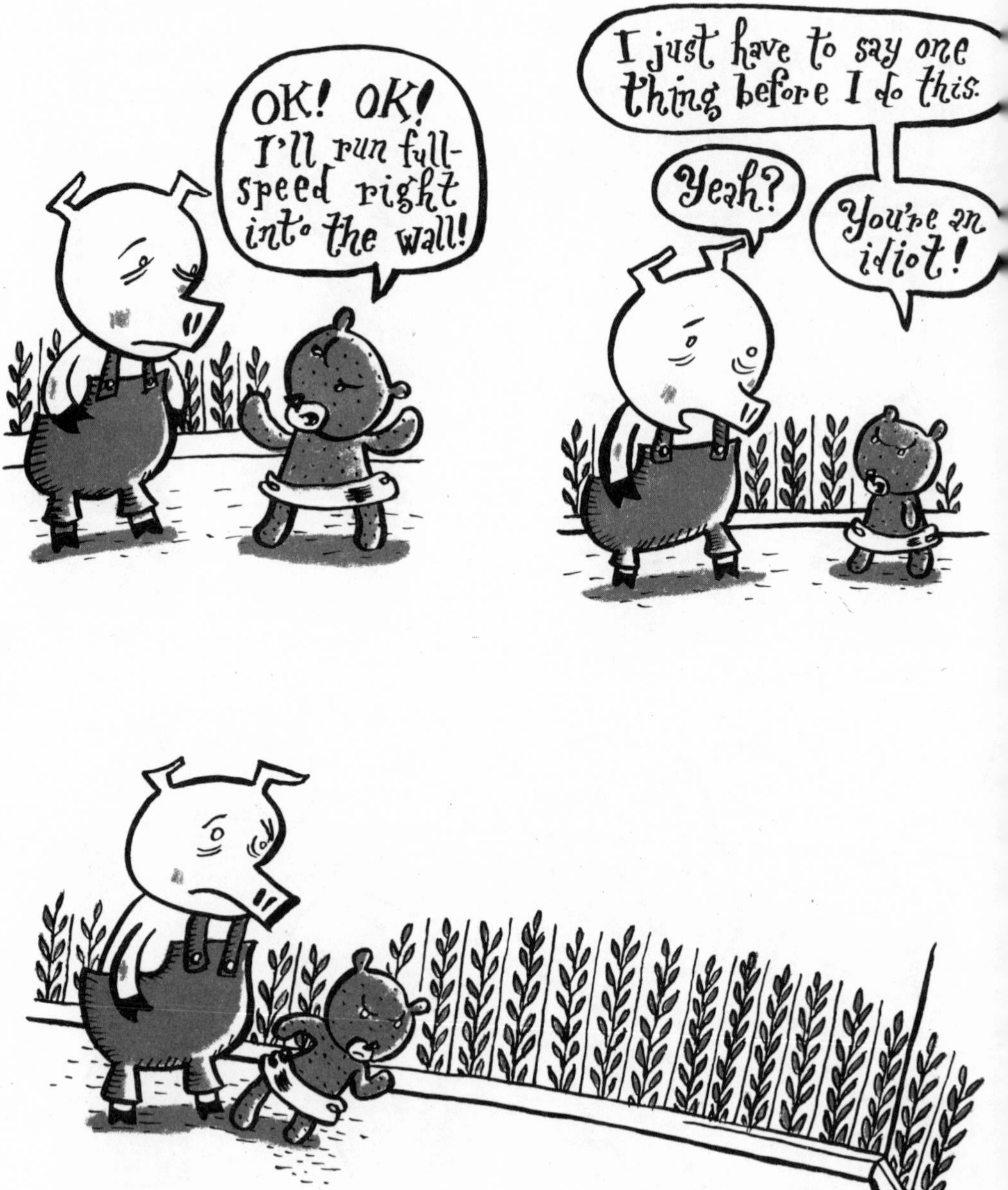
OK! OK! I'll run full-speed right into the wall!
I just have to say one thing before I do this.
Yeah?
You're an idiot!

CRASH!

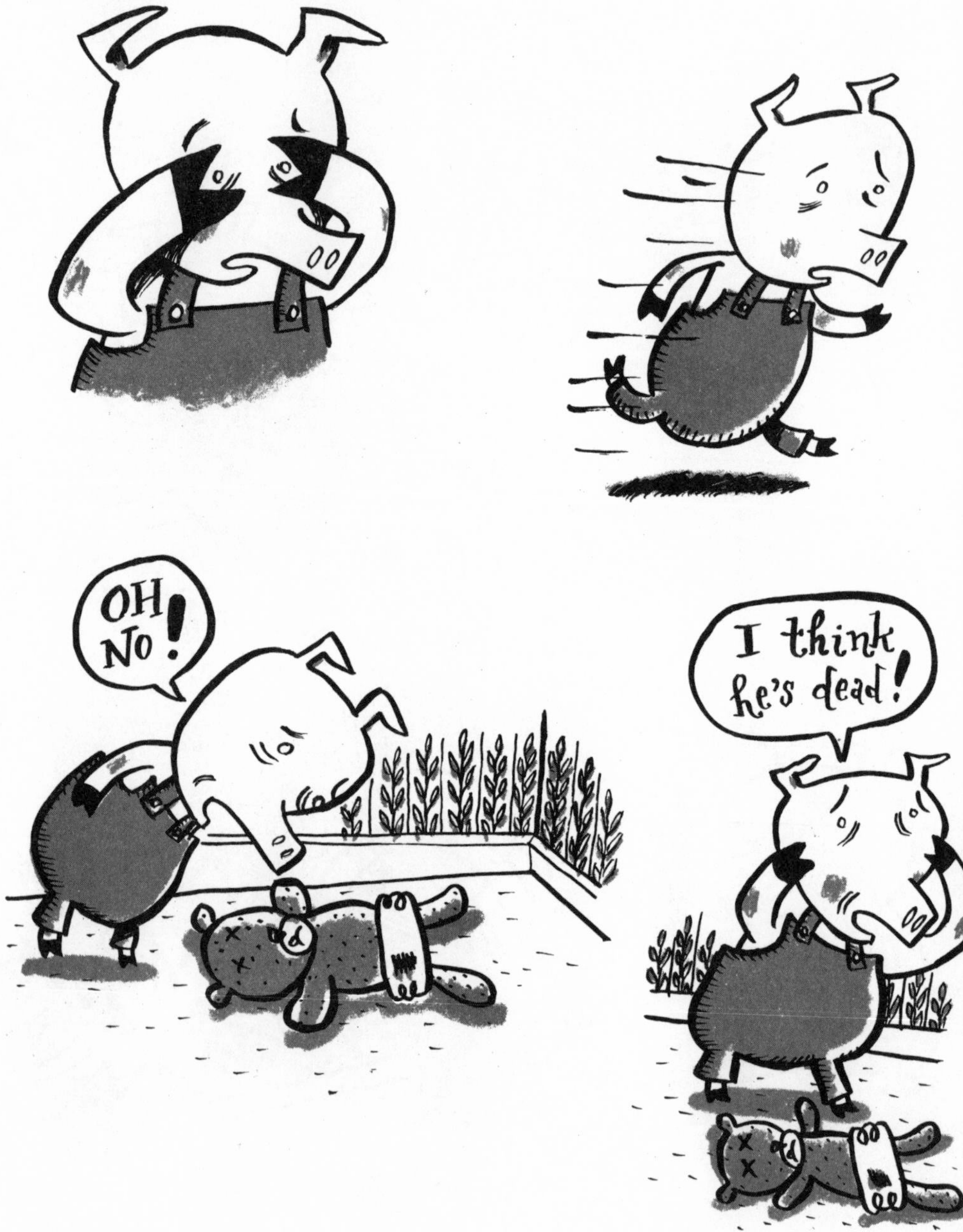
OH NO!
I think he's dead!

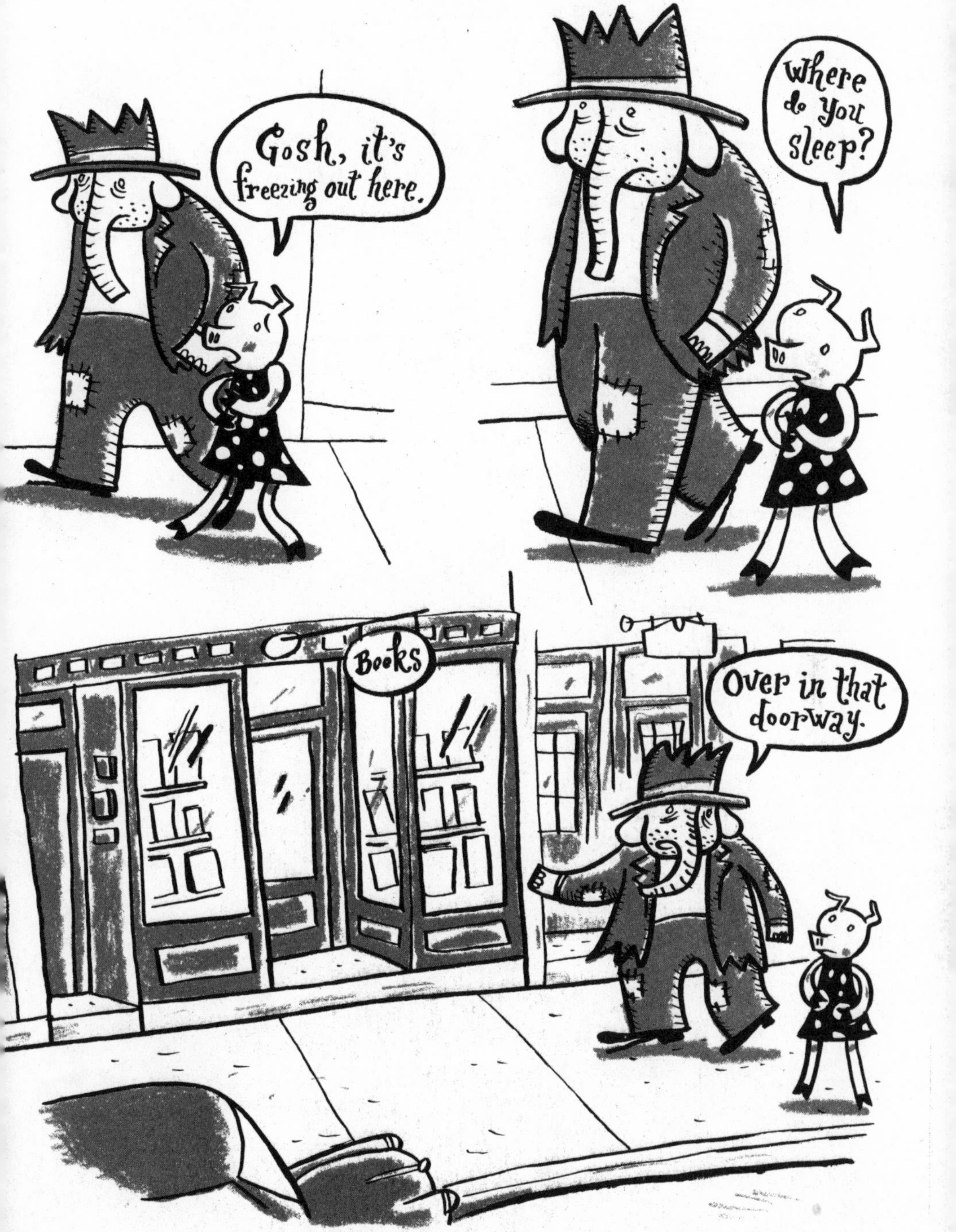
Gosh, it's freezing out here.
Where do you sleep?
Books
Over in that doorway.

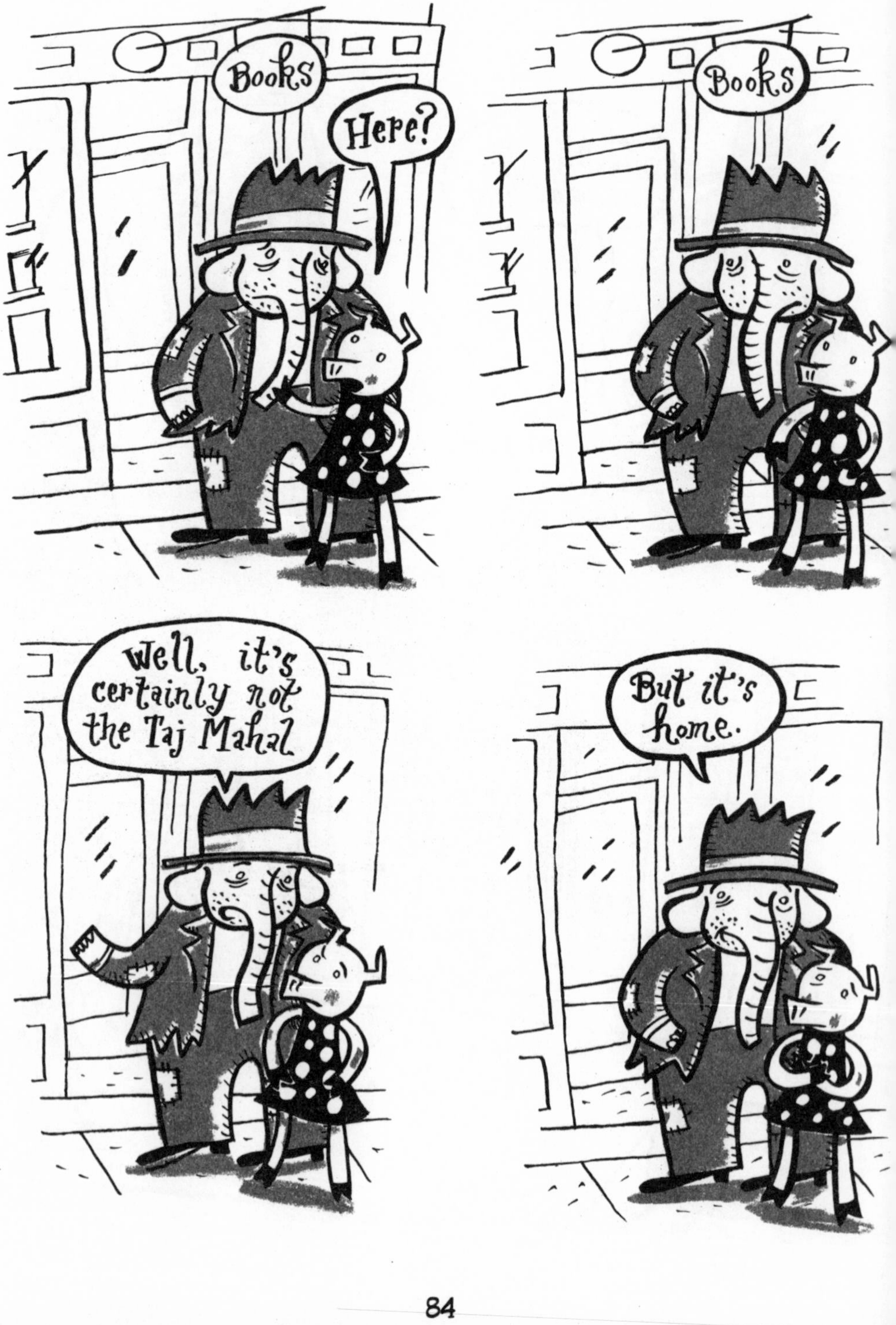
BooKS
Here?
BooKS
Well, it's certainly not the Taj Mahal
But it's home.

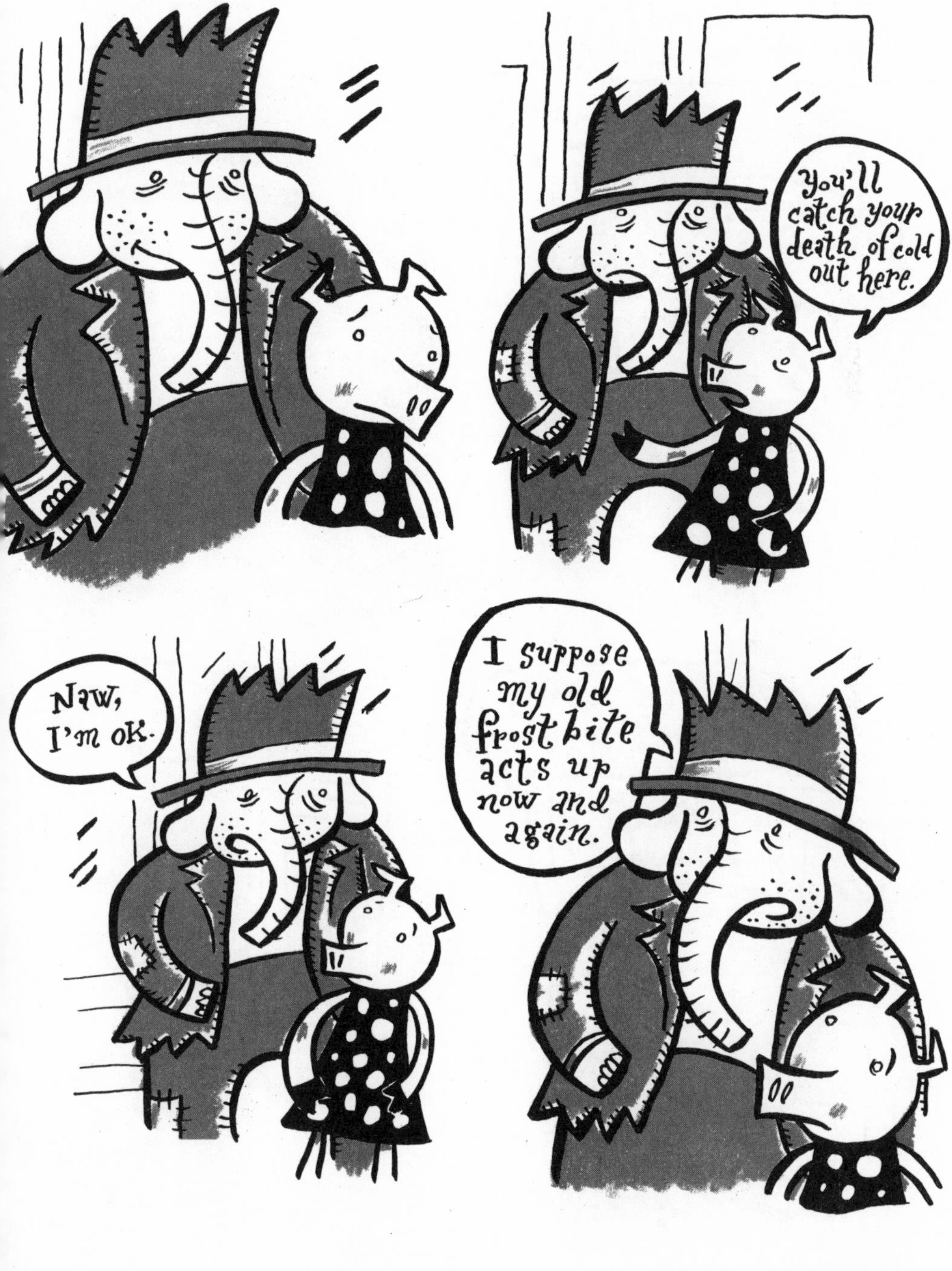
You'll catch your death of cold out here.
Naw, I'm OK.
I suppose my old frost bite acts up now and again.

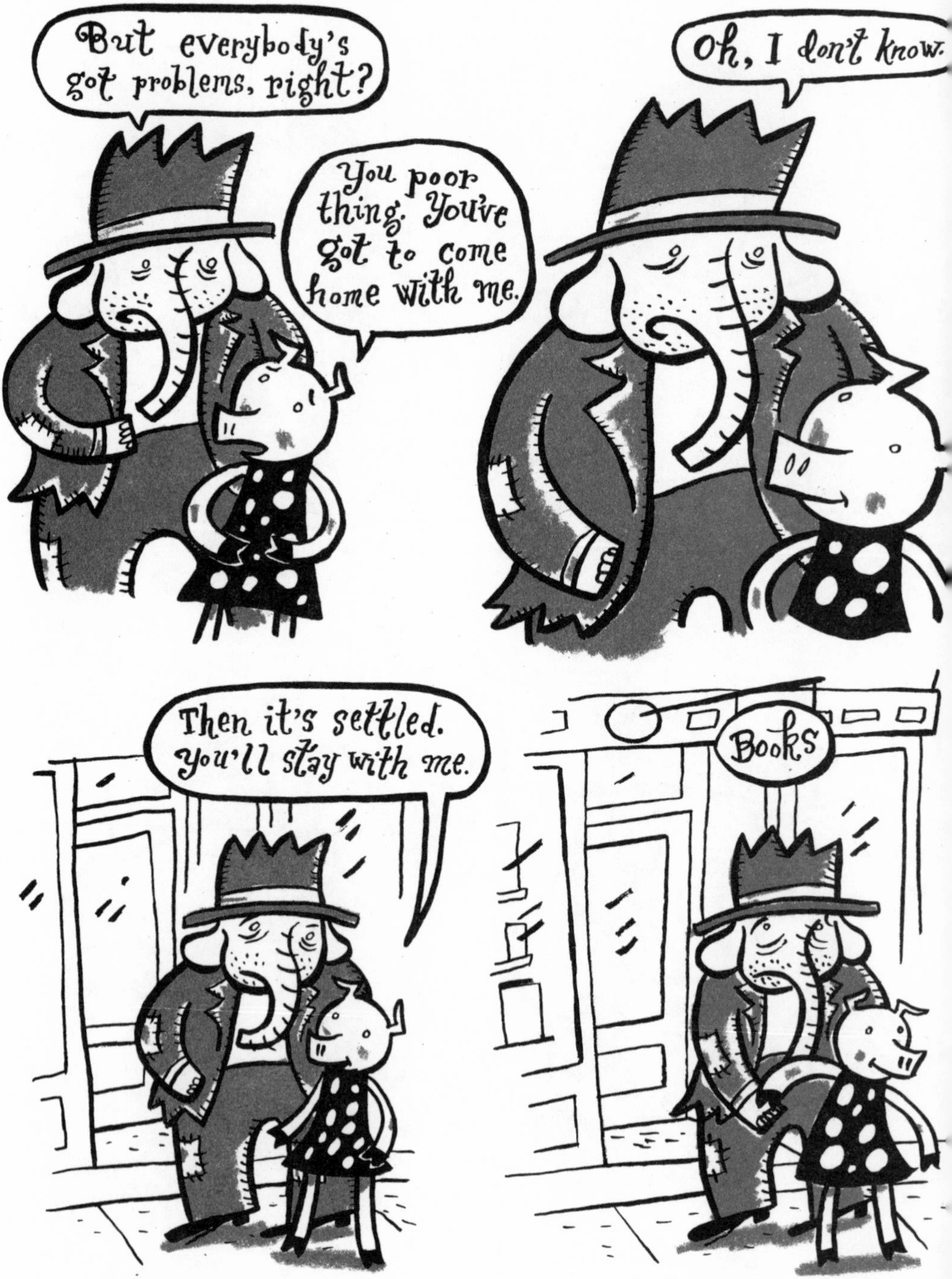
But everybody's got problems, right?
You poor thing. You've got to come home with me.
Oh, I don't know.
Then it's settled. You'll stay with me.
Books

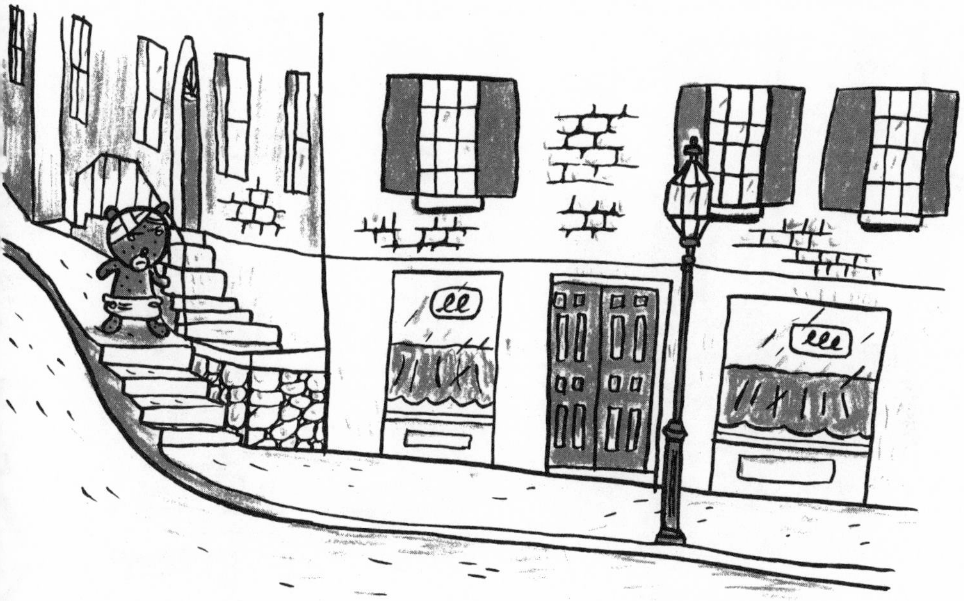

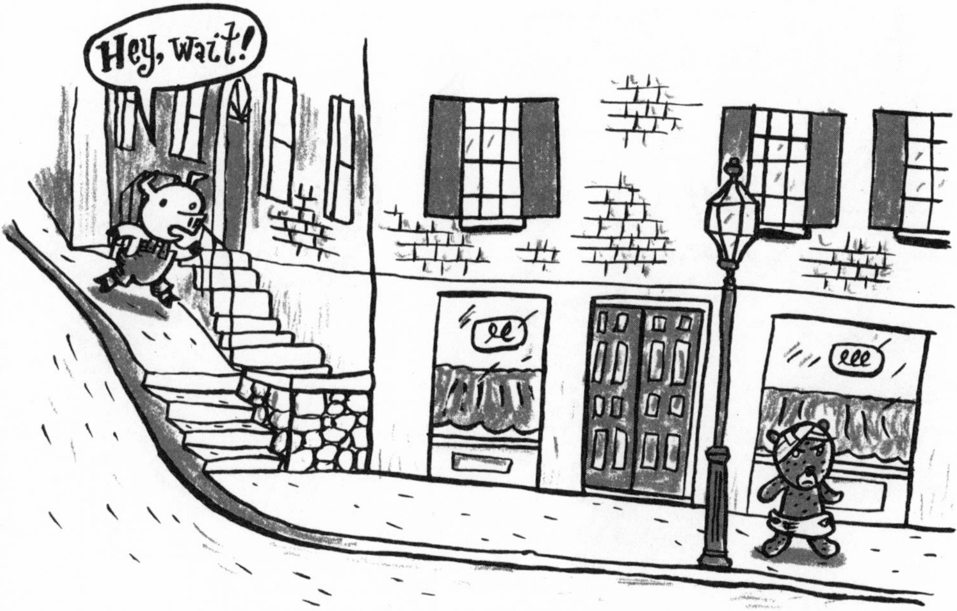
Hey, wait!

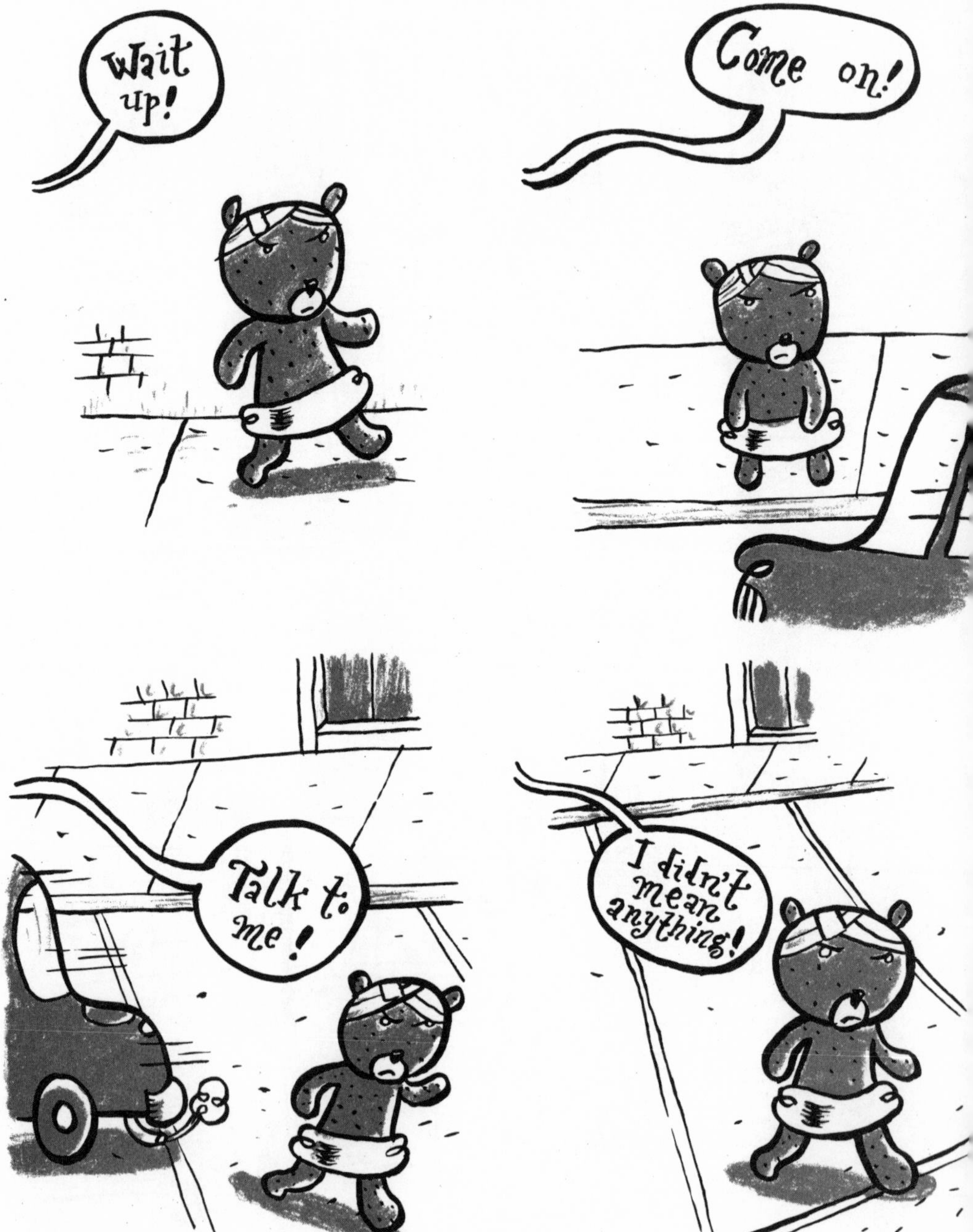
Wait up!
Come on!
Talk to me!
I didn't mean anything!

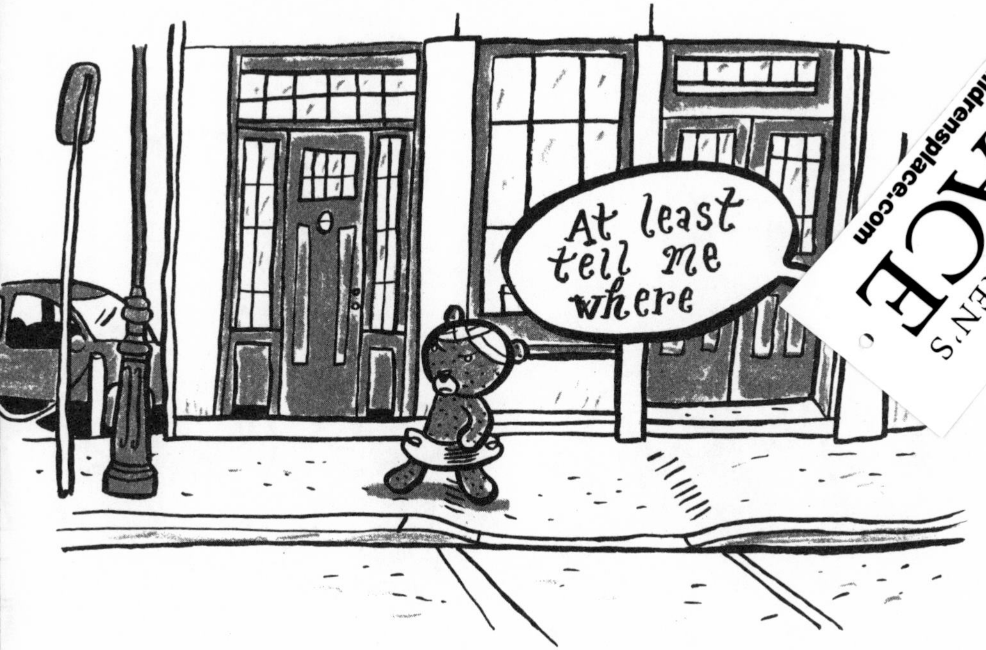
At least tell me where

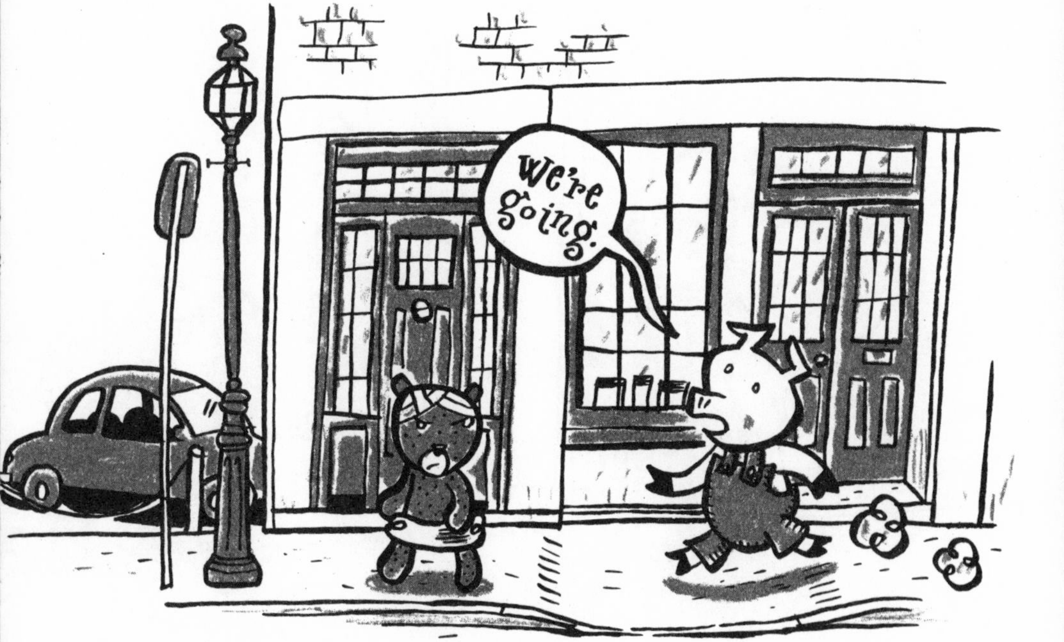
We're going.

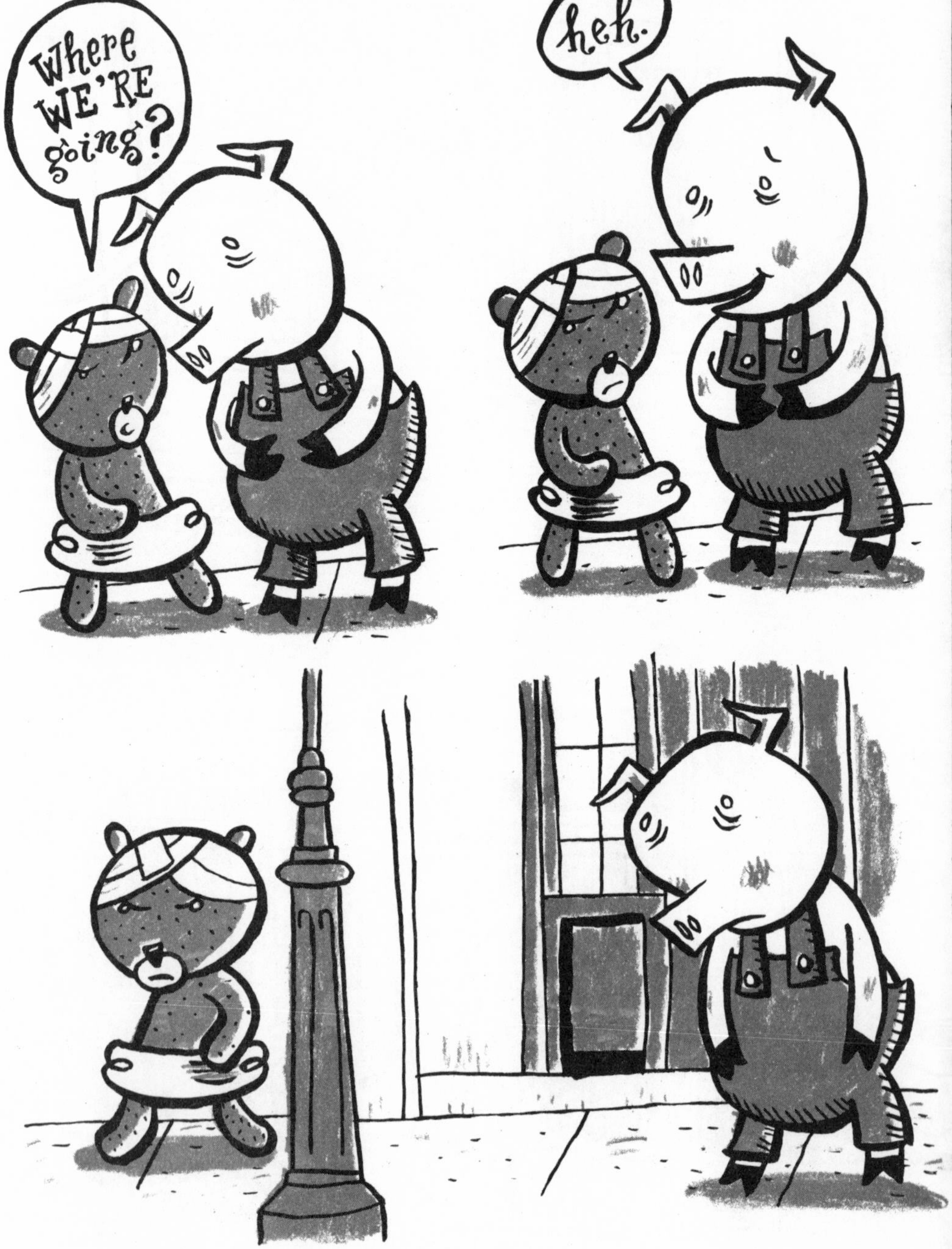
Where WE'RE going?
heh.

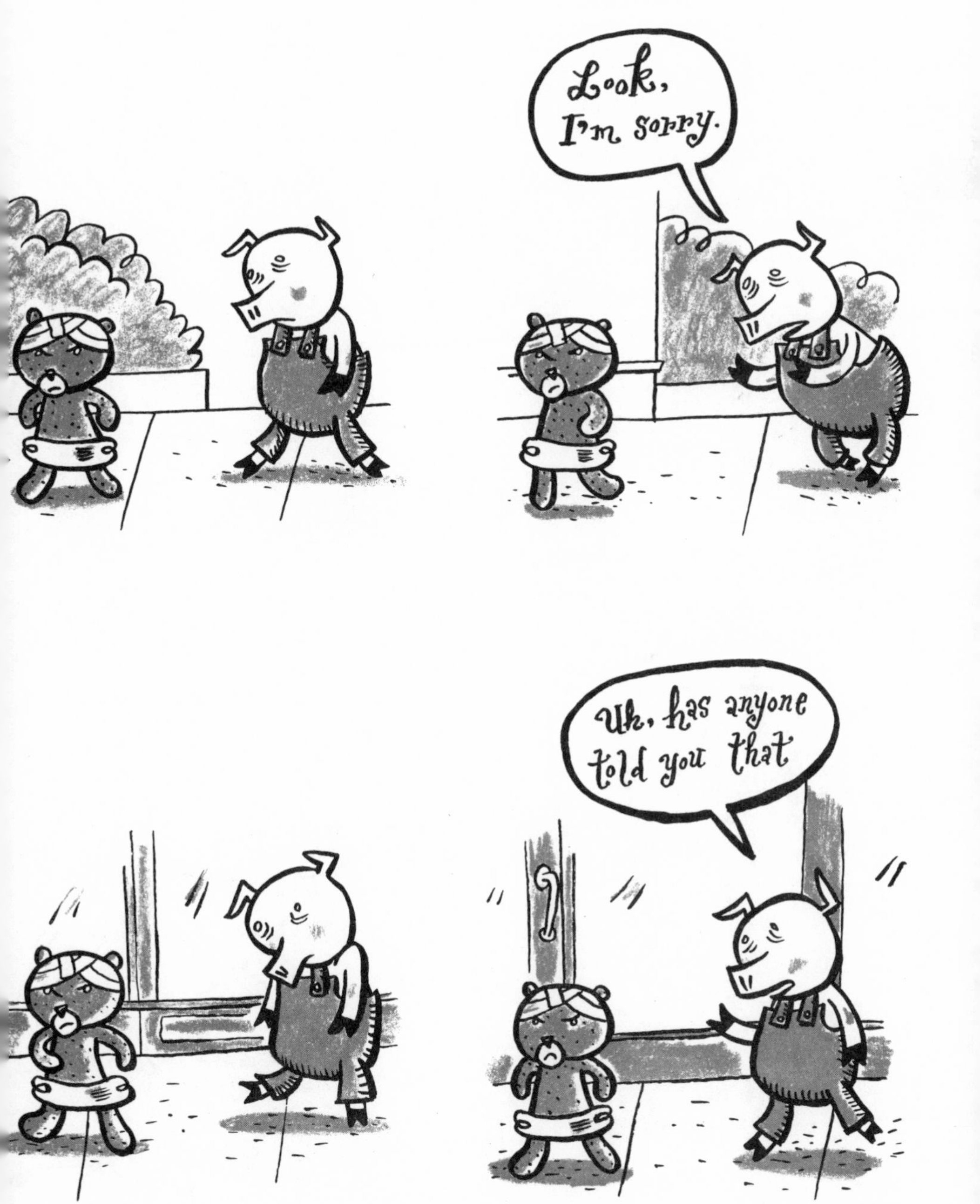
Look, I'm sorry.
Uh, has anyone told you that

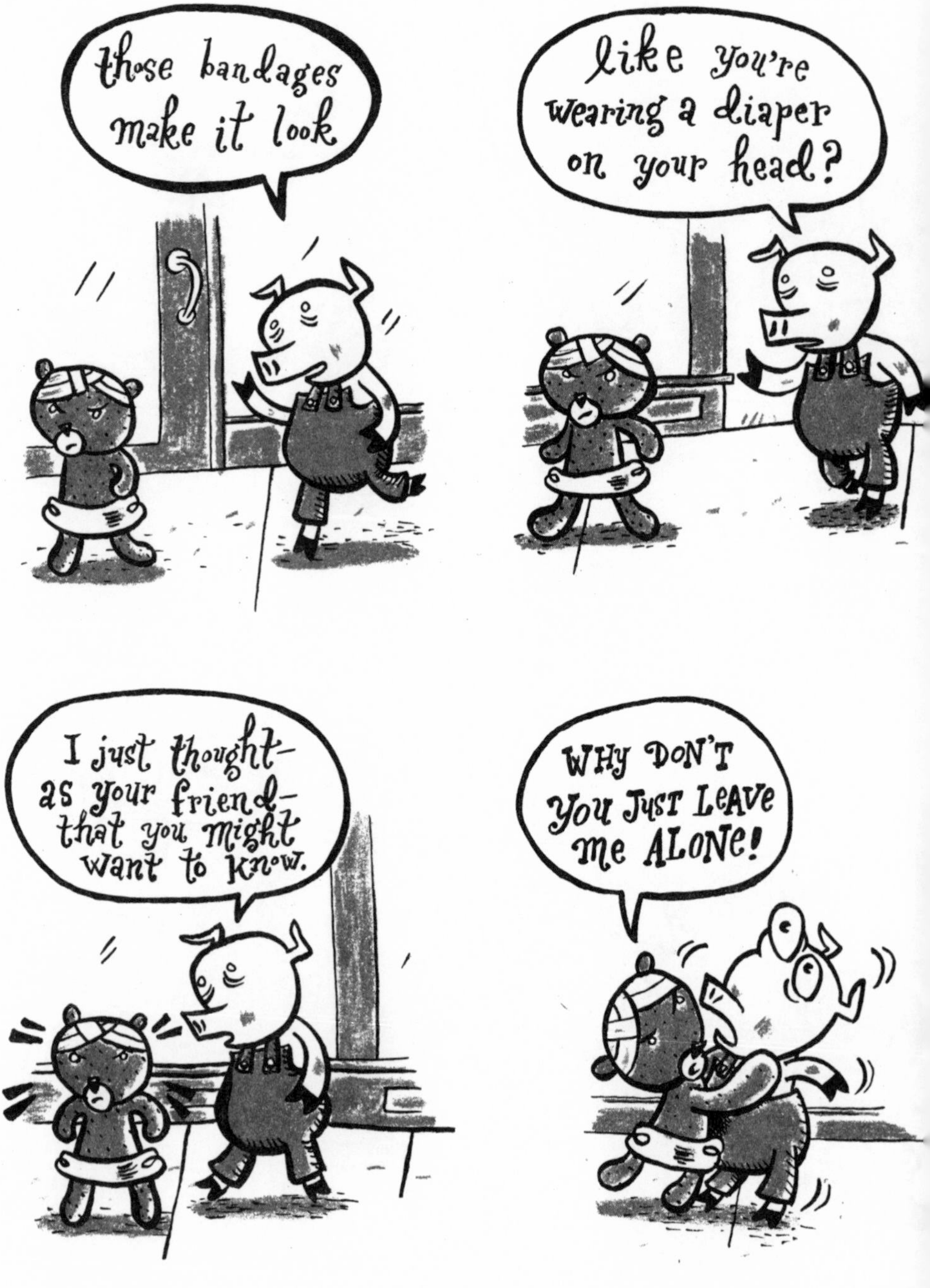
those bandages make it look
like you're wearing a diaper on your head?
I just thought- as your friend- that you might want to know.
WHY DON'T YOU JUST LEAVE ME ALONE!

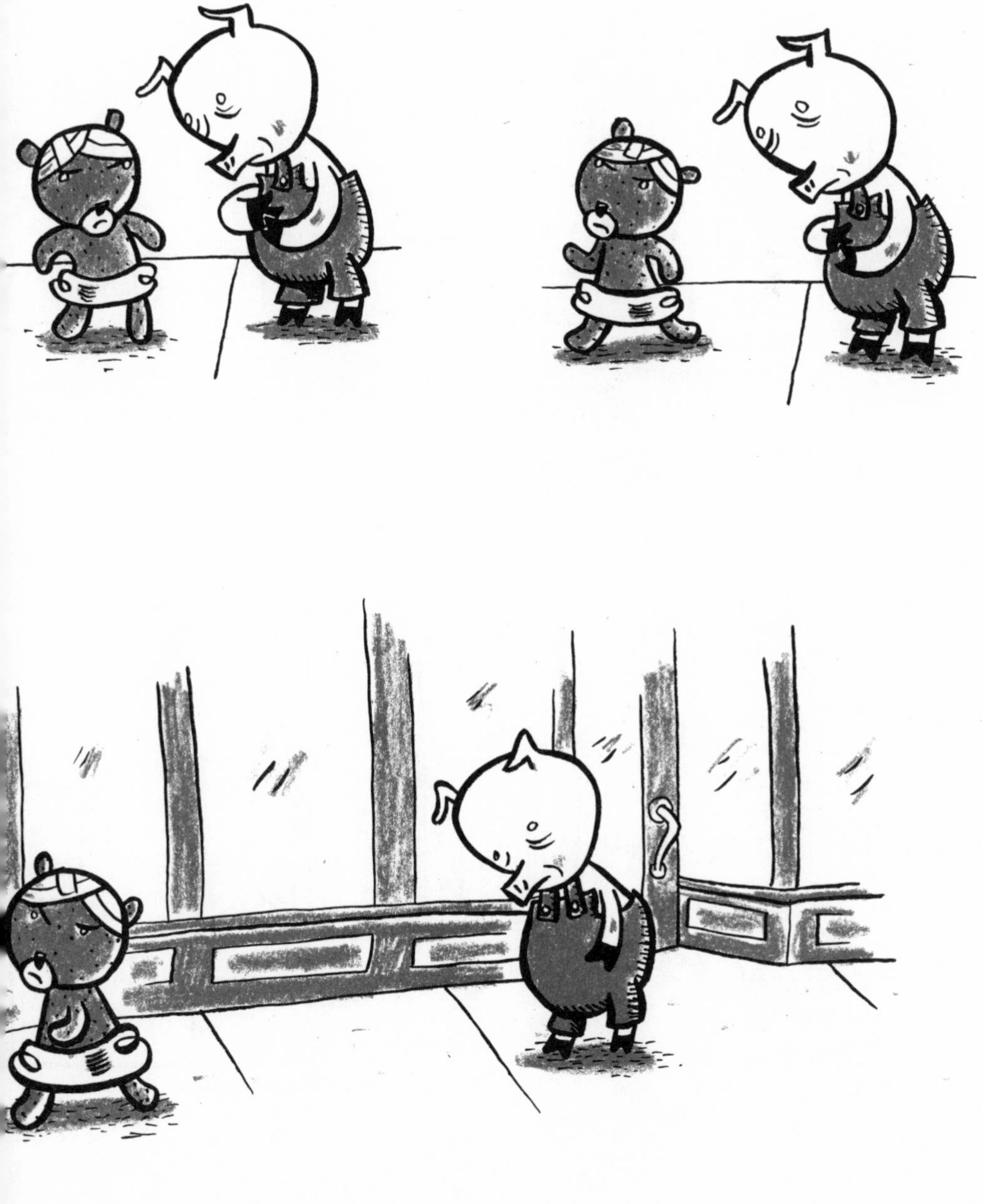

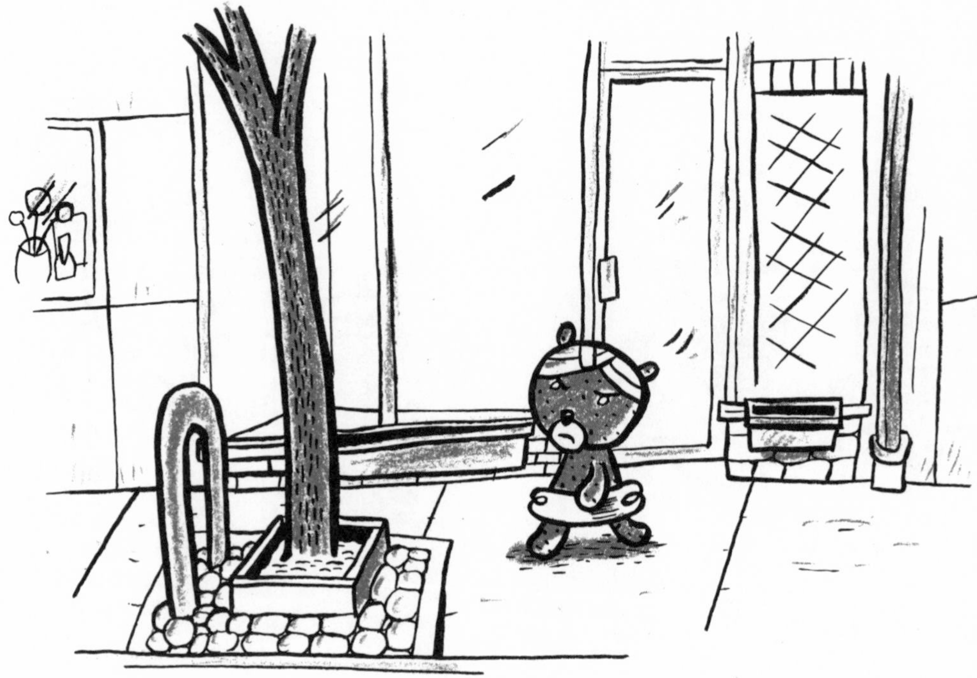

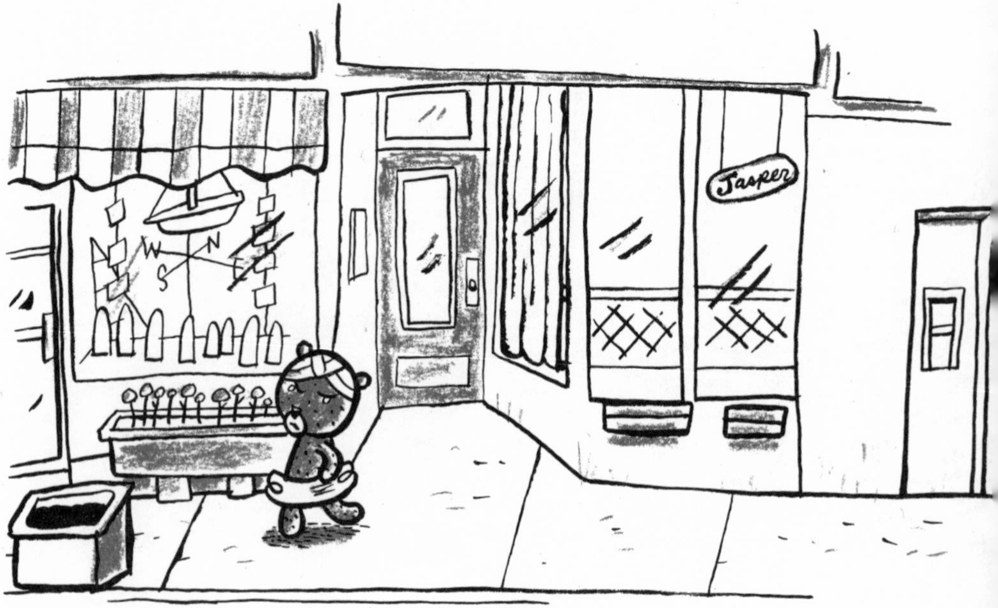
W
N
S
E
Jasper

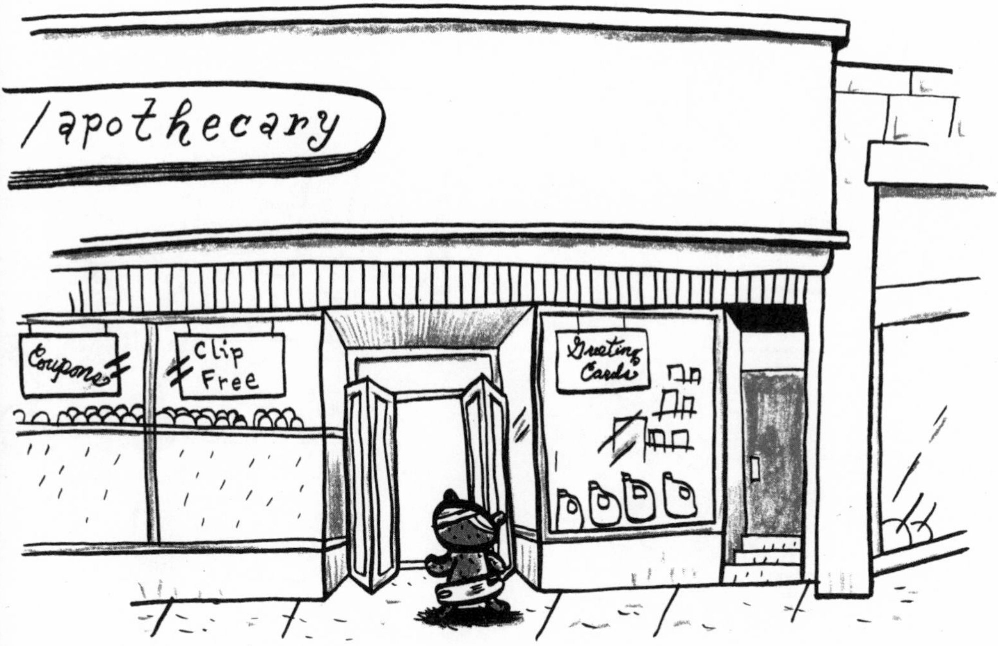
/apothecary
Coupons
Clip Free
Greeting Cards

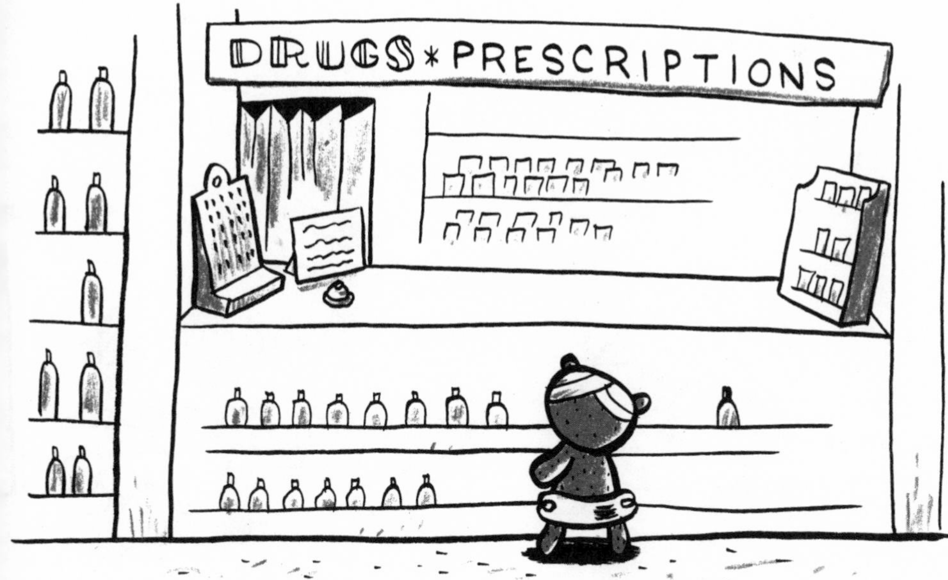
DRUGS * PRESCRIPTIONS

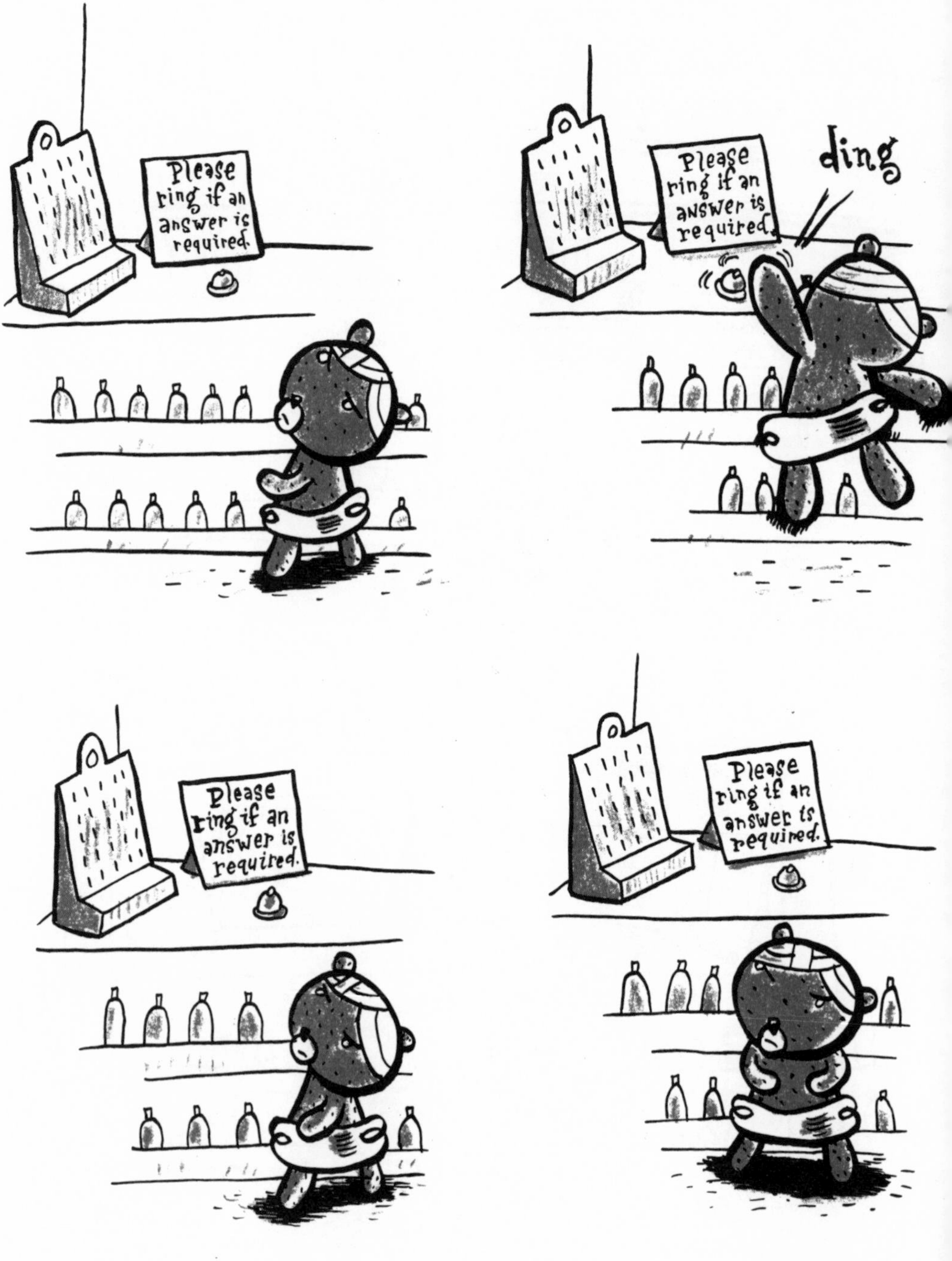
Please ring if an answer is required.
Please ring if an answer is required.
ding
Please ring if an answer is required.
Please ring if an answer is required.

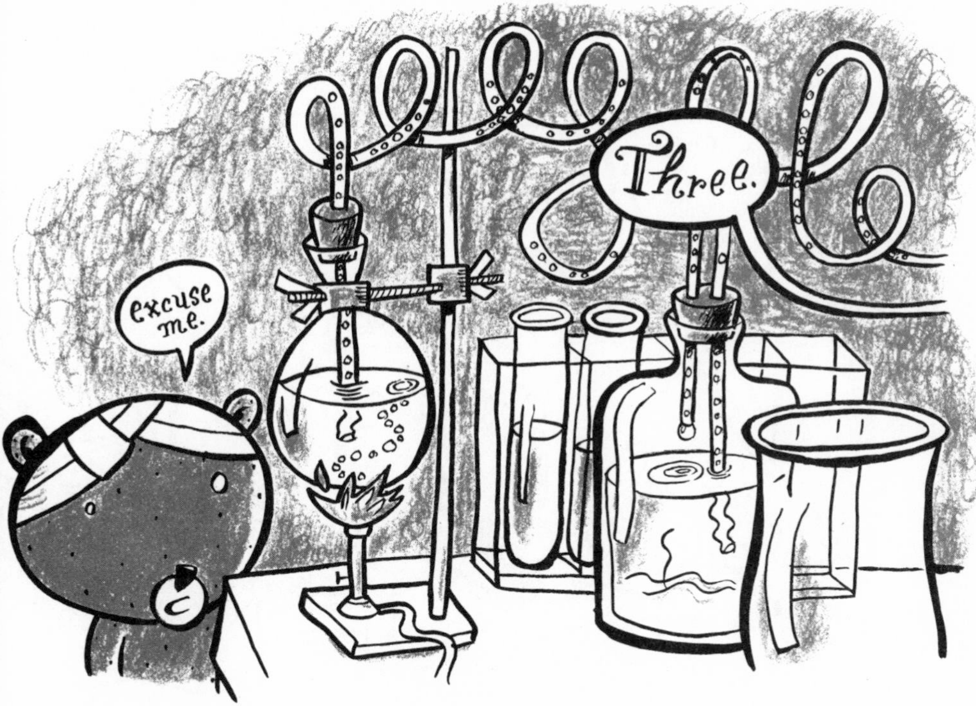
Three.
excuse me.

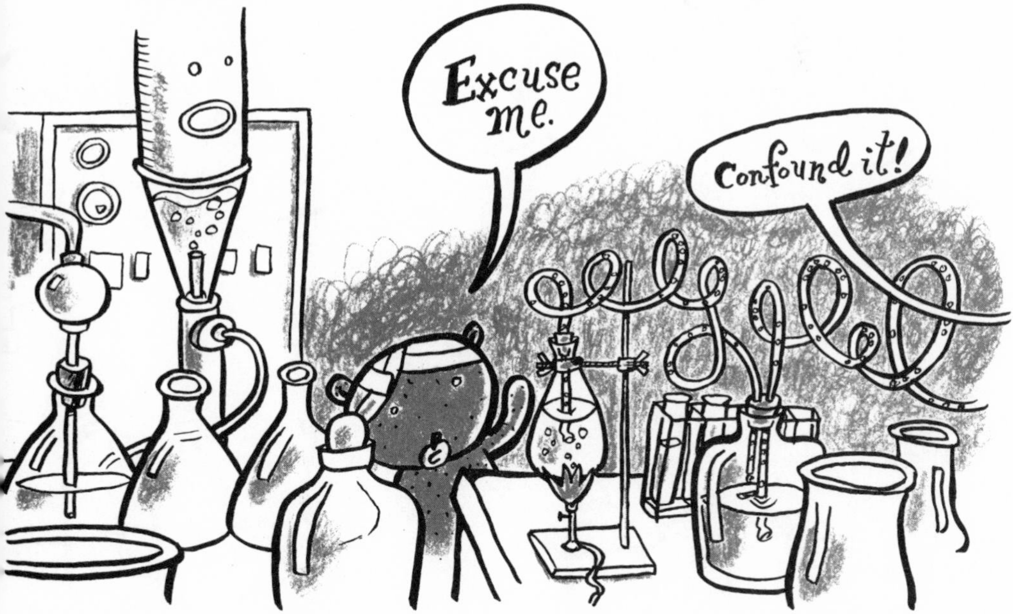
Excuse me.
Confound it!

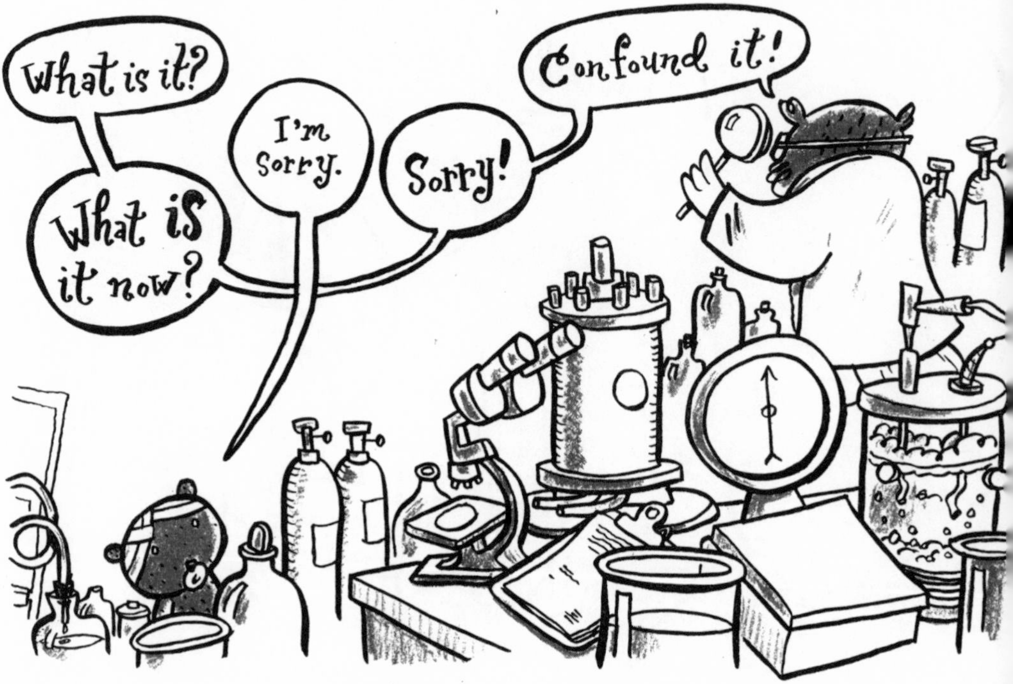
What is it?
What IS it now?
I'm sorry.
Sorry!
Confound it!

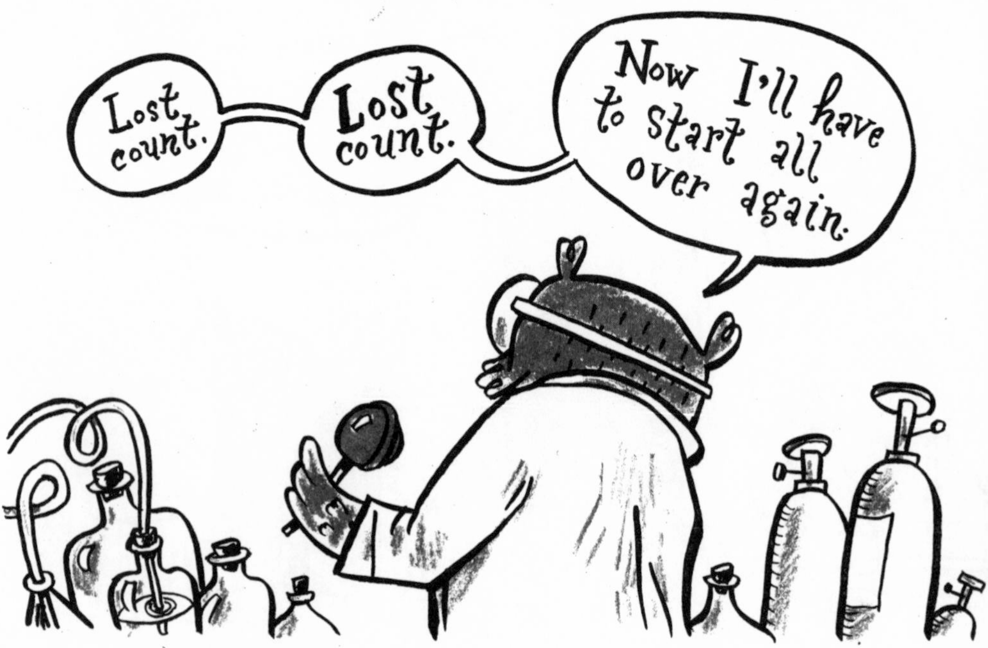
Lost count.
Lost count.
Now I'll have to start all over again.

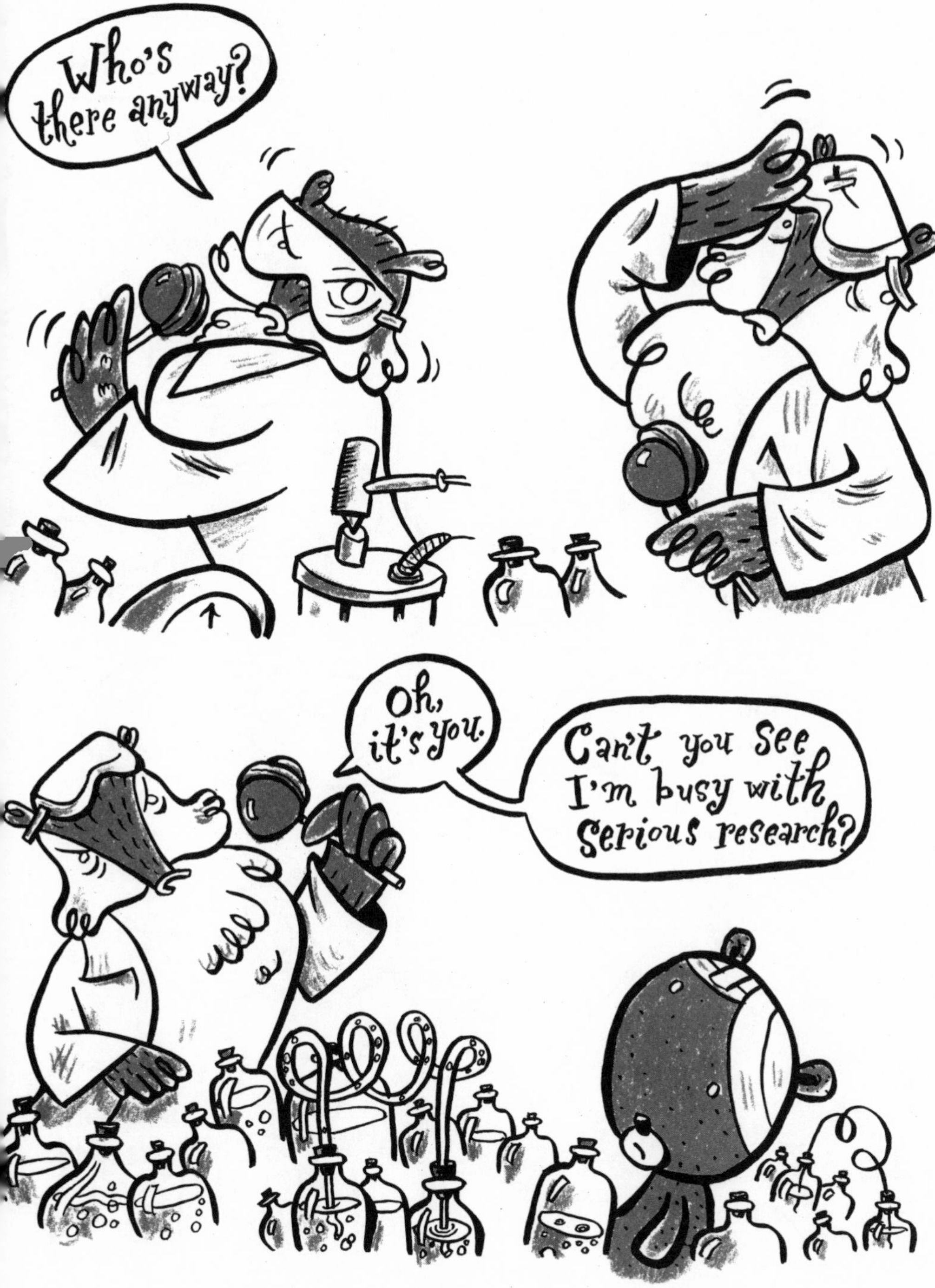
Who's there anyway?
Oh, it's you.
Can't you see I'm busy with serious research?

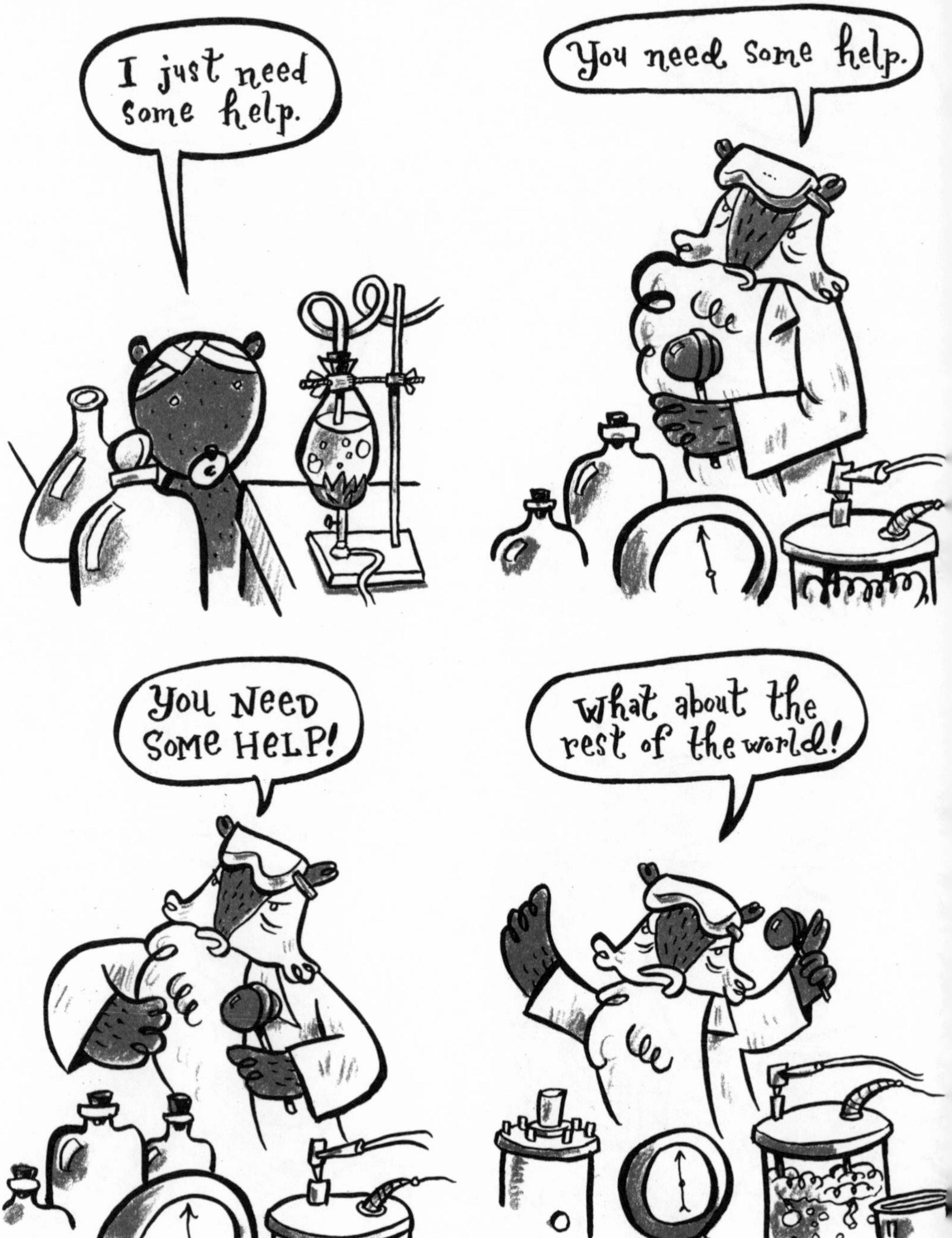
I just need some help.
You need some help.
You NEED SOME HELP!
What about the rest of the world!

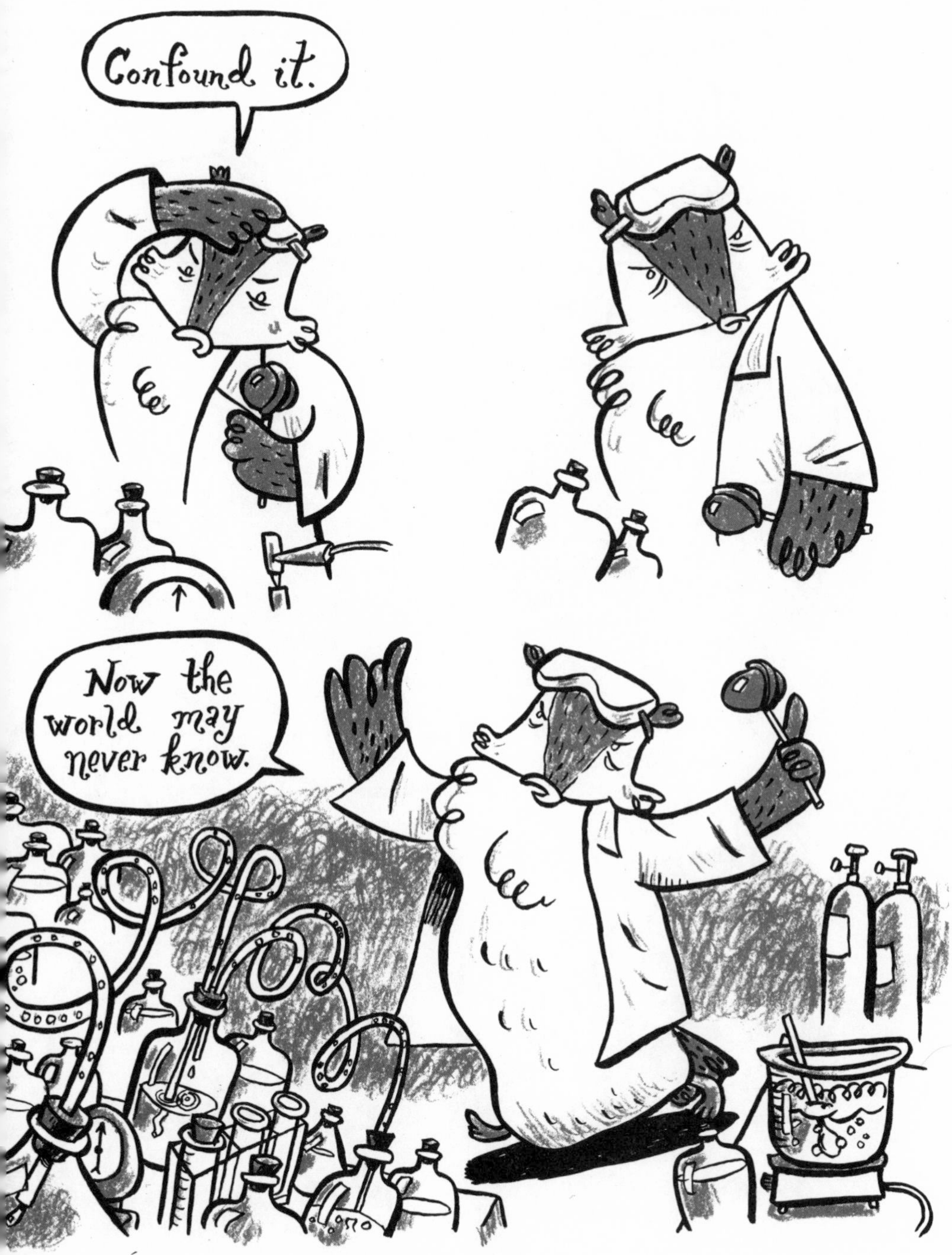
Confound it.
Now the world may never know.

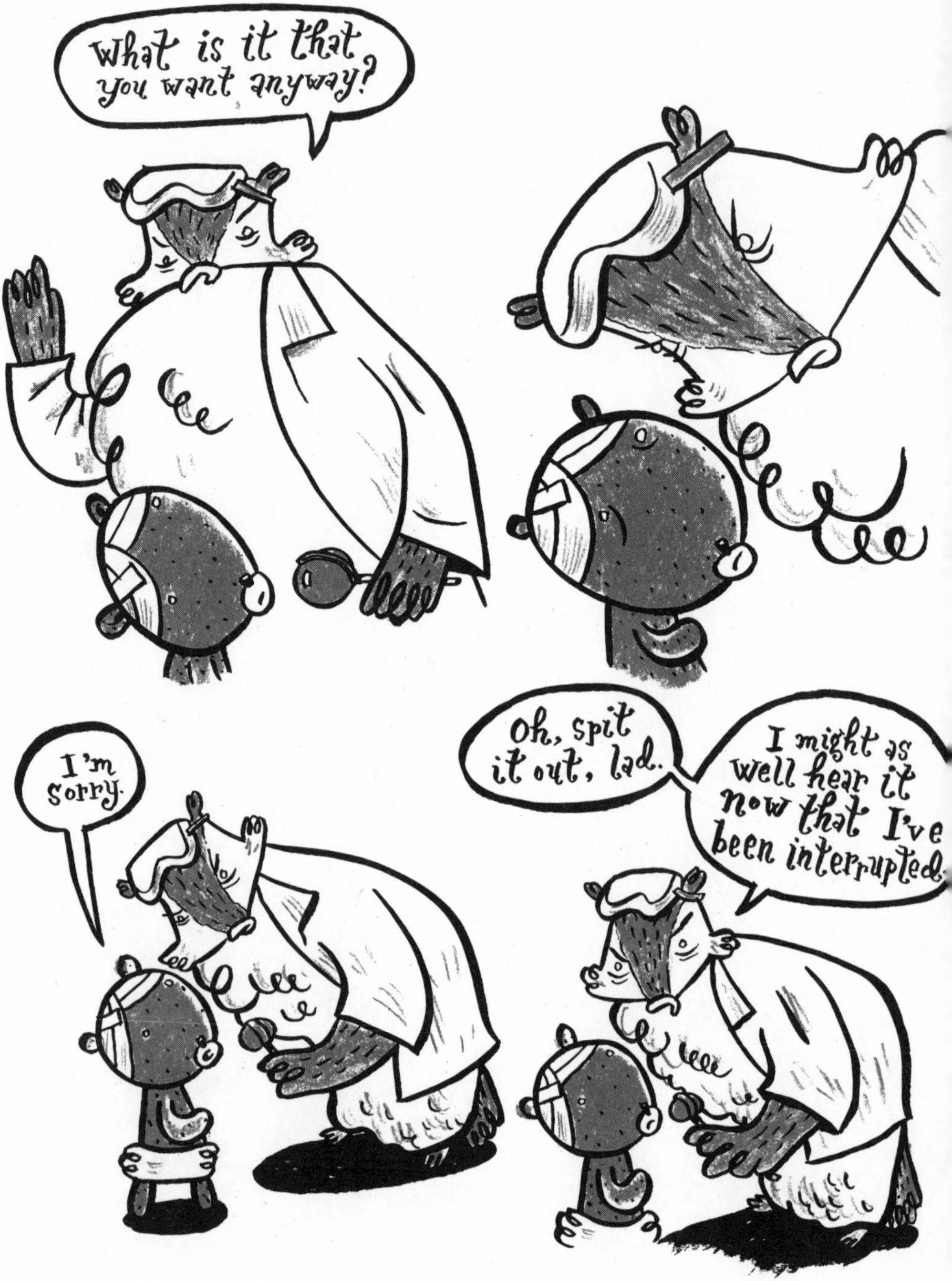
What is it that you want anyway?
I'm sorry.
Oh, spit it out, lad.
I might as well hear it now that I've been interrupted.

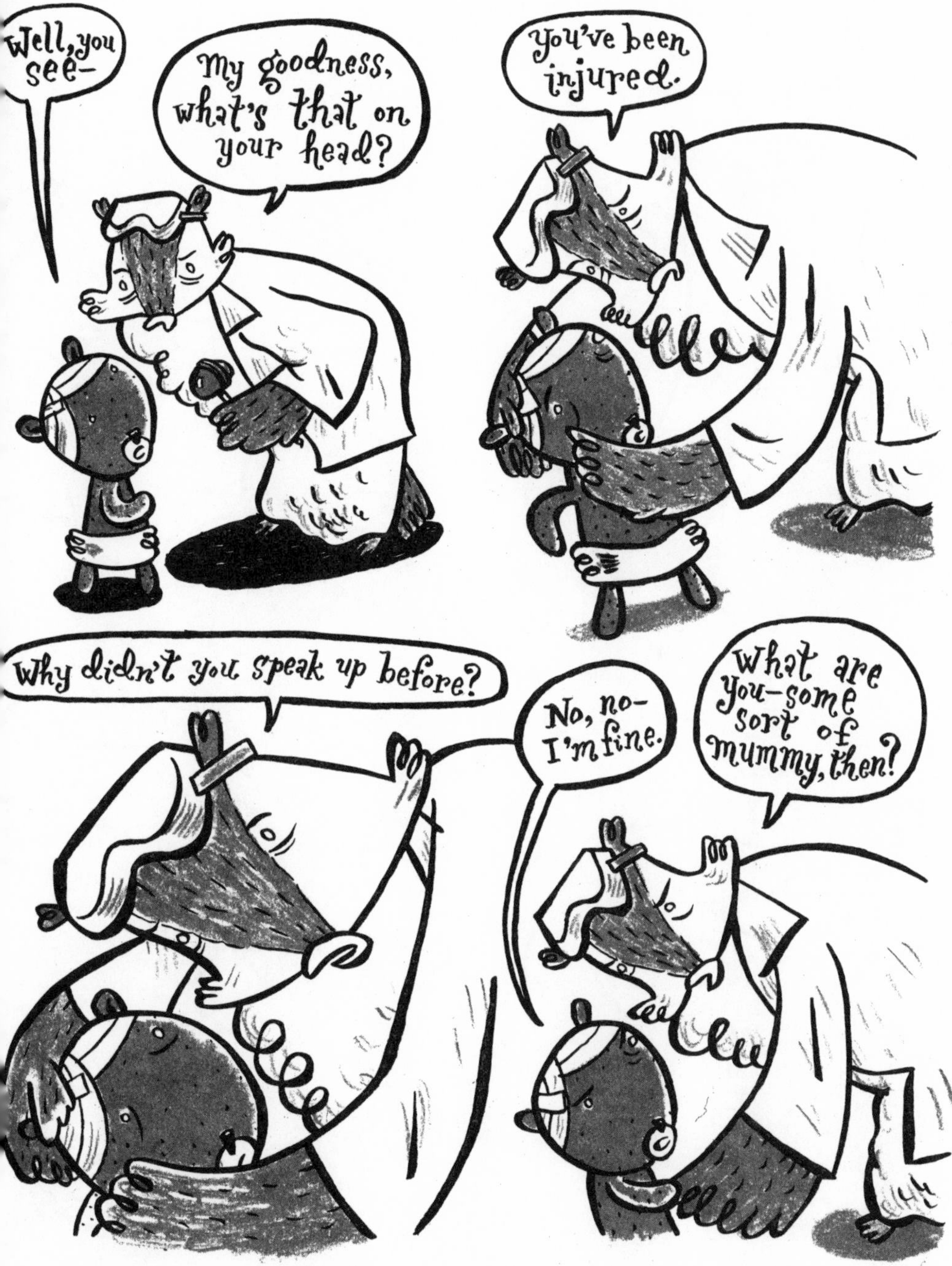
My goodness, what's that on your head?
Well, you see-
You've been injured.
Why didn't you speak up before?
No, no- I'm fine.
What are you-some sort of mummy, then?

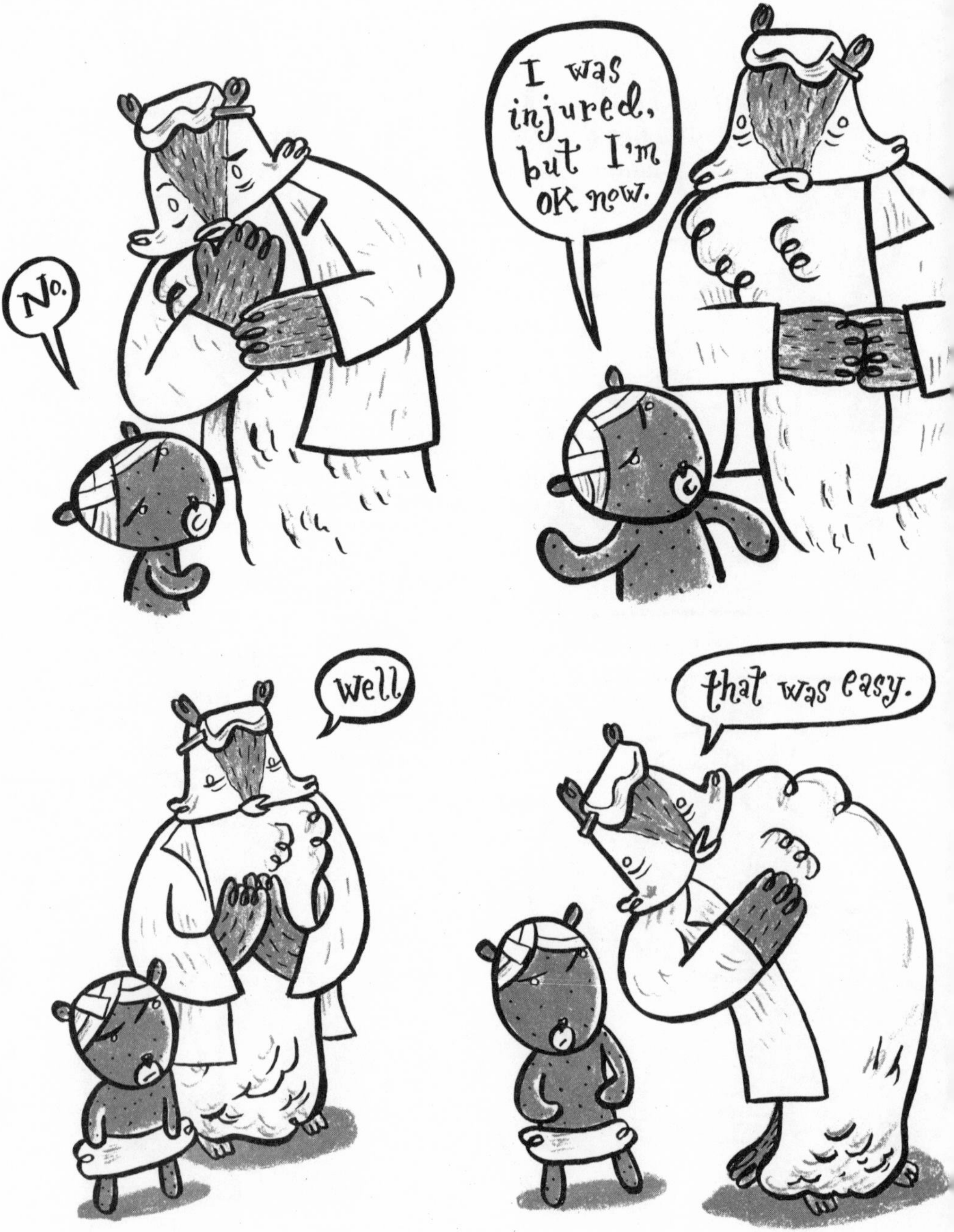
No.
I was injured, but I'm OK now.
well
that was easy.

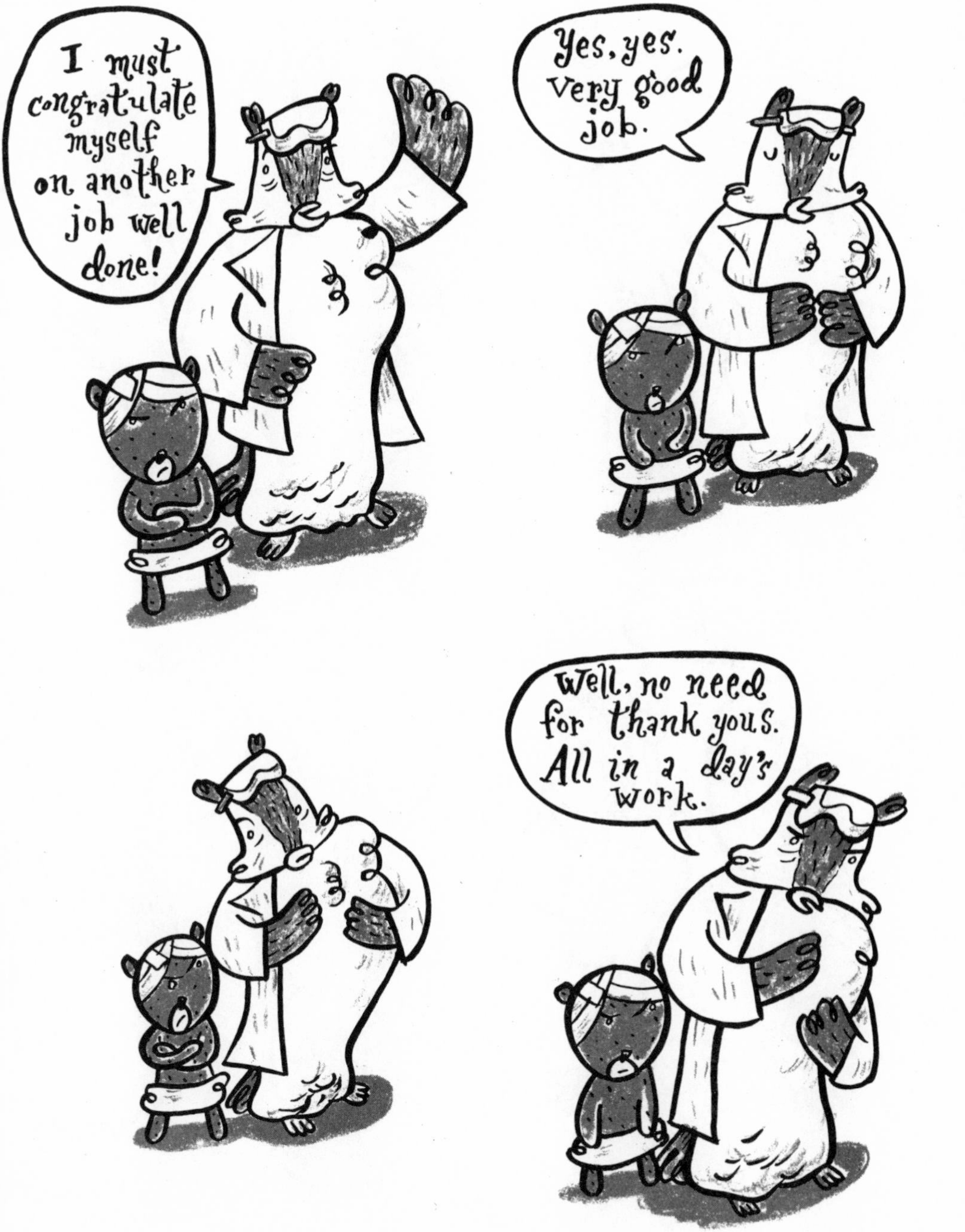
I must congratulate myself on another job well done!
Yes, yes. very good job.
Well, no need for thank yous. All in a day's work.

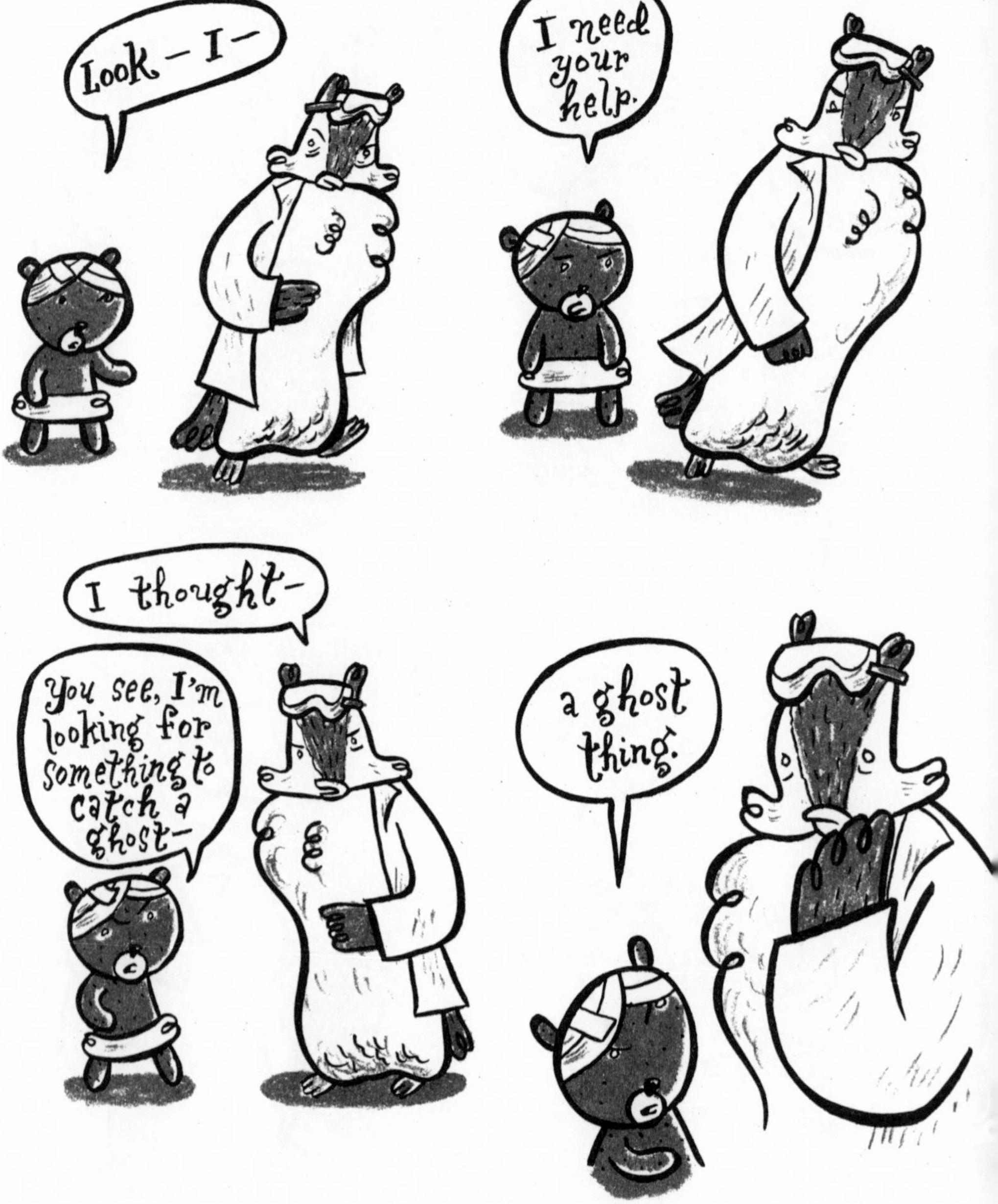

Look — I—
I need your help.
I thought—
You see, I'm looking for something to catch a ghost—
a ghost thing.

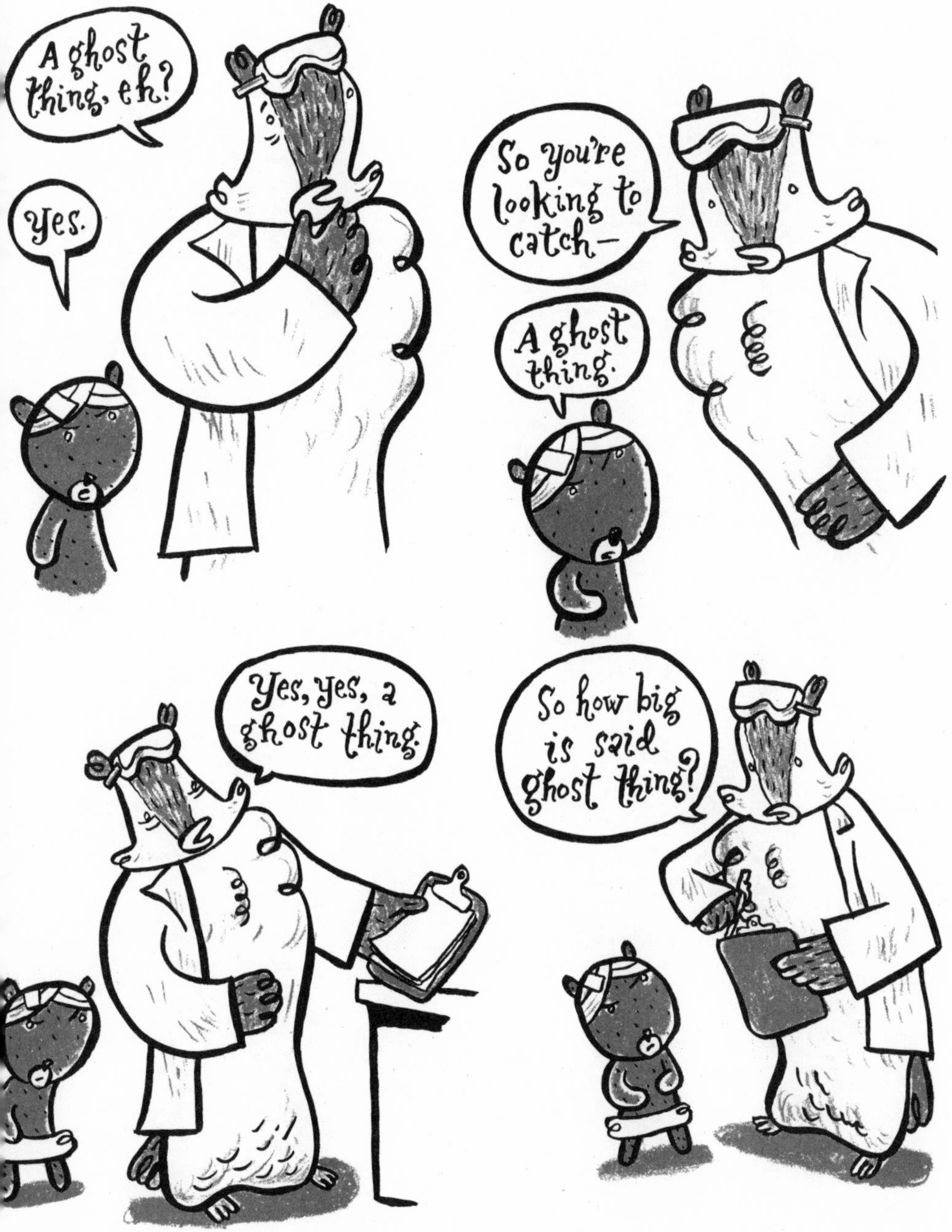
A ghost thing, eh?
Yes.
So you're looking to catch—
A ghost thing.
Yes, yes, a ghost thing.
So how big is said ghost thing?

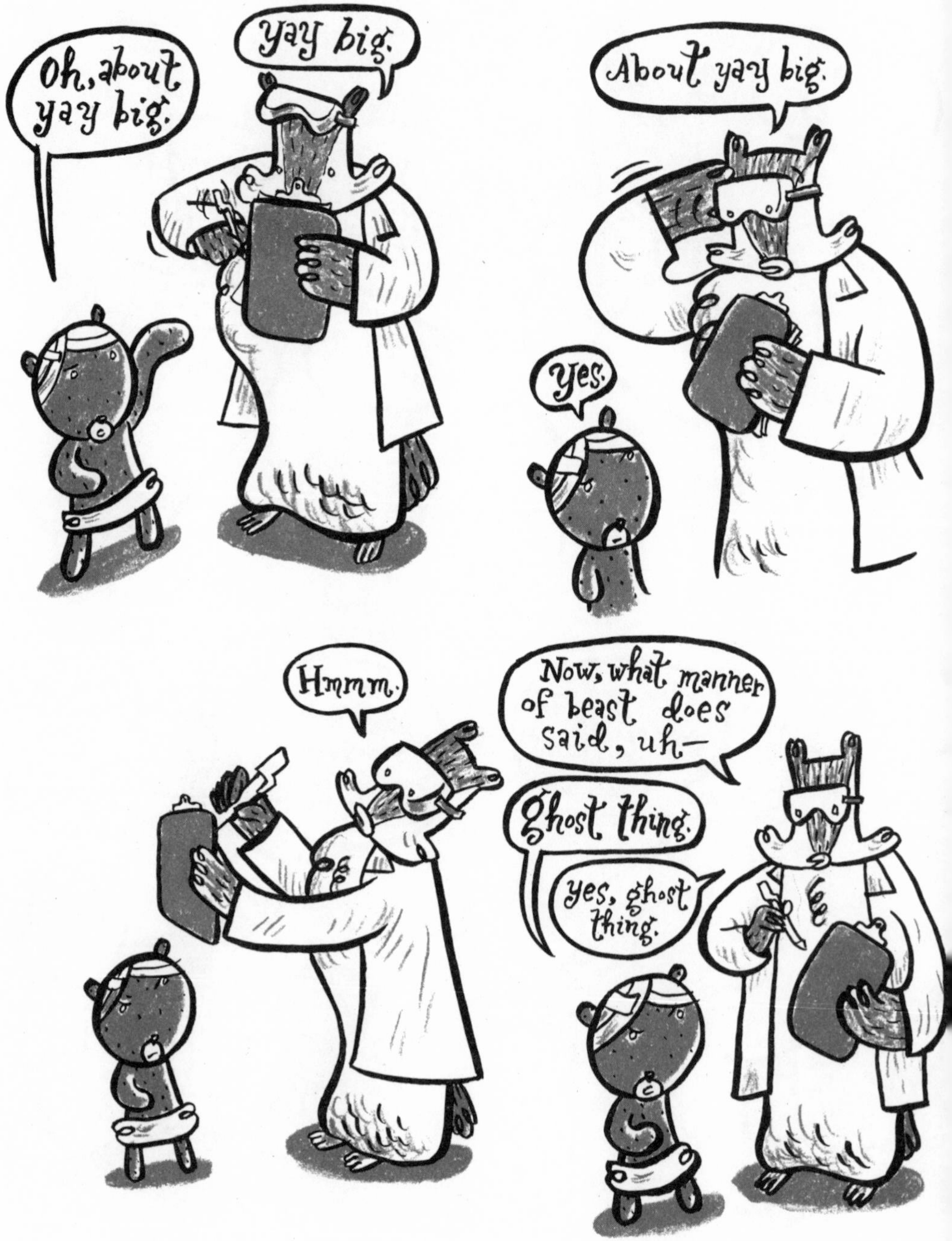

Oh, about yay big.
yay big.
About yay big.
Yes.
Hmmm.
Now, what manner of beast does said, uh—
ghost thing.
yes, ghost thing.

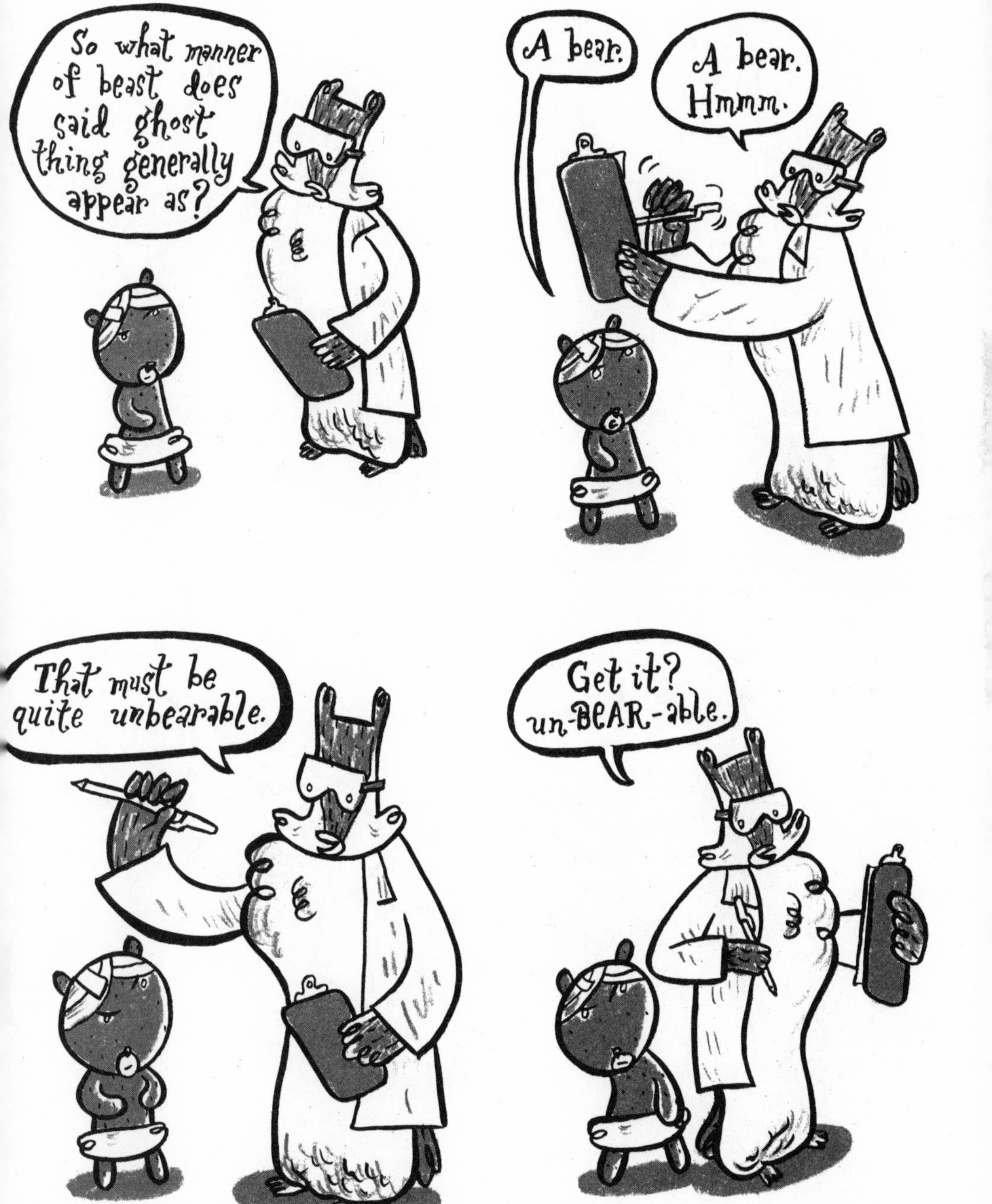
So what manner of beast does said ghost thing generally appear as?
A bear.
A bear. Hmmm.
That must be quite unbearable.
Get it? un-BEAR-able.

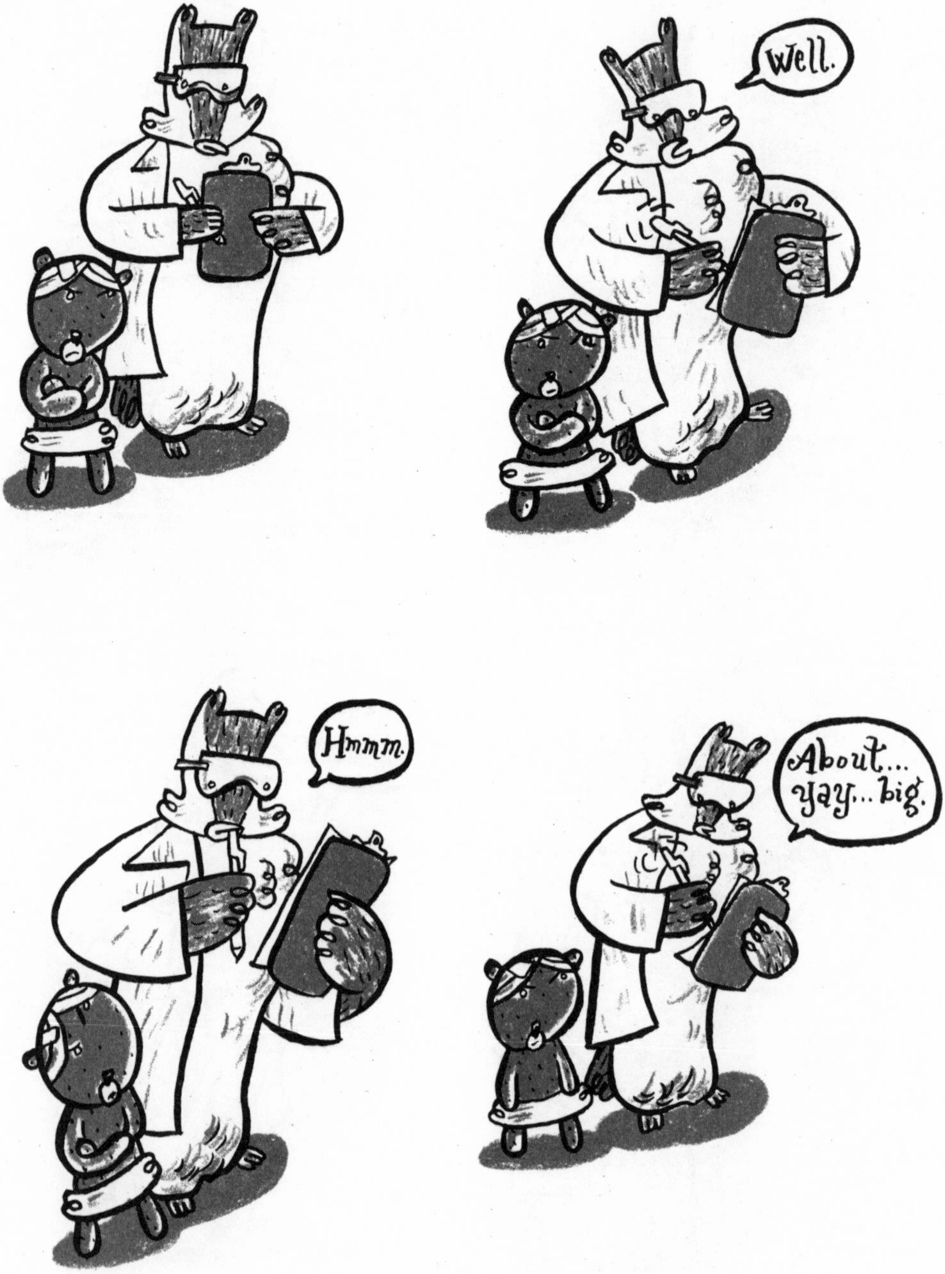
Well.
Hmmm.
About...
yay...big.

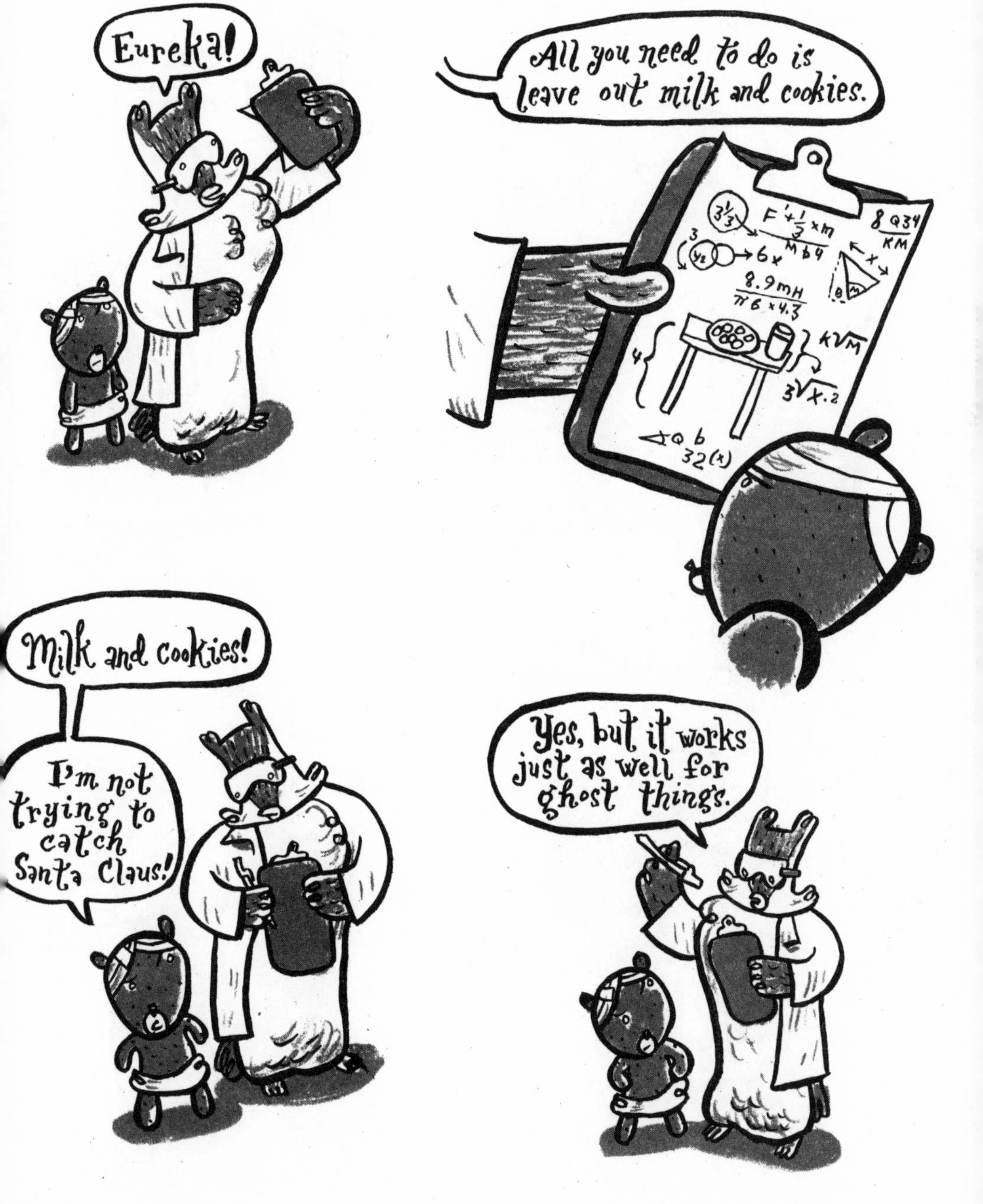
Eureka!
All you need to do is leave out milk and cookies.
Milk and cookies!
I'm not trying to catch Santa Claus!
Yes, but it works just as well for ghost things.

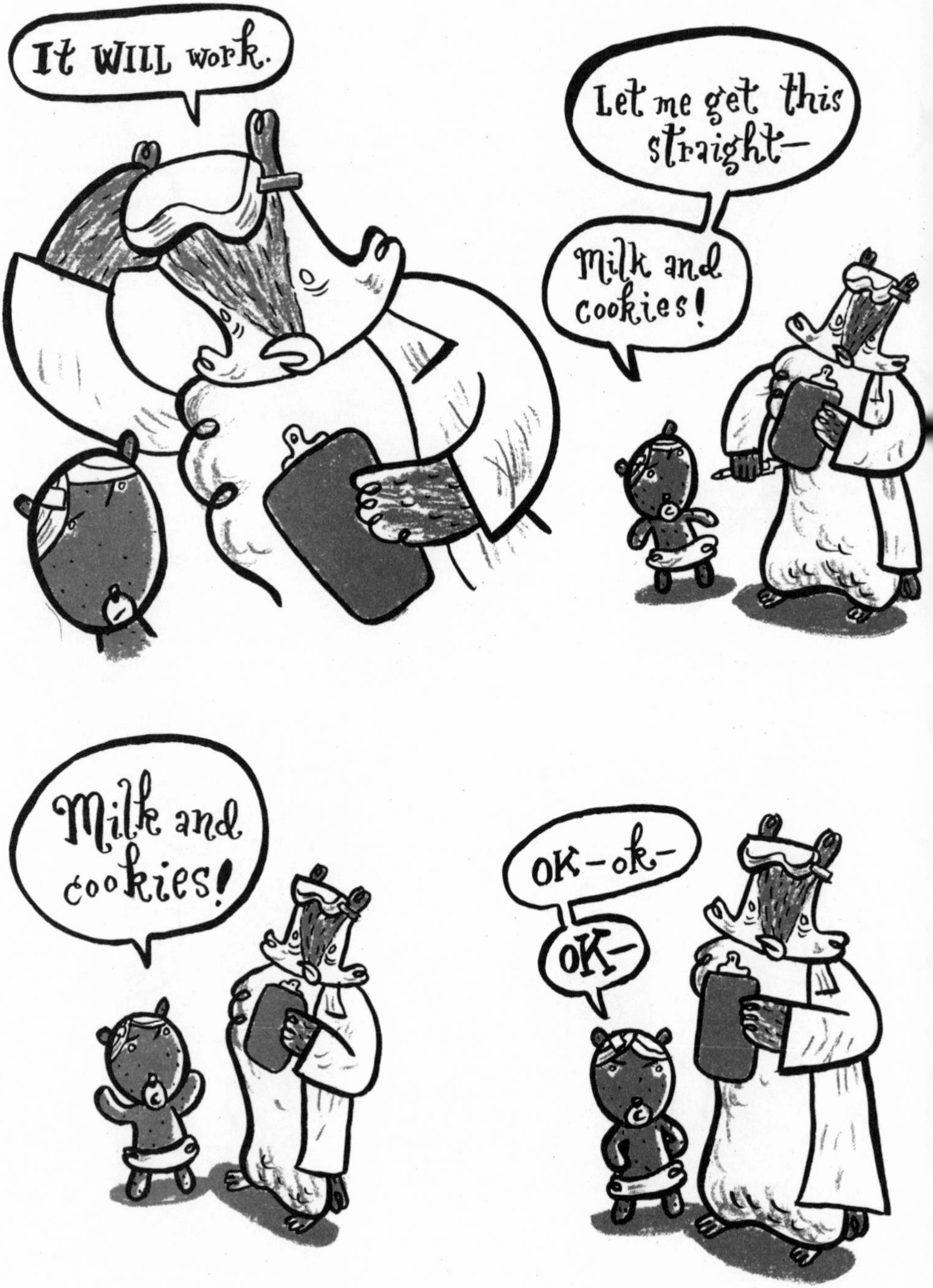
It WILL work.
Let me get this straight—
Milk and cookies!
Milk and cookies!
OK–ok–
OK–

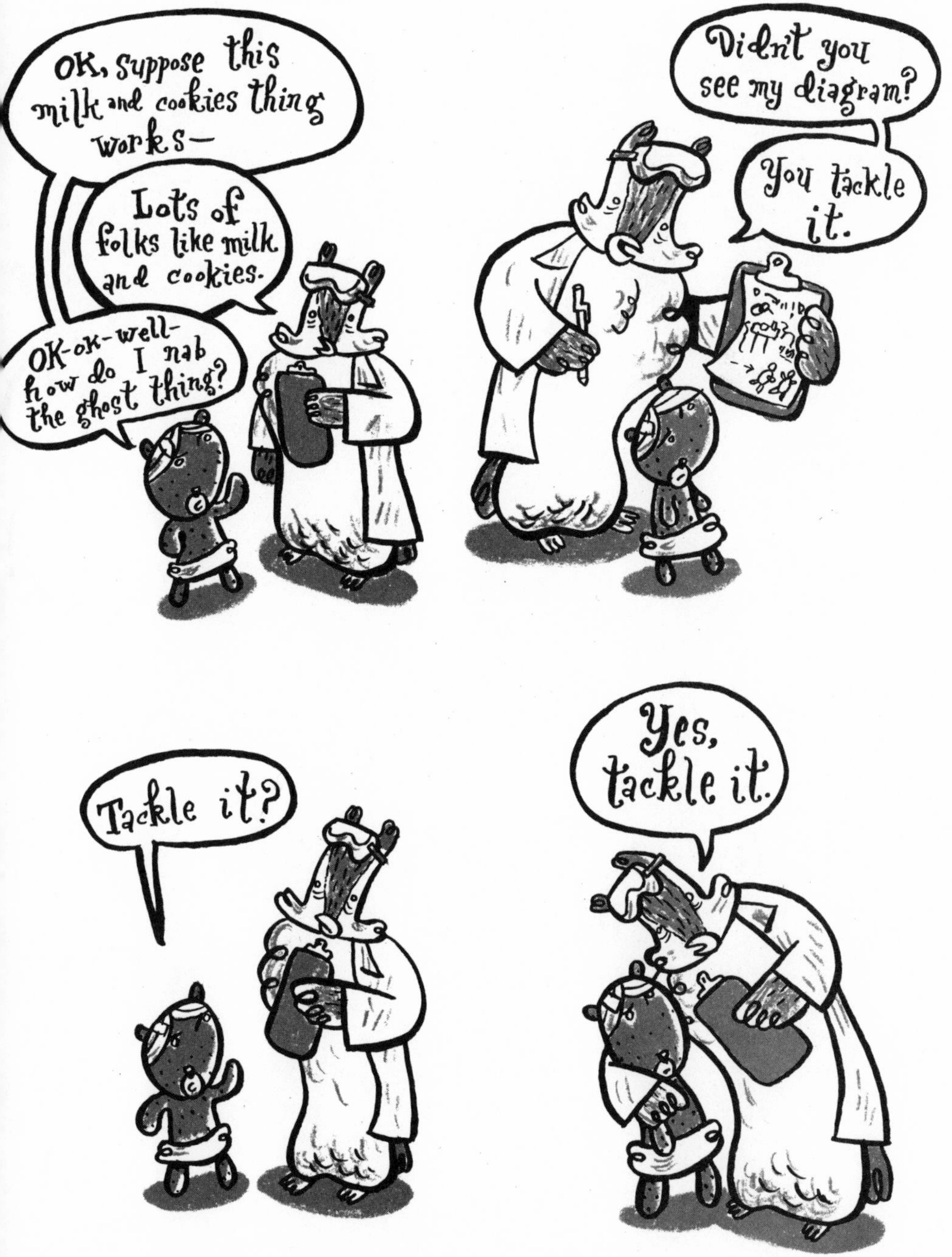
OK, suppose this milk and cookies thing works—
Lots of folks like milk and cookies.
OK-ok-well- how do I nab the ghost thing?
Didn't you see my diagram?
You tackle it.
Tackle it?
Yes, tackle it.

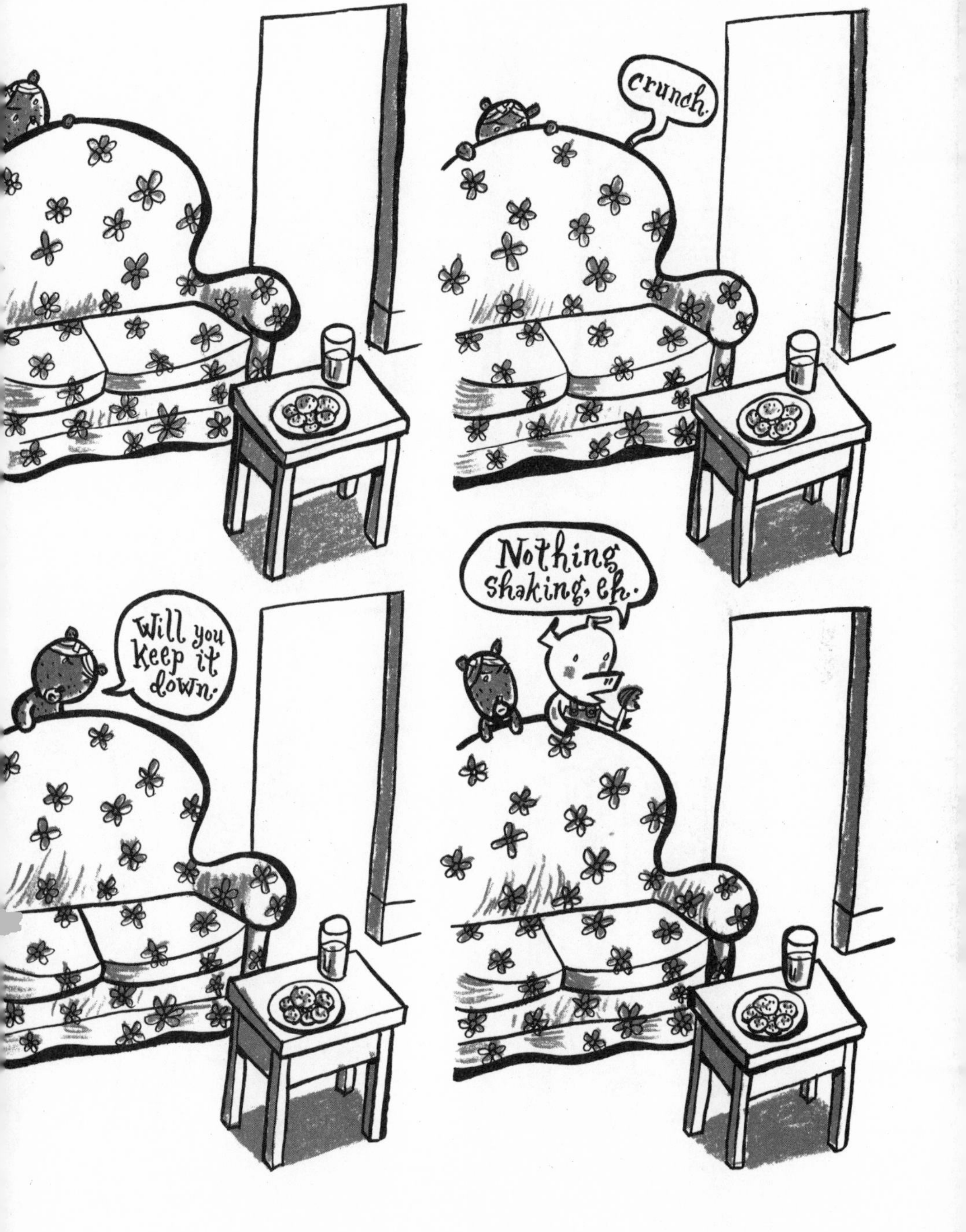
crunch.
Will you keep it down.
Nothing shaking, eh.

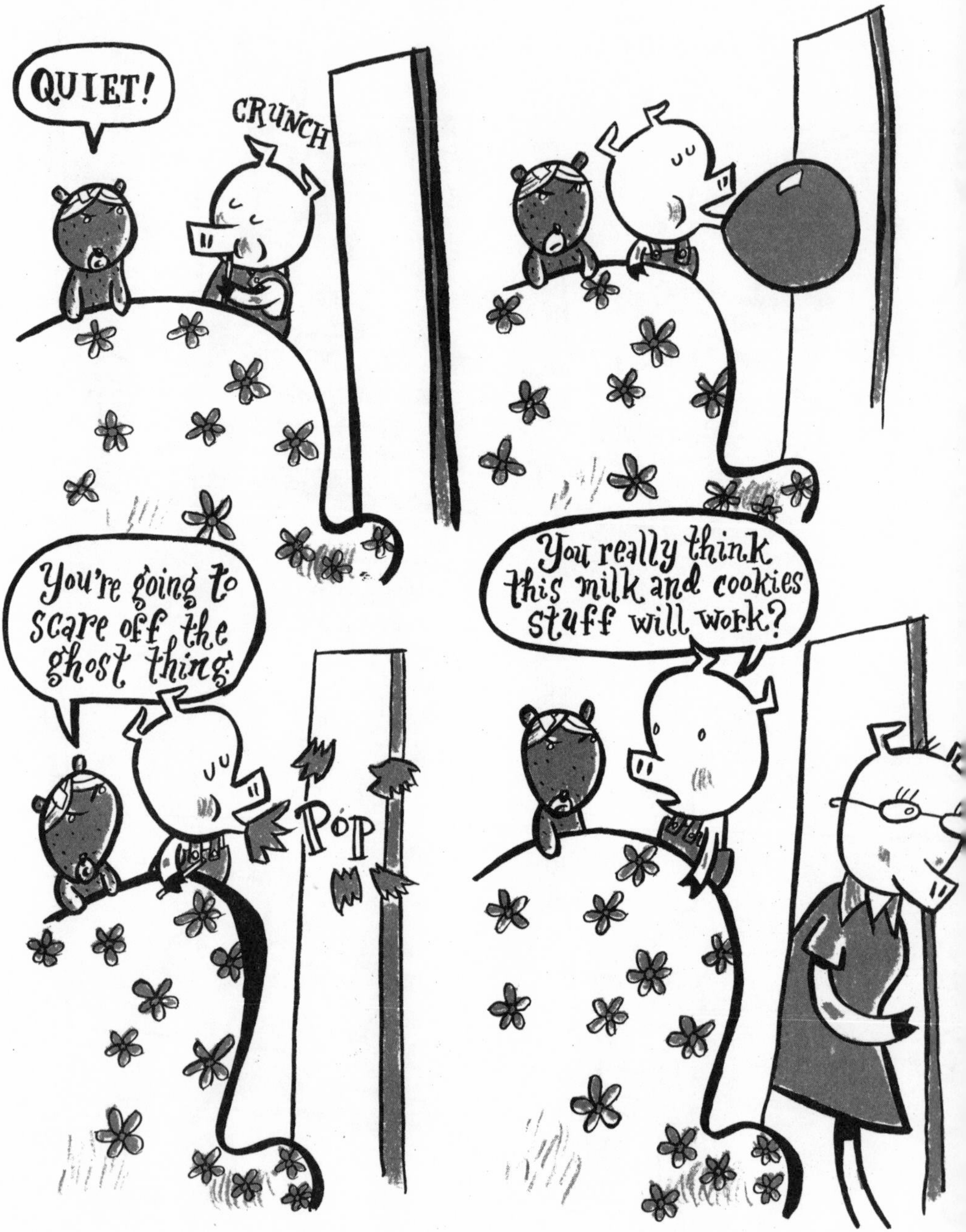
QUIET!
CRUNCH
You're going to scare off the ghost thing.
POP
You really think this milk and cookies stuff will work?

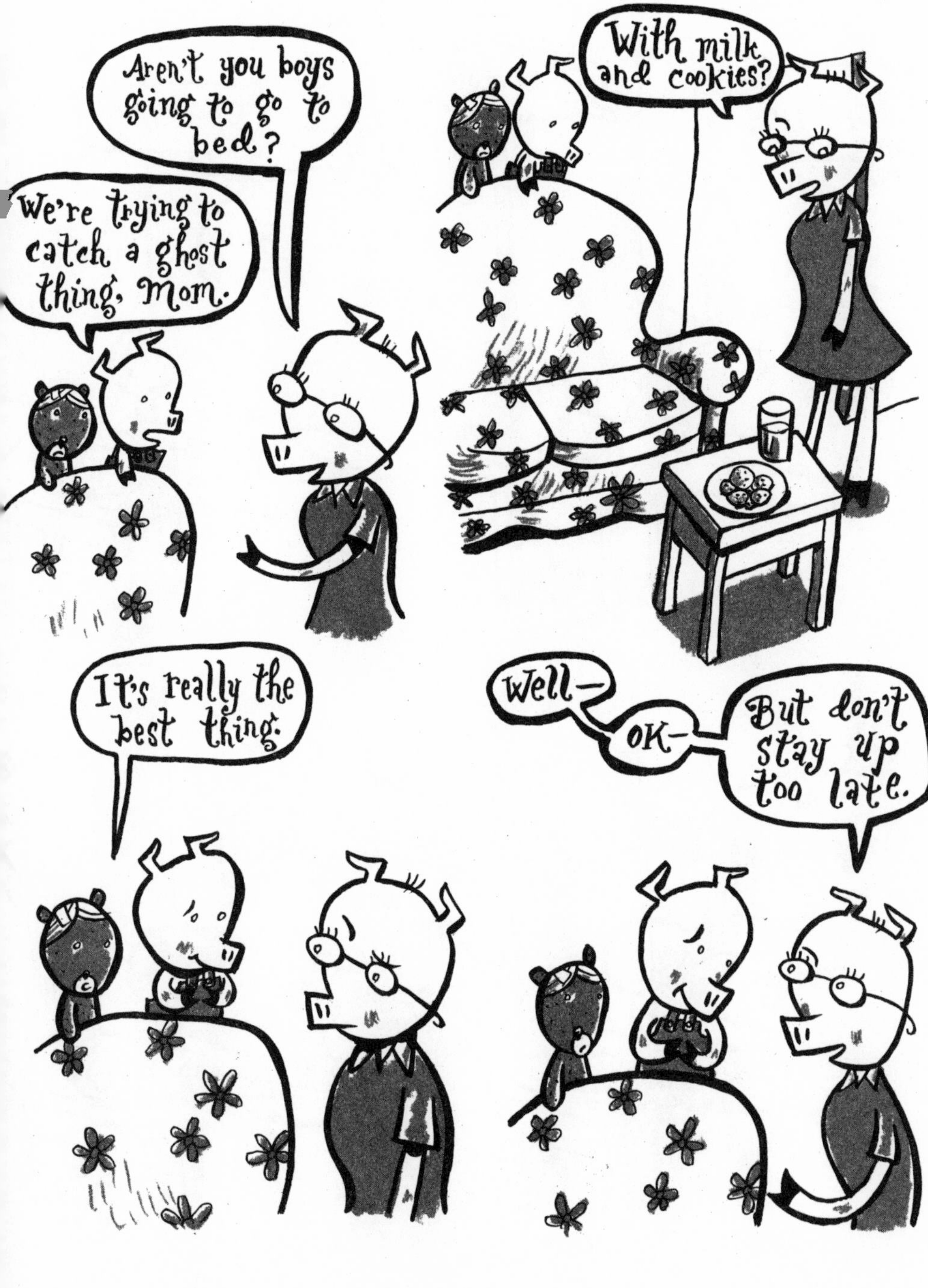
Aren't you boys going to go to bed?
We're trying to catch a ghost thing, Mom.
With milk and cookies?
It's really the best thing.
Well—
OK—
But don't stay up too late.

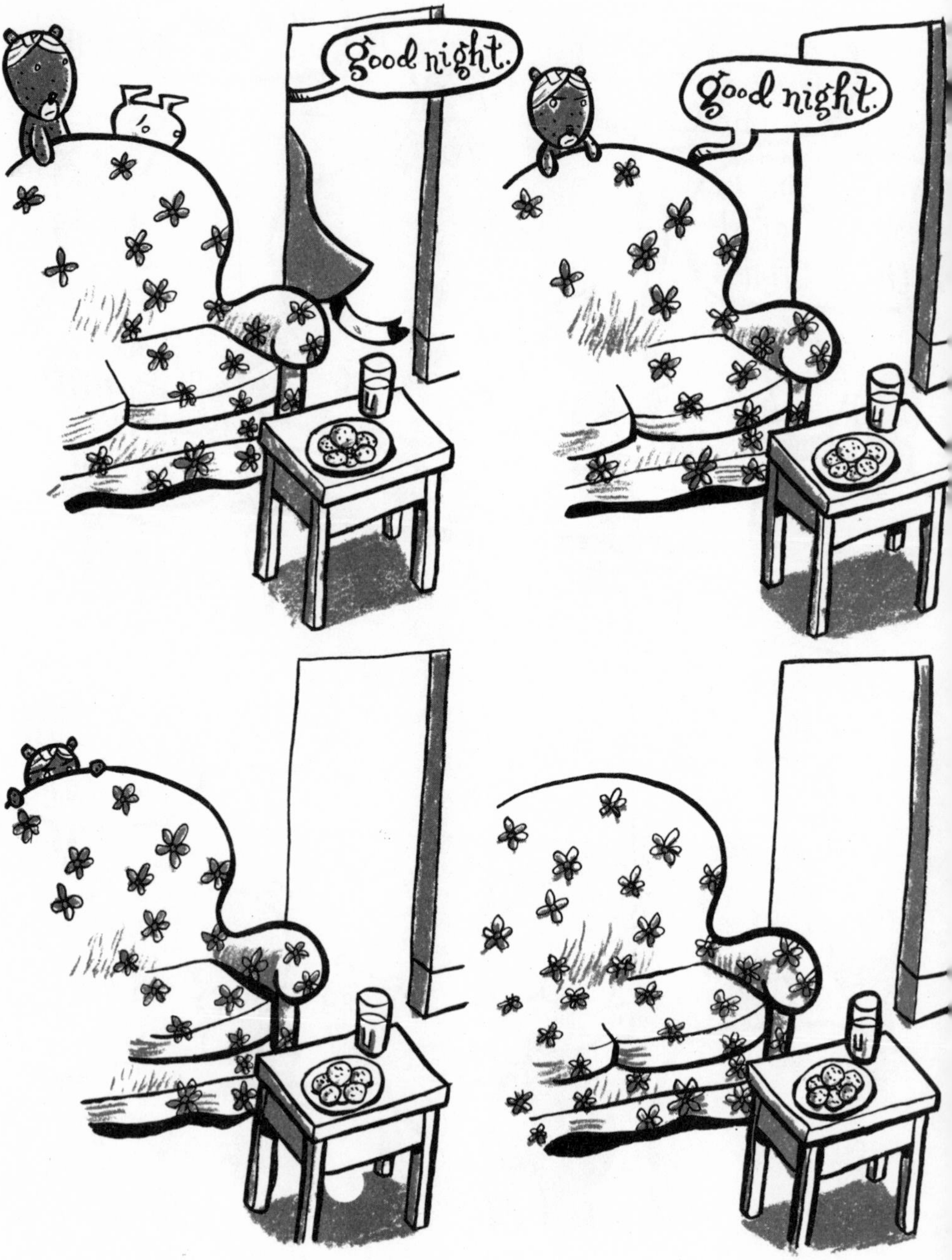
good night.
good night.

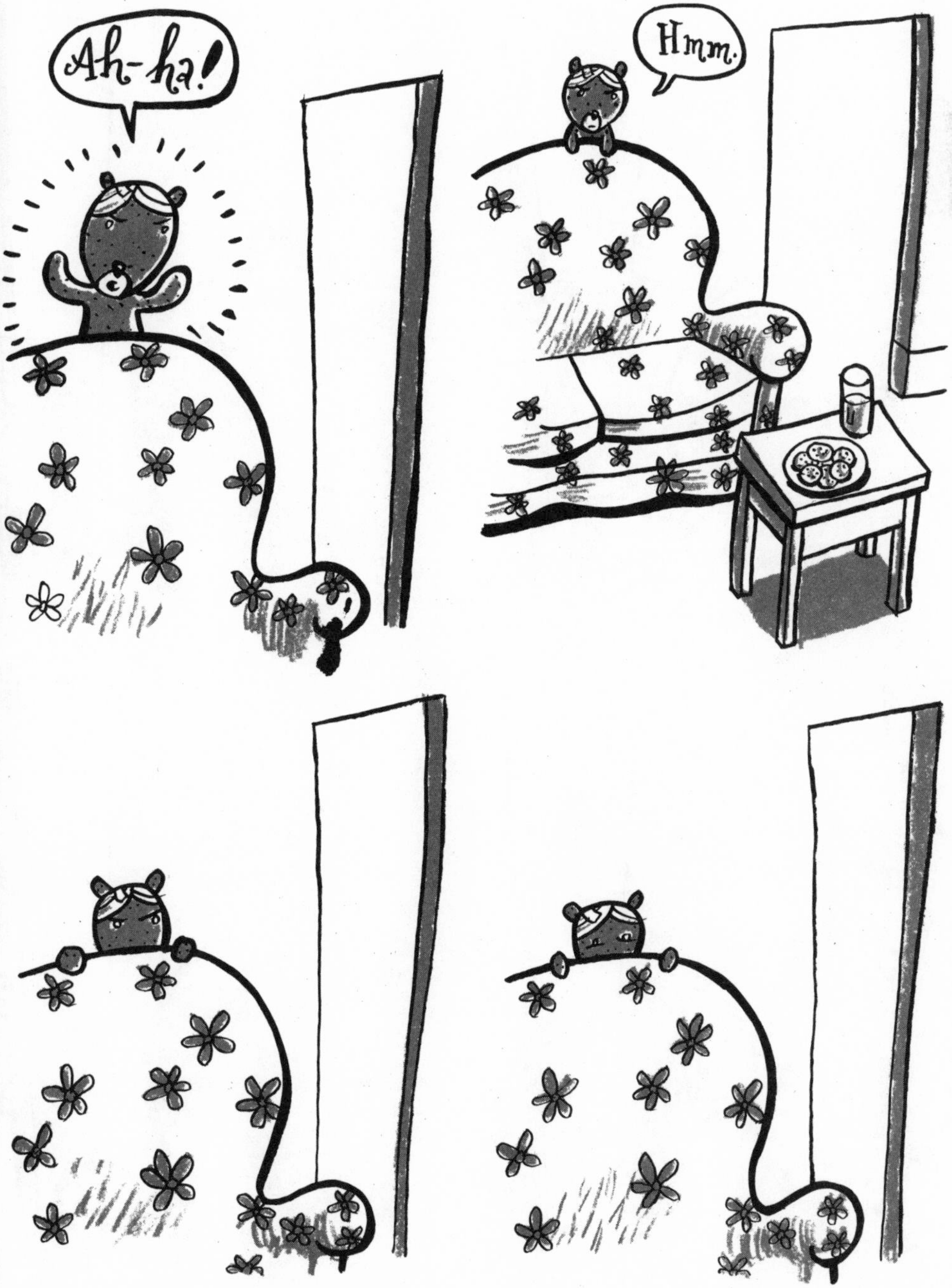
Ah-ha!
Hmm.

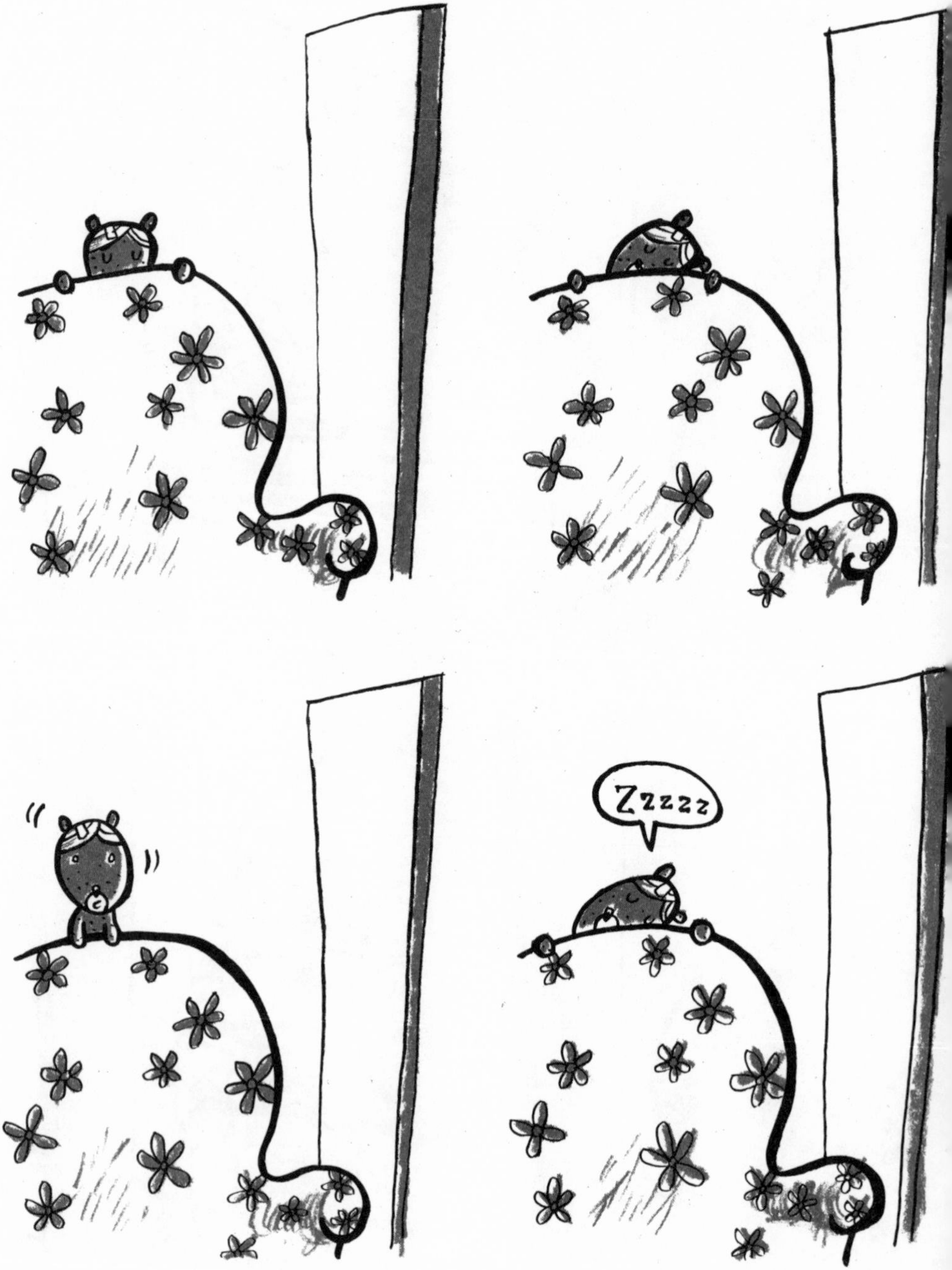
Zzzzz

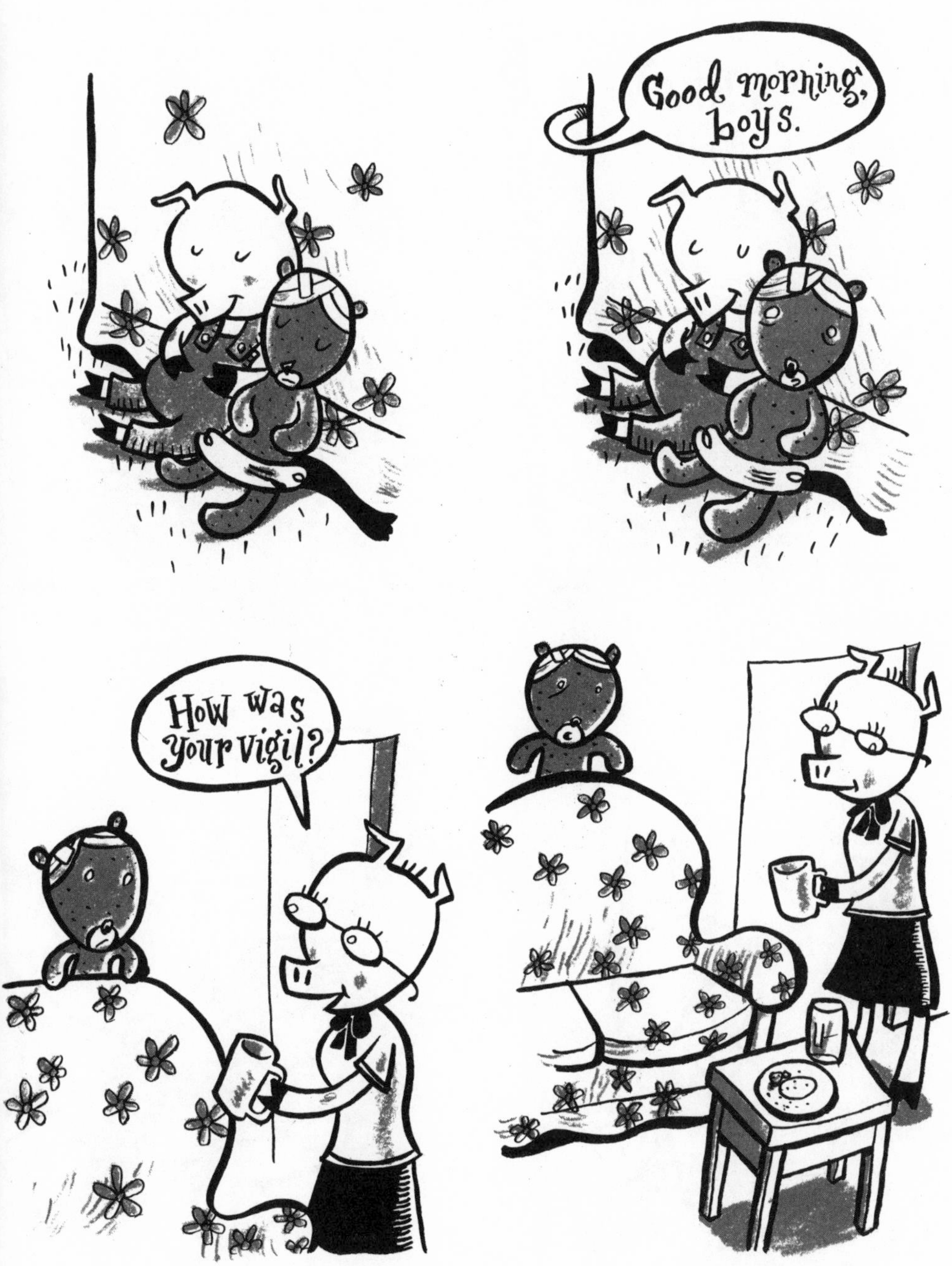
Good morning, boys.
How was your vigil?

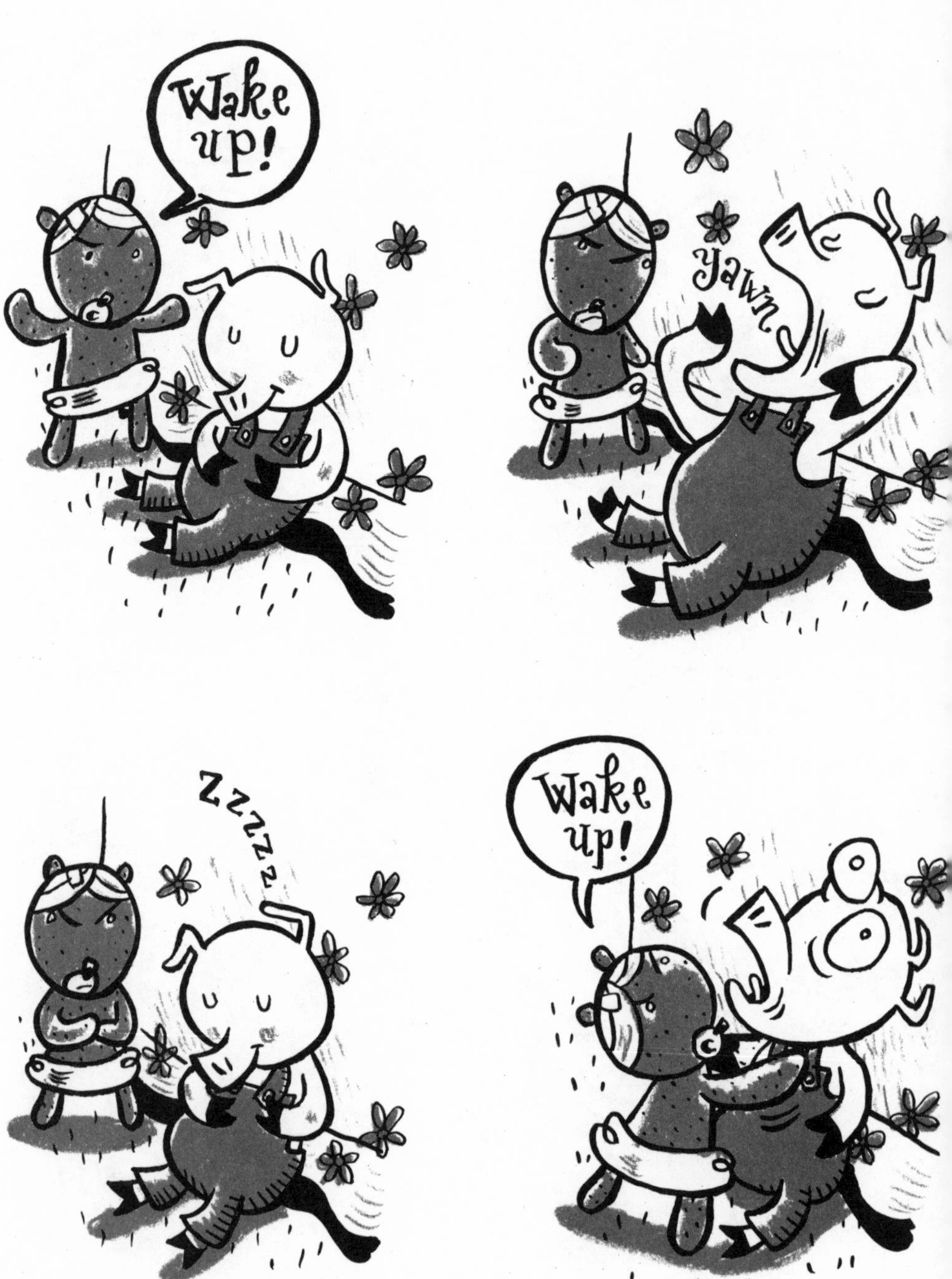
Wake up!
Yawn
ZZZZZZ
Wake up!

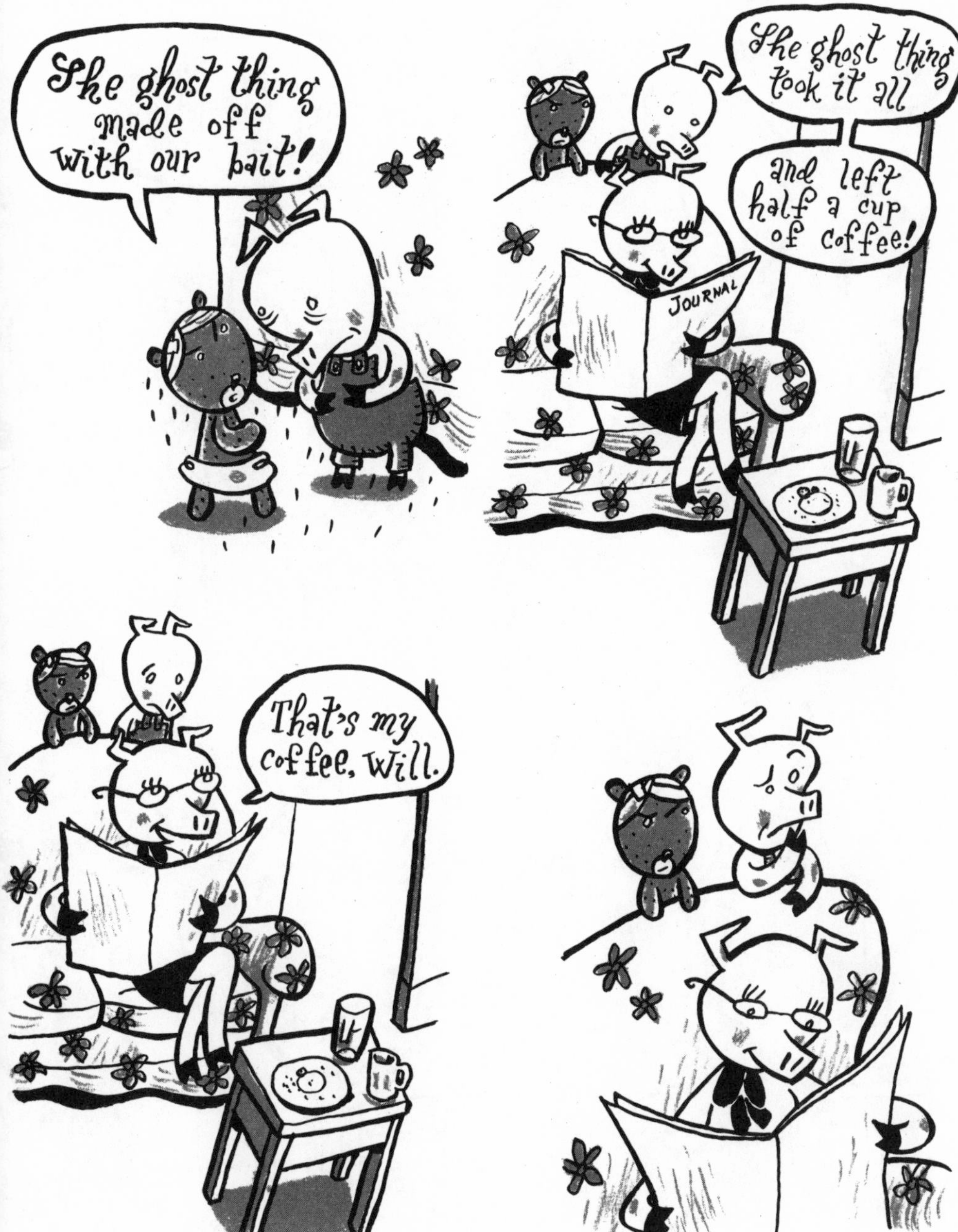
The ghost thing made off with our bait!
The ghost thing took it all
and left half a cup of coffee!
JOURNAL
That's my coffee, Will.

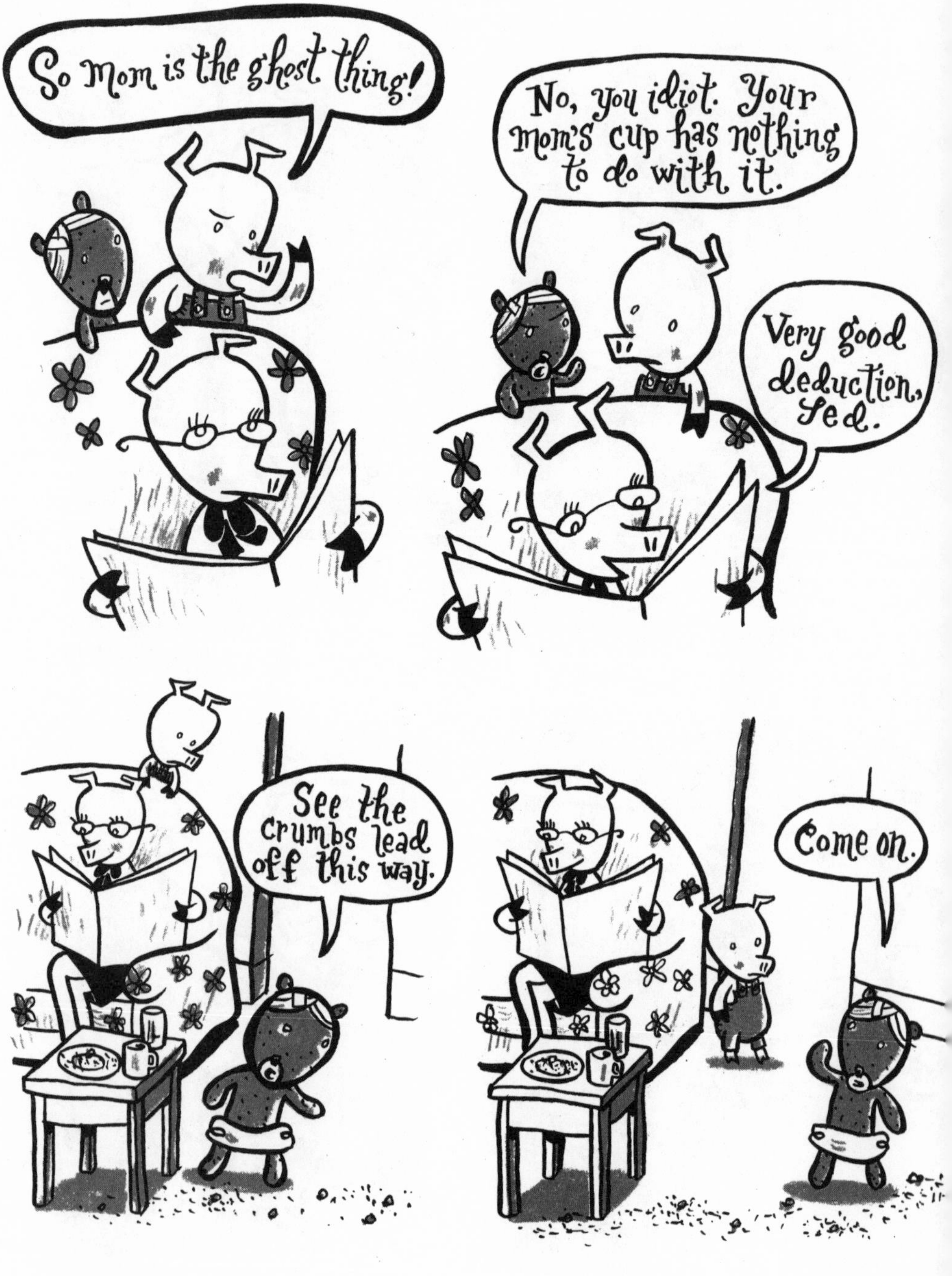
So Mom is the ghost thing!
No, you idiot. Your mom's cup has nothing to do with it.
Very good deduction, Sed.
See the crumbs lead off this way.
Come on.

Help me follow them.
Now where is it?
Oh, here it is.
Errr.

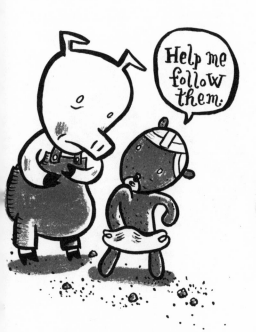

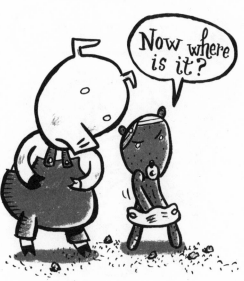

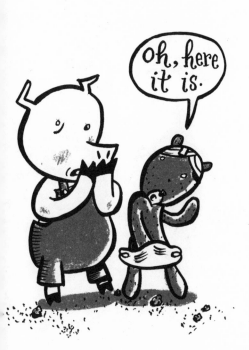

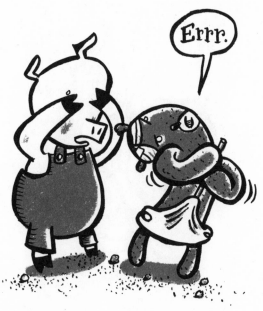

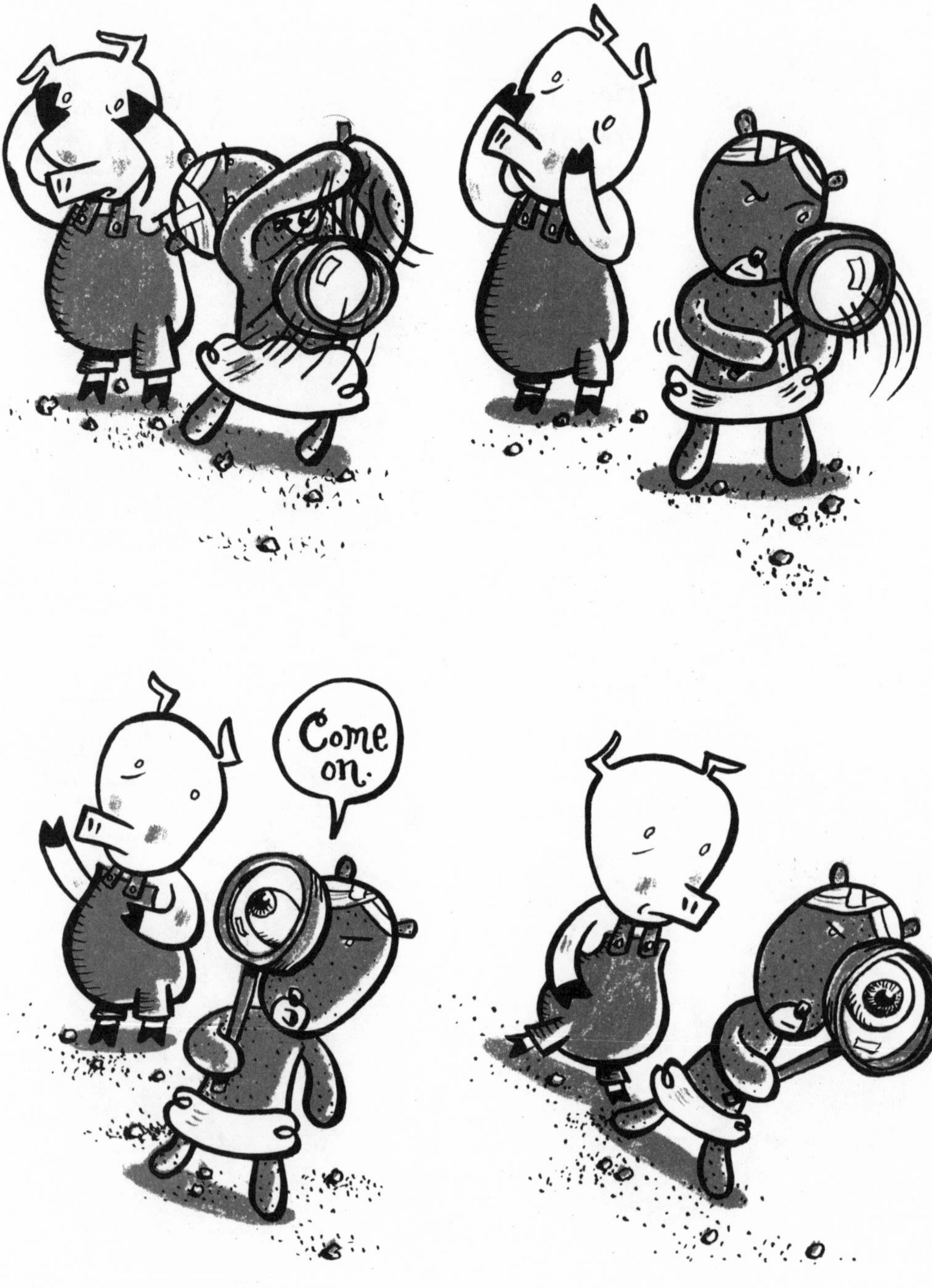
Come on.

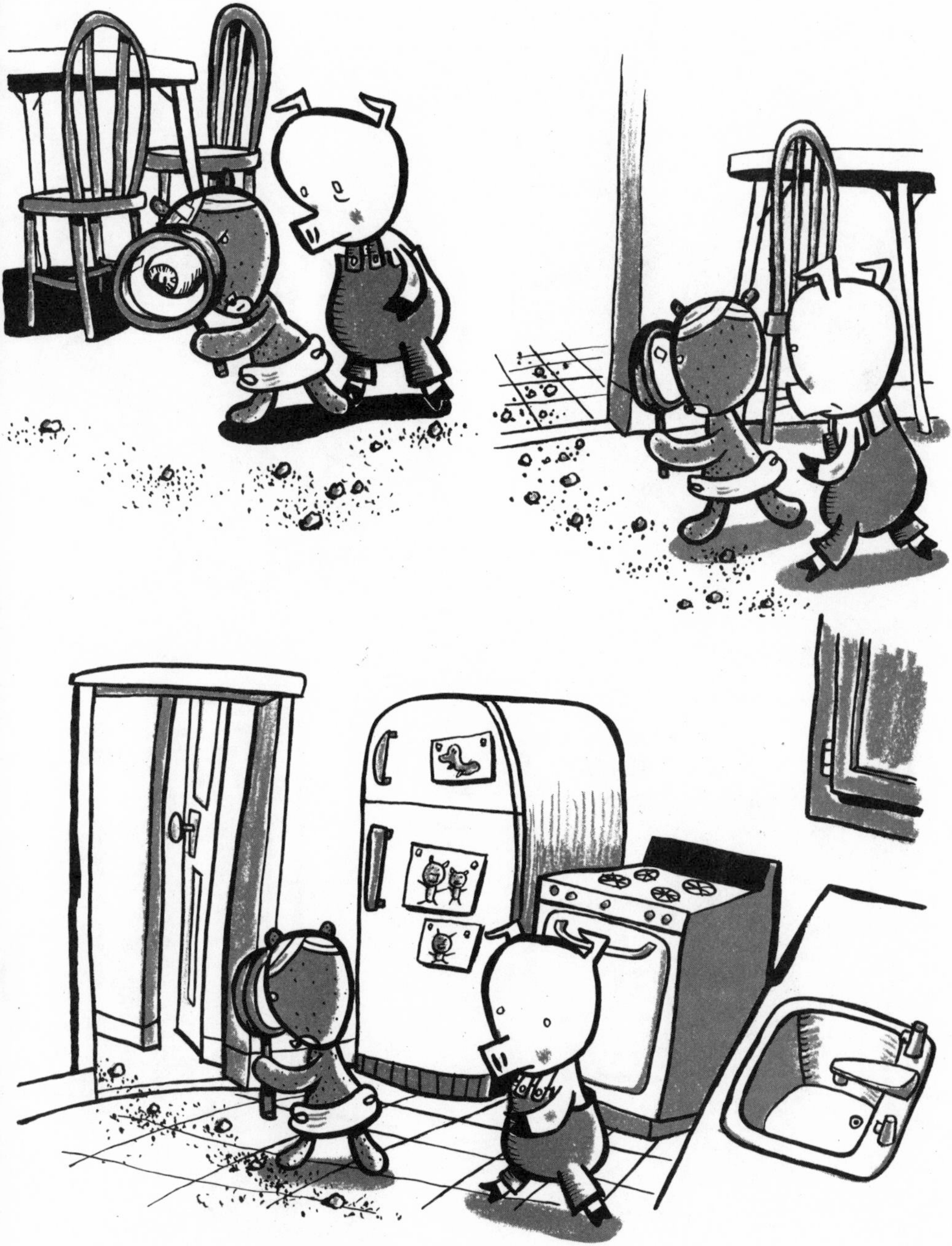

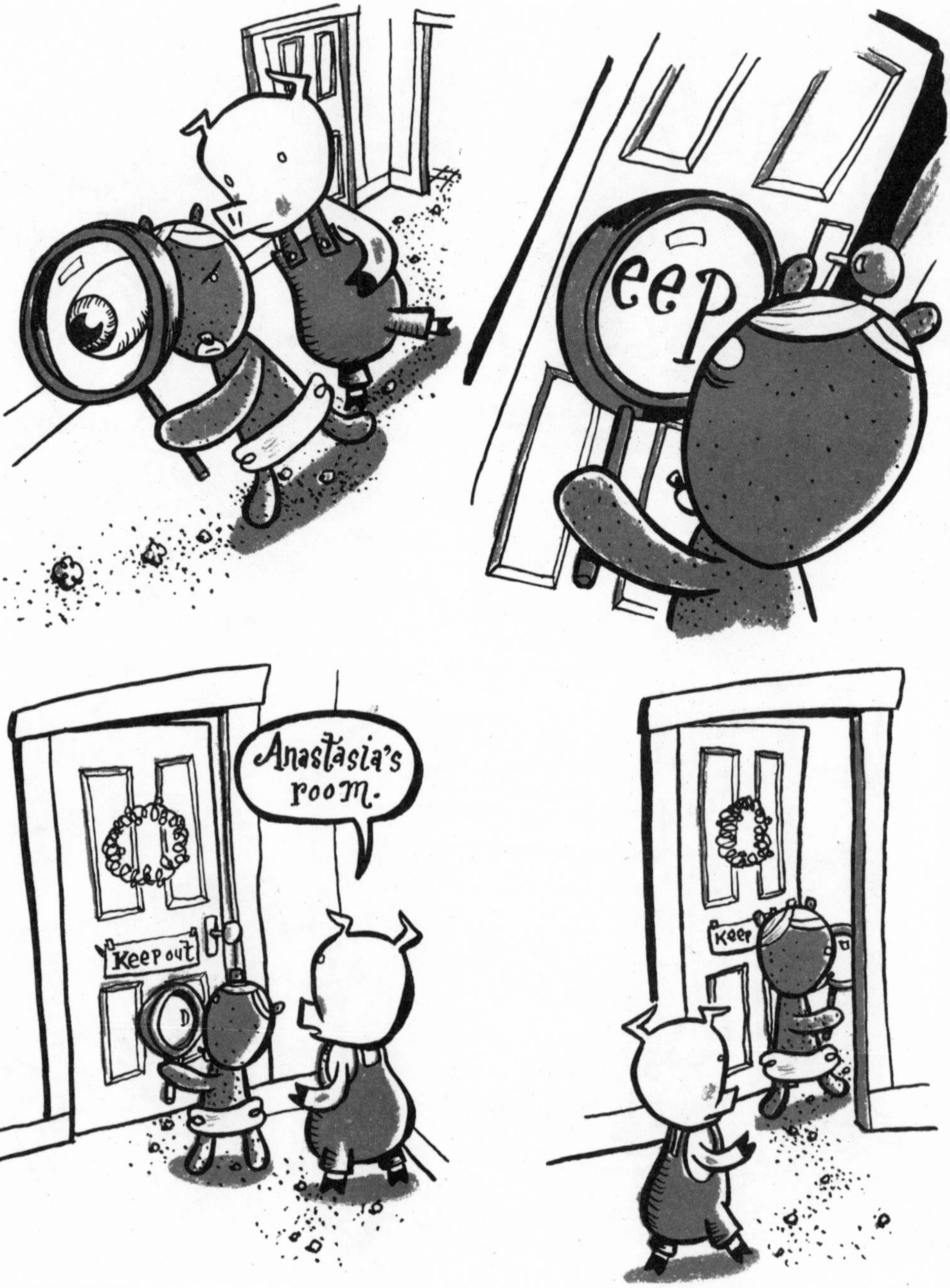
eep
Anastasia's room.
Keep out
Keep

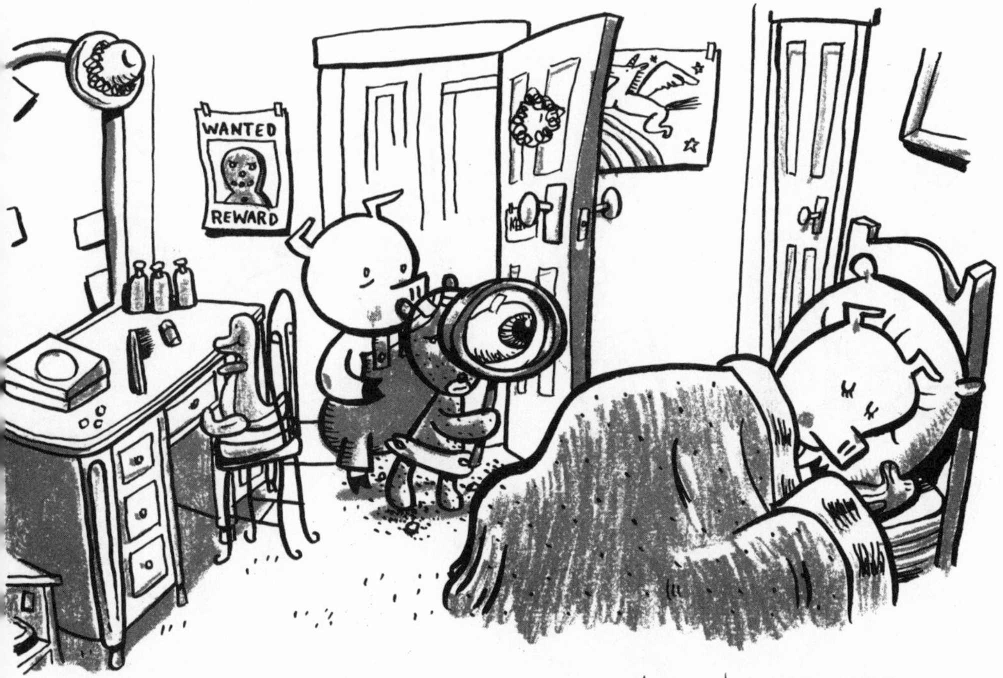
WANTED
REWARD

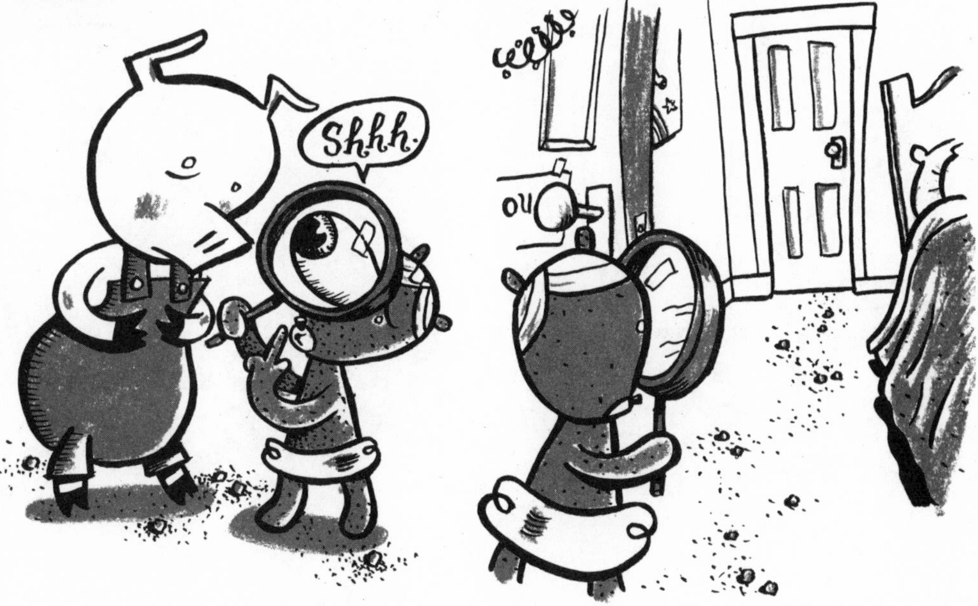
Shhh.

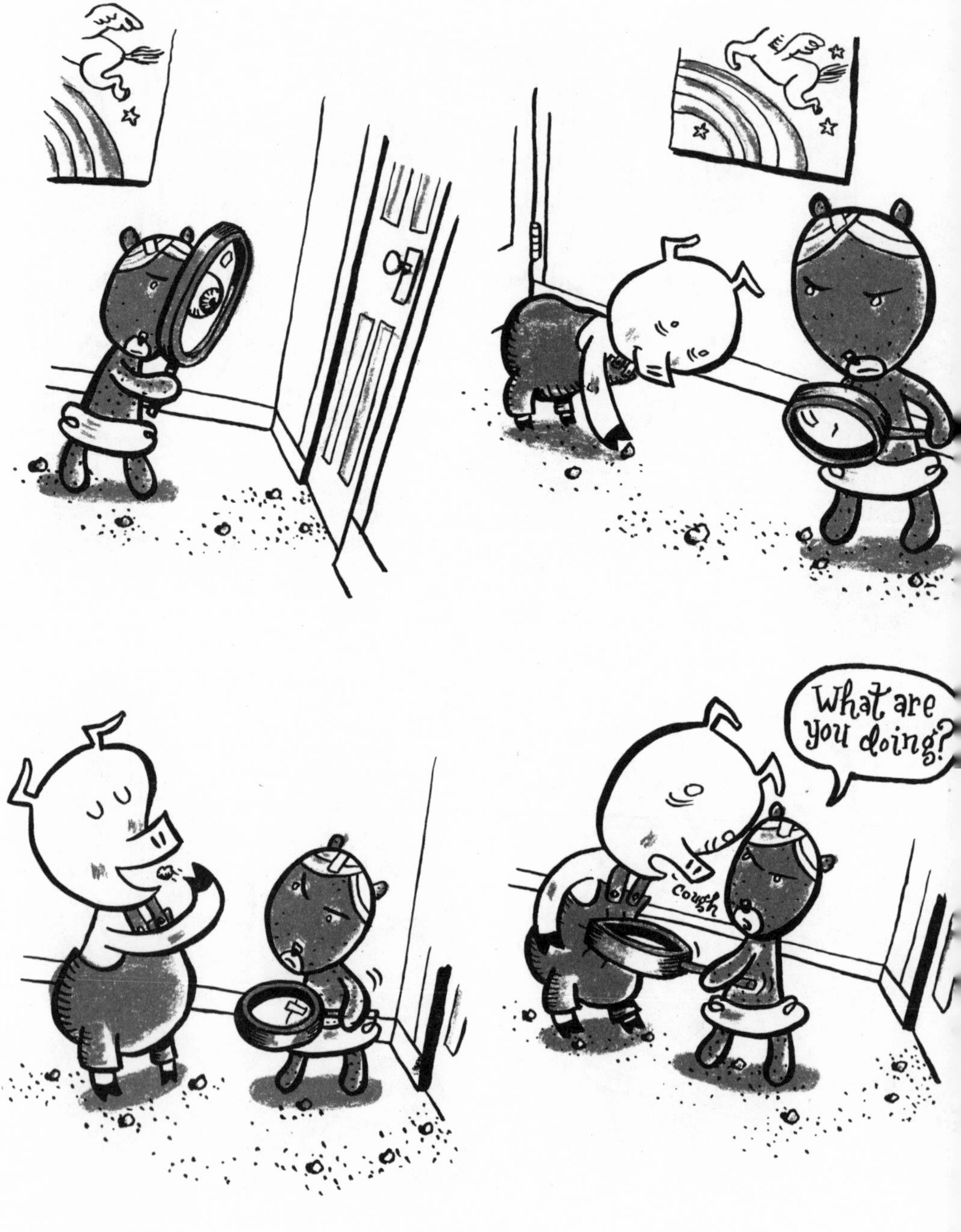
What are you doing?
cough

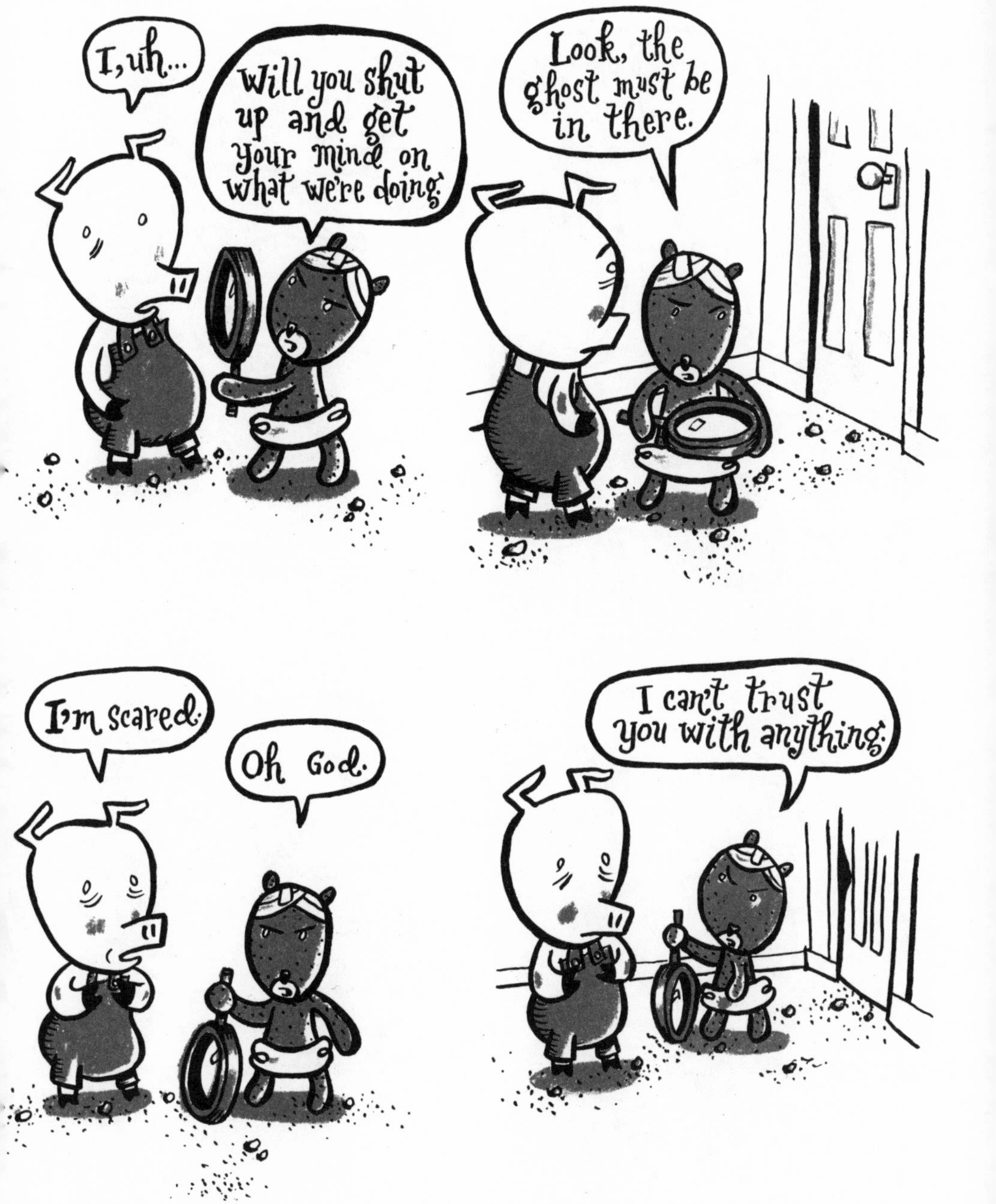
I, uh...
Will you shut up and get your mind on what we're doing.
Look, the ghost must be in there.
I'm scared.
Oh God.
I can't trust you with anything.

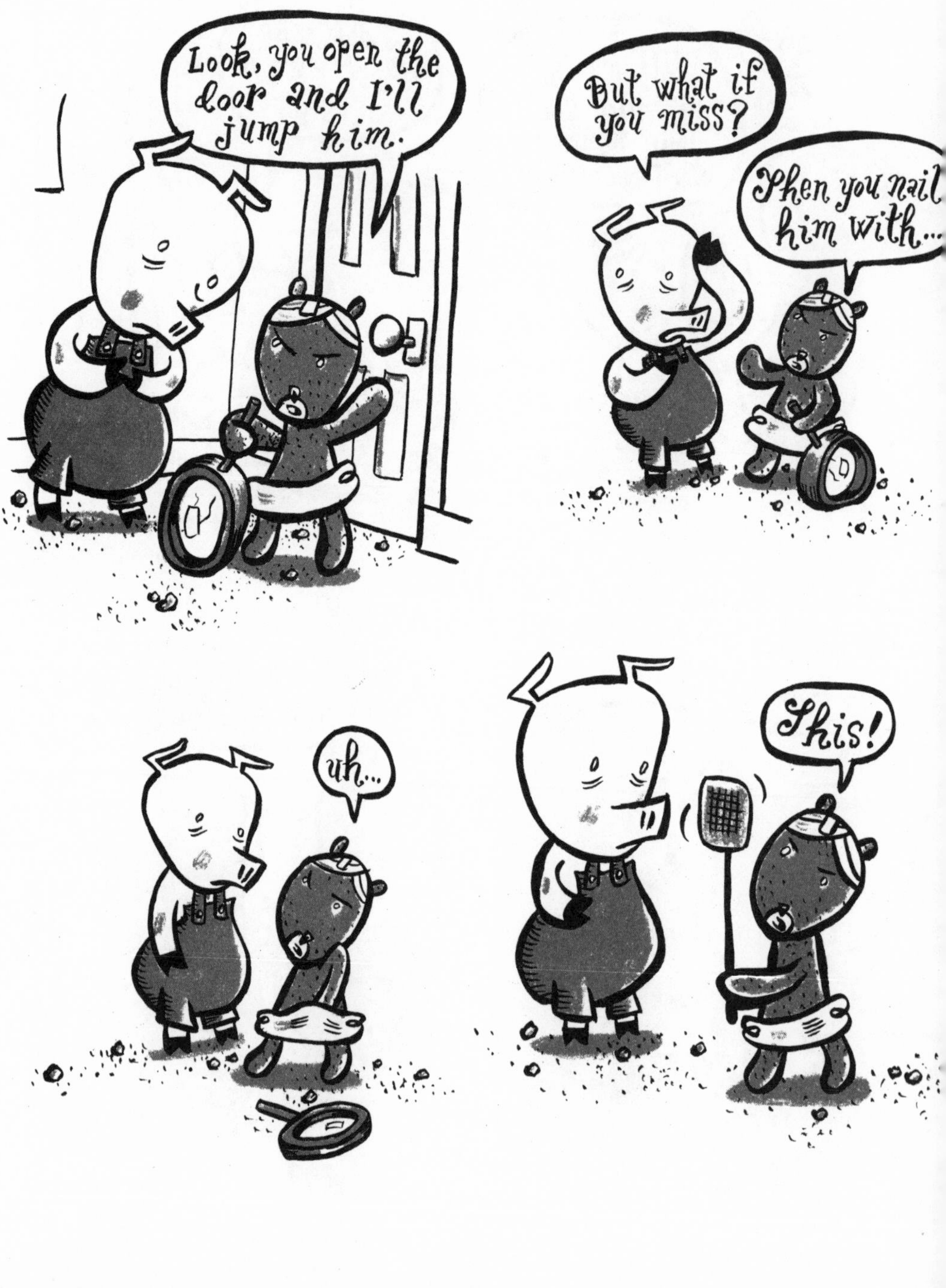
Look, you open the door and I'll jump him.
But what if you miss?
Then you nail him with...
uh...
This!

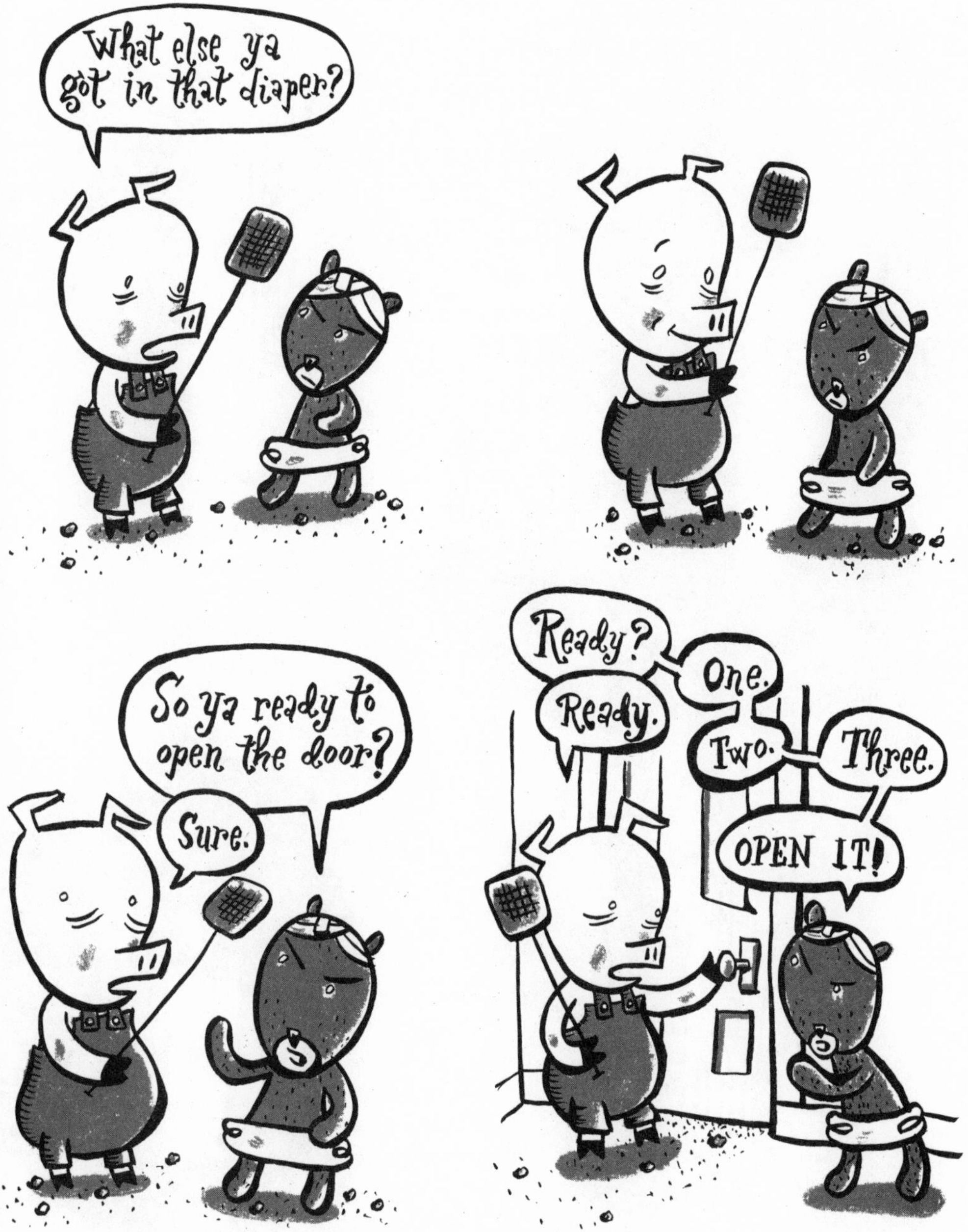
What else ya got in that diaper?
So ya ready to open the door?
Sure.
Ready?
Ready.
One.
Two.
Three.
OPEN IT!

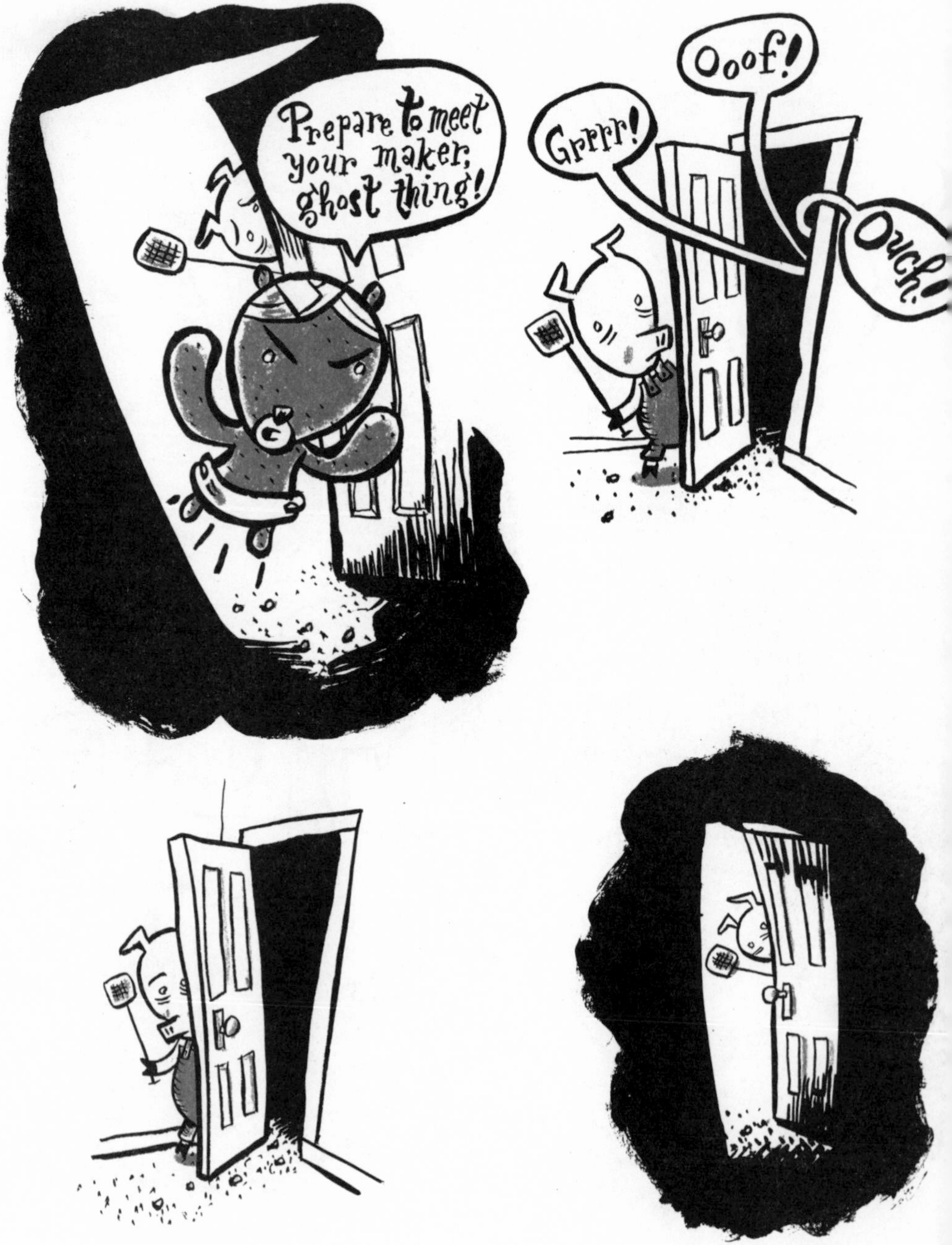
Prepare to meet your maker, ghost thing!
Grrrr!
Ooof!
Ouch!

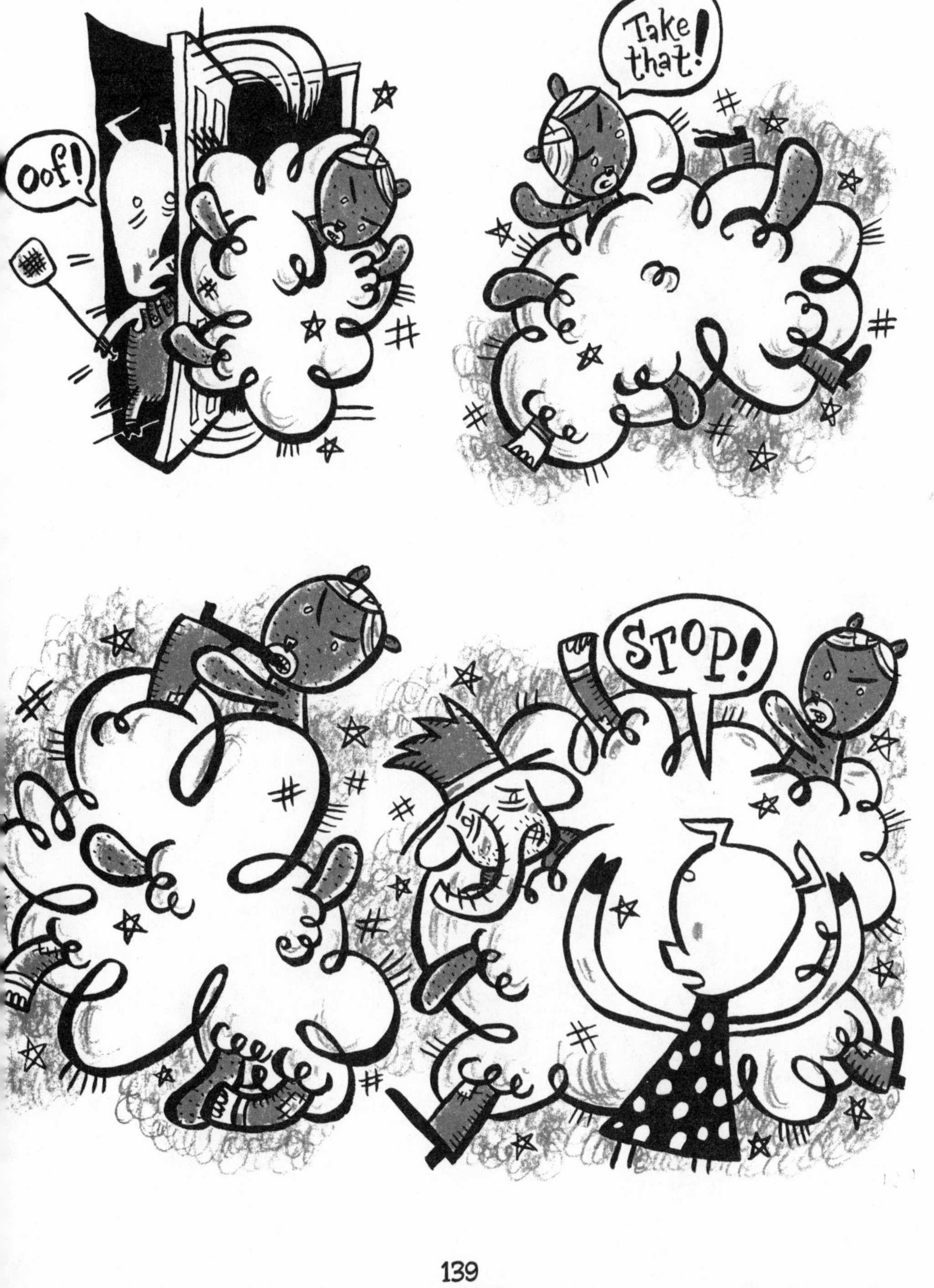
Oof!
Take that!
STOP!

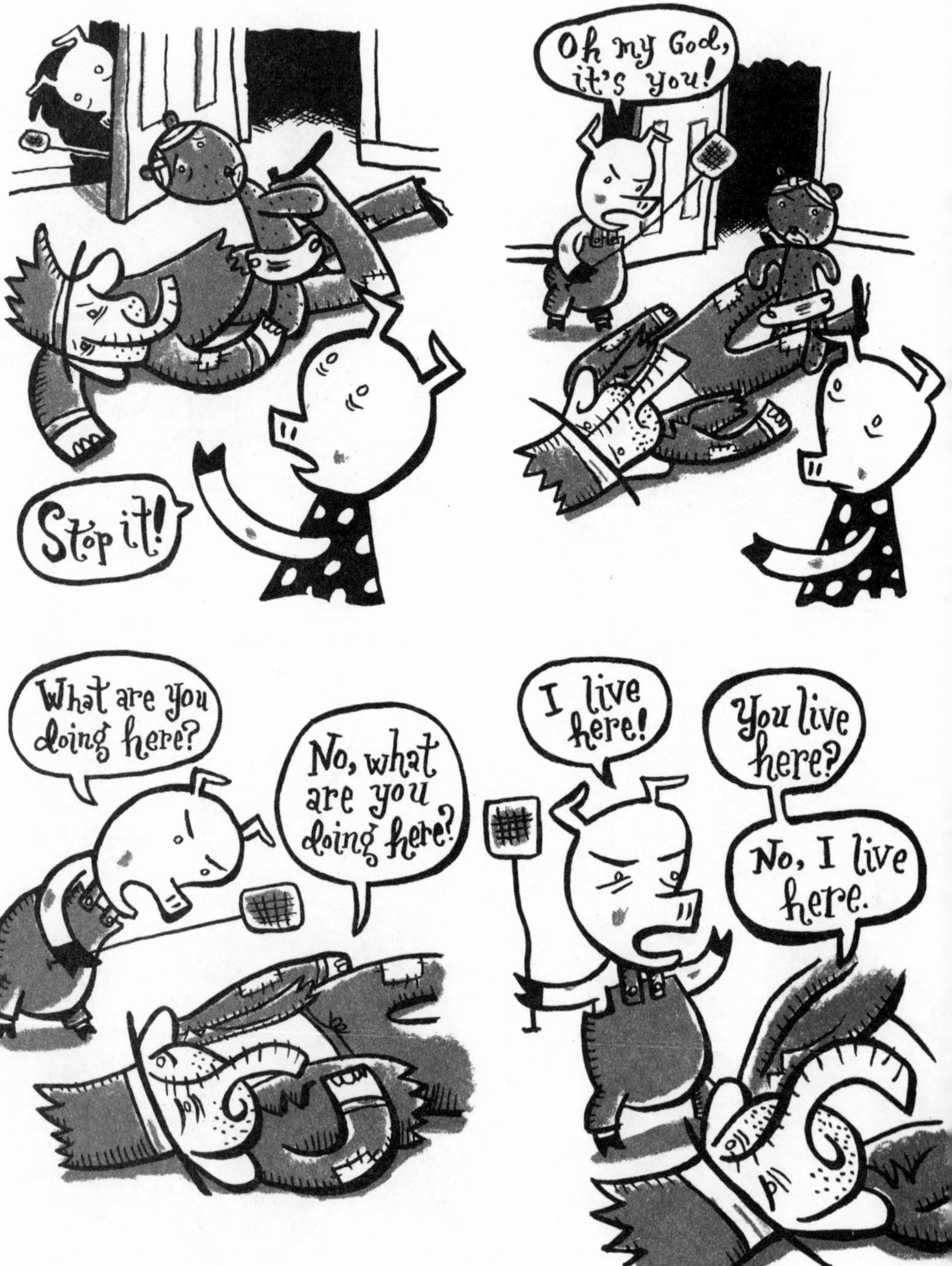
Stop it!
Oh my God, it's you!
What are you doing here?
No, what are you doing here?
I live here!
You live here?
No, I live here.

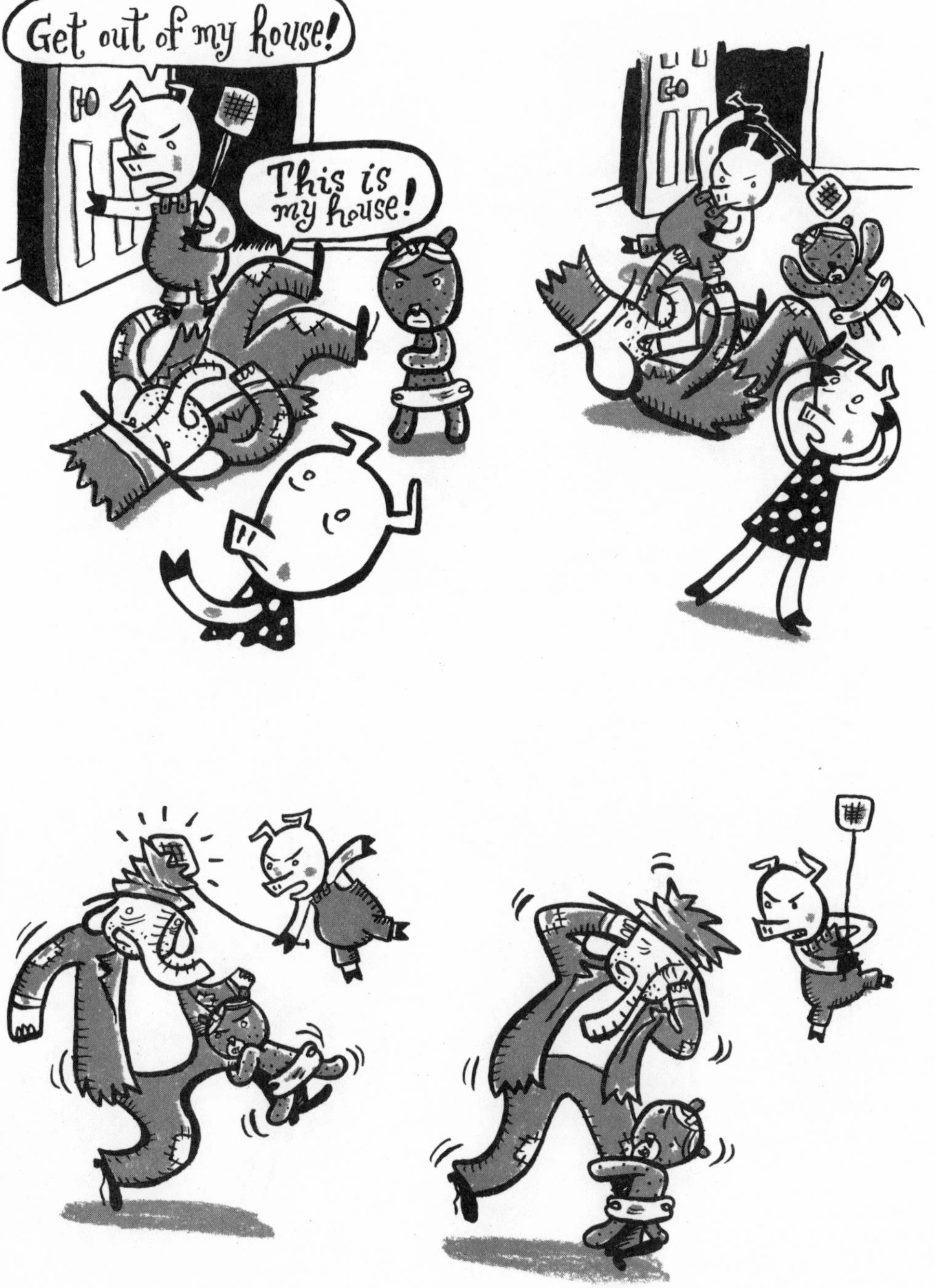
Get out of my house!
This is my house!

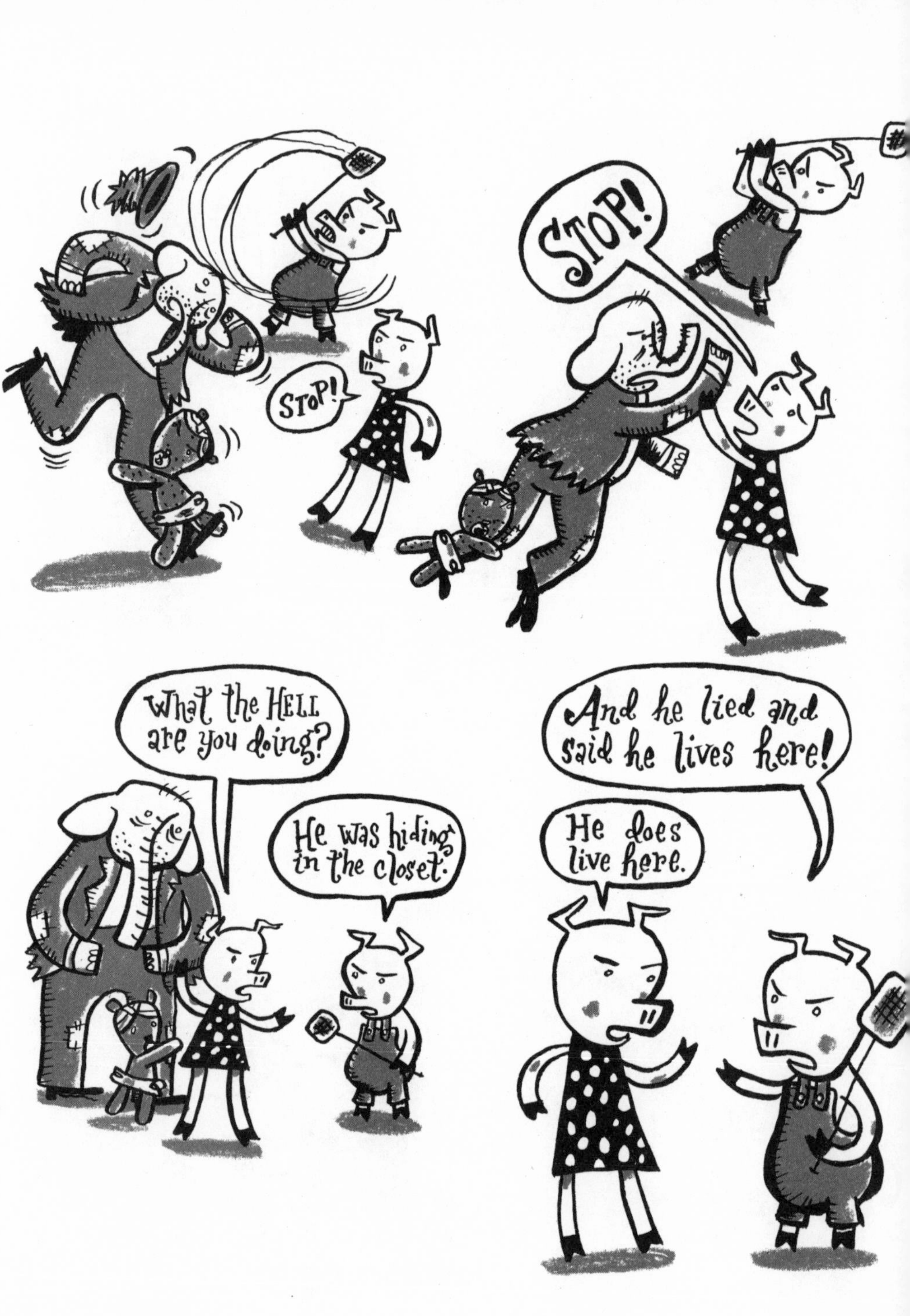
STOP!
STOP!
What the HELL are you doing?
He was hiding in the closet.
And he lied and said he lives here!
He does live here.

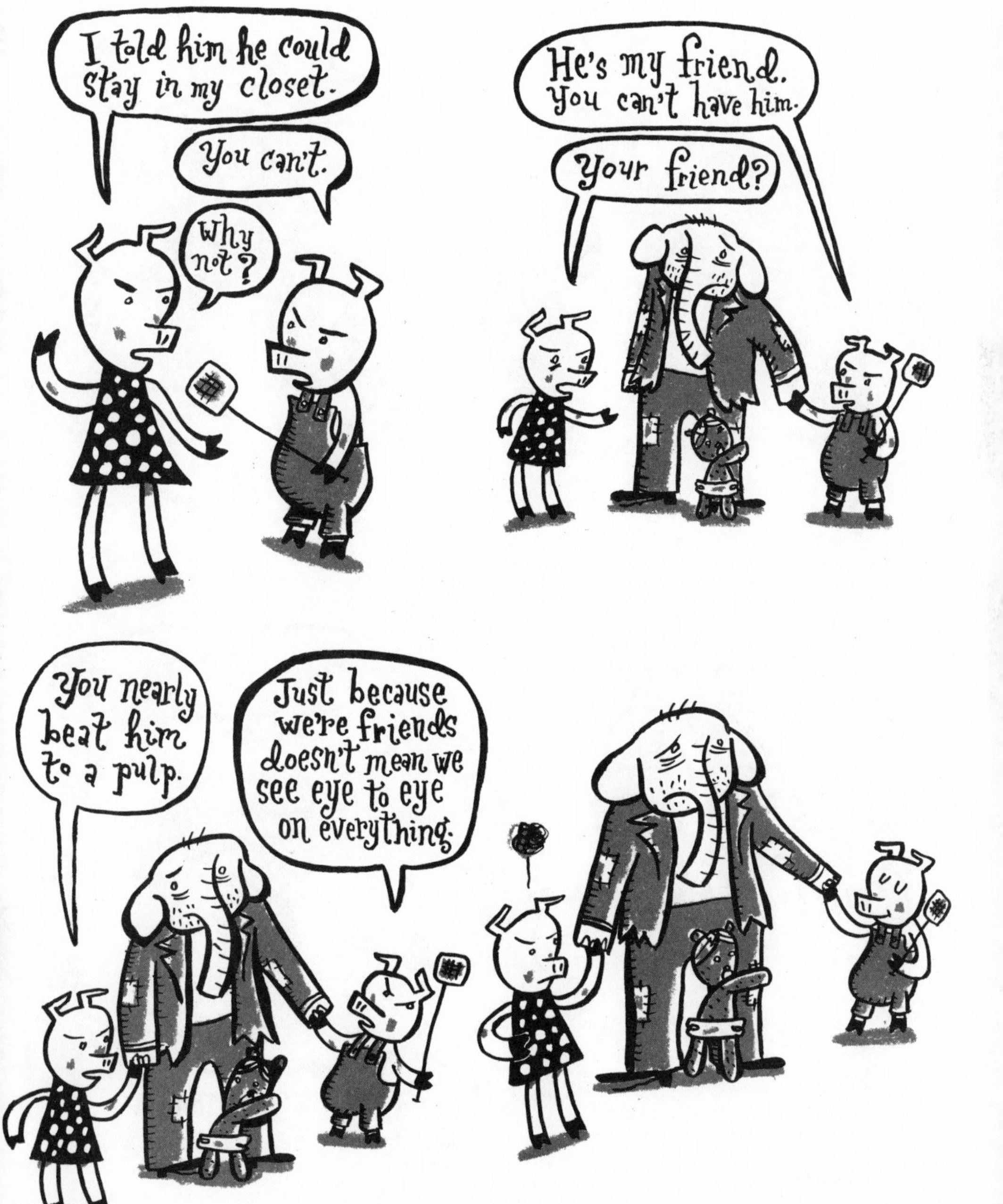
I told him he could stay in my closet.
You can't.
Why not?
He's my friend. You can't have him.
Your friend?
You nearly beat him to a pulp.
Just because we're friends doesn't mean we see eye to eye on everything.

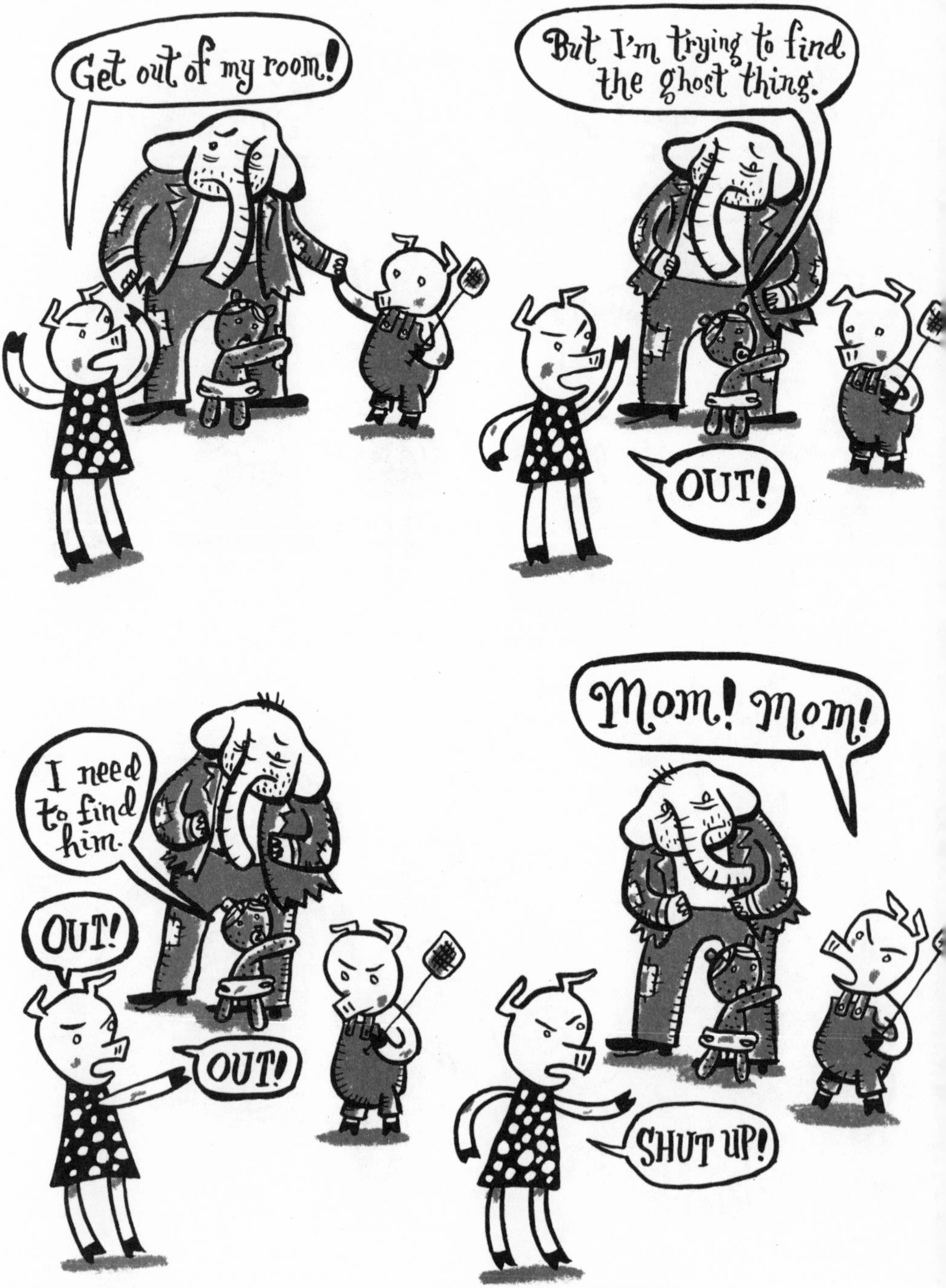
Get out of my room!
But I'm trying to find the ghost thing.
OUT!
I need to find him.
OUT!
OUT!
Mom! Mom!
SHUT UP!

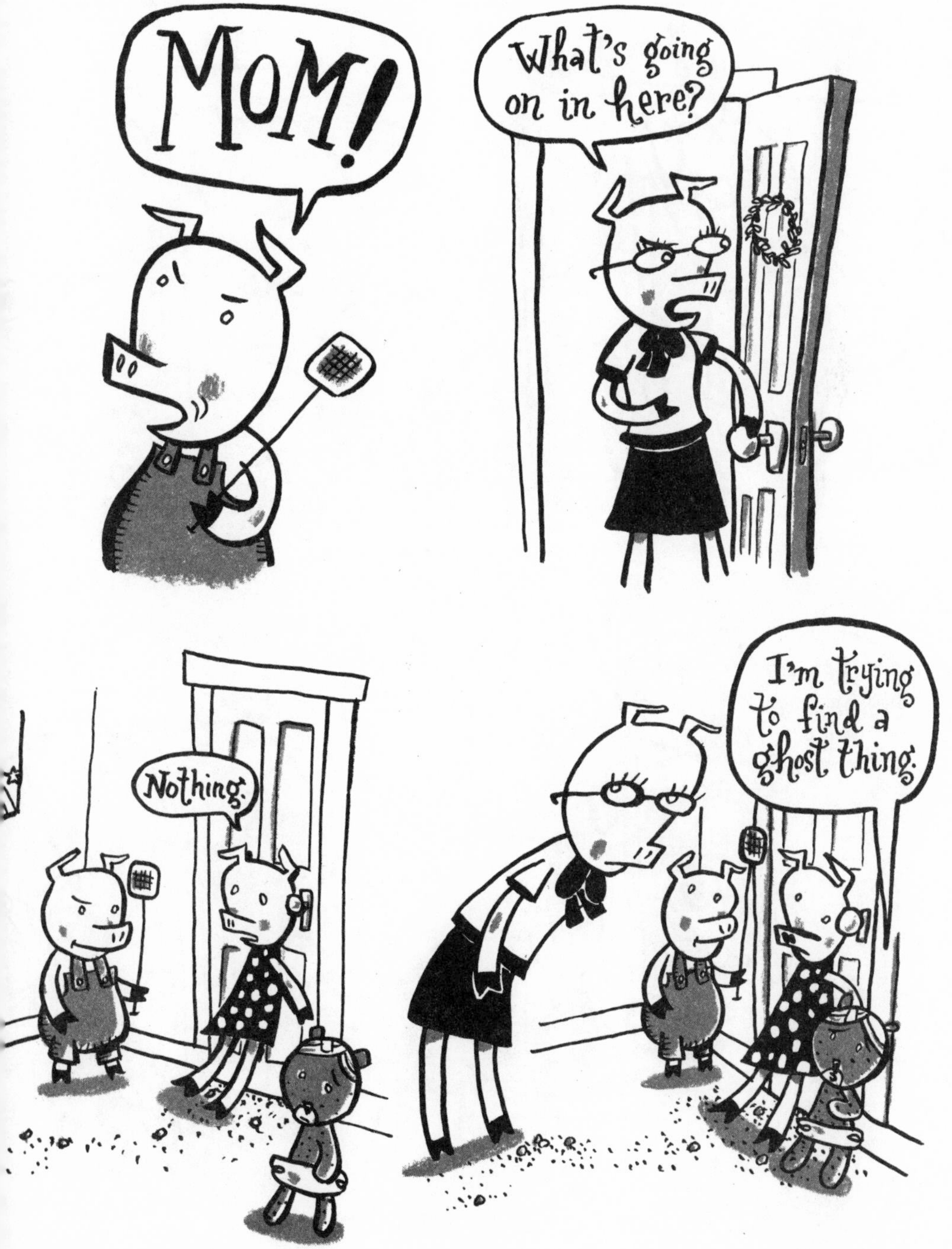
MOM!
What's going on in here?
Nothing.
I'm trying to find a ghost thing.

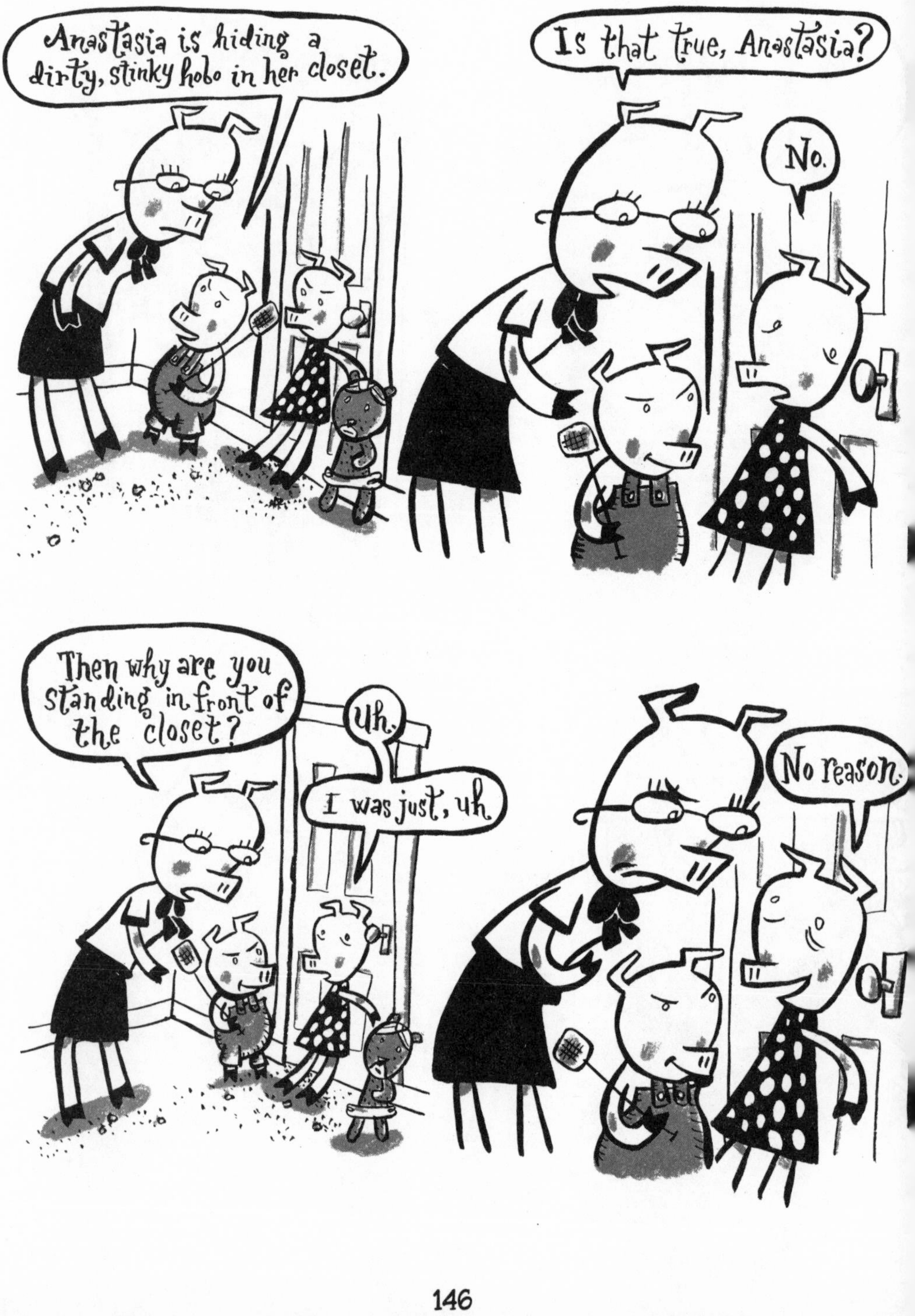
Anastasia is hiding a dirty, stinky hobo in her closet.
Is that true, Anastasia?
No.
Then why are you standing in front of the closet?
Uh.
I was just, uh.
No reason.

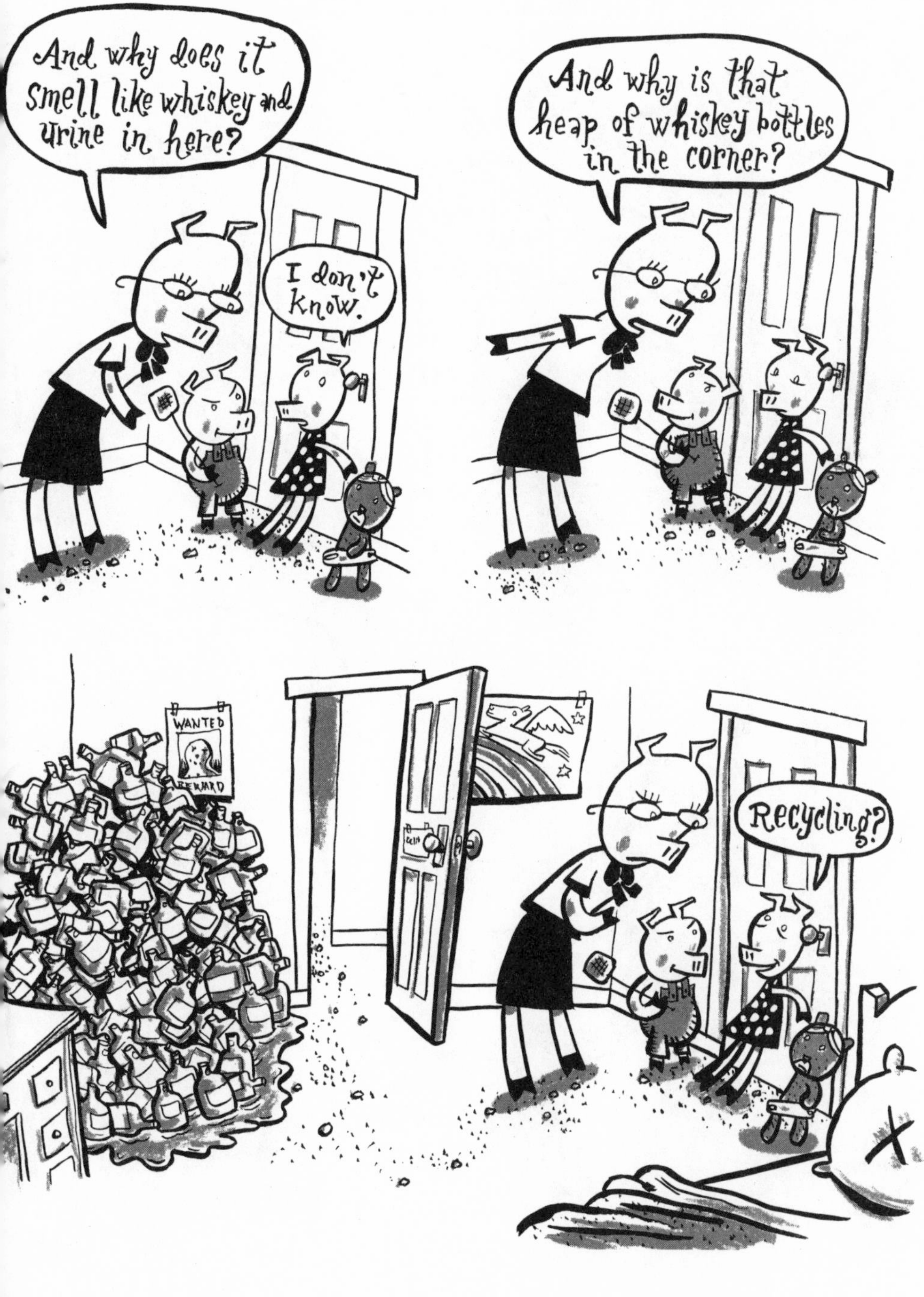

And why does it smell like whiskey and urine in here?
I don't know.
And why is that heap of whiskey bottles in the corner?
WANTED
REWARD
Recycling?

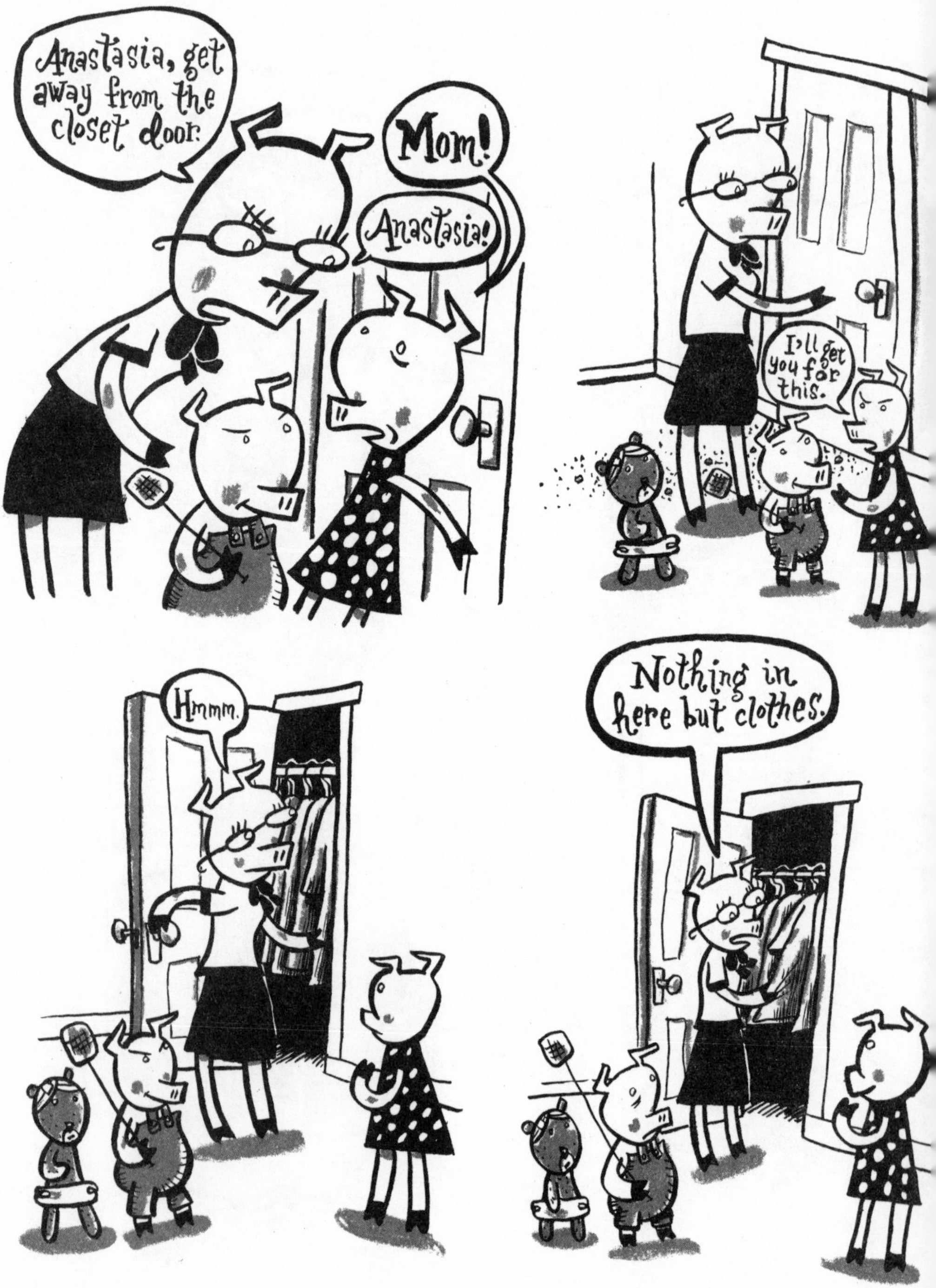
Anastasia, get away from the closet door.
Mom!
Anastasia!
I'll get you for this.
Hmmm.
Nothing in here but clothes.

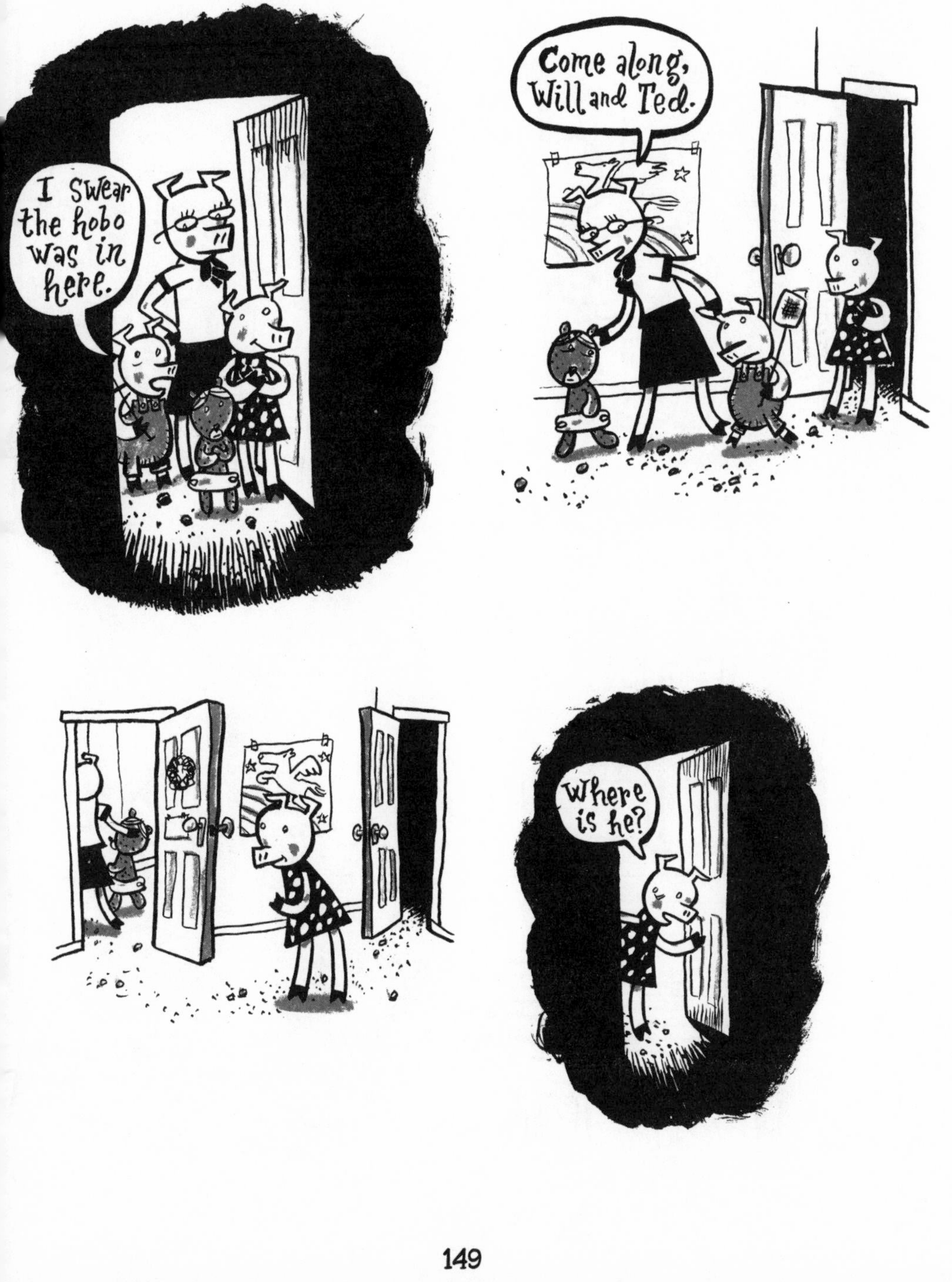
I swear the hobo was in here.
Come along, Will and Ted.
Where is he?

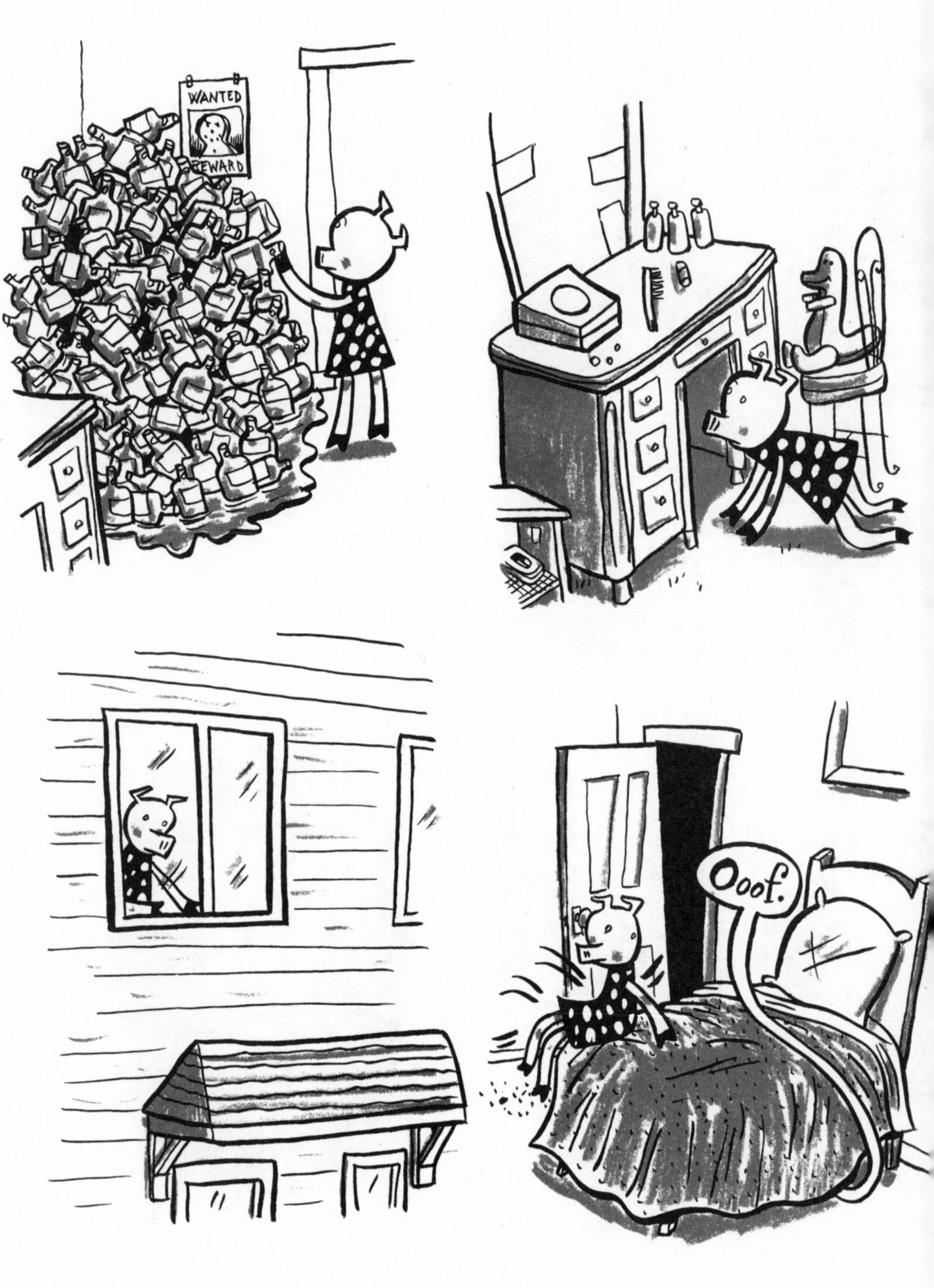
WANTED
Ooof.

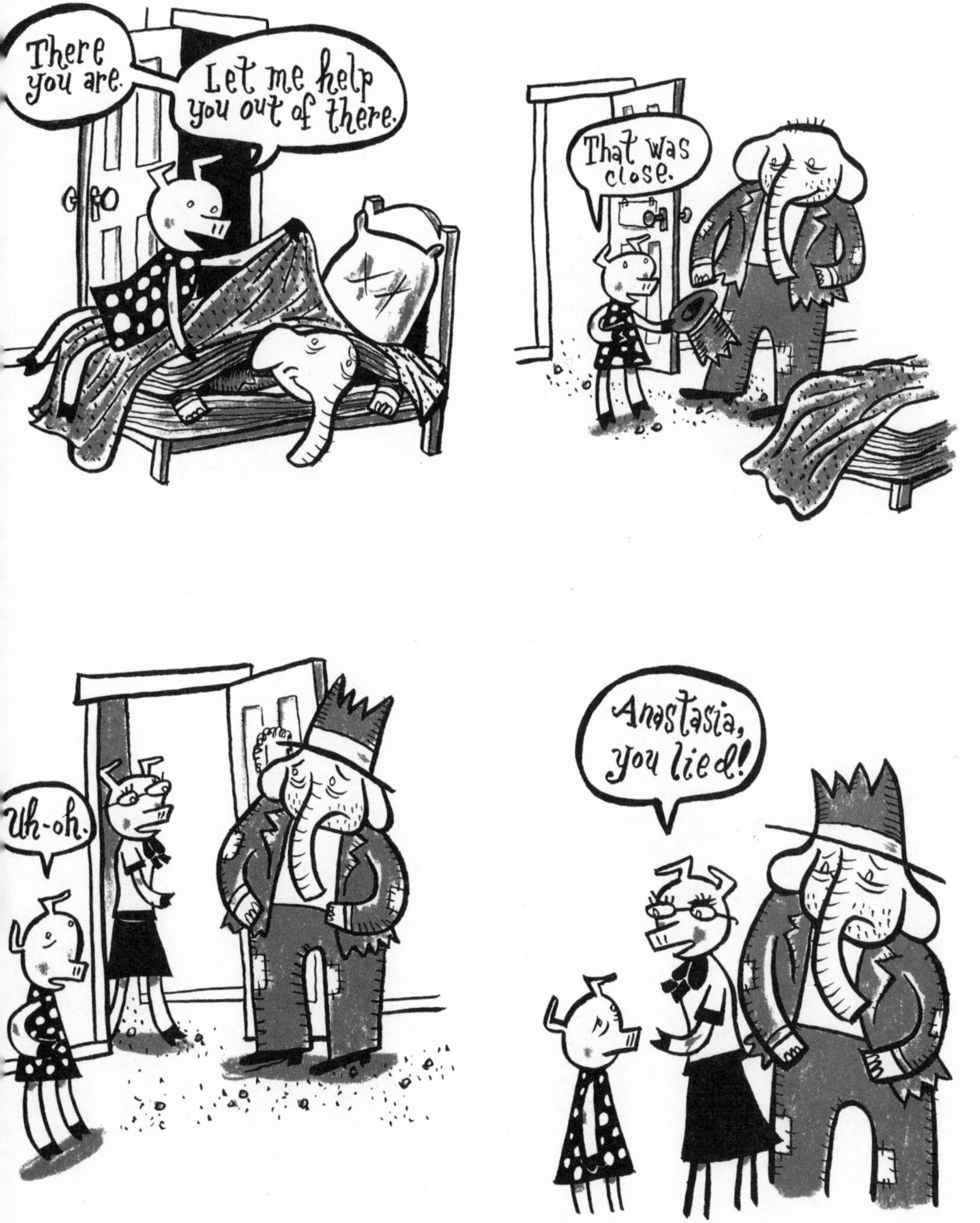
There you are.
Let me help you out of there.
That was close.
Uh-oh.
Anastasia, you lied!

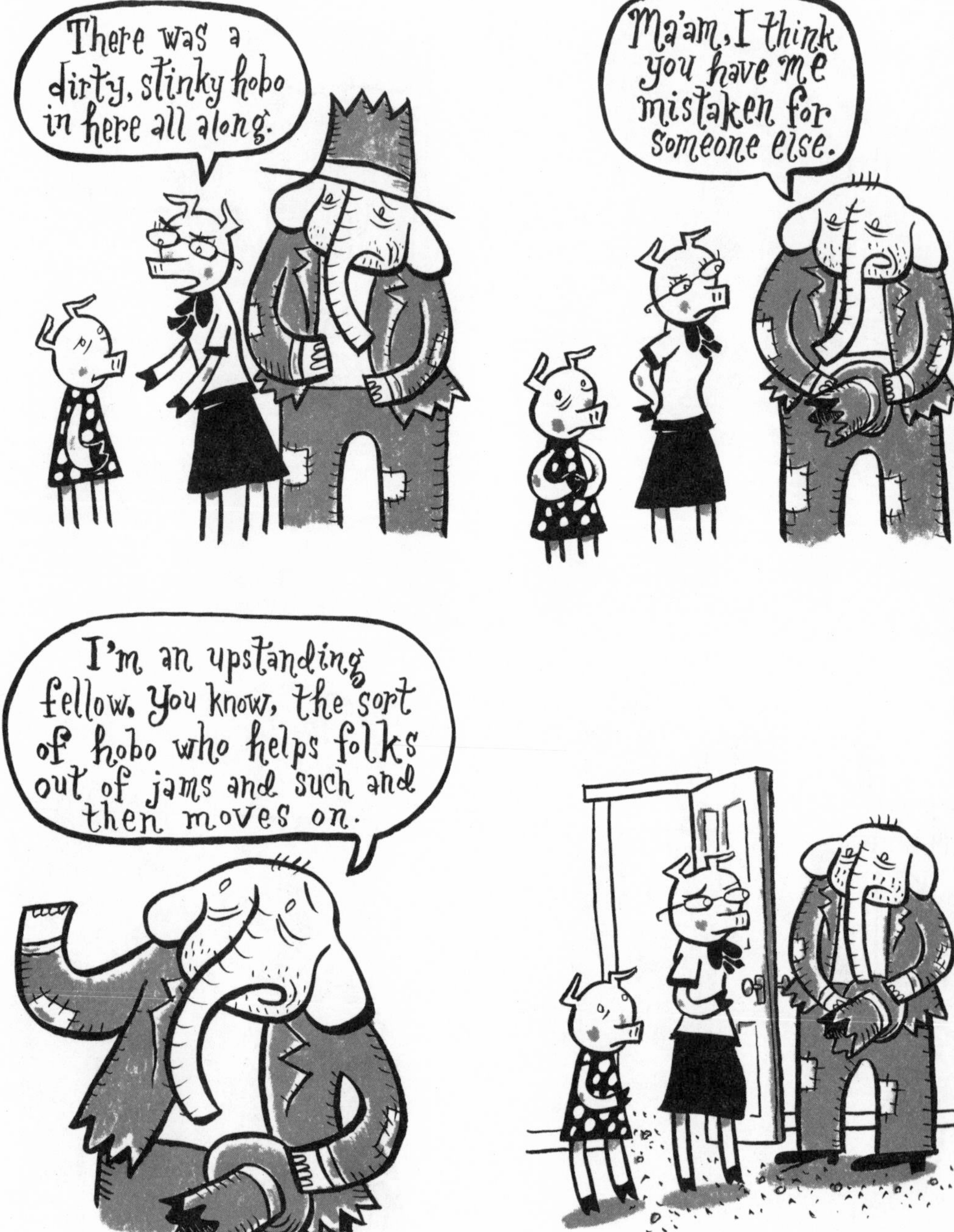
There was a dirty, stinky hobo in here all along.
Ma'am, I think you have me mistaken for someone else.
I'm an upstanding fellow. You know, the sort of hobo who helps folks out of jams and such and then moves on.

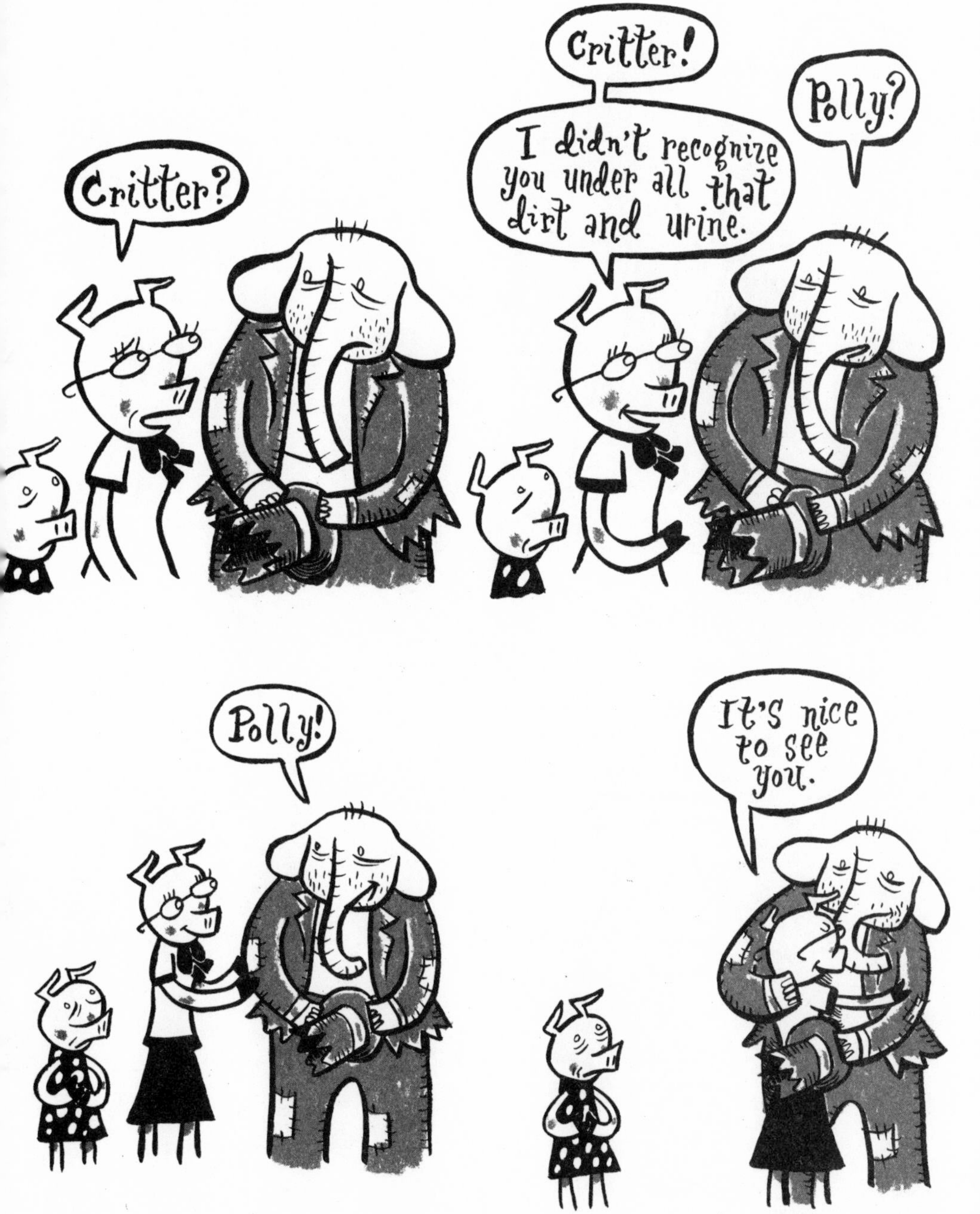
Critter?
Critter!
I didn't recognize you under all that dirt and urine.
Polly?
Polly!
It's nice to see you.

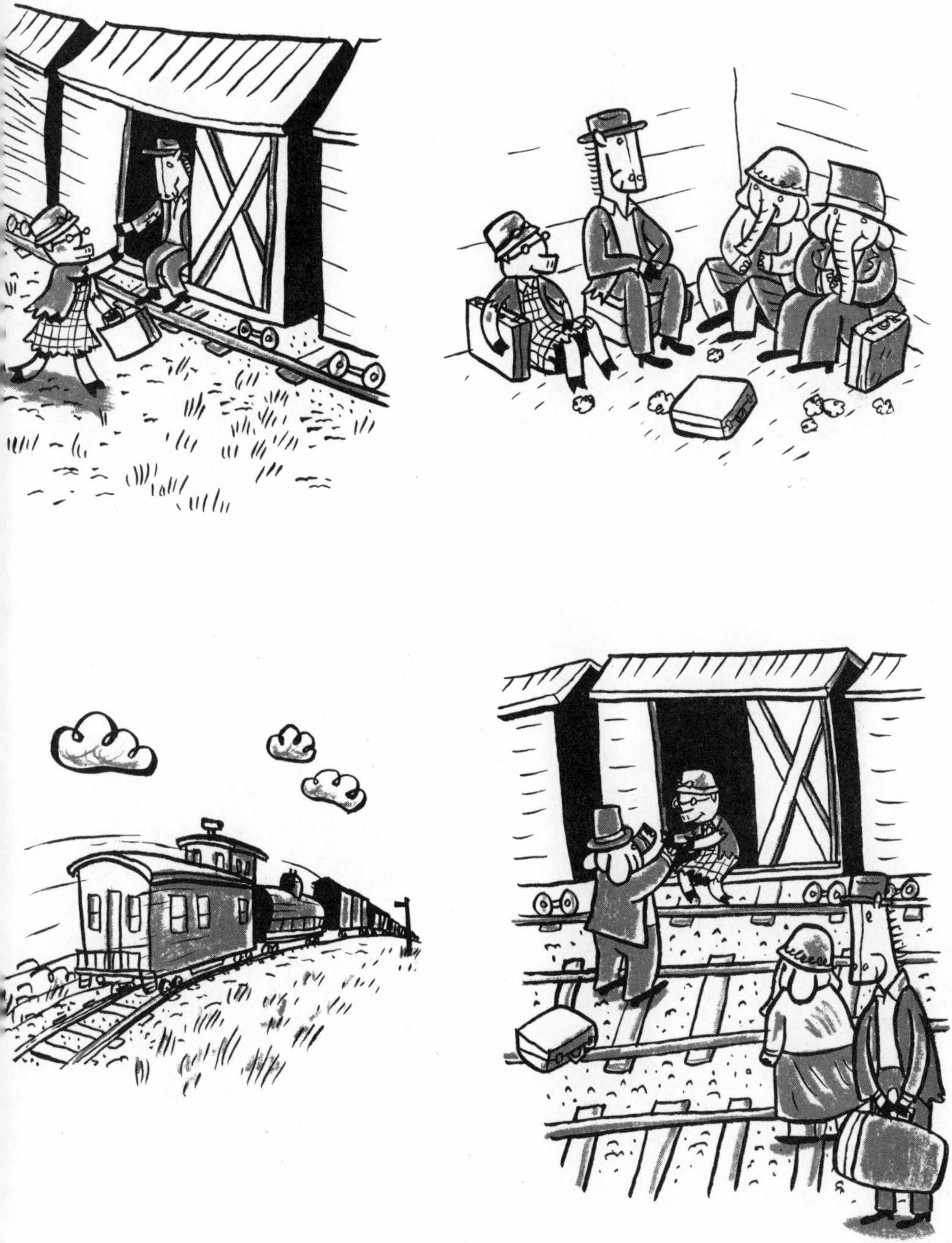

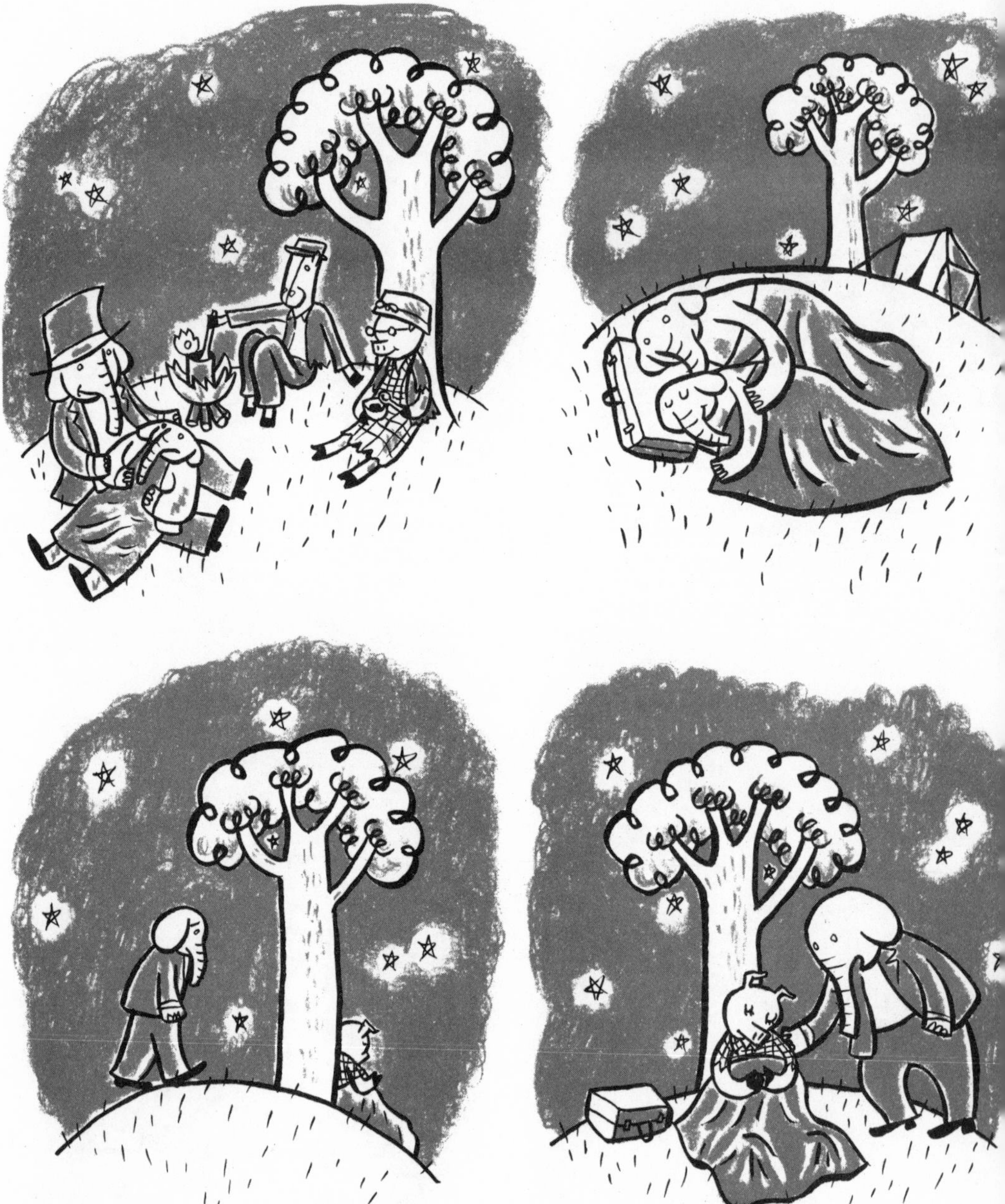

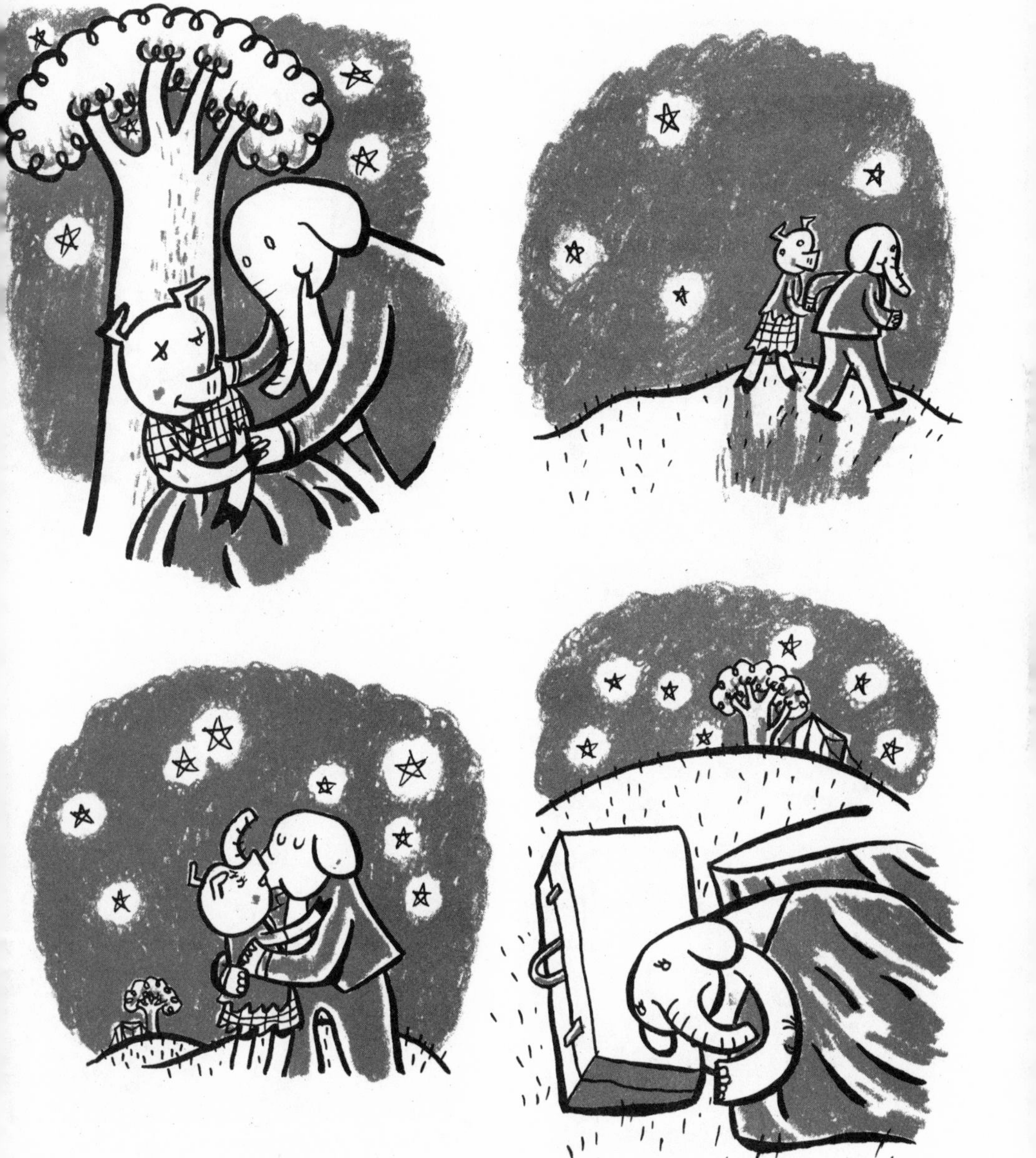

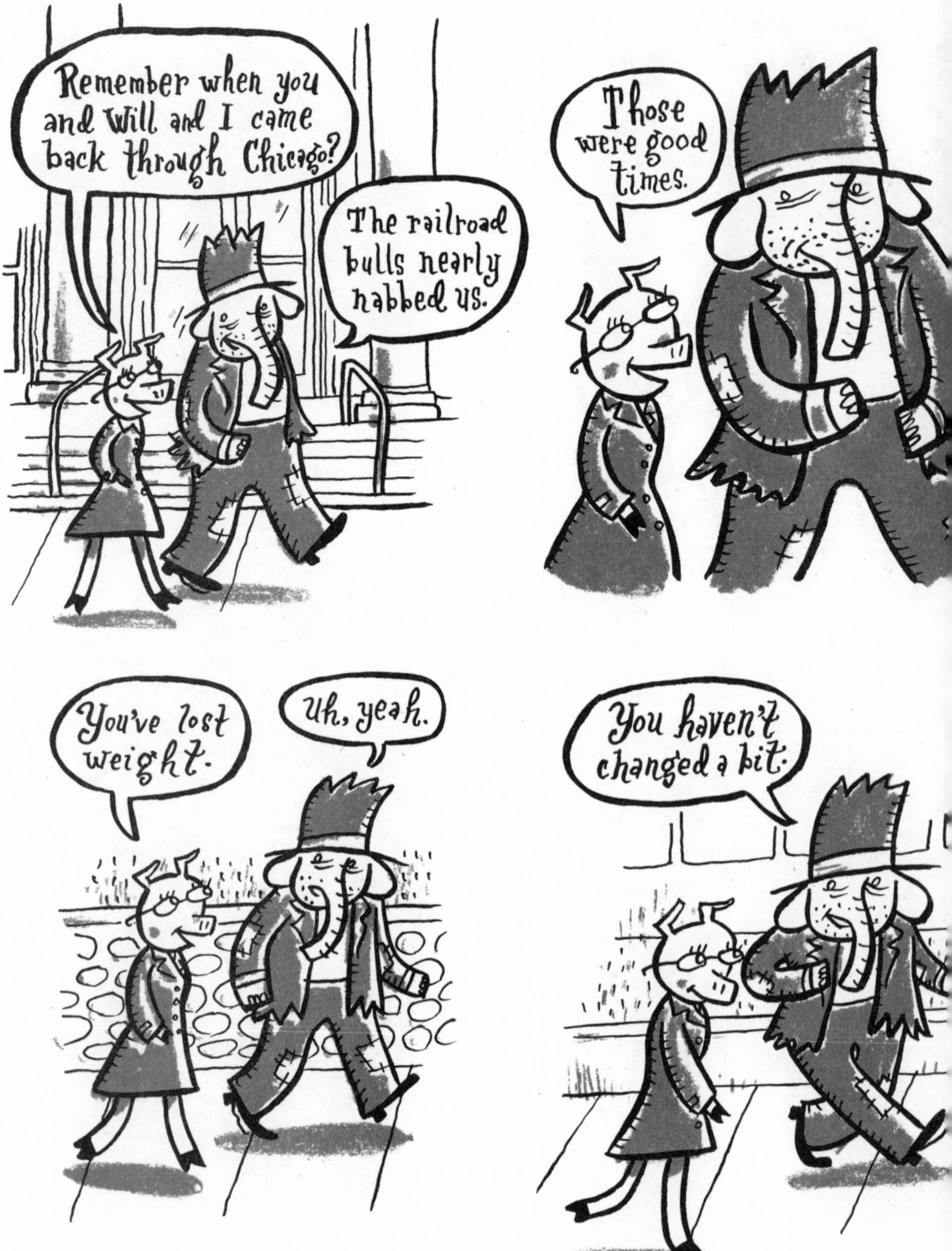

Remember when you and Will and I came back through Chicago?
The railroad bulls nearly nabbed us.
Those were good times.
You've lost weight.
Uh, yeah.
You haven't changed a bit.

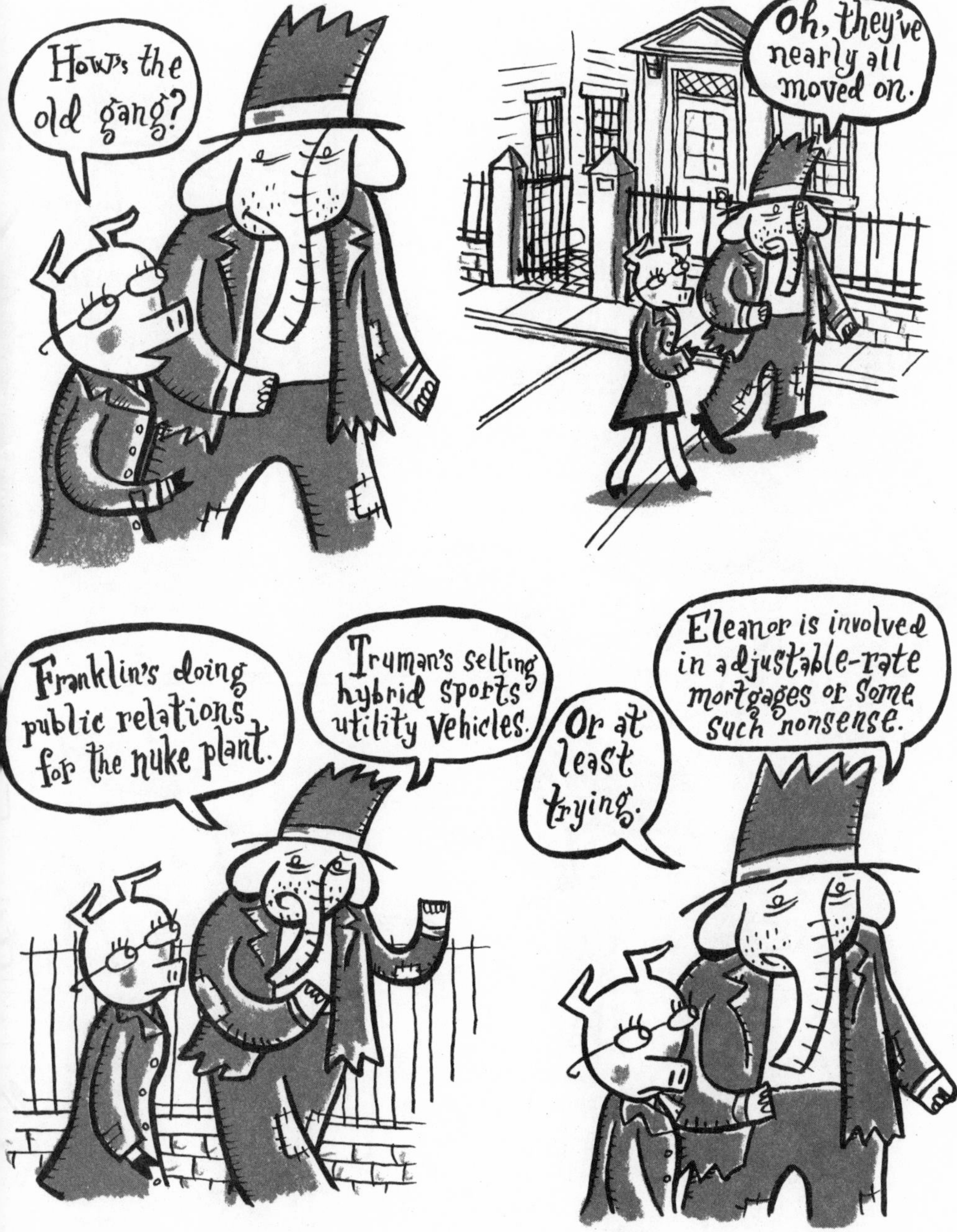
How's the old gang?
Oh, they've nearly all moved on.
Franklin's doing public relations for the nuke plant.
Truman's selling hybrid sports utility vehicles.
Or at least trying.
Eleanor is involved in adjustable-rate mortgages or some such nonsense.

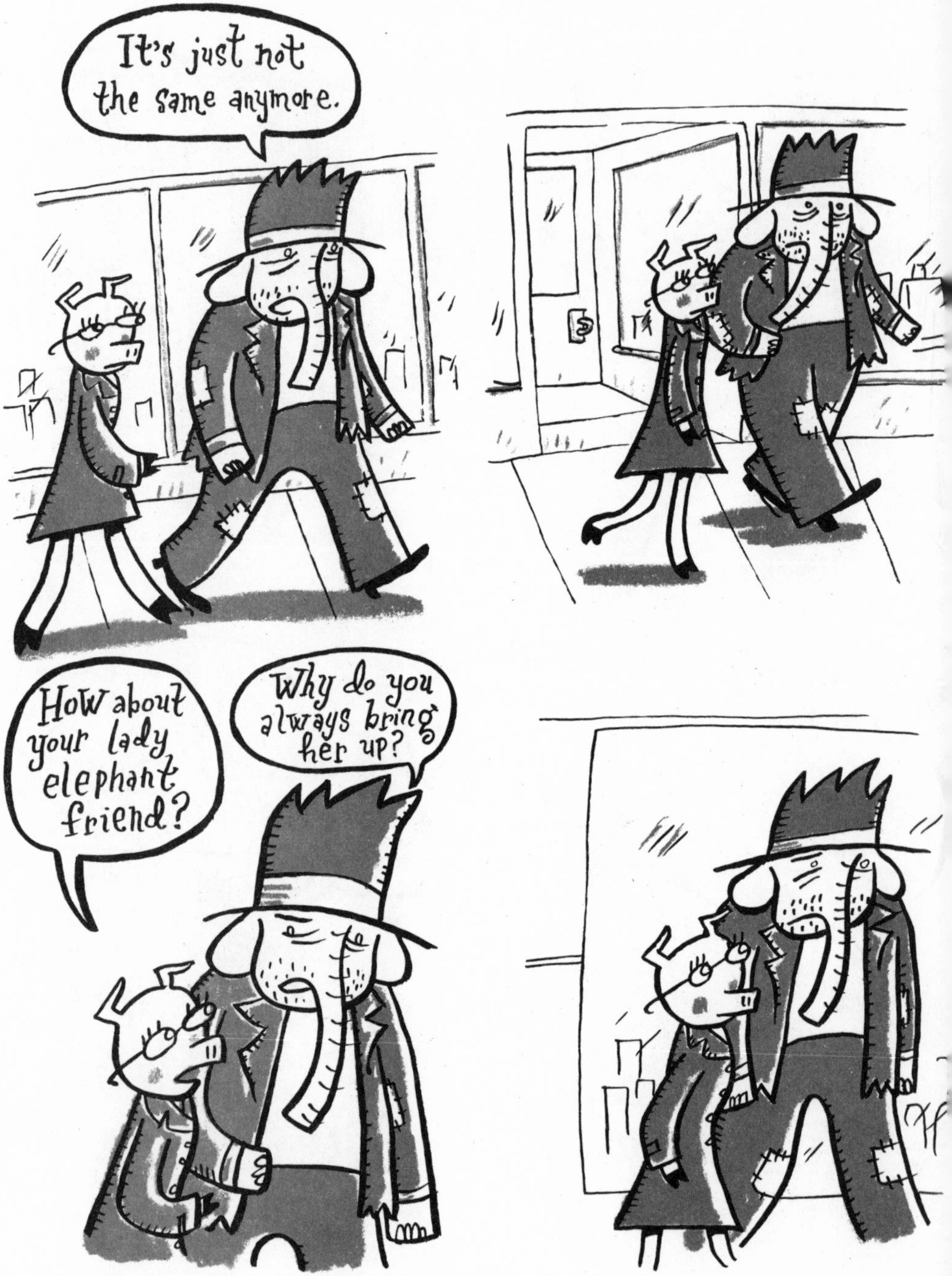
It's just not the same anymore.
How about your lady elephant friend?
Why do you always bring her up?

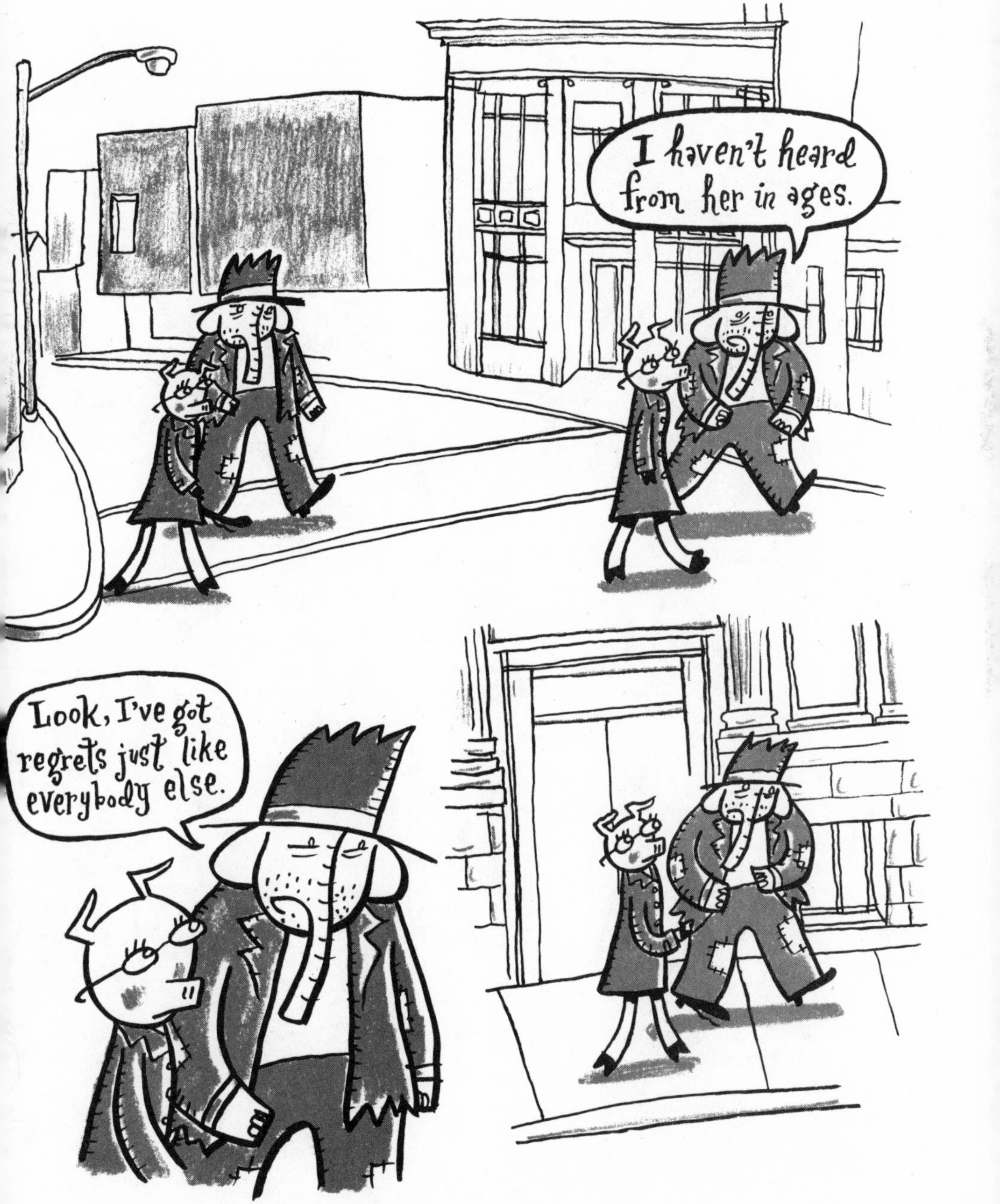

I haven't heard from her in ages.
Look, I've got regrets just like everybody else.

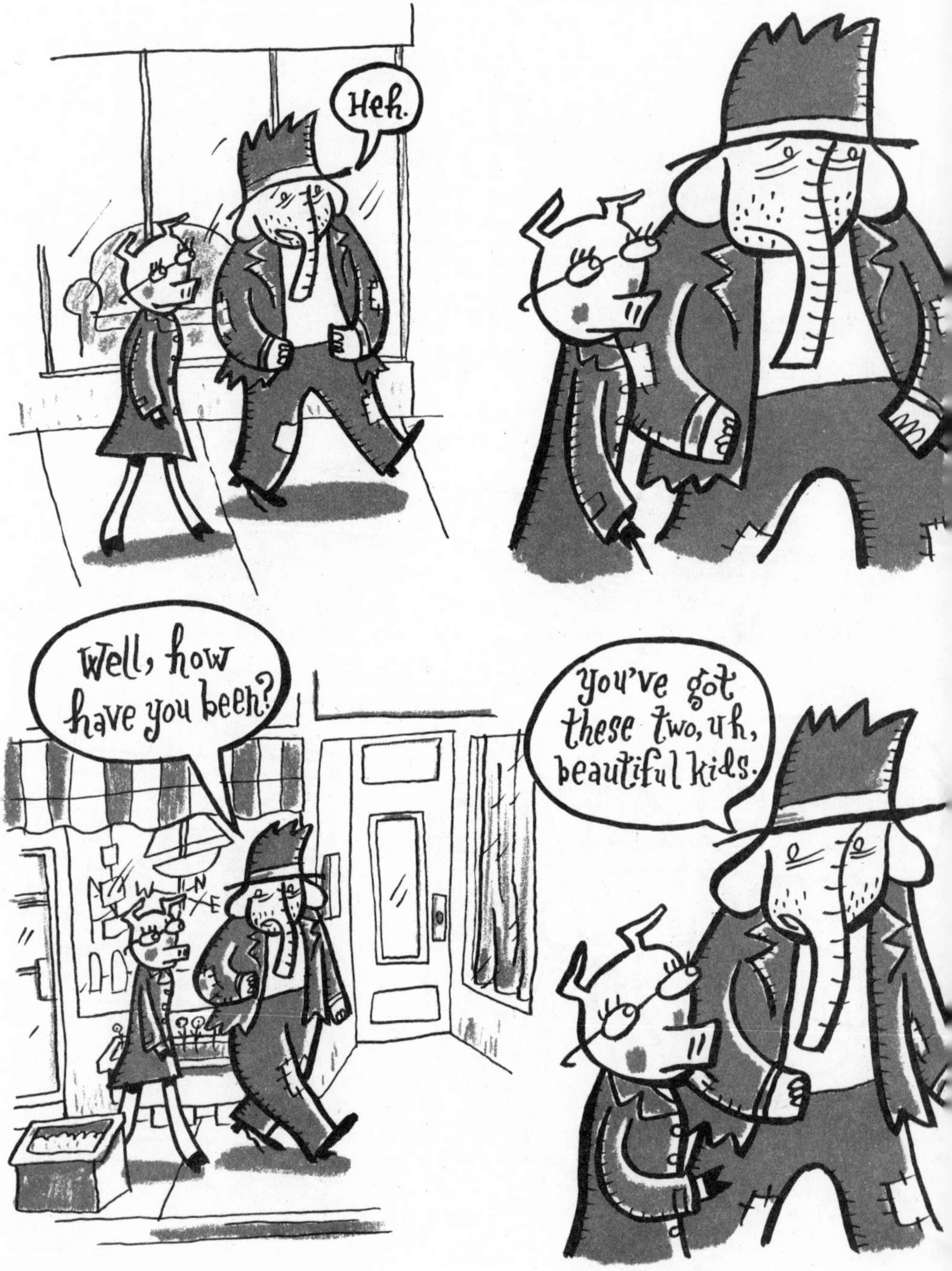
Heh.
Well, how have you been?
W N E
You've got these two, uh, beautiful kids.

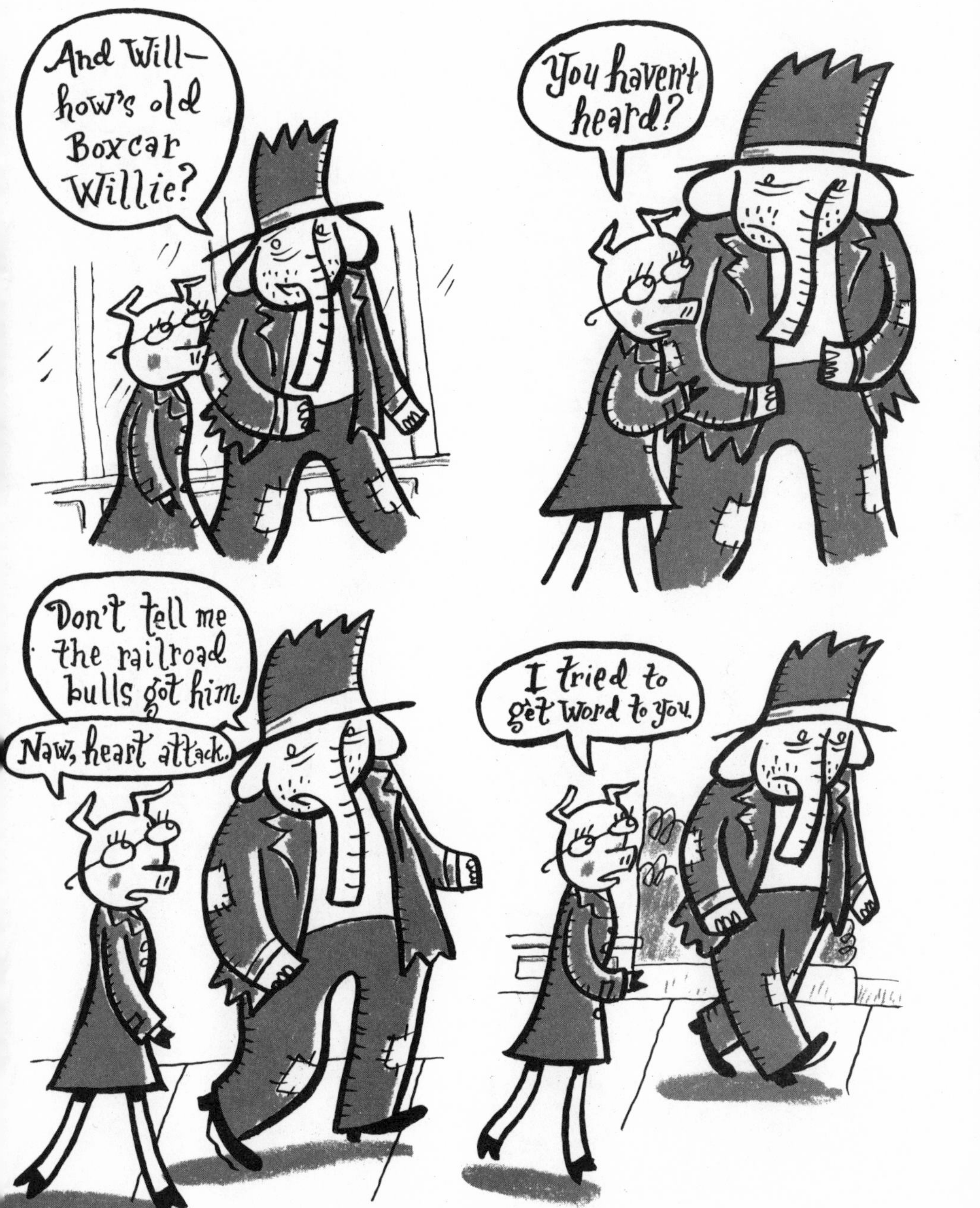
And Will—
how's old
Boxcar
Willie?
You haven't
heard?
Don't tell me
the railroad
bulls got him.
Naw, heart attack.
I tried to
get word to you.

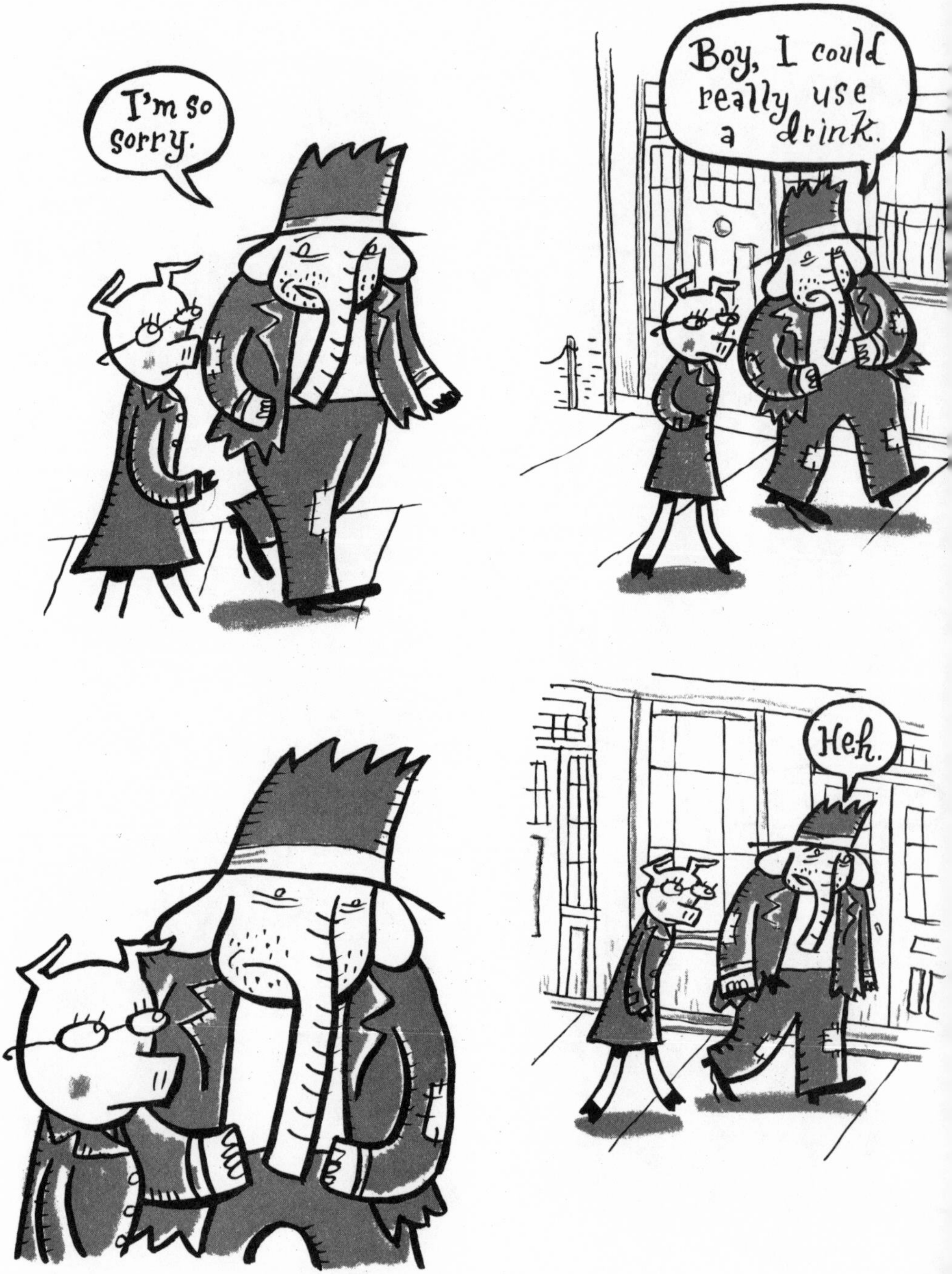
I'm so sorry.
Boy, I could really use a drink.
Heh.

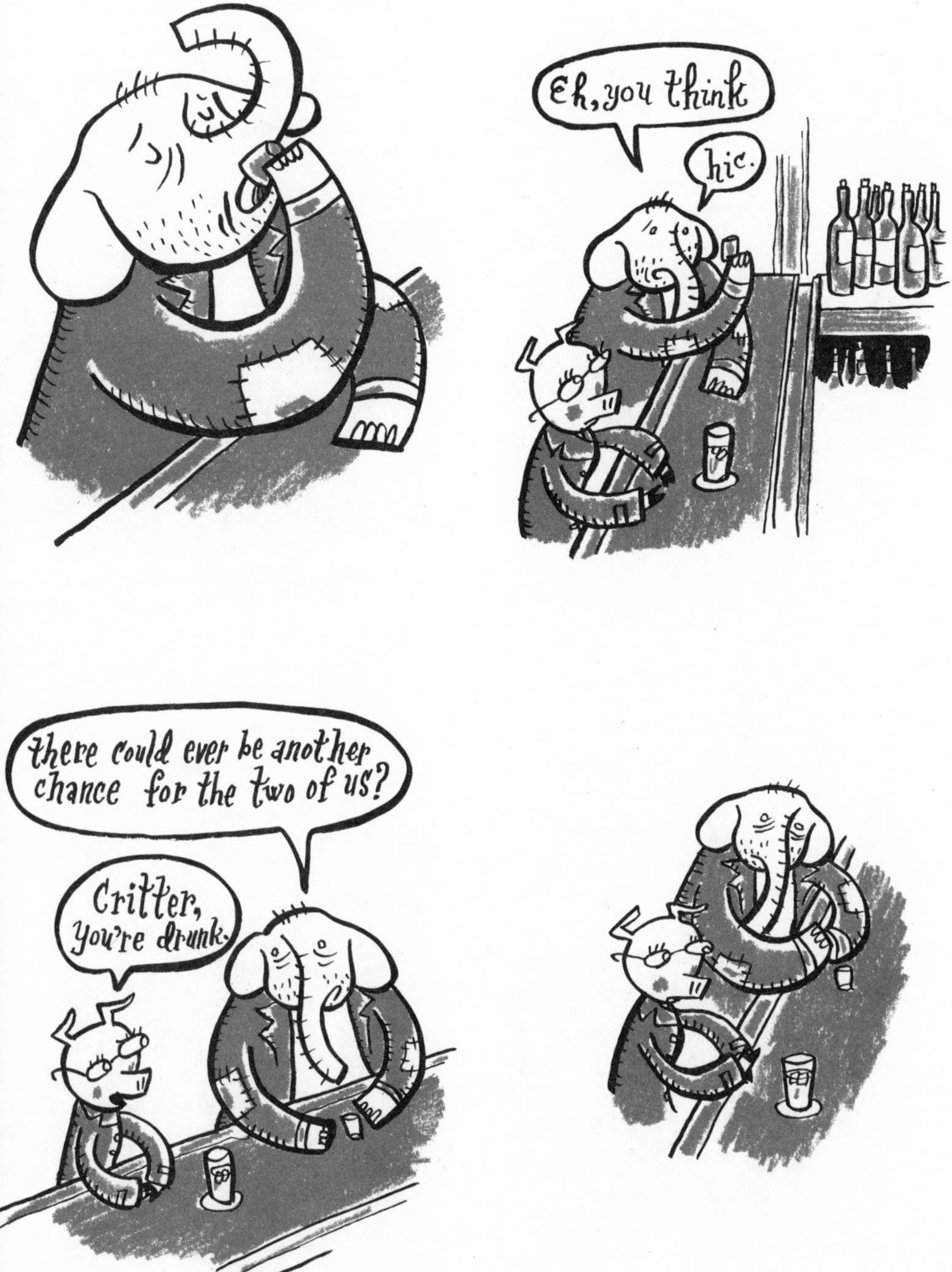
Eh, you think
hic.
there could ever be another chance for the two of us?
Critter, you're drunk.

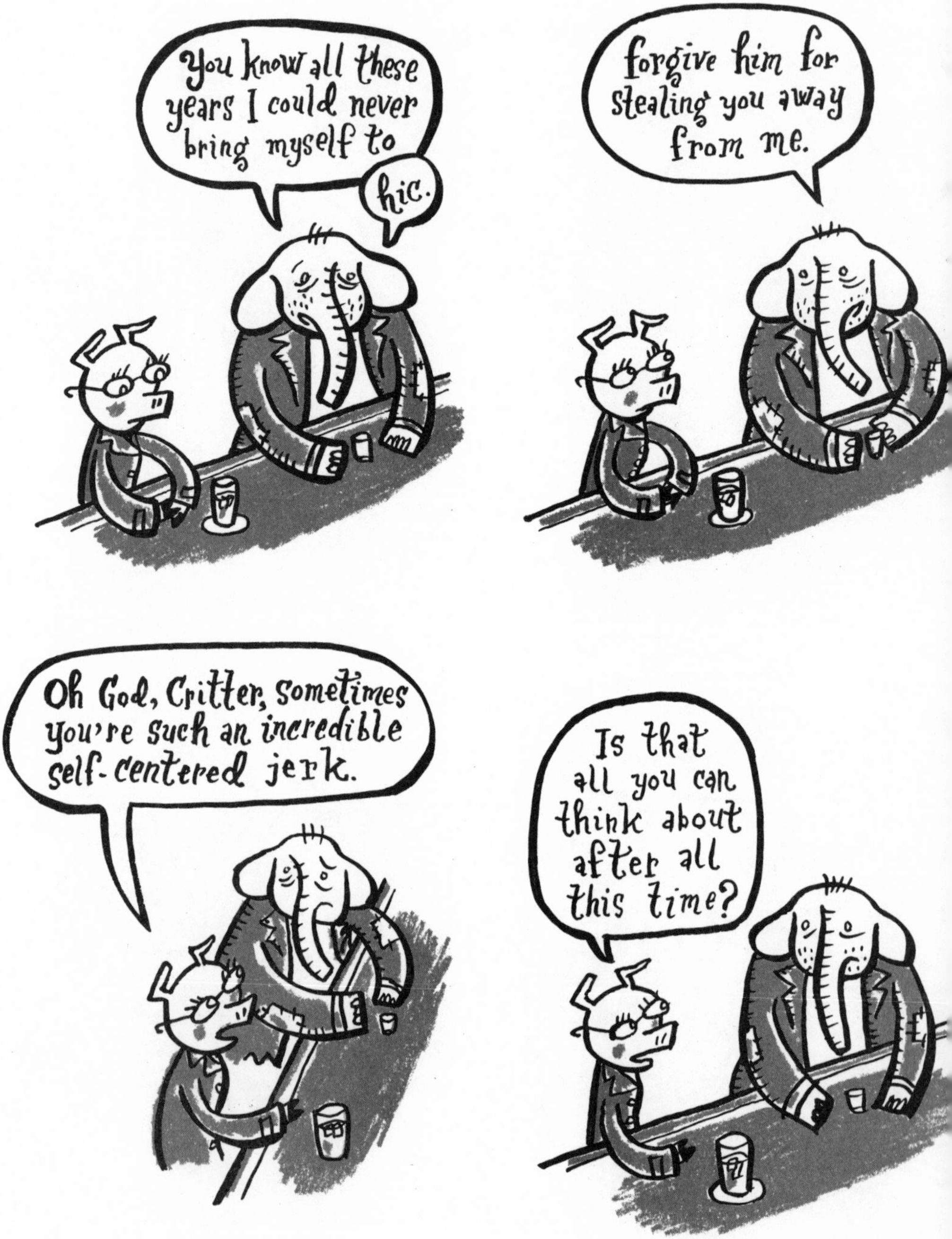
You know all these years I could never bring myself to
hic.
forgive him for stealing you away from me.
Oh God, Critter, sometimes you're such an incredible self-centered jerk.
Is that all you can think about after all this time?

You've got to be kidding me.
It wasn't up to Will anyway.
It was my choice.

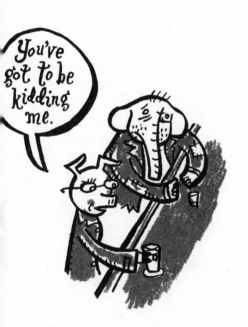

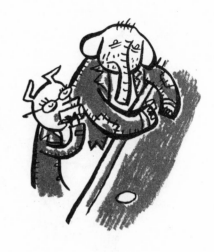

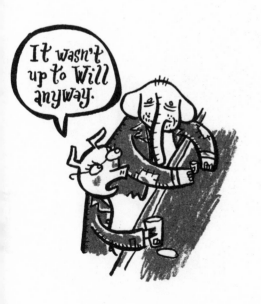

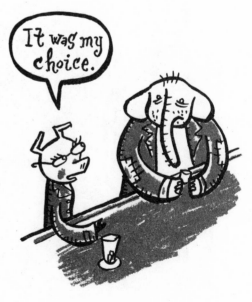

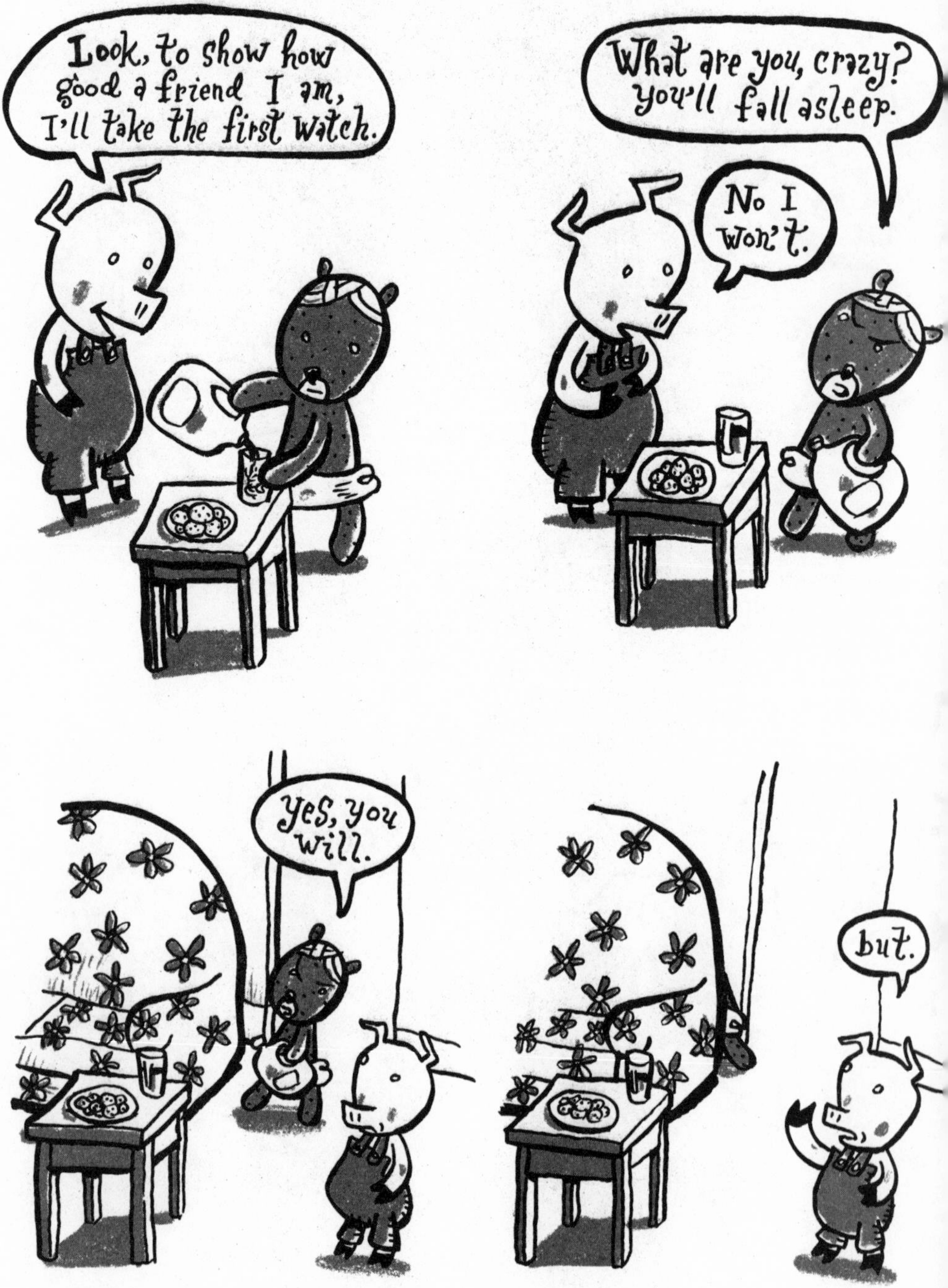
Look, to show how good a friend I am, I'll take the first watch.
What are you, crazy? You'll fall asleep.
No I won't.
Yes, you will.
But.

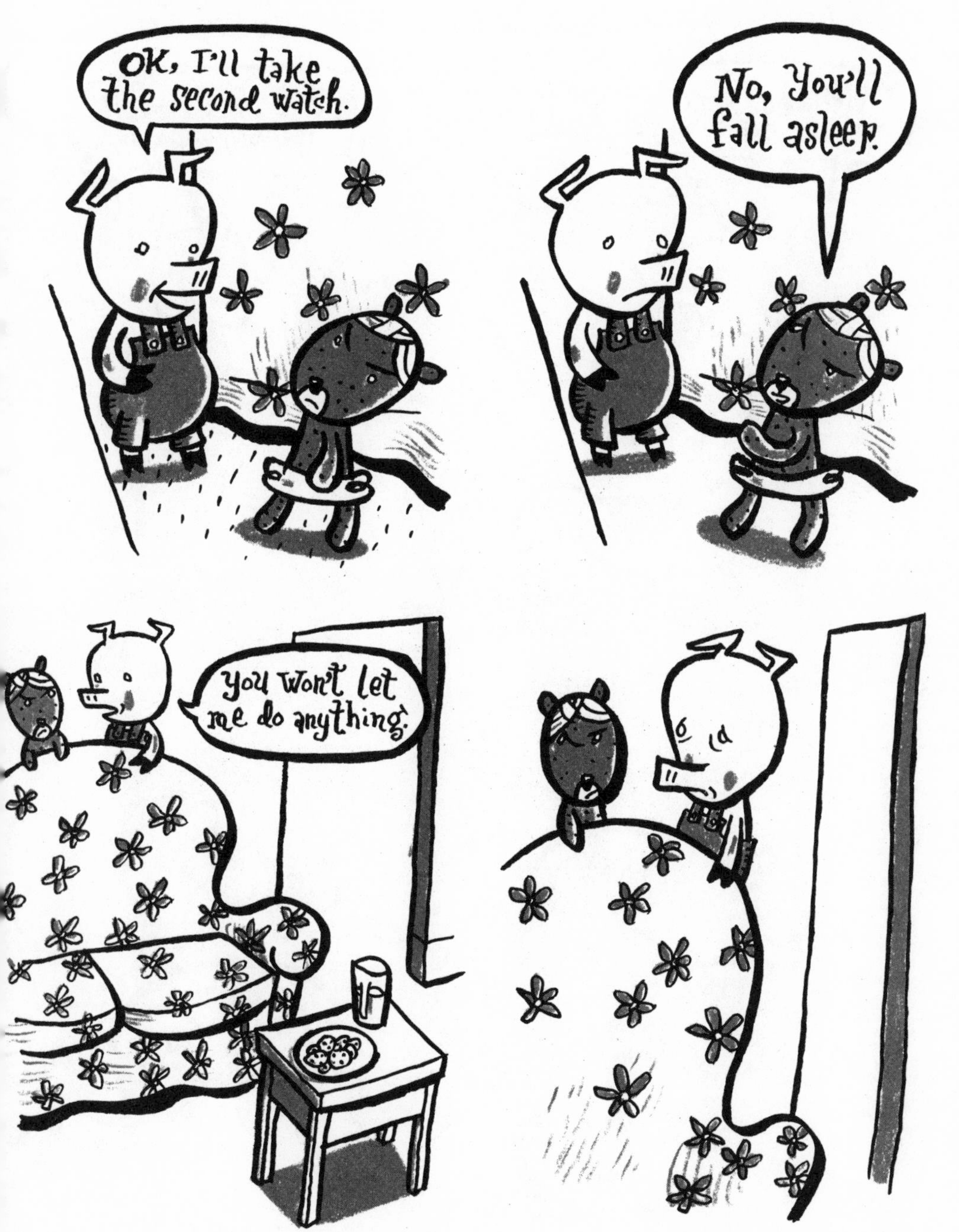
OK, I'll take the second watch.
No, You'll fall asleep.
You won't let me do anything.

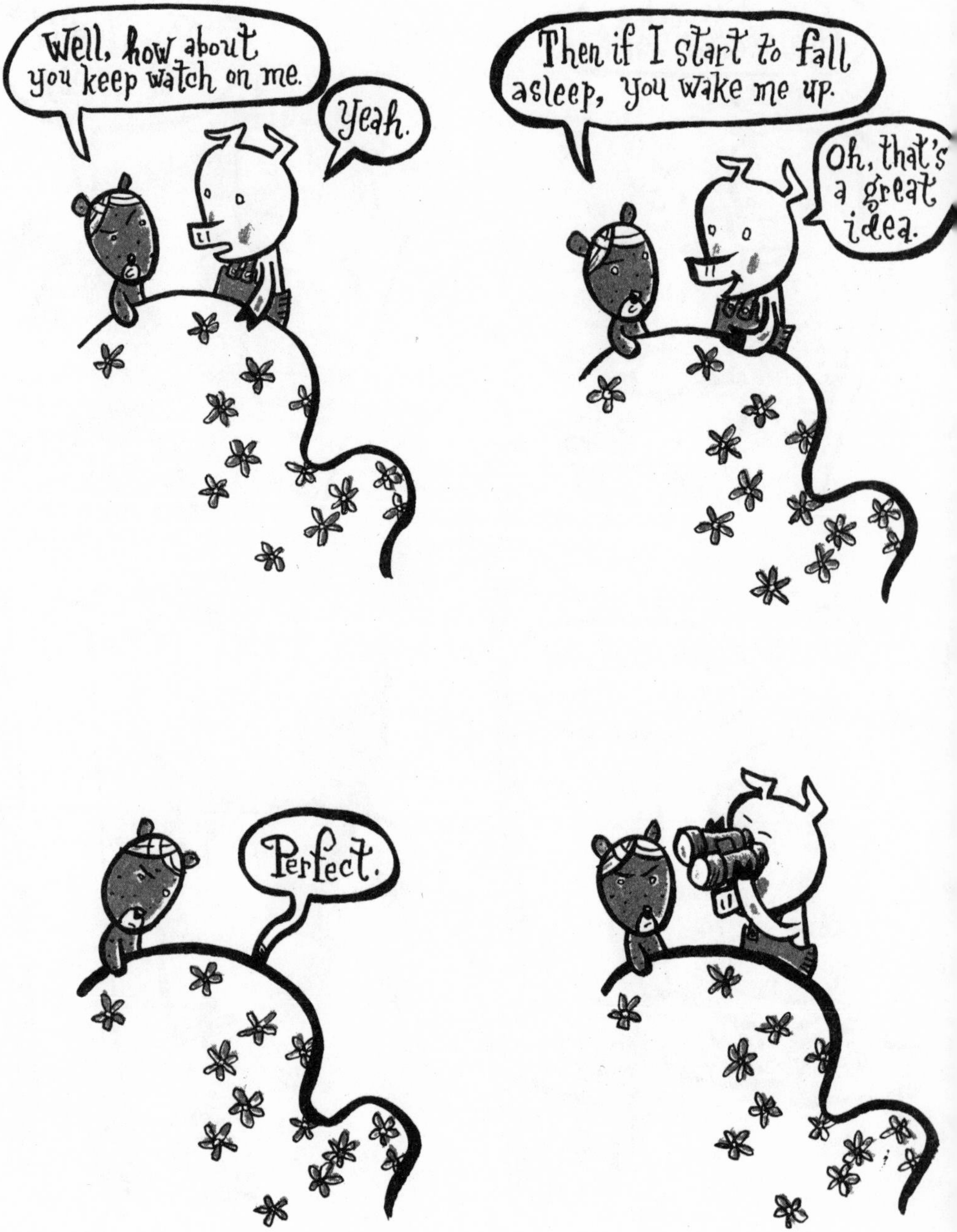
Well, how about you keep watch on me.
Yeah.
Then if I start to fall asleep, you wake me up.
Oh, that's a great idea.
Perfect.

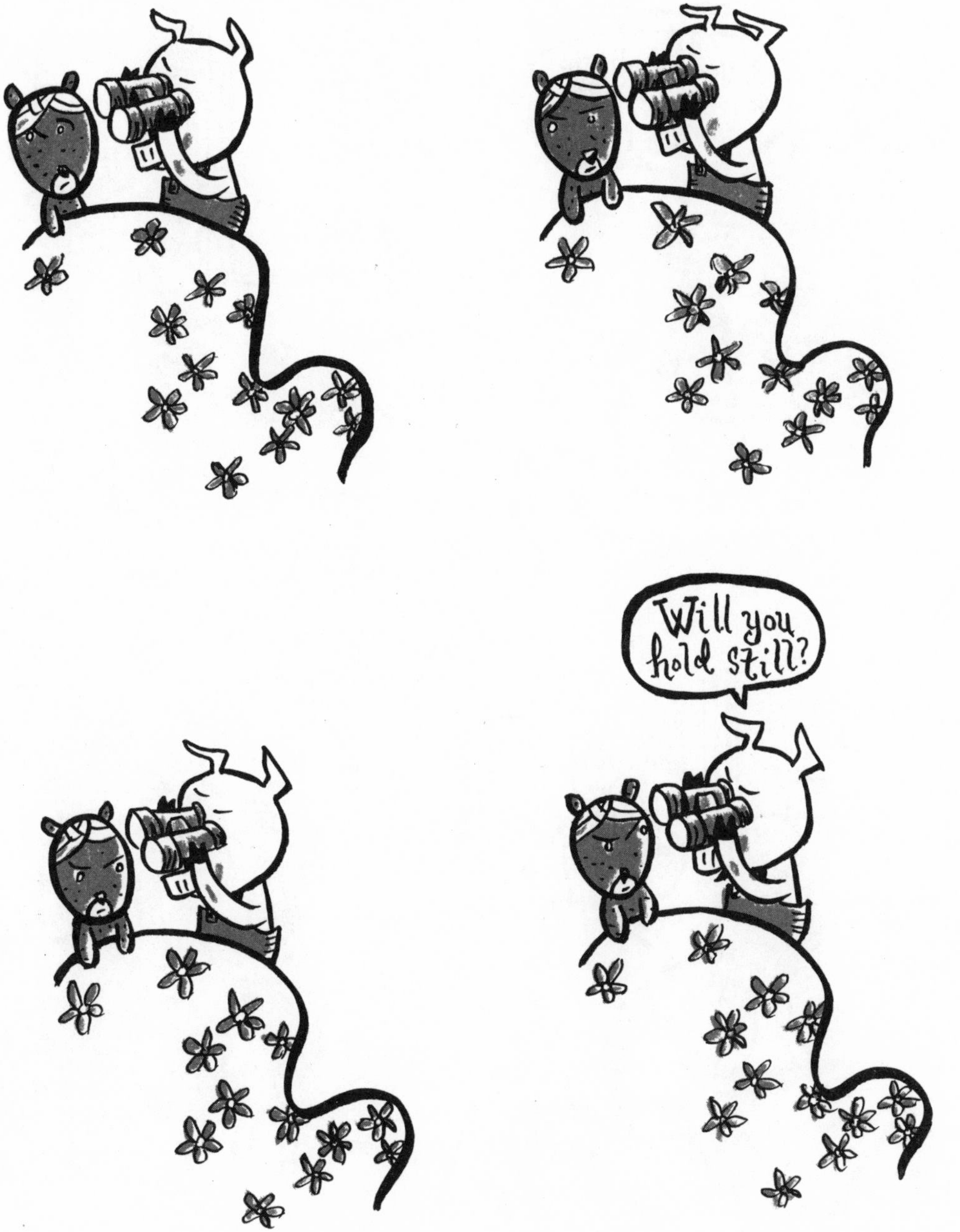
Will you hold still?

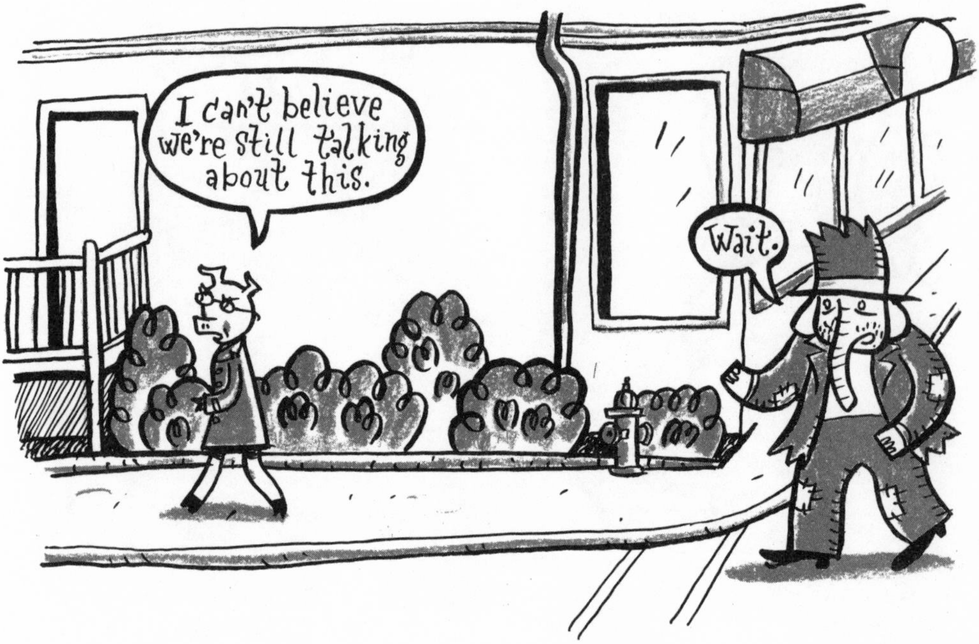
I can't believe we're still talking about this.
Wait.

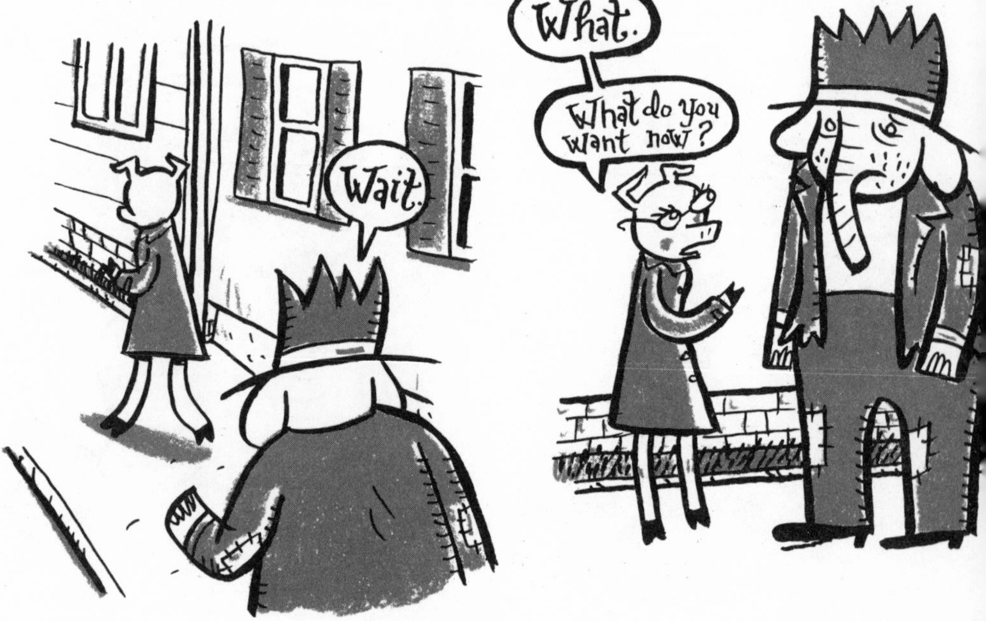
Wait.
What.
What do you want now?

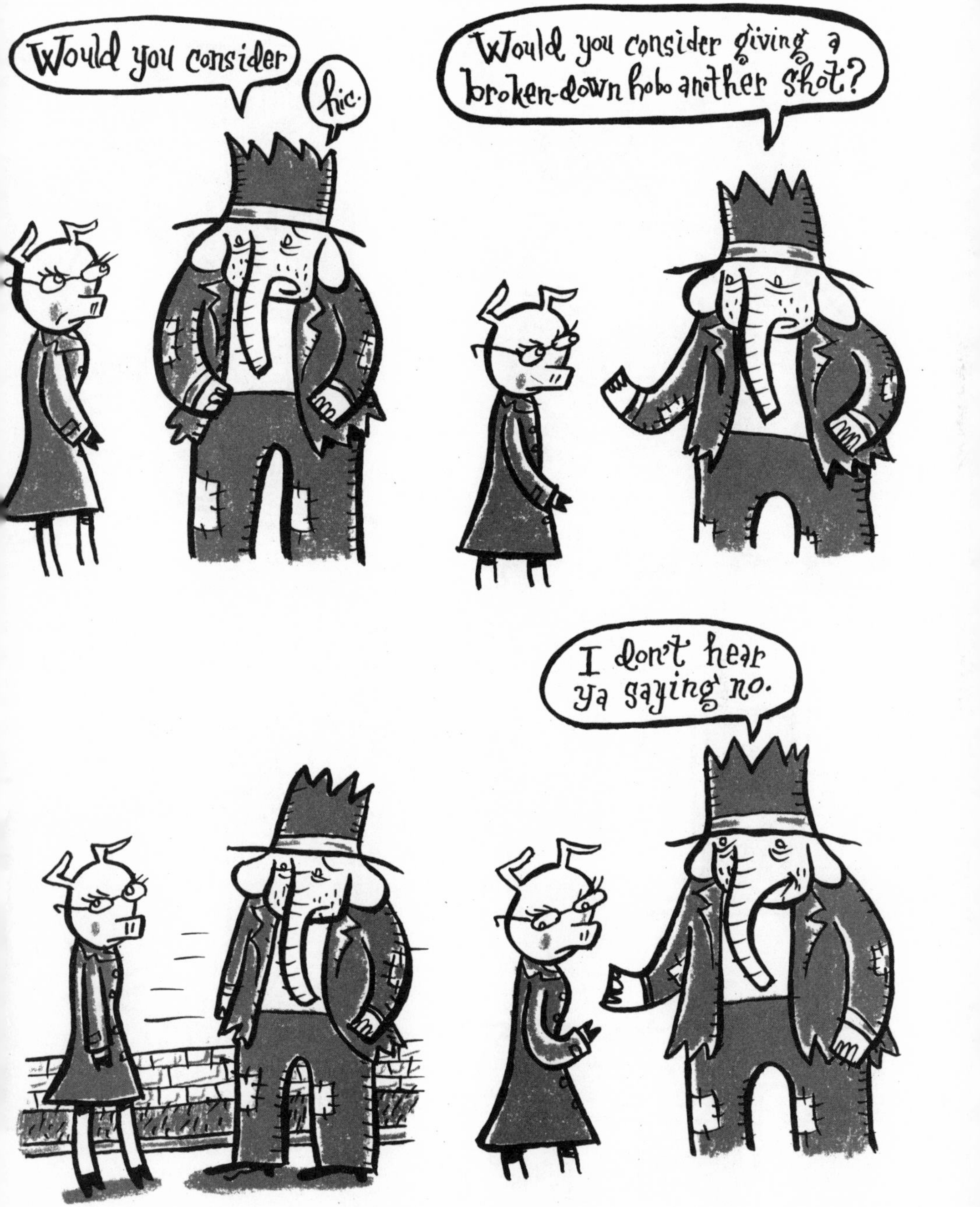
Would you consider
hic.
Would you consider giving a broken-down hobo another shot?
I don't hear ya saying no.

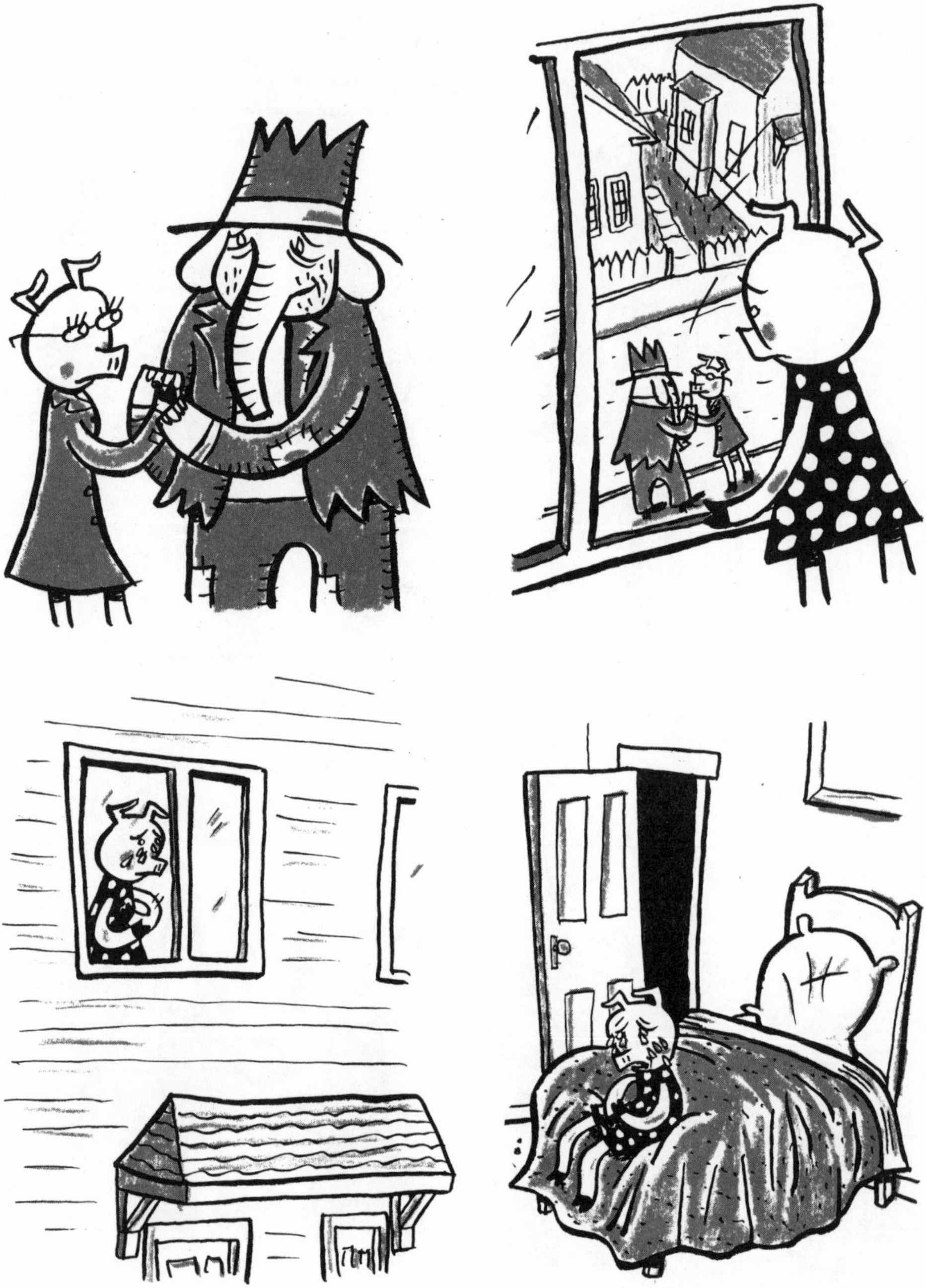

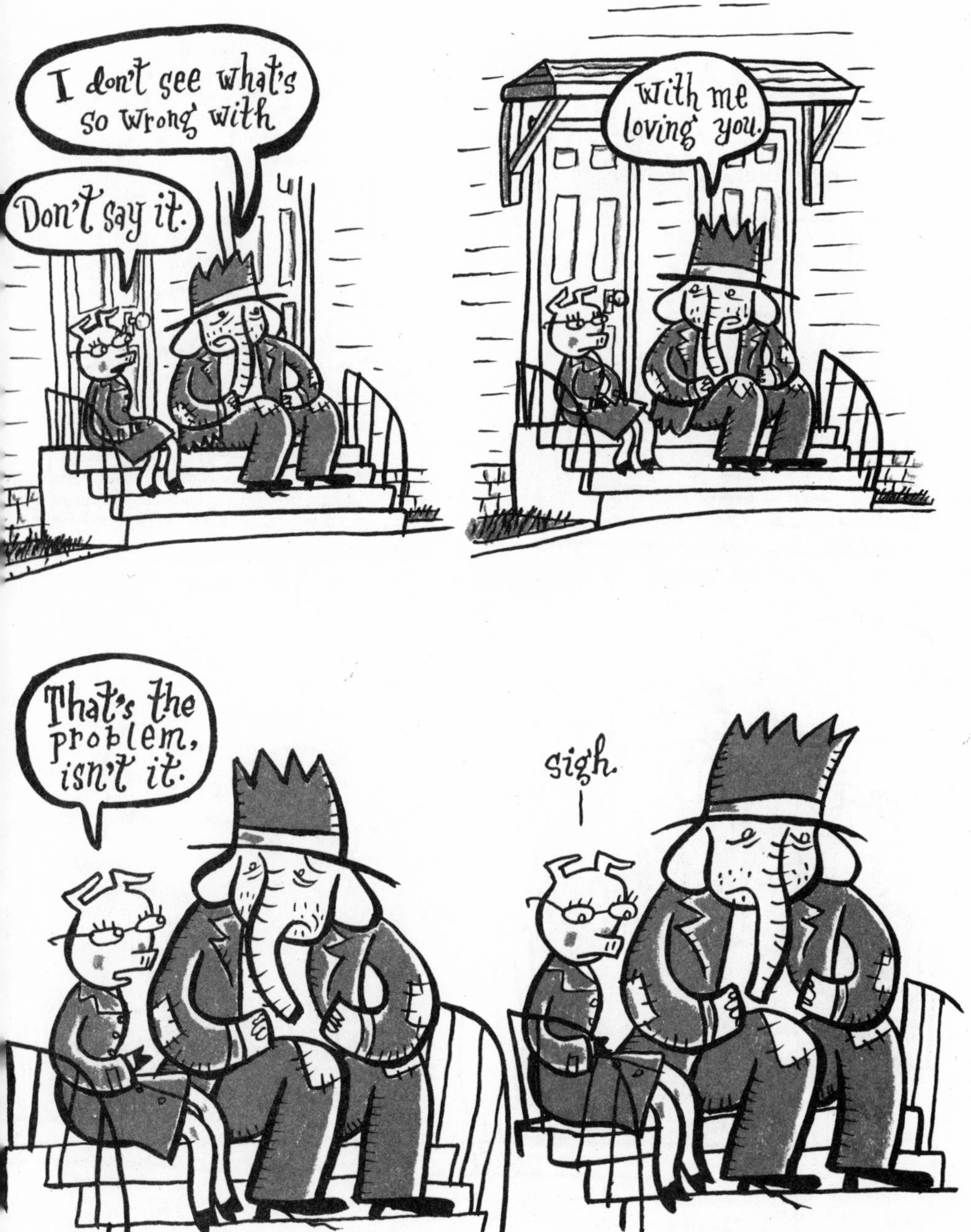
I don't see what's so wrong with
Don't say it.
With me loving you.
That's the problem, isn't it.
sigh.

Critter, it didn't work between us then and it isn't going to work now.
Besides the rails are no place to raise children.
I've got a place now.
You're living in my daughter's closet!

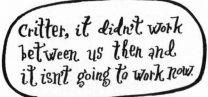

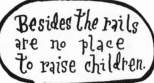

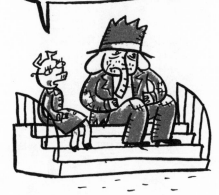

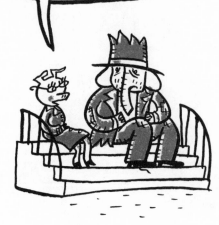

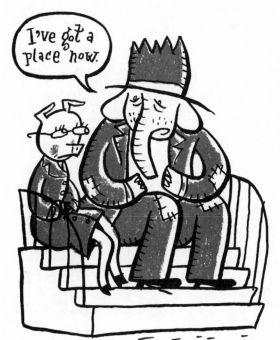

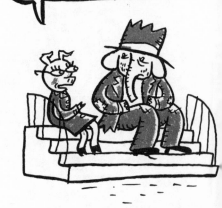

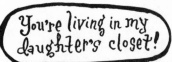

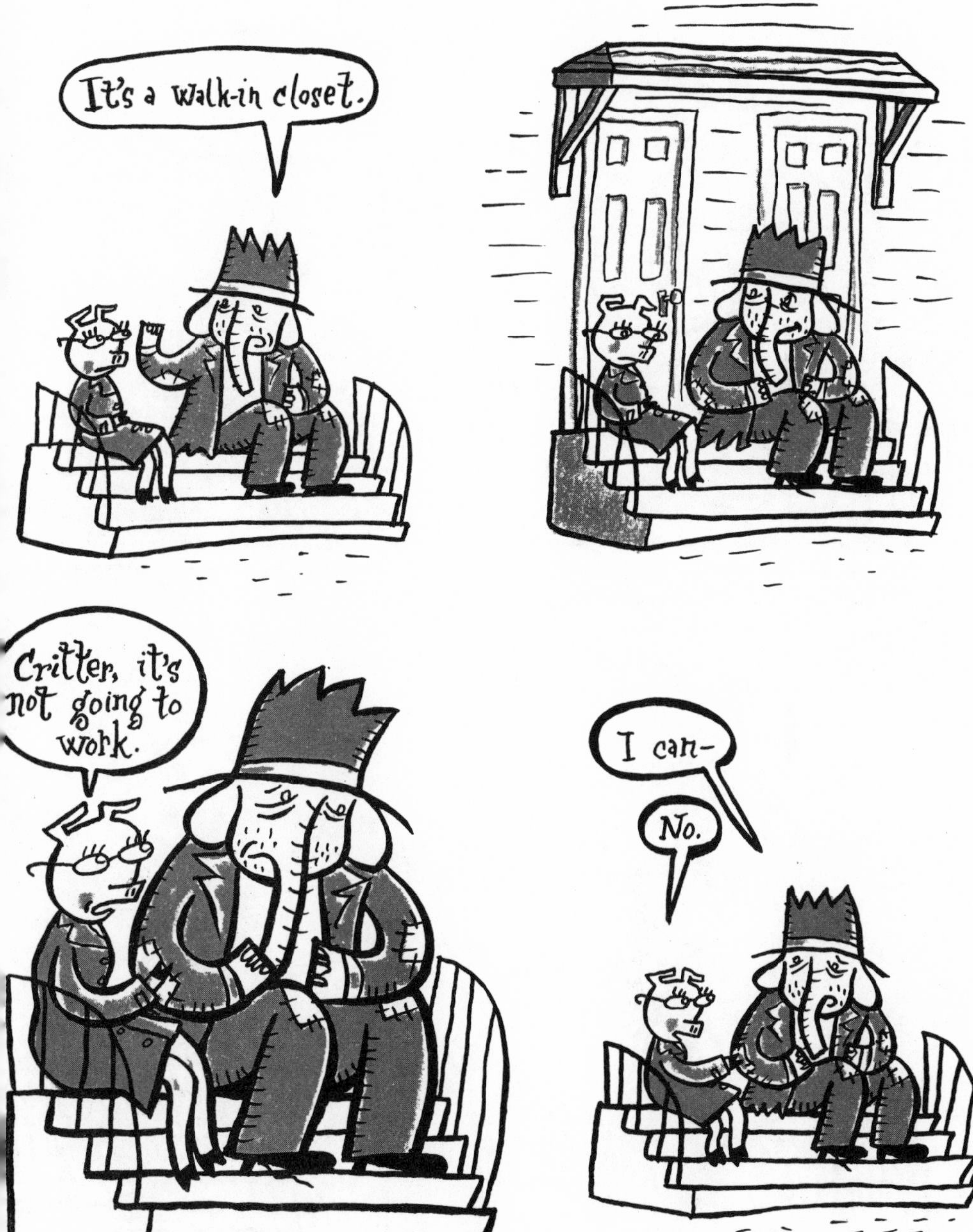
It's a walk-in closet.
Critter, it's not going to work.
I can-
No.

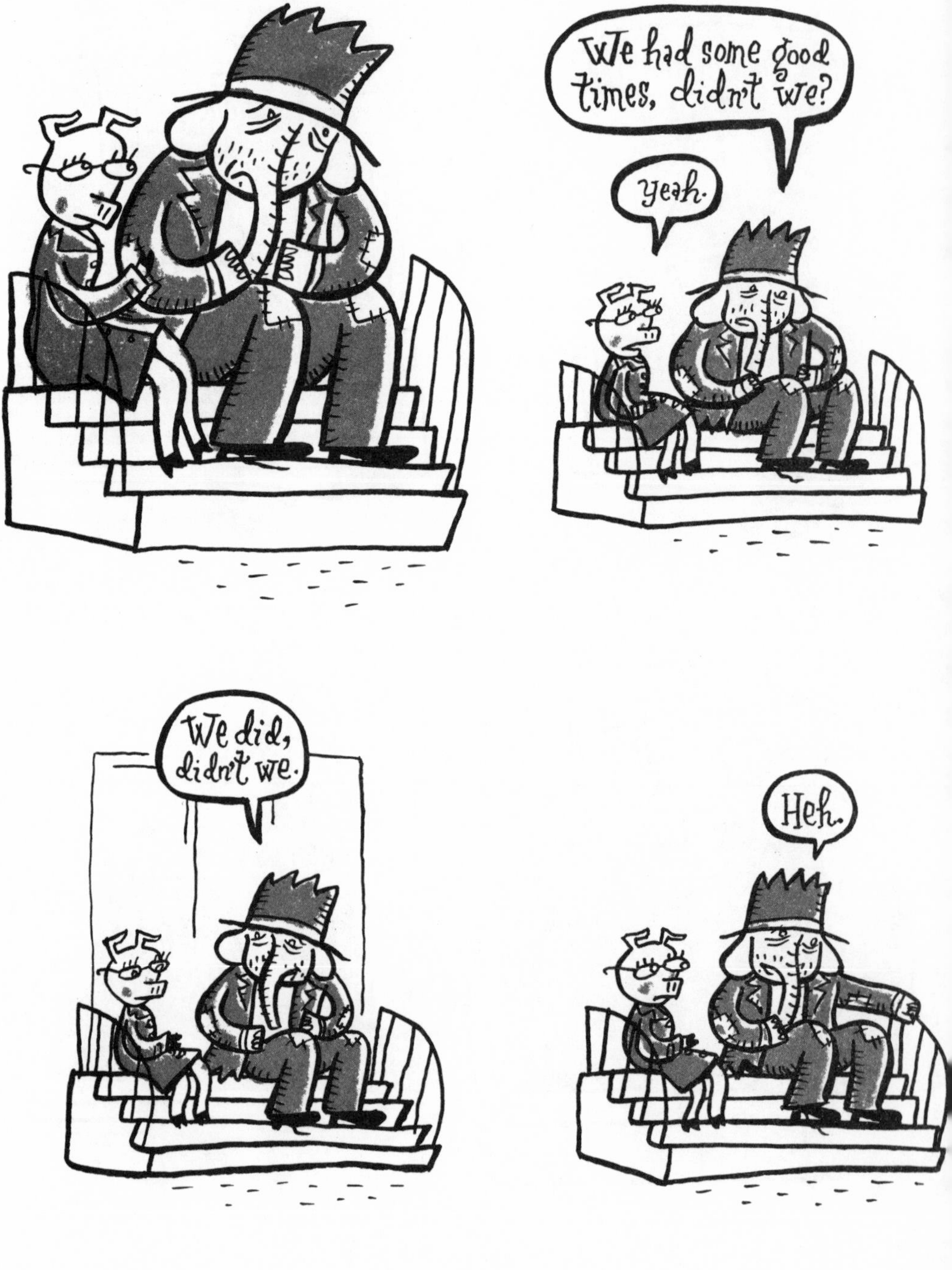
We had some good times, didn't we?
yeah.
We did, didn't we.
Heh.

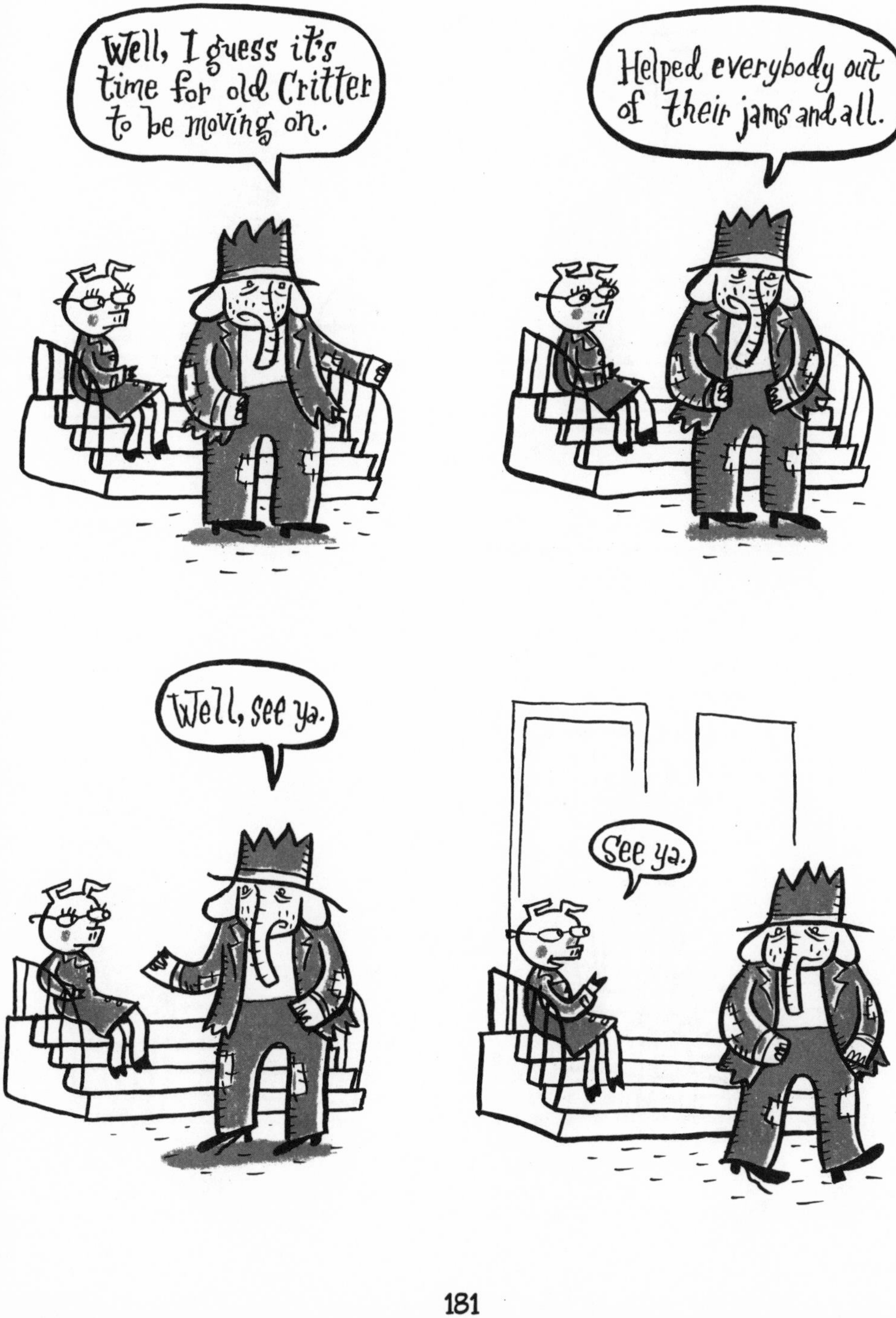
Well, I guess it's time for old Critter to be moving on.
Helped everybody out of their jams and all.
Well, see ya.
See ya.

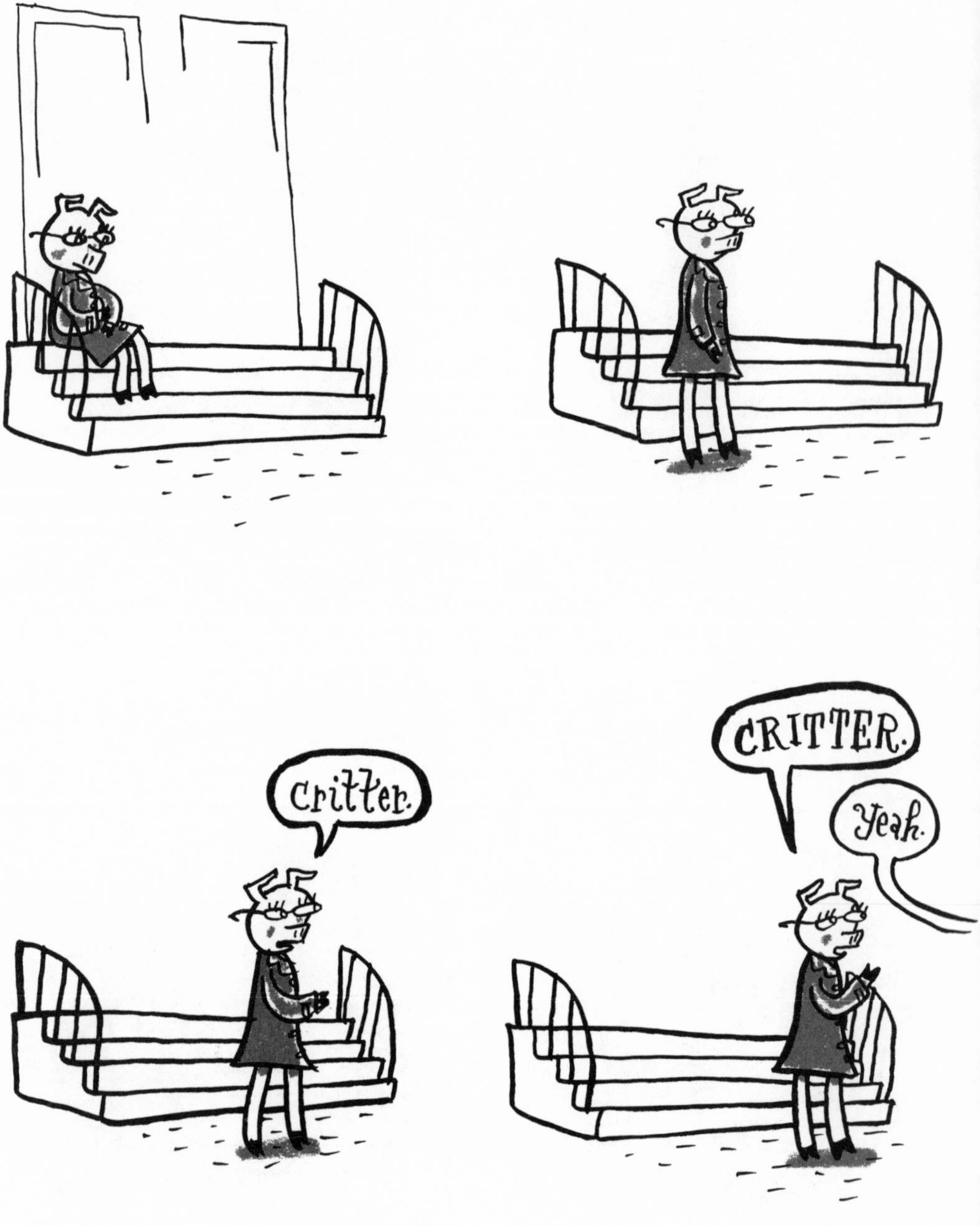
critter.
CRITTER.
Yeah.

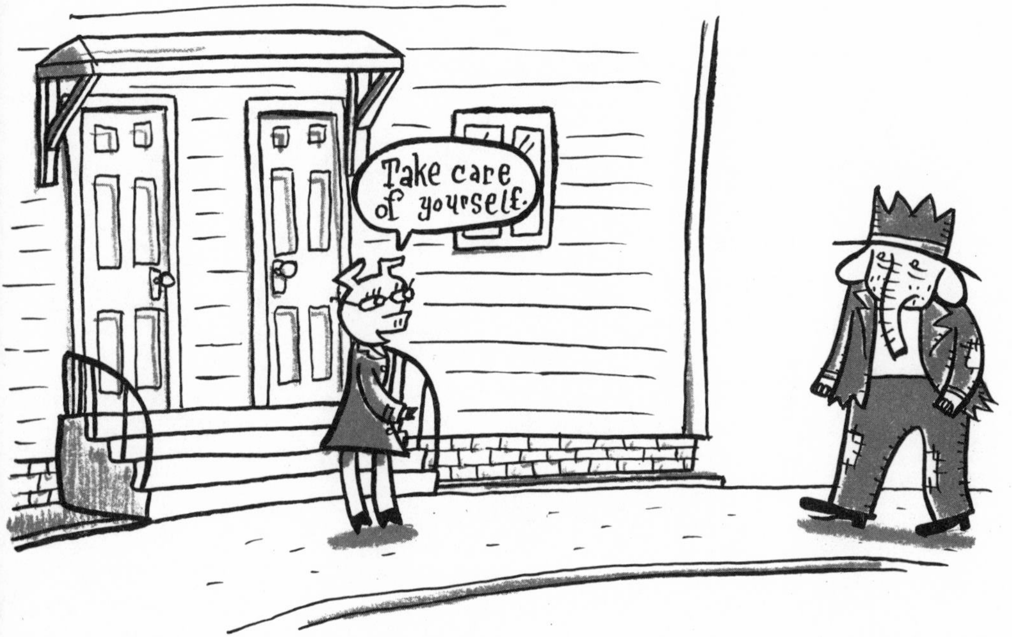
Take care of yourself.

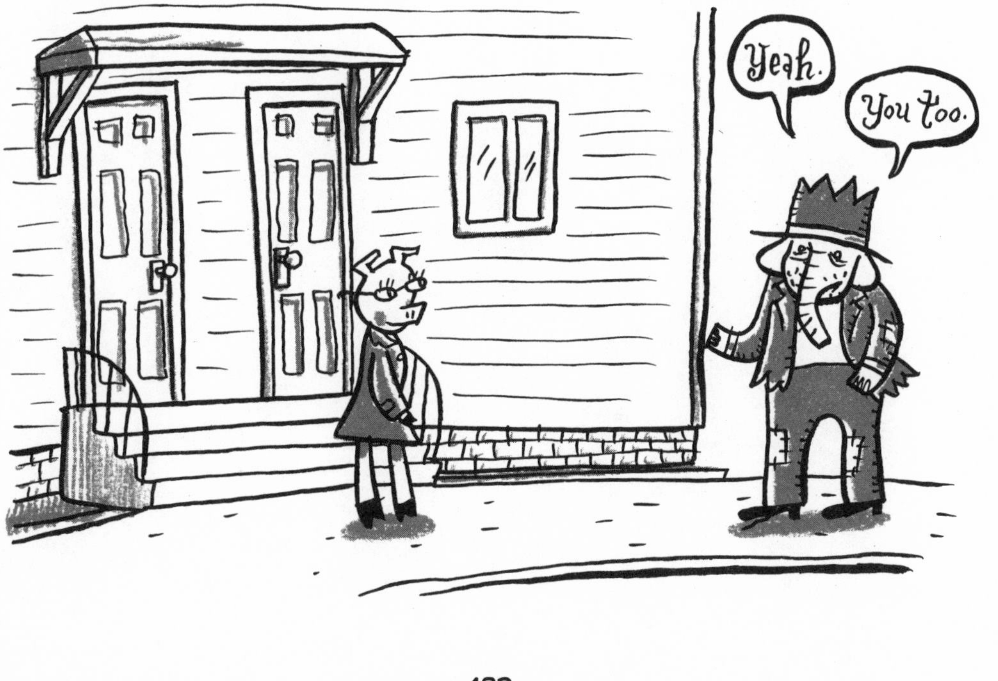
Yeah.
You too.

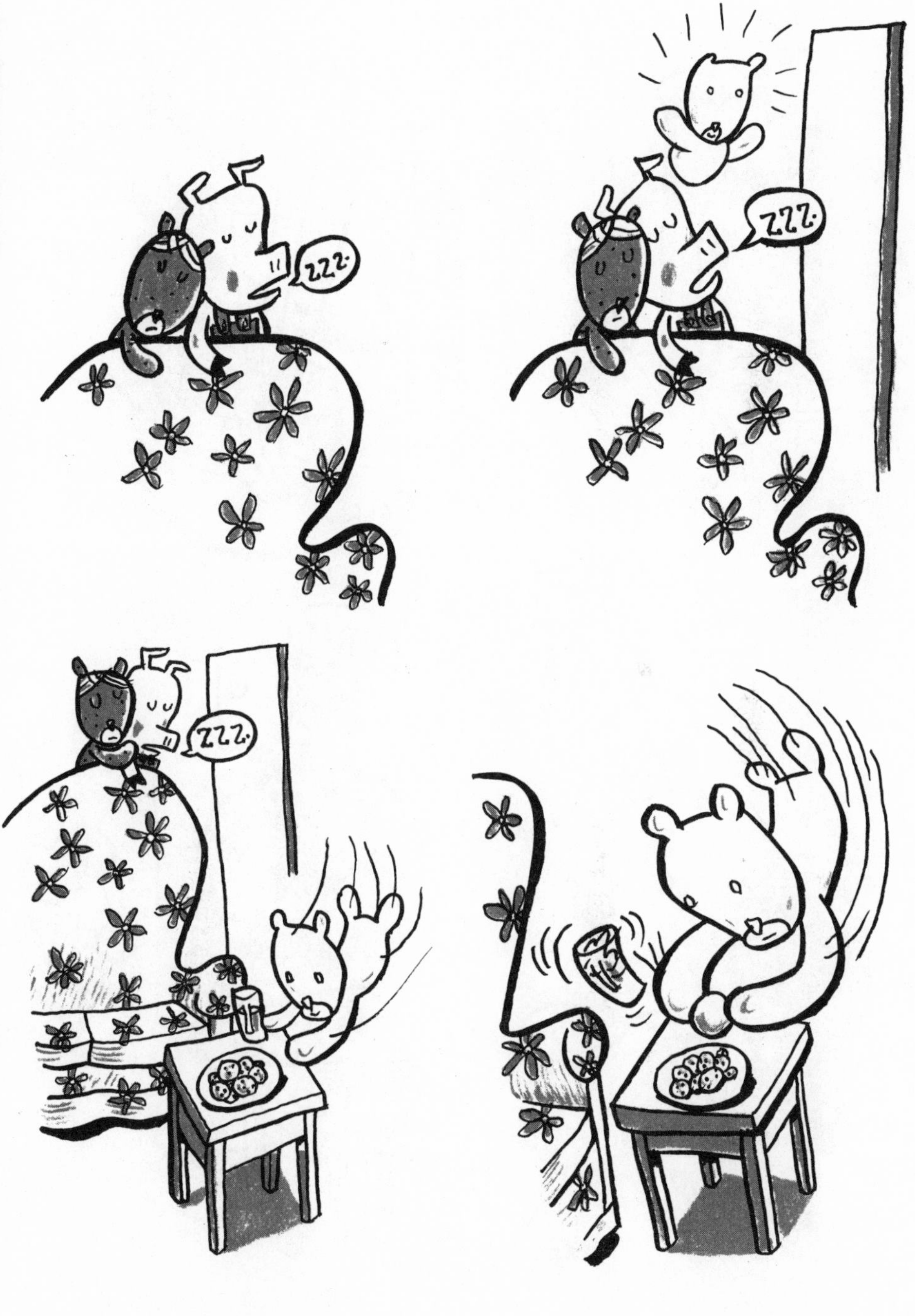
ZZZ.
ZZZ.
ZZZ.

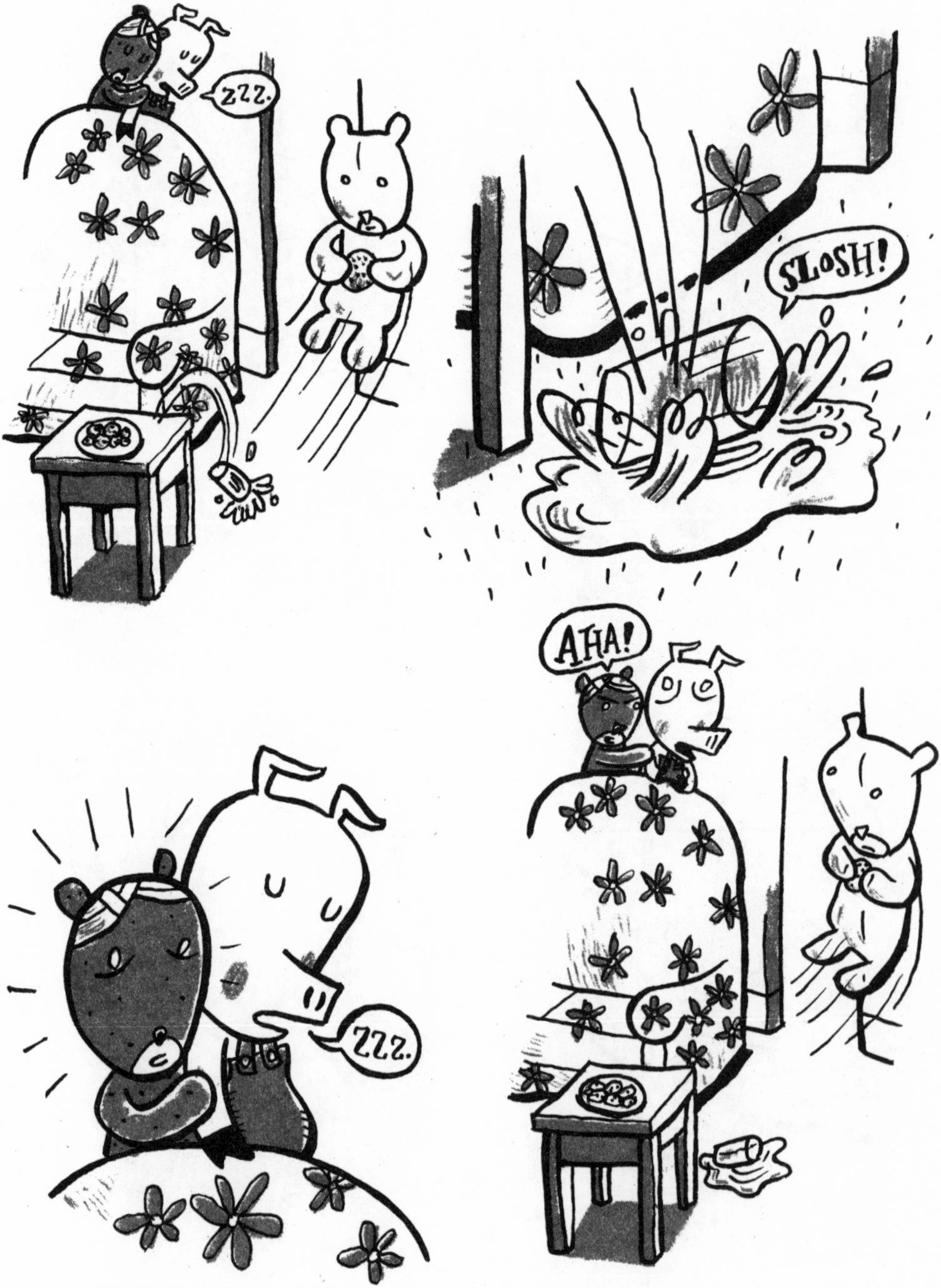
ZZZ.
SLOSH!
ZZZ.
AHA!

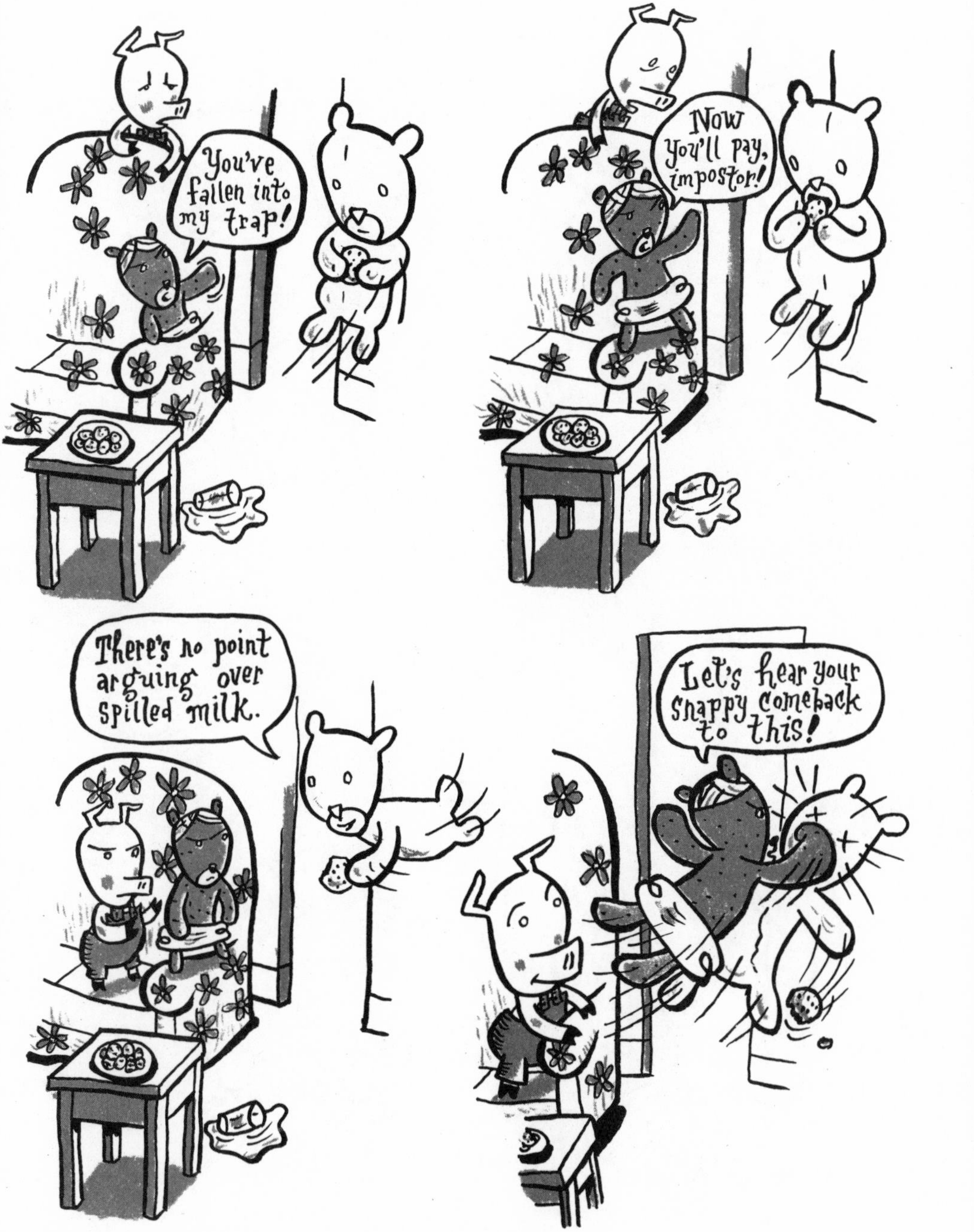
You've fallen into my trap!
Now you'll pay, impostor!
There's no point arguing over spilled milk.
Let's hear your snappy comeback to this!

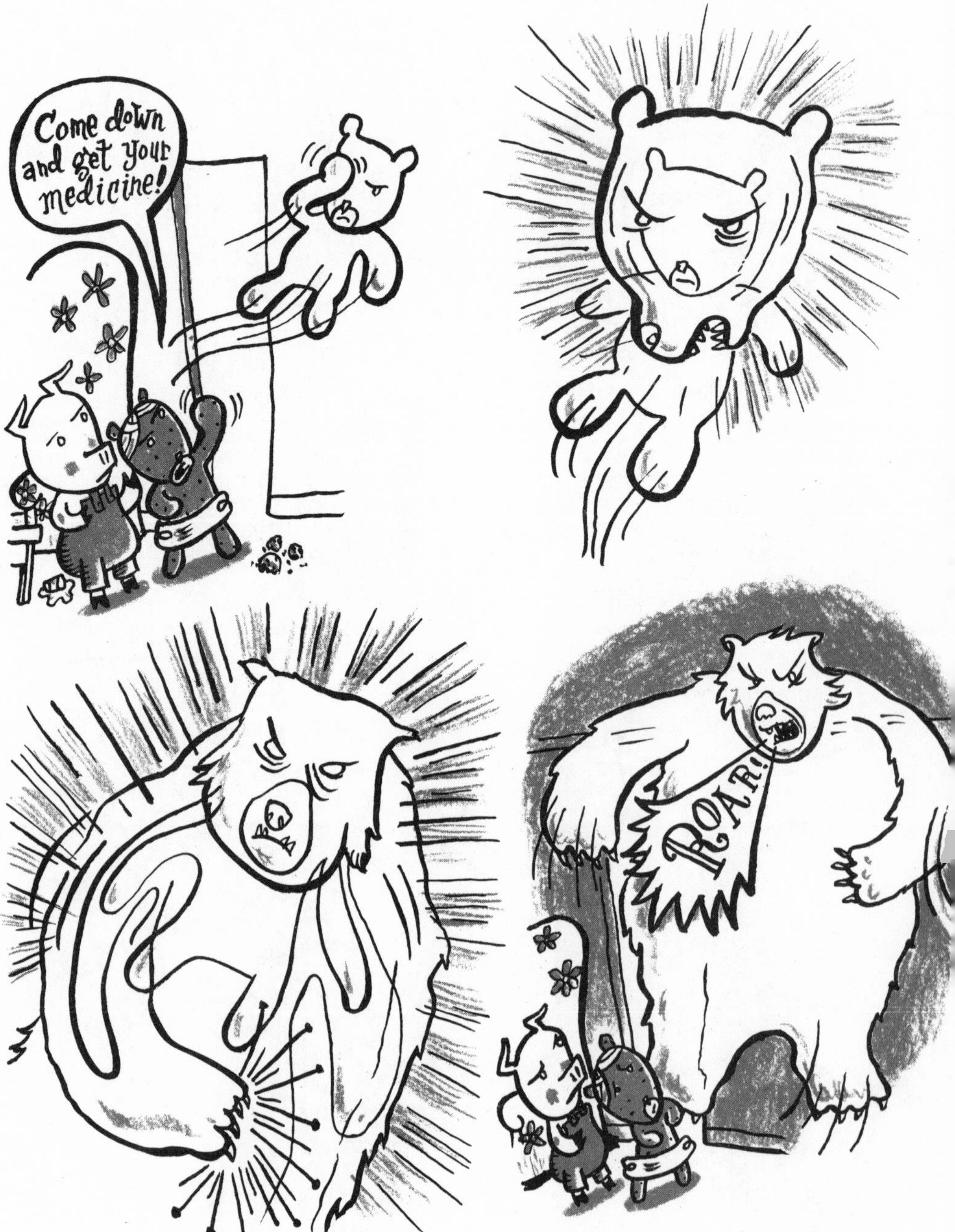
Come down and get your medicine!
ROAR!

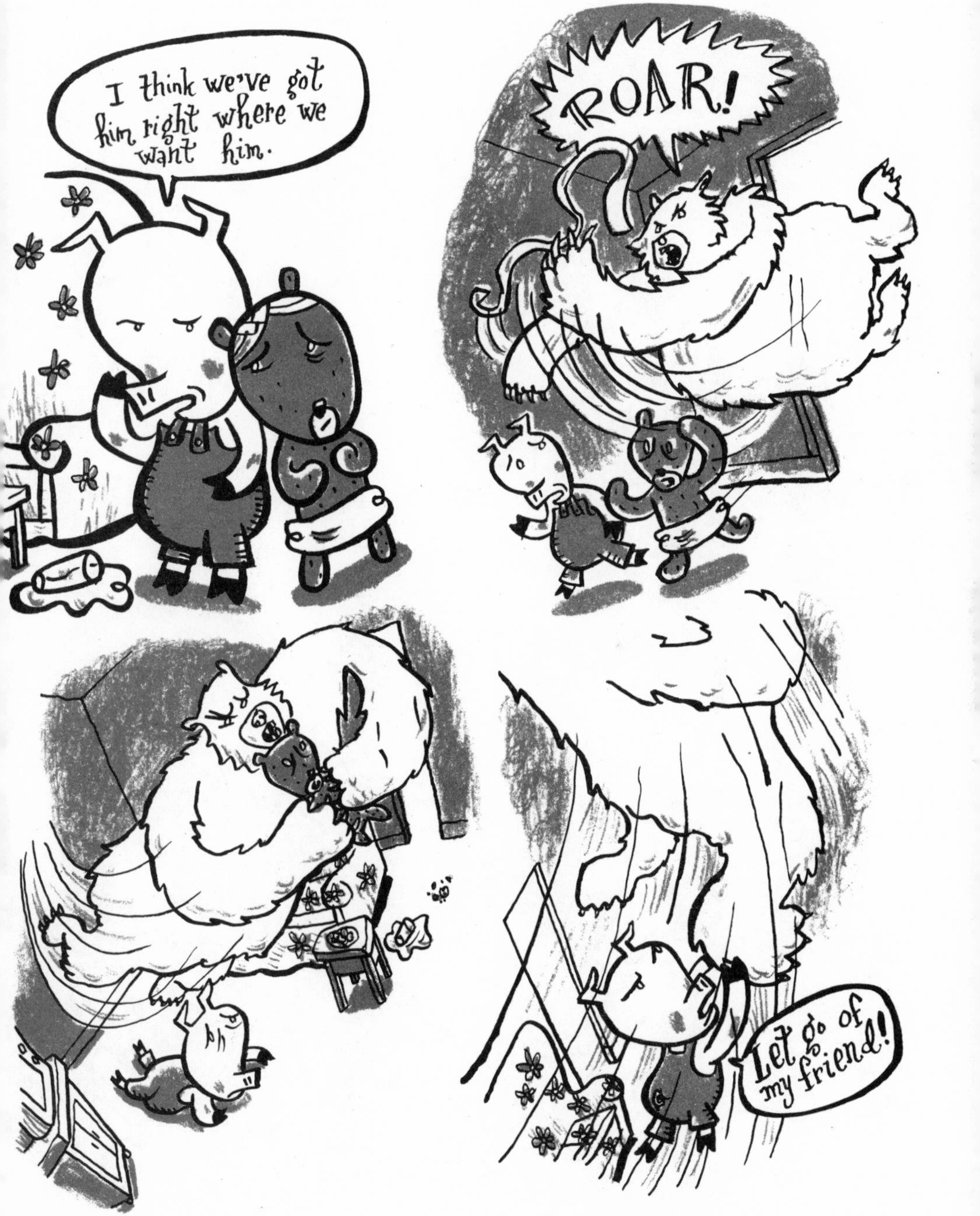
I think we've got him right where we want him.
ROAR!
Let go of my friend!

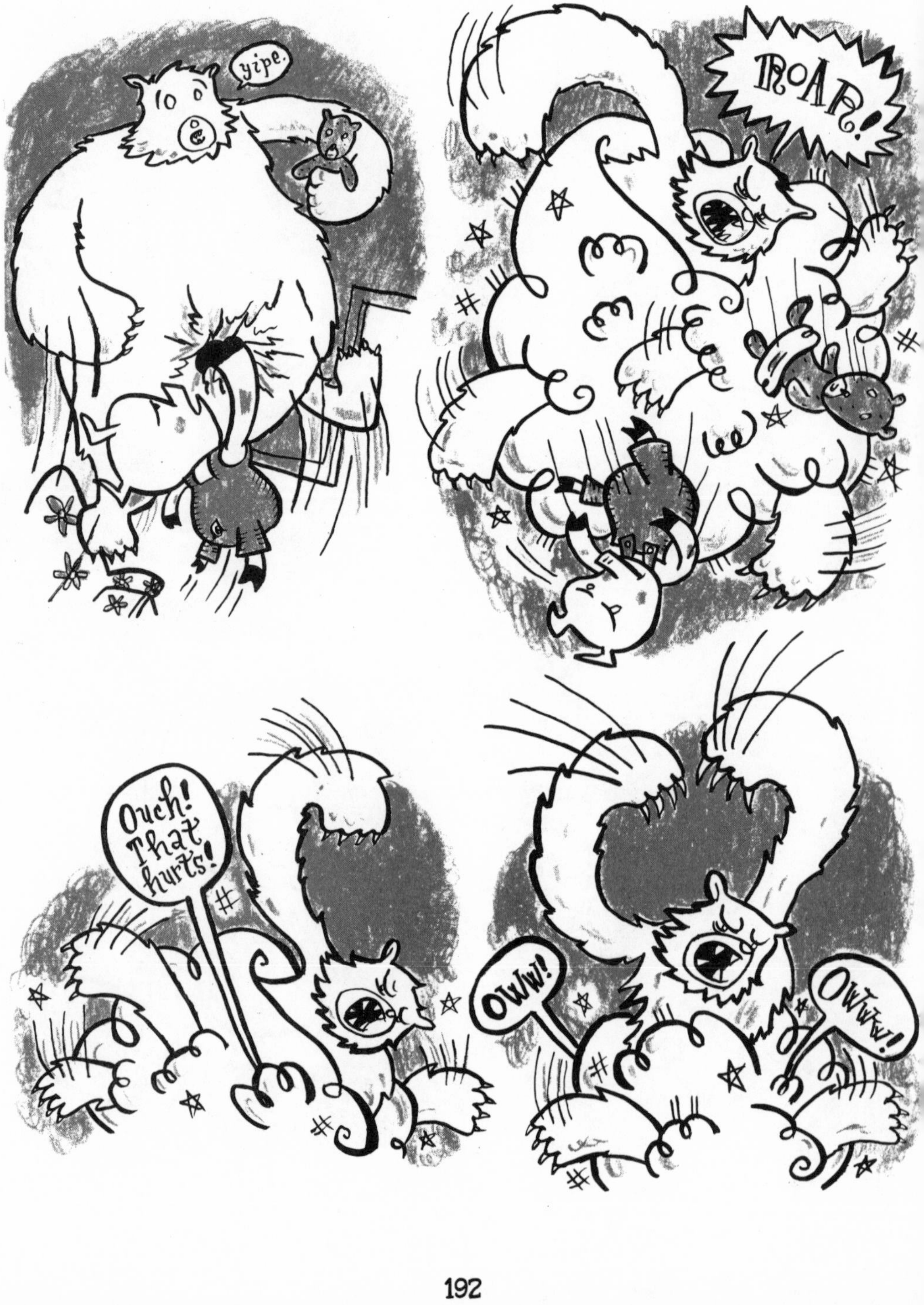
yipe.
ROAR!
Ouch! That hurts!
OWW!
OWWWW!

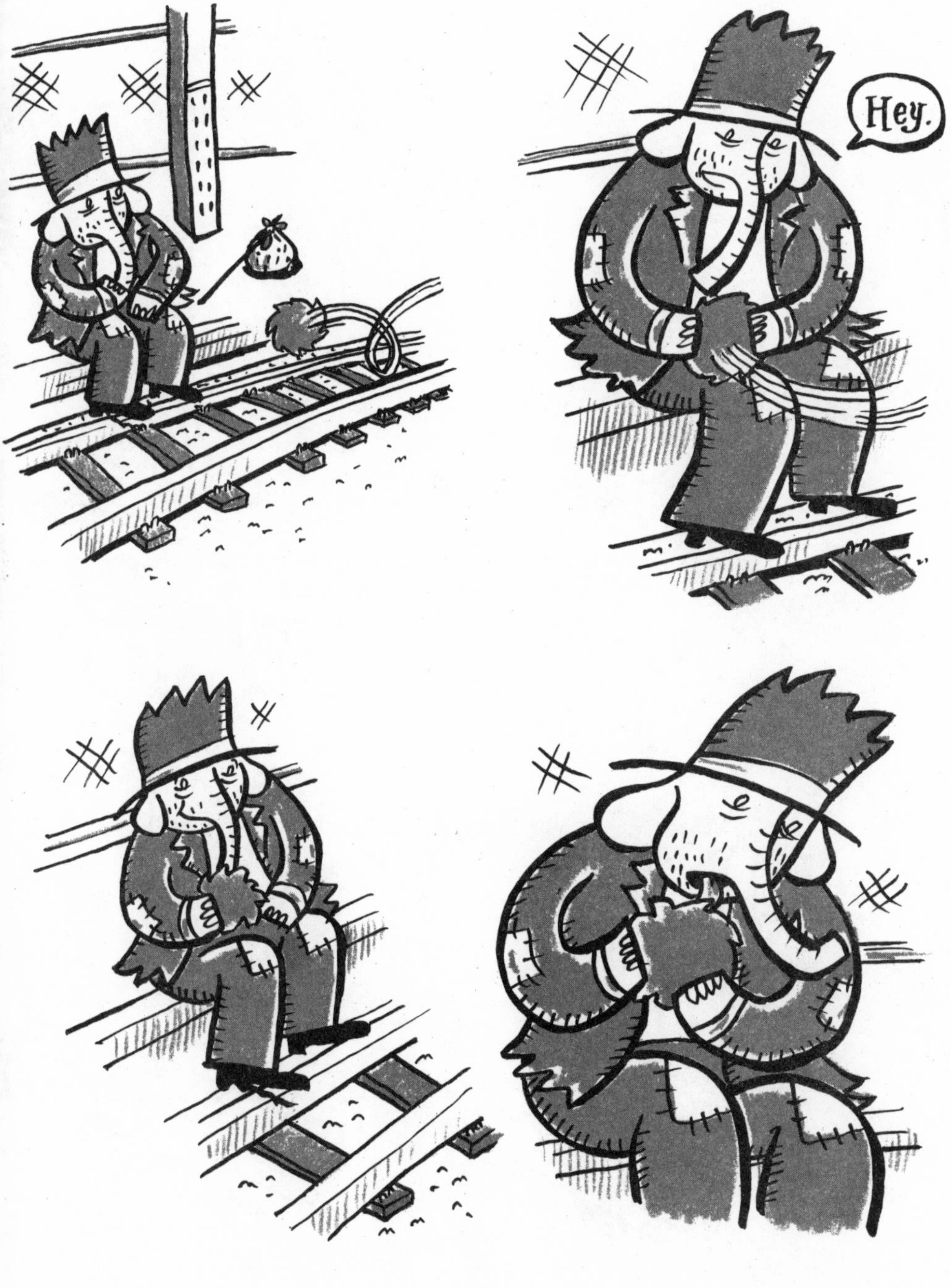
Hey.

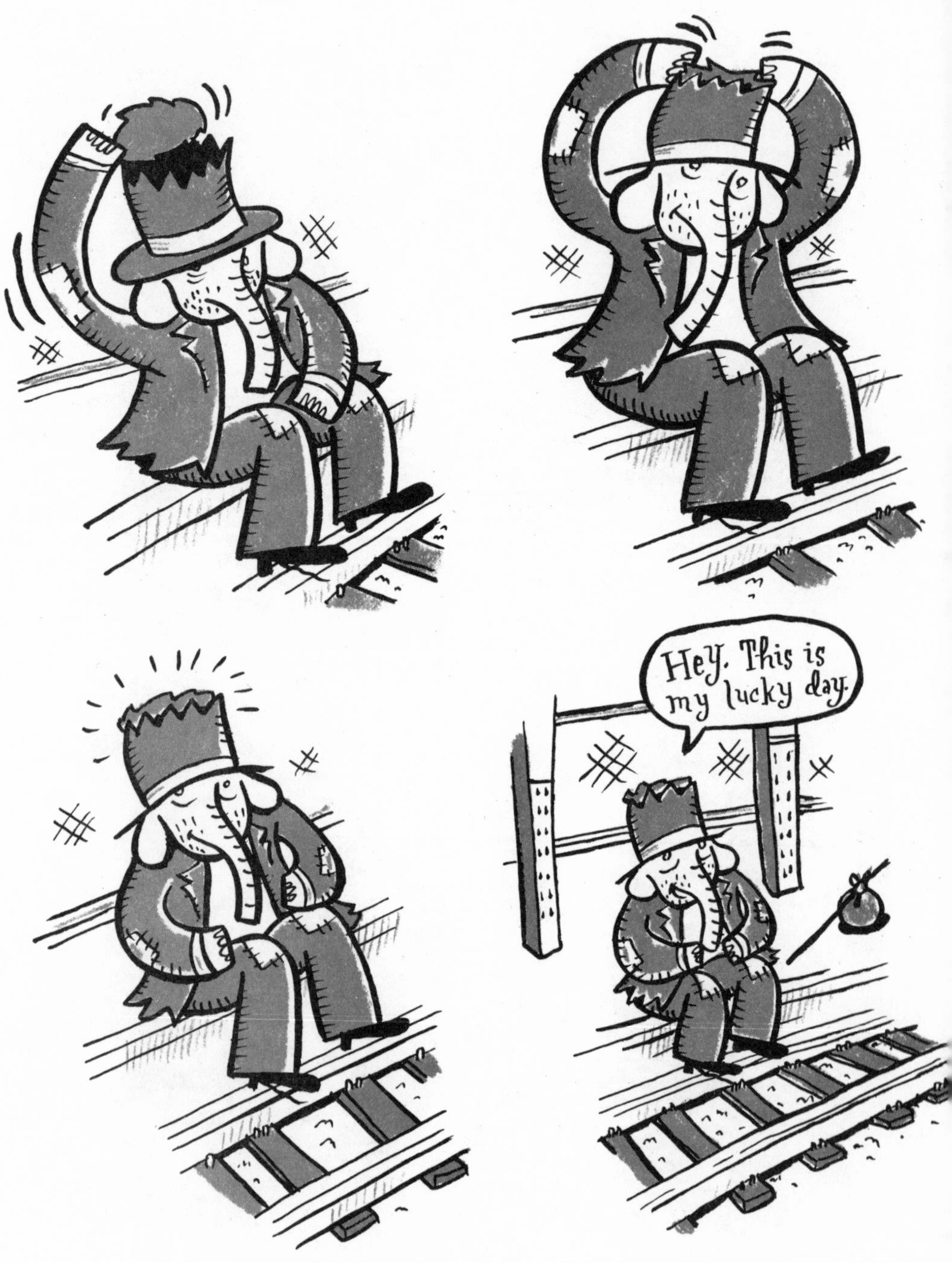
Hey. This is my lucky day.

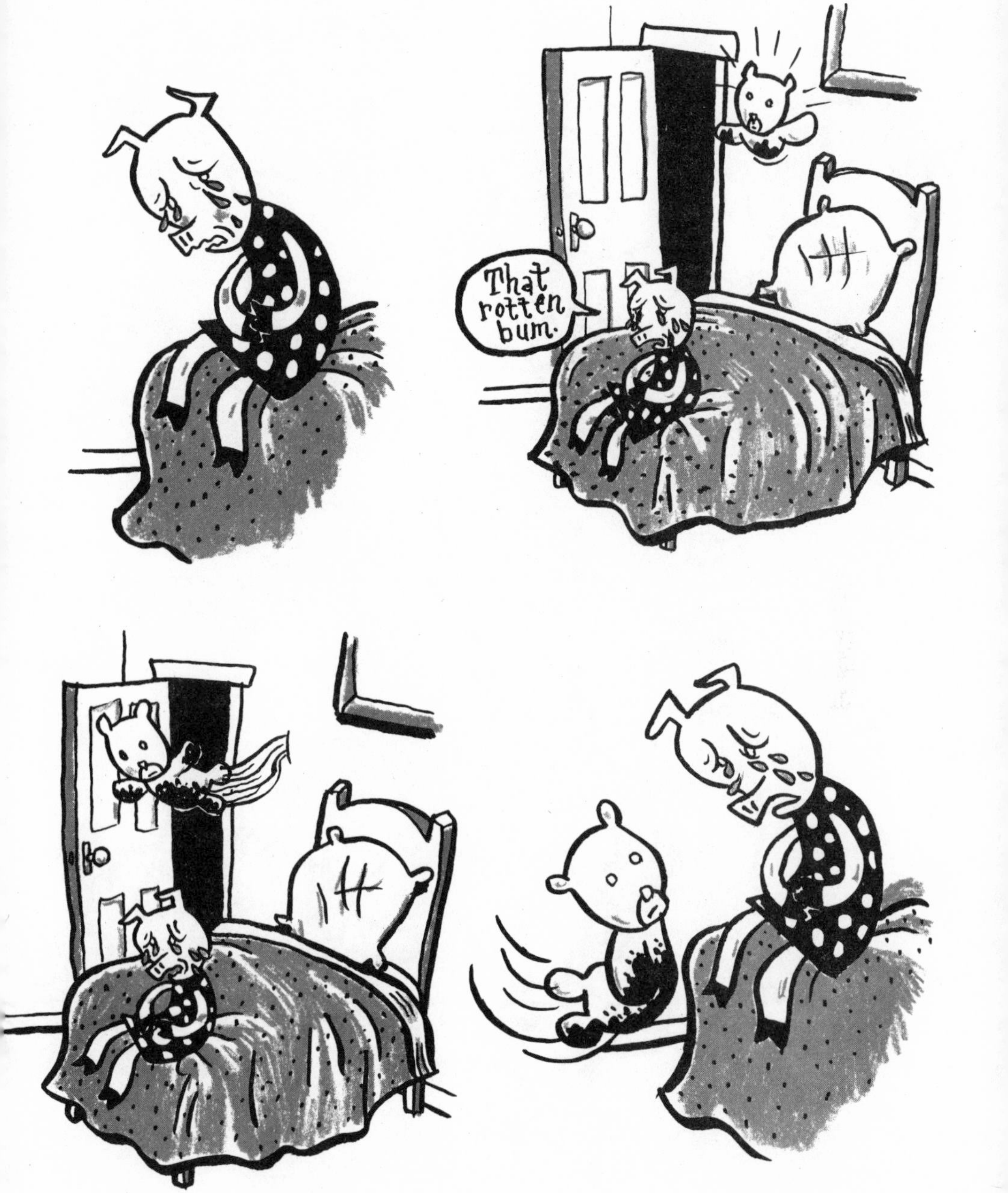
That rotten bum.

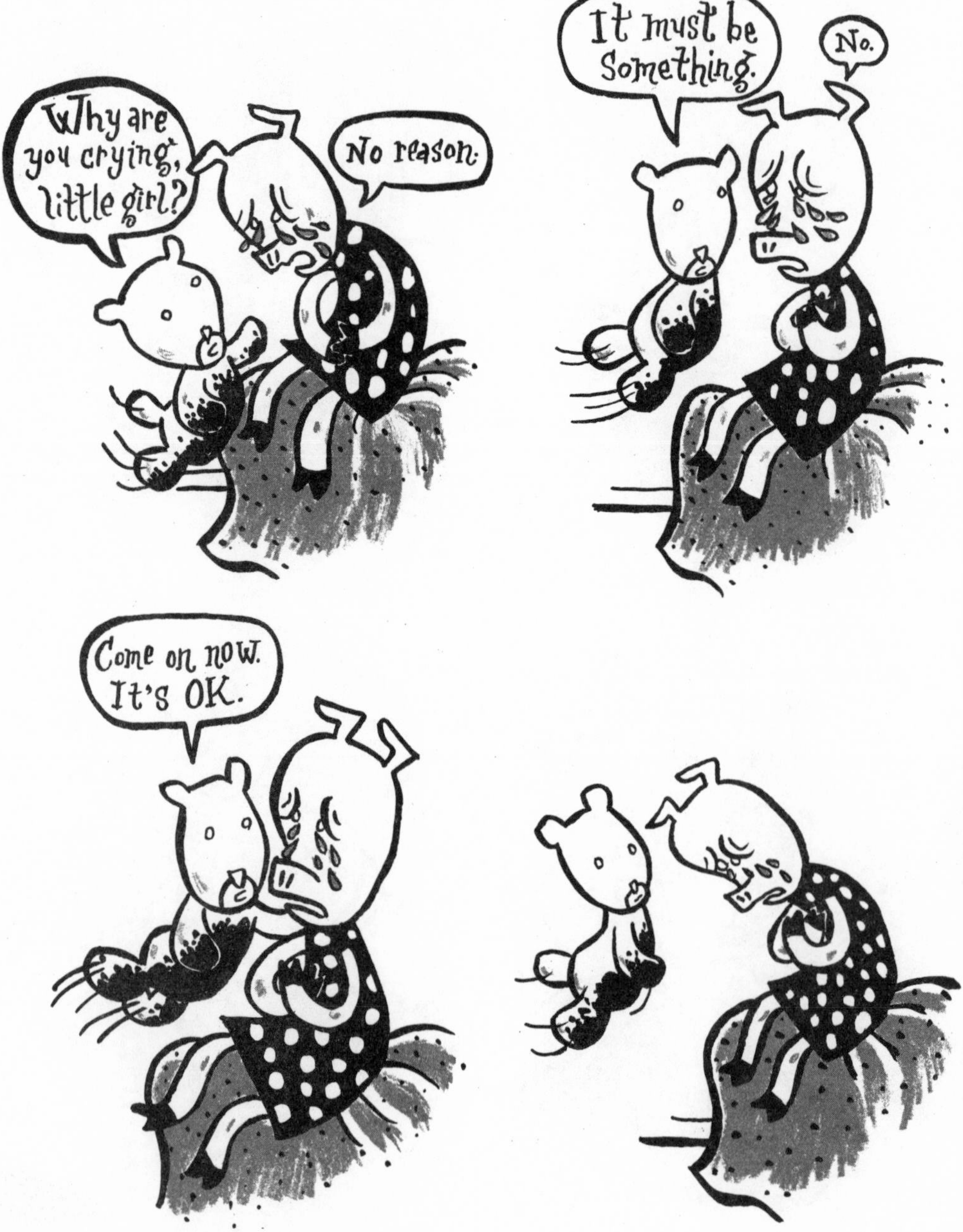
Why are you crying, little girl?
No reason.
It must be something.
No.
Come on now. It's OK.

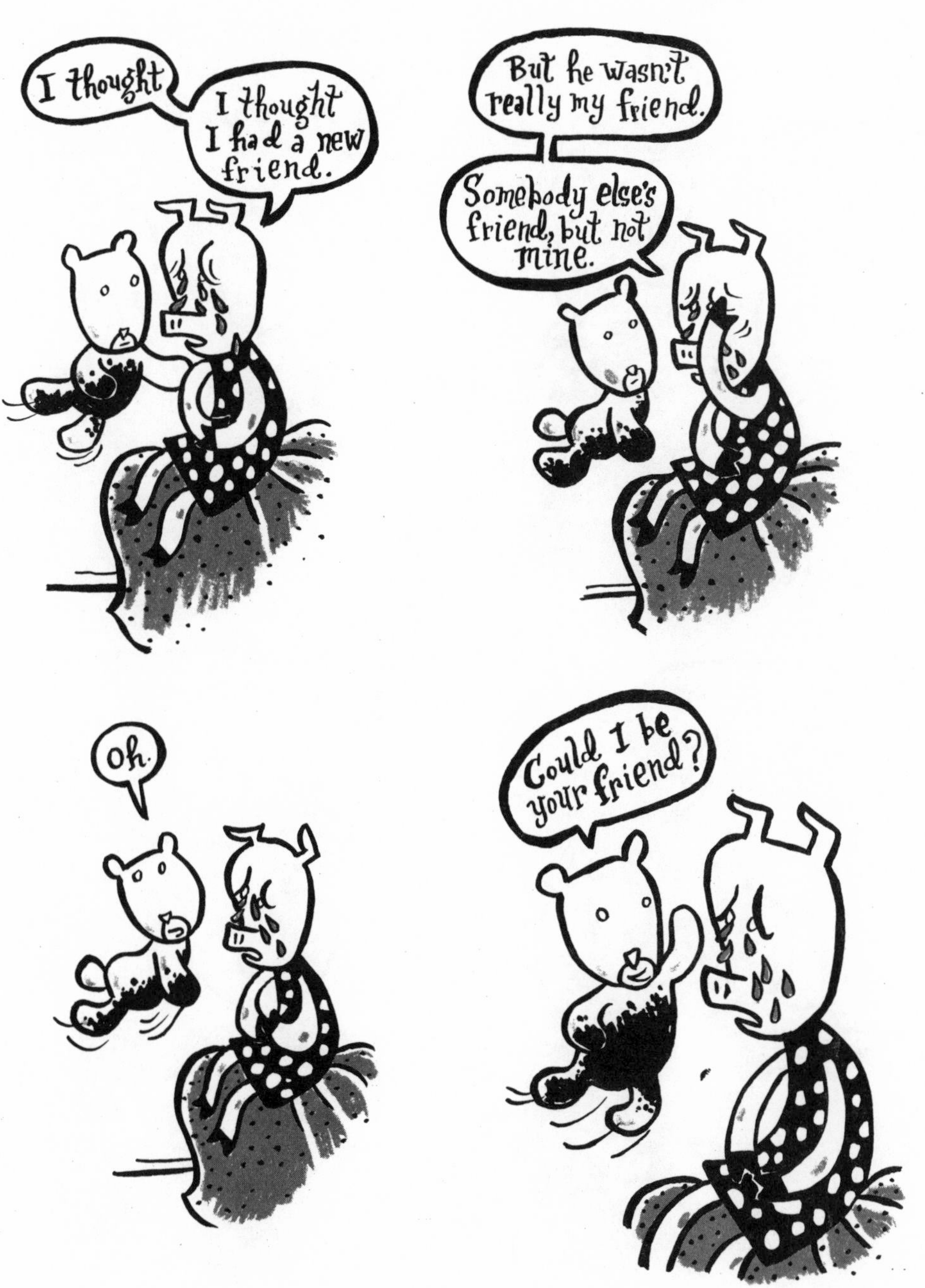
I thought
I thought I had a new friend.
But he wasn't really my friend.
Somebody else's friend, but not mine.
Oh.
Could I be your friend?

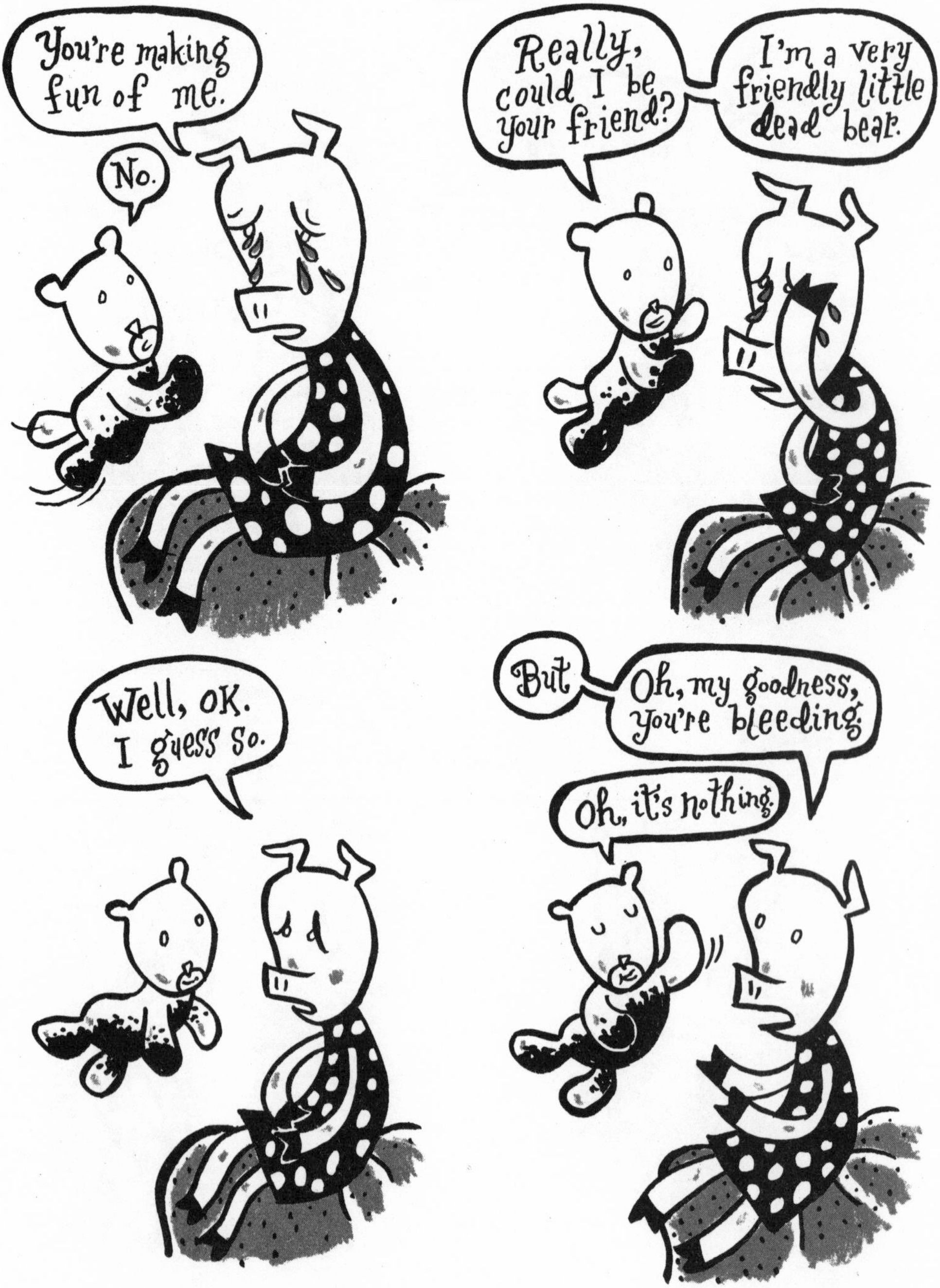
You're making fun of me.
No.
Really, could I be your friend?
I'm a very friendly little dead bear.
Well, OK. I guess so.
But
Oh, my goodness, you're bleeding.
Oh, it's nothing.

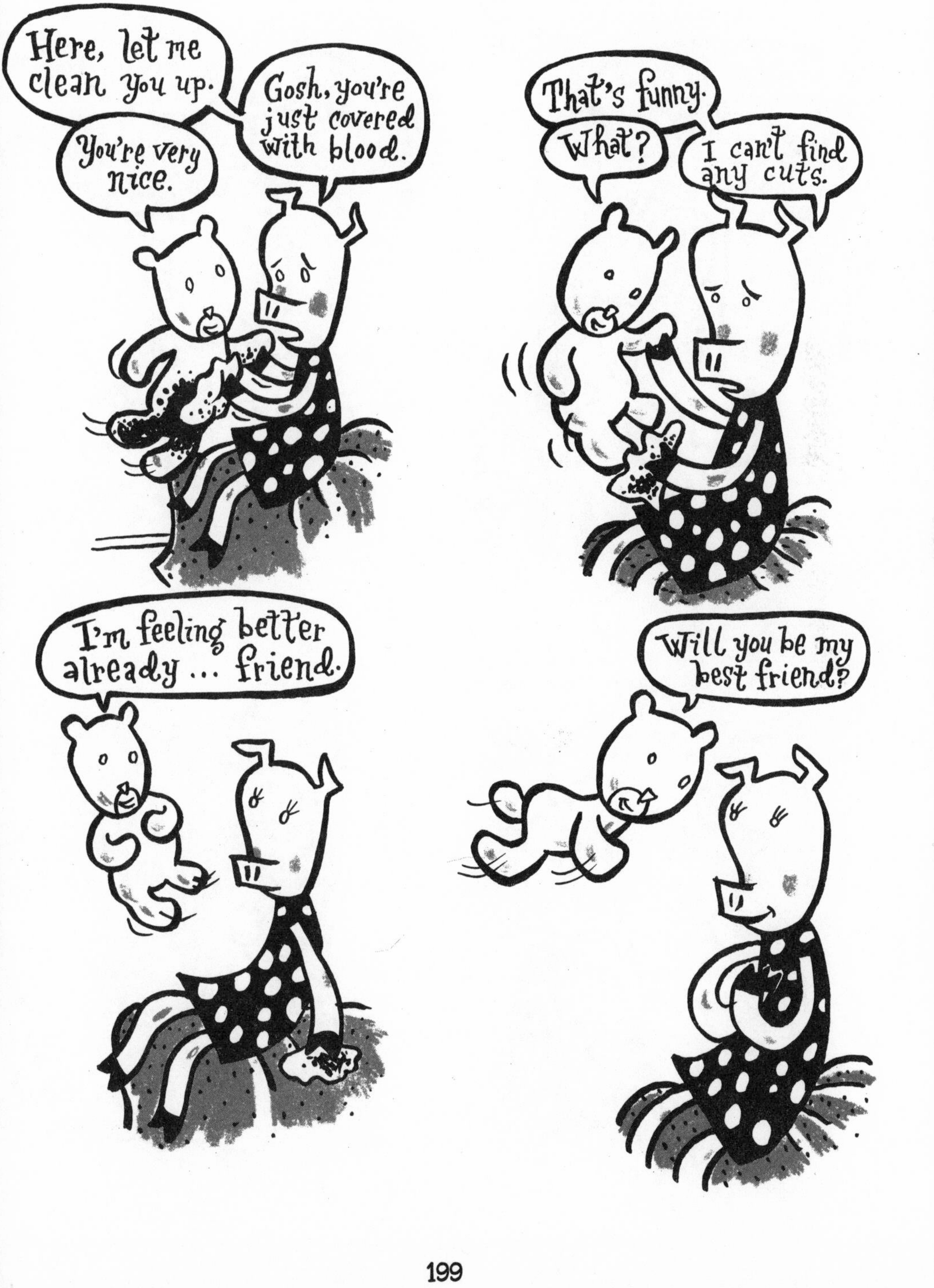
Here, let me clean you up.
Gosh, you're just covered with blood.
You're very nice.
That's funny.
What?
I can't find any cuts.
I'm feeling better already ... friend.
Will you be my best friend?

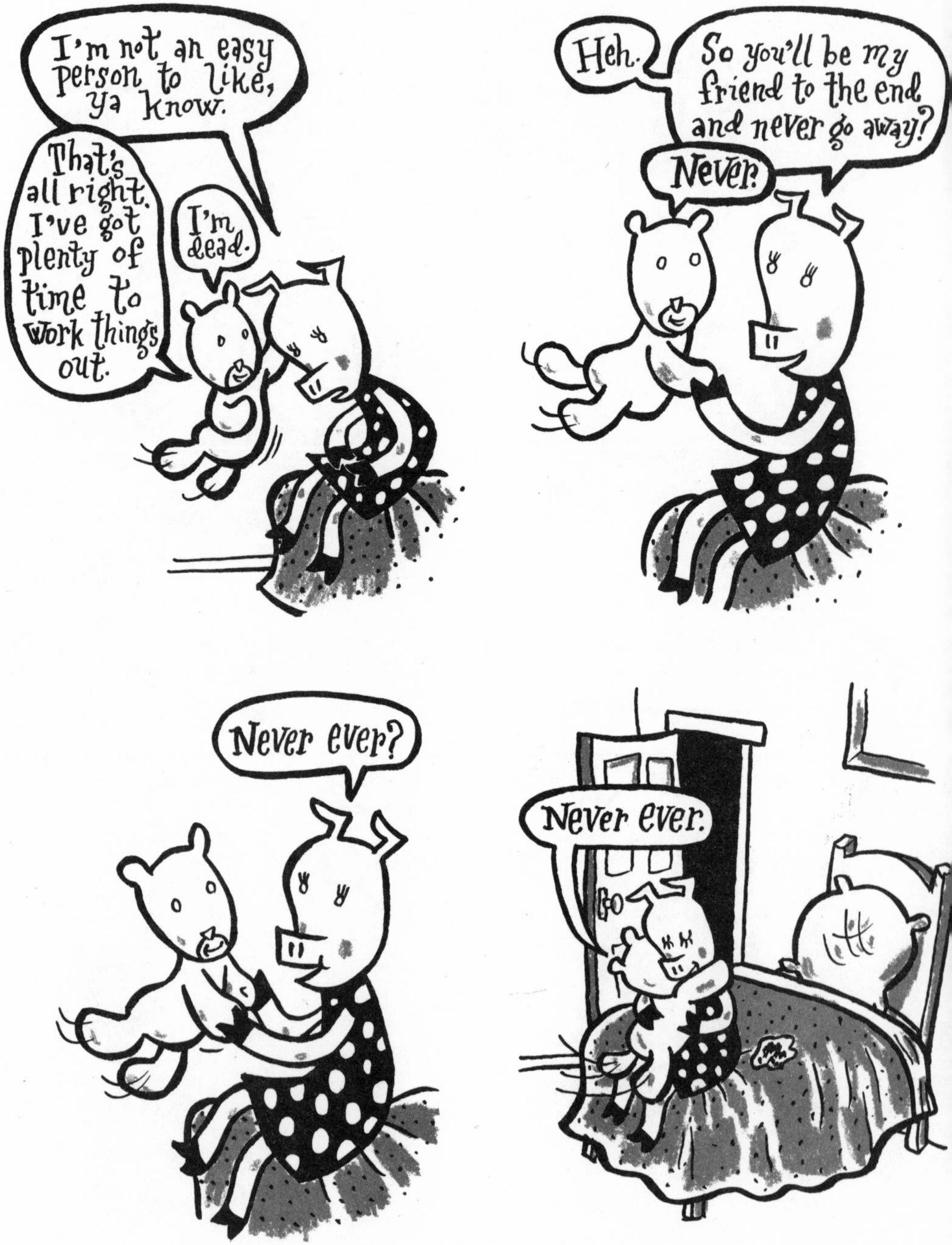
I'm not an easy person to like, ya know.
That's all right. I've got plenty of time to work things out.
I'm dead.
Heh.
So you'll be my friend to the end and never go away?
Never.
Never ever?
Never ever.